Dynamics of Labor Market and Economics in the 21st Century

Dynamics of Labor Market and Economics in the 21st Century

Edited by **Liam Hopkins**

New York

Published by Willford Press,
118-35 Queens Blvd., Suite 400,
Forest Hills, NY 11375, USA
www.willfordpress.com

Dynamics of Labor Market and Economics in the 21st Century
Edited by Liam Hopkins

International Standard Book Number: 978-1-68285-248-4 (Hardback)

Contents

Preface

There has been an enormous shift in the global labor market and economies in last five decades due to various factors like globalization, economic recession, migration and global unrest. This book is an assimilation of concepts such as revenue generation and earning by firms, effect of migration on labor supply, employment and poverty, evaluating skill level of labor in emerging economies, etc. From theories to research to practical assessments related to all contemporary topics of relevance to this field have been included in this book. It will help the readers in keeping pace with the rapid changes in this field.

All of the data presented henceforth, was collaborated in the wake of recent advancements in the field. The aim of this book is to present the diversified developments from across the globe in a comprehensible manner. The opinions expressed in each chapter belong solely to the contributing authors. Their interpretations of the topics are the integral part of this book, which I have carefully compiled for a better understanding of the readers.

At the end, I would like to thank all those who dedicated their time and efforts for the successful completion of this book. I also wish to convey my gratitude towards my friends and family who supported me at every step.

Editor

What happened to real earnings in Egypt, 2008 to 2009?

Paul Cichello[1]*, Hala Abou-Ali[2] and Daniela Marotta[3]

* Correspondence:
paul.cichello@bc.edu
[1]Economics Department, Boston College, 140 Commonwealth Ave, Chestnut Hill, MA 02467, USA
Full list of author information is available at the end of the article

Abstract: Nominal earnings in Egypt did not respond to the increase in inflation between February 2008 and February 2009, resulting in a 12.3 (9) percent decline in average (median) real earnings among 25 to 60 years old workers. Changes in earnings differ significantly by groups: (i) those with higher initial earnings (reported and predicted) suffered the largest declines in earnings; (ii) men lost more than women but after controlling for initial earnings, women lost considerably more than men; (iii) those who were initially in agriculture also had greater declines despite rising food prices.

JEL classification codes: J62; J16; J42; J43; O15; O17

Keywords: Earnings mobility; Egypt; Inflation; Gender; Wage differentials; Segmented labor market

1. Introduction

The returns to labor are critical for ensuring household economic well-being in Egypt, as elsewhere. As such, government leaders are concerned if they observe more labor lying dormant when unemployment rates rise or if they see the returns to labor fall when real earnings fall. In trying to better understand the workings and outcomes of the labor market and the returns to labor a multitude of studies have analyzed the Egyptian labor market. A number of these studies have examined earnings changes using cross-sectional data, illuminating important features of the Egyptian labor market (Arabsheibani 2000; Belhaj-Hassine 2012; Datt and Olmstead 2004; Said 2009, 2012). However, comparisons of cross-sectional data from two points in time do not allow us to follow the same individual over time when trying to determine who is getting ahead and who is falling behind.

Recently, panel data has been collected that allows researchers to track the same individual over time. By following individuals over time, we can identify how an individual's earnings level in the current year compares to his or her earnings in the previous period. We can also investigate how such earnings mobility experiences vary across individuals. This allows us to map the changes in earnings to the standard covariates, such as gender and education levels, and also to include new covariates such as the poverty level of the individual's household and the earnings level of the individual in the initial period. Inclusion of these items can have an important impact on how we interpret the observed changes in the economy and resulting policy implications.

To our knowledge, this study represents the first analysis of earnings mobility in Egypt to incorporate initial earnings into analysis of earnings changes for both wage and non-wage workers[1]. We initially viewed this project as a study designed to establish baseline statistics for "typical" earnings mobility patterns in the Egyptian labor market.

However, given the significant inflation shock that occurred between interviews, we recognize that this may be a rather unique period in the labor market and should not be thought of as "typical". Therefore we proffer this study as a window into the changes in the labor market in a time of severe stress on real wages due to an external shock of rising commodity prices.

Aggregate employment outcomes and nominal earnings or profits among prime-aged workers are shown to be fairly non-responsive despite the increased prices. Instead, inflation severely erodes the real earnings that individuals receive, implying an adjustment process that relies heavily on reduced real earnings. On average, a worker earns approximately 10 percent less than he or she did in the previous year.

The inability of workers to garner higher wages helped to keep inflation from continuing on an upward spiral[2]. The self-employed and employers also experienced declines in real profits suggesting that they either did not try or were not able to raise the prices of their goods and services in order to keep their real earnings constant or growing[3].

The lack of labor market response to inflation in aggregate employment and nominal earnings outcomes should not be construed as a signal of rigidity of experiences at the individual level. As is typical in such studies, there is a large degree of heterogeneity in the earnings changes experienced by individuals. We identify key determinants associated with earnings mobility using a variety of descriptive regression techniques.

There is a strong association between initial earnings and subsequent earnings changes, with those initially earning more experiencing larger declines than their counterparts. As such changes can be caused by temporary fluctuations in earnings and/or measurement errors; this effect is taken with some caution. Nonetheless, we find these results generally robust to methods that address measurement error concerns, such as using predicted earnings in place of actual earnings. Additionally, other determinants of earnings changes that one would assume would be quite powerful predictors of earnings change—such as workers changing the sector of employment (agriculture, industry, or services)—have a limited ability to predict earnings mobility.

Changes in earnings also differ significantly by gender. On average, the earnings changes are far *more* negative for men than for women. However, this gender effect is completely reversed if one controls for initial earnings; i.e. for men and women who have the same initial earnings (and otherwise similar job characteristics), the earnings changes tend to be *less* negative for men than for women. In contrast, the average difference in log earnings is relatively similar across gender, with men having a slight advantage. This advantage for males is dramatically magnified if one controls for initial log earnings.

The rest of the paper is organized as follows. Section 2 first describes the context of our study, and explains the context of the Egyptian economy during this time, including a review of the rise in inflation. Section 3 depicts the panel data used in this study. Section 4 portrays the empirical approach. Section 5 introduces the results. Section 6 provides a discussion of these results and presents the relevance to policy and future research.

2. Background discussion of the Egyptian economy

The World Bank study, "Poverty in Egypt 2008–2009: Withstanding the global economic crisis," includes a substantive review of the Egyptian economy leading up to 2008 (World Bank 2011). In this section, we review some of its critical findings relevant to our study.

From 2004 to mid-2008, Egypt experienced a period of steady economic growth with an average real GDP annual growth of 6.4 percent. This growth period was followed by a series of economic shocks starting in the second half of 2008 and continuing for most of 2009, namely:

(i) the slowdown in economic growth, which followed the global downturn in the world economy;

(ii) a simultaneous and related fall in remittances; and

(iii) a sudden acceleration in prices, mostly driven by exogenous factors such as the commodities price shock.

The economic developments over the period 2004–2009 are summarized in Figure 1. Note that the table begins in the last quarter of 2004 using the calendar year (second quarter of the fiscal year). For reference, the panel data analyzed in this study were collected in the first quarter of 2008 and the first quarter of 2009. They are denoted by the vertical strips at the third quarter of fiscal year 2008 and 2009, respectively.

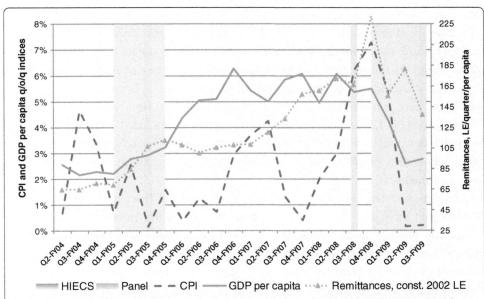

Figure 1 Quarterly GDP growth, inflation rate and remittances in Egypt, 2004–2009. Reprinted from The World Bank (2011). Data from CAPMAS and Ministry of Economic Development. *Note:* The quarterly GDP per capita data were annualized before determining the percent increase or decrease in the quarter-on-quarter index. CPI data were not annualized.

At first glance, Egypt weathered the global crisis relatively well. Despite an abrupt economic slowdown, from seven percent growth in 2008 to 4.7 percent in 2009, growth remained positive. However, employment growth stalled in absolute terms (employment was flat during 2008 and the first quarter of 2009), and unemployment started to rise again (to 9.4 percent in the first quarter of 2009). According to the Labor Force Sample Survey (LFSS) conducted by the Central Agency for Public Mobilization and Statistics (CAPMAS), there was a seven percent reduction in employment in manufacturing in the first quarter of 2009 (compared to the first quarter of 2008), and a 15 percent drop in the restaurants and hotel sectors. Meaning that, both sectors are most exposed to global trends and thus more susceptible to global shocks.

These changes came during a period of accelerating inflation, which peaked at 20 percent (annual average) in the summer of 2008. After peaking to an unprecedented level in August 2008 (23.7 percent), inflation remained exceptionally high for two quarters, only to stabilize at 9.9 percent between May and July-09. Inflation was almost completely imported, as a result of the sharp acceleration in global commodities prices (mostly fuel and food, including fruits and vegetables). Some components of the inflation basket, such as food and non-alcoholic beverages, remained high (up by 13.4 percent y-to-y in July-09) even after and despite the steep fall in international prices since mid-2008.

By the last quarter of 2009, the Egyptian economy showed signs of rebounding, and since then has been growing at five percent and higher each quarter. The employment losses were soon recovered (at least in absolute figures). Thus, our earnings mobility analysis may overestimate some of the long term decline in earnings that individuals faced from this period.

3. Data

The data used in this analysis come from the Household Income, Expenditure and Consumption Panel Survey (HIECPS), which is a subcomponent of the Household Income, Expenditure and Consumption Survey (HIECS). This is a nationally representative panel survey. However, as there were relatively few observations from the frontier governorates, we exclude the border region from our analysis.

Households were interviewed in February 2008 and those same households were interviewed again in February 2009. Information gathered included individual labor market outcomes, wages and profits from enterprises run by household members, as well as standard demographic information such as age, gender, and education level of all household members.

Earnings were constructed at the individual level. Earnings from household enterprises were split among all household members engaged in the enterprise, including those typically referred to as "unpaid workers[4]". Unless clearly denoted as nominal earnings, all earnings are deflated over both time and space and represent the purchasing power of the 2005 Egyptian pound (EGP) spent in the metropolitan area.

The analysis is limited to those who were 25 to 58 years old in 2008, unless explicitly stated. We are most interested in the changes in earnings of those actively engaged in the labor market and do not want large earnings changes by those retiring or moving to part time jobs in a pseudo-retirement phase to cloud our analysis. Additionally, large gains from recent entrants (or entrants into full time work) can disrupt our analysis. This is not to say that we are not interested in the important issues of youth (15–24 years) unemployment or earnings. We simply feel they should be analyzed separately. We will discuss how the inclusion of these younger workers affects some of our key results below.

Additionally, we limit earnings mobility analysis to those who are employed in both periods[5]. We use 3,481 observations of dual employed individuals with valid data.

One concern of such panel studies is that not every person interviewed in 2008 can be found again (or is willing to be re-interviewed) in 2009. This can have a particularly pernicious effect on our analysis if those who were not re-interviewed tend to have (extremely) positive or (extremely) negative earnings changes compared to those who are similar to them but were re-interviewed. There is some empirical evidence that such movers, particularly those that move farther away, tend to have more positive earnings changes than those left behind (Beegle et al. 2011). However, the existing evidence is quite limited and not from Egypt. Additionally, there are some common sense theoretical arguments that suggest that such missing individuals could be worse off. This question remains open as we do not have enough evidence to answer it in one direction or the other.

The fact that attrition rates in this panel are relatively low (just three percent of 2008 households are not re-interviewed in 2009) is therefore reassuring. As is typical in such studies, the individual attrition rate, 9.1 percent, is higher than the household attrition rate. Among 25 to 58 year olds, the individual attrition rate is 8.7 percent.

Overall, attrition appears to be driven more by who a person is and general life-cycle effects than by an individual's productive characteristics or outcomes. The first column of Table 1 shows the results of a linear probability model (LPM) predicting individual attrition. The dependent variable is 1 if the individual is not re-interviewed and 0 if the individual is re-interviewed. Those who were not married, were either very young or very old, were male and lived in the Metropolitan region were more likely to be missing at the 2009 interview. Meanwhile, joint significance tests on education level, initial sector of work, and relationship with employer categories were not found to have a significant effect at the ten percent level. An exception to this general trend is the fact that those who had higher initial earnings were found to be more likely to attrite. This was statistically significant at the five percent level, with change of one standard deviation in real earnings in 2008 resulting in a change in the predicted probability of attrition of 0.009 percentage points, ceteris paribus. A probit model was also run (see rightmost column of Table 1). The results of the probit model generally corroborate the LPM findings. One potential exception is that individuals working in the manufacturing and construction and trades and services sectors are less likely to attrite than those working in agriculture[6].

4. Empirical approach

We identify the typical change in earnings experienced by different types of Egyptian workers using empirical approaches that are common in the earnings and income mobility literature. We start by reporting mean and median earnings changes and move on to control for an increasing set of covariates. Techniques are similar to some of

Table 1 Determinants of attrition

	Dep. Var. (Attrition = 1)	
	Linear Prob. Model	Probit dF/dx
Metropolitan (omitted)		
Lower Urban	−0.061***	−0.039***
Lower Rural	−0.056***	−0.043***
Upper Urban	−0.045**	−0.029**
Upper Rural	−0.063***	−0.046***
Male	0.041***	0.030***
Working Housewife	−0.024	−0.029*
Married	−0.091***	−0.059***
Age	−0.022***	−0.017***
Age-squared	0.000***	0.0001***
Illiterate/no formal schooling (omitted)		
Basic education/literacy	0.008	0.010
Completed Primary	0.004	0.006
Secondary education	−0.005	−0.003
University degree	0.025	0.022
wage worker public (omitted)		
wage worker private	0.018	0.015
employer	−0.019	−0.015
self employed	−0.002	−0.001
unpaid worker	0.007	0.002
Agriculture (omitted)		
Manu/Const	−0.032*	−0.025**
Trade/Services	−0.021	−0.022*
Log per capita consumption	0.008	0.009
Earnings in 2008	−0.000**	0.000
Constant	0.635***	
n	4160	4160
R-squared / Pseudo R-squared	0.076	0.112

Notes: legend: * $p < 0.10$; ** $p < 0.05$; *** $p < 0.01$. Probit dF/dx evaluated at the mean of all other variables. Dummy variables show difference from 0 to 1.
Source: HIECPS, Feb 2008 to Feb 2009 (CAPMAS 2009).

those used in Cichello et al. (2005), Fields et al. (2003a/2003b), and Fields and Sanchez-Puerta (2010). Fields (2008) provides a literature review of such micro-mobility studies and provides a description of methods. There is a particular emphasis on controlling for initial earnings.

The goal of this empirical approach is to identify who has experienced the most severe declines in earnings, who has been able to avoid such severe declines in earnings, and which variables are consistently associated with the changes in earnings experienced by Egyptian workers. While all of the analysis, even the multivariate regression analysis, is descriptive rather than causal, one can confidently identify which groups of workers have been most or least adversely affected[7]. One can also piece together strong circumstantial evidence regarding some of the major drivers of earnings change.

Theories of what caused the changes in earnings should, at a minimum, be consistent with these descriptive results.

Our analysis will use both the change in earnings and the change in log earnings as the outcome variables of interest. The former is self-explanatory while the latter conforms roughly to the percentage change in earnings. Given that utility functions are concave, determining that earnings have fallen more on average for those who started with higher earnings may not necessarily suggest a lower welfare loss[8]. Also, in the context of an inflation shock, one may not be overly surprised if those with higher initial earnings have greater earnings declines. However, if the log earnings falls more for those with higher initial earnings, this goes beyond just the changes due to inflation.

We assess the change in earnings across a variety of characteristics. These include demographic variables (gender, age, marital status), location/region (urban and rural), and education level. We take these variables as exogenous variables that individuals bring to the labor market[9]. We also include a number of 2008 outcomes which may well be co-determined with the earnings change process. These include an individual's sector of employment (agriculture, industry or construction, trade or services); relationship with employer (public wage worker, private wage worker, employer, self-employed, unpaid worker); and formal or informal worker status, with formal workers defined as those covered by the social insurance system. We also include whether one lives in a poor household, defined as having consumption levels below the household specific poverty line[10]. In our multivariate analysis, these variables will be right hand side determinants of the change in log earnings.

Additionally, the relationship between the change in earnings and initial earnings is explored using flexible estimation approaches. The non-parametric lowess estimator estimates a smoothed change in log earnings value, y_i^s, for each observation by running n observation specific regressions of the change in log earnings (y_i) on initial log earnings (x_i) and calculating the predicted value of y_i. Weights for each observation in the regression are determined based on the distance from the x_i value of the current observation. More emphasis is placed on observations that are close to the current observation, even going so far as to give a zero weight to observations outside the bandwidth. The lowess estimator in STATA uses the tri-cube weight of Cleveland (1979) and we apply a bandwidth of 0.8 throughout these figures[11].

Measurement error can be particularly problematic when determining the change in earnings to initial earnings. For example, assume the relationship between these variables is linear and we would like to run a simple regression of change in reported earnings Δy_i^r, on initial reported earnings $y_{08,i}^r$.

$$\Delta y_i^r = \beta_0 + \beta_1 y_{08,i}^r + \varepsilon_i, \tag{1}$$

This can be re-written incorporating the potential for measurement error, signified by μ. We use y_k to represent the true level of earnings in year k.

$$\Delta y_i + \left(\mu_{09,i} - \mu_{08,i}\right) = \beta_0 + \beta_1 \left(y_{08,i} + \mu_{08,i}\right) + \varepsilon_i, \tag{2}$$

Even if measurement error is assumed to be mean zero, independent across individuals, independent across time for a given individual and independent of an individual's earnings level, the problems are more than the standard attenuation concerns that typically accompany a classical measurement error. The realized measurement error in year 2008 turns up on both the left hand and right hand sides of this equation causing a spurious negative correlation. To the extent that the measurement error is not perfectly auto-correlated, this can lead to a problem identical in nature to Galton's Fallacy. A negative relationship between initial earnings and the change in earnings *might* simply be due to random reporting errors.

Running the above regression will not give us the desired regression coefficient,

$$\hat{\beta}* = \frac{Cov(\Delta y, y_{08})}{Var(y_{08})} \tag{3}$$

Instead, as shown in a more general form in Fields et al. (2003a), we obtain:

$$\hat{\beta} = \hat{\beta}* * \frac{Var(y_{08})}{Var(y_{08}) + Var(\mu_{08})} - \frac{Var(\mu_{08})}{Var(y_{08}) + Var(\mu_{08})} \tag{4}$$

The first term identifies the standard attenuation bias issue while the second term accounts for the spurious negative correlation caused by the measurement error being on both the right and left side of the equation.

A simple example will illustrate why addressing this issue is of fundamental importance to our analysis. Suppose $\hat{\beta}* = 0.50$, implying that for each additional pound of earnings in 2008, on average, the individuals experiences a change in earnings that is a half a pound more (i.e. less negative). Also, suppose that the variance in measurement error is exactly equal to the variance in initial earnings. In this case, the attenuation bias would shrink the estimate from 0.5 to 0.25 and the second term would take away another 0.50. In other words, we would observe a coefficient of –0.25 in our analysis. Our story would be one of converging earnings, but the reality would be significant divergence of earnings in this sample. This example, while extreme, shows how powerful the impact of these biases can be on our results. It also highlights that the extent of the problem is driven in part by our assumption of how large the variance of the measurement error is relative to the variance of the initial earnings. For example, if we assumed the variance of μ was ten percent of the variance of initial earnings, the coefficient would observe would be 0.35 rather than 0.50[12].

In order to assess the robustness of our results given this potential problem, two approaches will be applied. First, initial earnings will be substituted by predicted initial earnings on the right hand side of equation (1) in the simple regression above (as well as in other methods). This process, i.e., the use of predicted values of initial values, should rid the right hand side of equation (1) of the spurious measurement error[13]. Of course, if our ability to predict initial earnings is weak, we may lose more than we gain from this approach. It should be noted that the key variables used to predict initial earnings are gender, age, education, place of residence, relationship with employer, sector of work, and log per capita consumption in the household.

The prediction regression results are shown in Table 2. When predicting initial earnings, the R-squared is 0.32. When predicting initial log earnings, the R-squared is .612. Thus, there is a relatively strong ability to predict initial earnings in levels and logs. The coefficient estimates are entirely reasonable; they are what we would expect in Egypt. Ceteris paribus, men have a strong initial advantage, earnings are concave with respect to age (turning point at roughly 45 years of age), those with higher education

Table 2 Regressions used to predict 2008 earnings and log earnings

	2008 earnings	2008 log earnings
Male	4517***	0.580***
Age	723***	0.090***
Age-squared	−8***	−0.001***
Working Housewife	603	−0.207***
Married	2873***	0.366***
Illiterate/no formal schooling (omitted)		
Basic education/literacy	414	0.094***
Completed Primary	1700***	0.155***
Secondary education	636*	0.115***
University degree	1406***	0.194***
Metropolitan (omitted)		
Lower Urban	−1035**	−0.007
Lower Rural	−1495***	−0.049*
Upper Urban	−563	0.033
Upper Rural	−439	−0.021
wage worker public (omitted)		
wage worker private	−356	−0.032
employer	3724***	0.388***
self employed	152	−0.114***
unpaid worker	−882	−0.509***
Agriculture (omitted)		
Manu/Const	1021**	0.148***
Trade/Services	775*	0.126***
log per capita consumption (08)	5748***	0.520***
Constant	−60681***	1.682***
n	3481	3481
R-squared	0.32	0.612

Notes: legend: * $p < 0.10$; ** $p < 0.05$; *** $p < 0.01$.
Source: HIECPS, Feb 2008 to Feb 2009 (CAPMAS 2009).

are earning considerably more than those with less education, wage workers outperform the self-employed and unpaid workers, but not employers, and agricultural workers earn less than others.

We will also assess whether such a classical measurement error can explain the results we observe in this dataset using a second approach. We assess the amount of measurement error that must be present, defined in terms of the variance, for measurement error to explain our observed regression coefficient if the true β coefficient is positive; i.e. if those higher initial earners experienced greater earnings gains. This is similar to a subset of simulations found in Fields et al. (Fields et al. 2003a). Additionally, in the annex, we use a simple simulation to demonstrate what our lowess graphs would look like given certain assumed levels of classical measurement error.

Under these assumptions, we consider it implausible that the negative coefficient on initial earnings from the simple regression was driven solely by classical measurement error. In order for this to be true, the variance of measurement error must be at least 1.56 times the variance of the true earnings level.

5. Findings

5.1 Transitions into and out of employment

Employment participation held steady and even increased slightly (68.2 to 69.6 percent), between February 2008 and February 2009 among panel members who were 25 to 58 years old in 2008. Thus, this is not a period where job losses were a dominant feature in the labor market for prime-aged workers[14].

Table 3 reveals that the aggregate participation rate masks strikingly different participation rates by gender, 94.5 percent for men versus 44.4 percent for women in 2008. The difference is largely due to many more women remaining outside the labor force.

Given the decline in real earnings between 2008 and 2009 (which is discussed in much more detail below), one might expect households to offset the erosion of real earnings by increasing the number of earners in the households. Since most men are already participating, this would require an influx of women into the labor market.

The "added worker effect" is discussed in the labor literature primarily with regard to married women entering the labor market in response to unemployment of the male (Lundberg 1985; Serneels 2002). The empirical evidence has been relatively weak for any large scale effects on employment rates in other countries, and often weak for even *desiring* more employment (Serneels 2002). Our situation differs from the often cited situation in that the male is not unemployed and therefore not necessarily "freely" available to substitute for the wife in the production of goods and services at the home. Additionally, the wife's real wage has also been reduced. Thus, we are not necessarily expecting a large change in female participation in response to the reduced earnings power of the male.

We find that the employment participation rates increase slightly for both males and females in 2009, to 94.9 percent and 46.7 percent respectively. These numbers do not suggest that households are adding workers as a major strategy for coping with inflation. Nor does the data suggest that firms fired large numbers of workers as a result of inflation[15]. These finding are consistent with findings of Roushdy and Gadallah (2011) which finds relatively little change in employment outcomes despite the economic downturn and large real earnings declines in 2009.

Table 4 takes advantage of the longitudinal nature of the data to allow us to see the flows into and out of each labor market status. The tables show the percentage of men (women) in each transition possibility, with the sum of all cells equaling 100 percent.

Most interesting is the large flow of women moving into and out of employment from the 'out of the labor force' category. Approximately one in six of women employed in 2008 are classified as out of the labor force in 2009, with roughly similar percentages of those out of the labor force in 2008 moving into employment in 2009. It is possible

Table 3 Labor force status of 25 to 58 year olds in 2008 and 2009, by gender

	All		Male		Female	
	2008	2009	2008	2009	2008	2009
Employed	68.2	69.6	94.5	94.9	44.4	46.7
Unemployed	1.9	1.6	1.7	1.5	2.1	1.7
Out of Labor Force	29.9	28.8	3.8	3.6	53.6	51.6

Notes: n = 5702.
Source: HIECPS, Feb 2008 to Feb 2009 (CAPMAS 2009).

Table 4 Labor force transitions of 25 to 58 year olds in 2008 and 2009, by gender

Male

Status in 2008	2009		
	Employed	Unemp	OLF
Employed	92.4	0.6	1.5
Unemployed	1.0	0.5	0.2
Out of Labor Force	1.6	0.3	1.9

Female

Status in 2008	2009		
	Employed	Unemp	OLF
Employed	36.2	0.4	7.8
Unemployed	0.4	0.7	1.0
Out of Labor Force	10.1	0.7	42.7

Notes: n = 2702 and 2995, respectively.
Source: HIECPS, Feb 2008 to Feb 2009 (CAPMAS 2009).

that some of this apparent flow is due to mis-measurement as women may not be declared employed in one period. However, it suggests that there are a large number of women who are capable of entering the labor force, at least for some time, if the household desires additional earnings. The story is similar if the data is restricted to only married women (not shown). Thus, there appears to be some scope culturally for many houses to add women workers to the labor force if needed. Finally, there is actually a slight decline in the unemployment rate for women, from 4.5 percent in 2008 to 3.5 percent in 2009.

While the bulk of men are employed in both periods, there is some evidence that the limited set of men who are unemployed may remain unemployed for some time. Thirty percent of those men who were unemployed in 2008 were unemployed again when interviewed in 2009 (as compared to just 0.7 percent who were employed at the time of the interview in 2008). The unemployment issue is similar for females as 31 percent of females who were unemployed in 2008 were unemployed again in 2009. However, in Egypt, unemployment is generally considered a luxury, where highly educated workers wait for a high paying job. For example, 85 percent of those unemployed in 2008 have secondary or university education, as compared to 45 percent of the entire prime-age working population.

5.2 A period of declining real earnings

Restricting our attention to the dual employed, the mean earnings change was a loss of 950 EGP, with the median change being a loss of 446 EGP. As will be detailed below, this decline in mean and median earnings was experienced by almost every type of worker. This is consistent with the erosion in real pay found by Said using the quarterly Egypt Labor Force Survey (ELFS) from 2007–2009 (Said 2012). The decline in real earnings is the dominant story of the labor market during this time period.

This decline in real earnings appears directly related to the increase in inflation. The mean (median) change in nominal earnings is just 107(330) EGP compared to a mean (median) of 9,858 (7,890) EGP in 2008 nominal earnings. Alternatively, if we apply the 2009 deflators to the 2008 nominal earnings, we project the average earnings fall from

7,755 EGP in 2008 to 6,727 EGP in 2009. In fact, the average real earnings in 2009 are 6,804 suggesting that workers earnings basically stagnated while inflation took away its buying power.

The improvement when comparing the median earnings level in each year is considerably better. The 6,237 EGP median earnings in 2008 would equate to 5,424 EGP using the 2009 deflators while the real median earnings in 2009 was 5,832EGP. Thus, comparing median earnings levels across distributions, workers were able to get back approximately 50 percent of the loss in earnings due to inflation. However, this seems to be an unusual point in the distribution of earnings. Corresponding values at the 25th and 75th percentiles are 16 percent and 23 percent. Figure 2 depicts the percentage of earnings lost to inflation that earners were able to recover due to increased nominal earnings for each percentile. At the top and bottom of the distributions, earnings appear to fall even in nominal terms. Overall, nominal earnings don't seem to increase much in response to the rapid rise in inflation, resulting in a significant loss of earnings power.

This result is in keeping with other findings from the Egyptian labor market. For example, Datt and Olmsted suggest that the rise and fall of real wages in Egypt between the mid-1970s and the early 1990s "masks a complex dynamic process by which nominal wages adjust in response to changes in food prices" (Datt and Olmsted 2004). The authors show a slow adjustment of nominal wages, with "a significant negative initial impact of rising food prices on real wages, though wages do catch up in the long run" (ibid).

Figure 3 depicts the real earnings changes using a density function of the change in log earnings for all but the top and bottom 2.5 percent of changes. The distribution is

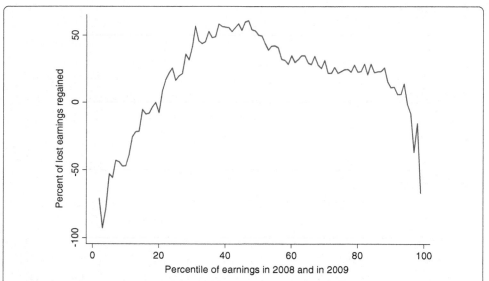

Figure 2 Percent of real earnings lost to inflation that was regained due to increased nominal pay, Egypt 2008 to 2009. *Source*: Authors' compilation from HIECPS (Feb 2008 to Feb 2009 (CAPMAS 2009)). *Notes*: This figure shows the change in nominal earnings for a given percentile in the earnings distribution as a percentage of the loss in real earnings that would have been experienced due to increased inflation if nominal earnings were the same in 2008 and 2009. The first percentile value (−161) has not been shown as it distorts the scale. Negative percentages imply that nominal earnings have declined between 2008 and 2009 for that percentile of the earnings distribution.

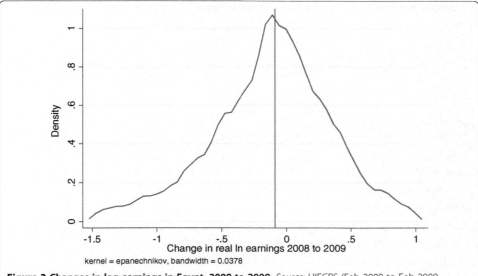

Figure 3 Changes in log earnings in Egypt, 2008 to 2009. *Source:* HIECPS (Feb 2008 to Feb 2009 (CAPMAS 2009)). *Notes:* Density function excludes top and bottom 2.5 percent of changes. The vertical line depicts the median change in log earnings.

centered below zero, with a median change in log earnings of negative 0.09 and a mean of negative 0.123.

Despite the substantial decline in earnings for measures of central tendency, the picture is indeed more complex than one where every individual earns 12 percent less than the year before: 41 percent of individuals experienced a gain in earnings over the time period; many individuals experienced positive and negative changes that were quite sizeable relative to their initial earnings; 31 percent of the changes in the density function above are greater than 0.5 or less than –0.5. While we would expect some differential across years due solely to the measurement error, we would expect that differentials of 50 percent in reported earnings would be extremely rare if an individual had the same earnings in both years[16].

As this is the first earnings mobility study in Egypt, we cannot say if this is more or less volatility in earnings than is the norm. What is clear is the following: while the aggregate employment numbers suggest a stagnant situation overall—with little change in employment status and average and median nominal wages—individuals are experiencing substantial fluctuations in their earnings. The rest of this paper seeks to explore which characteristics are associated with changes in earnings at the individual level.

5.3 The influence of initial earnings

There is a strong negative relationship between initial earnings and the ensuing earnings change. Using simple regression, Table 5 shows a statistically significant relationship. The coefficient estimate implies that the predicted earnings change is 0.61 EGP less for every additional Egyptian pound of reported initial earnings.

Table 5 shows that the negative relationship between earnings change and initial earnings holds up even if one replaces reported initial earnings with predicted initial earnings, although the coefficient falls to –0.29. Predicted initial earnings should not be

Table 5 Simple regression of change in earnings on initial earnings

Regression	Coeff.	st. error	p-value
Δy on y	−0.61	0.097	0.000
Δy on predicted y	−0.29	0.052	0.000
$\Delta \ln(y)$ on ln(y)	−0.23	0.017	0.000
$\Delta \ln(y)$ on predicted ln(y)	−0.04	0.026	0.131

Notes: Standard errors account for strata and clusters in sample survey design. Standard errors are bootstrapped when using predicted earnings or predicted log earnings.
Source: HIECPS, Feb 2008 to Feb 2009 (CAPMAS 2009).

correlated with the measurement error term under standard classical measurement error assumptions, although the random error in the predicted value of initial earnings may result in attenuation bias.

We consider it implausible that the negative coefficient on initial reported earnings from the simple regression was driven solely by classical measurement error. In order for this to be true, under the assumptions outlined above and the resulting equation (4), the variance of measurement error must be at least 1.54 times the variance of the true earnings level.

The analysis is repeated using log earnings. For every one percent increase in initial earnings, the predicted change in earnings decreases by approximately 0.23 percent. This result is statistically significant at the 1 percent level. In this case, again using equation (4), the variance of measurement error need only be 30 percent of the variance of the true earnings level for it to entirely explain the observed negative coefficient[17]. Additionally, we find that the predicted change in earnings decreases by 0.04 percent for every 1 percent increase in predicted initial log earnings. However, the p-value for this coefficient lies slightly outside the ten percent range for statistical significance. Thus, we are not confident that the true coefficient is negative.

This analysis assumes a linear relationship between initial earnings and earnings change. Next we allow more flexible approaches of establishing this relationship. Table 6 presents the mean and median change in earnings for each quintile of initial earnings.

Table 6 Change in earnings by initial earnings quintile

Initial reported earnings quintile	Change in earnings			Change in log earnings		
	Mean	Median	% positive	Mean	Median	% positive
1st (Lowest)	567	122	56%	0.086	0.071	56%
2nd	502	142	54%	−0.045	0.035	54%
3rd	119	−245	45%	−0.080	−0.040	45%
4th	−914	−1,148	31%	−0.200	−0.143	31%
5th	−5,026	−3,825	19%	−0.375	−0.294	19%

Initial Predicted (Log) Earnings Quintile

	Mean	Median	% positive	Mean	Median	% positive
1st (Lowest)	20	−45	48%	−0.124	−0.073	45%
2nd	−290	−295	44%	−0.103	−0.039	47%
3rd	−417	−306	45%	−0.062	−0.055	45%
4th	−867	−939	36%	−0.133	−0.111	37%
5th	−3,199	−1,880	32%	−0.193	−0.161	32%
TOTAL	−950	−446	41%	−0.123	−0.090	41%

It also documents the percent of individuals in each group that experienced positive changes in earnings.

The results clearly demonstrate a downward trend in the change in earnings as initial earnings quintile increases each step. The change between the first and second quintiles is rather limited, but other changes are quite large. This result is fairly consistent when comparing the change in earnings across predicted earnings quintiles. There is a clear downward trend in mean, median and percent positive earnings change across initial predicted earning quintile, except some bunching or minor reversal at the second and third quintiles.

When comparing the change in log earnings across initial log earnings quintiles, the results demonstrate a clear downward trend by initial earnings quintile. When comparing the change in log earnings across initial predicted log earnings, however, the data shows some potential for an inverted U shape, where those in the middle earnings category were able to buffer their losses (in percentage terms) as compared to those in the lowest earnings quintiles. Overall, however, the typical decline is far worse for those at the highest earnings levels as compared to those initially at the lowest earnings levels.

The severe decline in earnings experienced by those in the highest quintile is consistent across all four models. Just 19 percent of those in the highest initial earnings category experienced positive earnings changes. The mean decline in earnings for this group was 5,026 EGP as compared to the average of 950 EGP across the full sample. The median decline in earnings was 3,825 EGP and the median difference in log earnings was −0.29.

Figure 4 presents a more flexible method for assessing the relation between changes in log earnings and initial log earnings using a locally weighted regression. The vertical lines denote the different quintiles of initial log earnings. These results confirm the

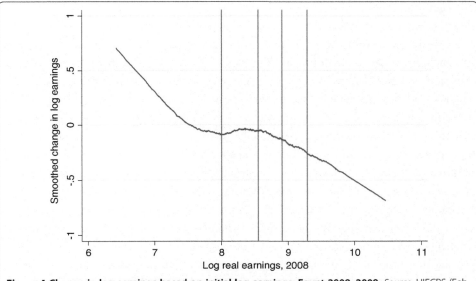

Figure 4 Change in log earnings based on initial log earnings, Egypt 2008–2009. *Source*: HIECPS (Feb 2008 to Feb 2009 (CAPMAS 2009)). *Notes*: Locally weighted regression was used to determine the predicted change in log earnings based on log real earnings in 2008. The top and bottom one percent of changes in log earnings are excluded. Vertical lines denote the 20th, 40th, 60th and 80th percentiles for 2008 log real earnings.

downward sloping relationship between the change in log earnings and initial log earnings, with bunching at the second and third quintile.

This result is consistent with previous examinations of real earnings that show declining inequality in periods when real earnings are falling in Egypt (Said 2009).

5.4 The role of characteristics besides initial earnings

Table 7 presents the mean and median earnings change and the percent of positive earnings changes for a series of additional characteristics that may be useful for either understanding more about the underlying process that drove the earnings changes during this time period and/or for understanding who was most adversely affected for the purpose of targeting assistance. This information is presented in columns (3) through (5), respectively. Columns (6) and (7) present the mean and median change in log earnings. Columns (1) and (2) are provided solely to assist the reader in understanding the composition of the labor force and relative earnings standings of each type of worker in the initial period.

Men had larger mean and median declines in real earnings than women, with an average decline of 1,189 EGP versus 391 EGP, respectively. This is not entirely unexpected in a period of rising inflation as men were initially earning more. Column (6) and (7) show a cloudier picture when it comes to differences across gender in terms of the average change in log earnings, or the percentage change in earnings. Men had a slightly larger median decline, but a slightly lower average decline. Thus, the story is less clear when it comes to the difference in log earnings.

Column (1) of Table 8 provides a simple regression of earnings change on each variable alone. This allows an easy way to identify the difference between groups relative to the omitted category (denoted by a 0) and whether this differential is statistically significant. The 798 EGP difference between average earnings for men and women is statistically significant.

Before reading too much into these average changes, one should consider controlling for initial earnings. Column (2) of Table 8 presents the regression results with initial earnings included as the sole additional right hand side variable. Compared to a female with the same initial earnings, a male is expected to have an earnings change that is 2,751 EGP better than his female counterpart. Thus, whether one considers this period a particularly bad period for male or female earners depends on whether we choose to consider male and female earners who are alike in their initial labor market outcomes or simply compare typical outcomes for each gender irrespective of their initial starting point. Similar analysis of the change in log earnings is presented in column (3), which has the average difference from the omitted group, and column (4) which includes log initial earnings on the right hand side. The minimal advantage that men had relative to women in the average change in log earnings expands dramatically (from 6 percent to 36 percent) once we control for initial log earnings.

Reviewing the results of Table 7 and columns (1) and (2) of Table 8, earnings declines were often larger for those groups who started with higher initial earnings, just as they were for men versus women. Examples include older workers, those in urban areas and the Metropolitan region, those who were employers in 2008, those who weren't unpaid workers in 2008, and those who lived in poor households in 2008. Consistent with this,

Table 7 Change in earnings and log earnings by individual characteristics, Egypt 2008 to 2009

2008			Change in earnings			Change in ln earnings	
(1)	(2)		(3)	(4)	(5)	(6)	(7)
Percent of panel workers	Median earnings	Individual characteristics	Mean	Median	Percent positive	Mean	Median
		TOTAL					
100%	6,237		-950	-446	41%	-0.12	-0.09
		Gender					
30%	2,964	Female	-391	-206	44%	-0.16	-0.08
70%	7,627	Male	-1,189	-628	40%	-0.11	-0.10
		Age					
31%	4,648	25-34	-459	-317	43%	-0.09	-0.08
34%	6,778	35-44	-803	-421	42%	-0.10	-0.07
35%	7,478	45-58	-1,518	-639	38%	-0.18	-0.12
		Education					
30%	4,047	Illiterate/no formal schooling	-781	-471	39%	-0.19	-0.14
12%	7,010	Basic education/ literacy	-1,534	-815	34%	-0.17	-0.16
10%	7,072	Completed Primary	-2,070	-699	41%	-0.14	-0.10
32%	6,503	Secondary education	-610	-287	43%	-0.07	-0.06
16%	8,490	University degree	-850	-349	46%	-0.04	-0.05
		Urban					
62%	5,316	Rural	-648	-404	41%	-0.14	-0.10
38%	7,783	Urban	-1,437	-516	42%	-0.10	-0.08
		Region					
17%	8,272	Metropolitan	-2,318	-817	39%	-0.13	-0.14
11%	8,481	Lower Urban	-413	-214	46%	-0.03	-0.03
38%	5,421	Lower Rural	-534	-287	43%	-0.11	-0.08
10%	6,859	Upper Urban	-1,053	-620	42%	-0.14	-0.08
24%	5,068	Upper Rural	-827	-522	37%	-0.18	-0.14
		Type of worker					
33%	7,400	wage worker public	-633	-117	47%	-0.03	-0.02
25%	5,914	wage worker private	-628	-504	41%	-0.10	-0.10
15%	9,324	employer	-2,809	-1,803	28%	-0.30	-0.21
16%	4,054	self employed	-1,077	-522	38%	-0.25	-0.16
10%	1,925	unpaid worker	214	-70	47%	-0.01	-0.04
		Informal worker					
53%	4,603	Informal	-838	-471	40%	-0.16	-0.13
47%	7,827	Formal	-1,074	-395	42%	-0.08	-0.06
		Industry					
31%	3,411	Agriculture	-829	-427	39%	-0.20	-0.17
19%	7,010	Manu/Const	-1,200	-645	37%	-0.12	-0.10
51%	7,151	Trade/Services	-931	-361	44%	-0.08	-0.06

Table 7 Change in earnings and log earnings by individual characteristics, Egypt 2008 to 2009 *(Continued)*

		Poor household in 2008					
84%	6,893	Non-poor	-1,171	-601	39%	-0.15	-0.11
16%	3,924	Poor	214	28	52%	0.00	0.01

Source: HIECPS, Feb 2008 to Feb 2009 (CAPMAS 2009).

but to a lesser degree, those who were formal workers and those who started outside of agriculture also had smaller mean and median changes. Working against this general trend, those with university education experienced smaller average losses than those with some primary schooling or complete primary schooling and those in the lower urban area seemed to withstand large losses relative to others despite high initial earnings. Yet, this relationship generally flips once one controls for initial earnings (or expands further in favor of the initially favored).

Columns (3) and (4) of Table 8 re-affirm this relationship with log earnings. The main difference is that the initial comparison between the favored and less favored groups is not as consistent. Besides the mixed results by gender, there are some notable exceptions where the log earnings changes of those who have low initial earnings are higher —such as for agricultural workers, informal workers, and those in rural regions. Results for age, education, employer relationship, and poor/non-poor household in 2008 generally conform to our previous analysis. Yet in almost all these cases, the initially favored group has much better average earnings changes once we control for initial log earnings is controlled.

With this in mind, we return to the flexible estimation approach of locally weighted regressions, mapping the relationship between earnings changes and initial earnings for particular groups of individuals.

Figure 5 shows that men consistently have *better* earnings change experiences than women who started at the same initial earnings[18]. The reason men had worse average and median earnings overall is because they started at higher initial earnings in 2008. This is clear through the fact that the area of support is pushed further to the right for men as compared to women. Thus, although men had larger declines on average, one might suspect that they actually had an advantage in responding to the surge in inflation.

Figure 6 assesses the change in log earnings based on the initial sector of work. Again, the negative relationship between log earnings change and initial log earnings is relatively consistent across all groups. In this case, the relationship in Table 7 is not overturned when controlling for initial earnings. Those who started out working in agriculture have consistently worse earnings changes than those working in other sectors.

Figure 7 suggests that there is no consistent differential for those who were in poor households in 2008 compared to those in non-poor households once one controls for initial earnings. There may be some gap at the lower and upper initial earnings, but those in poor households have a slight advantage in the middle range of shared initial earnings. Thus, the earnings mobility disadvantages that some individuals face do not appear rooted in initial year poverty status.

Column (7) in Table 7 shows the regression coefficient from bivariate regressions of earnings change on the category of interest, controlling for initial earnings. By looking across columns (6) and (7), we can see that there are multiple cases where our

Table 8 Earnings changes by individual characteristics, with relation to initial earnings

Dependent variable	Change in earnings		Change in log earnings	
	(1)	(2)	(3)	(4)
Individual Characteristics	no controls	with income as a control	no controls	with log income as a control
Gender				
Male	−798***	2,751***	0.06**	0.38***
Age				
35-44	−344	1,218***	−0.01	0.06**
45-58	−1,059***	1,018***	−0.09***	0.01
Education				
Basic education/literacy	−754*	1,181***	0.02	0.17***
Completed Primary	−1,290	1,155***	0.04	0.20***
Secondary education	171	1,709***	0.11***	0.25***
University degree	−70	3,513***	0.14***	0.37***
Urban				
Urban	−789*	1,624***	0.03	0.16***
Region				
Lower Urban	1,905**	1,096	0.10*	0.09*
Lower Rural	1,784**	−1,355***	0.02	−0.12***
Upper Urban	1,265	−560	−0.01	−0.07
Upper Rural	1,491*	−1,651***	−0.05	−0.20***
Type of worker				
wage worker private	5	−1,263***	−0.07**	−0.14***
employer	−2,175***	−516	−0.27***	−0.19***
self employed	−444	−2,495***	−0.22***	−0.42***
unpaid worker	848**	−3,657***	0.02	−0.44***
Informal Worker				
Formal	−236	2,279***	0.08***	0.27***
Industry				
Manu/Const	−371	1,967***	0.09**	0.31***
Trade/Services	−102	2,335***	0.13***	0.35***
Poor household in 2008				
Poor	1,385***	−1,053***	0.15***	0.01
Initial earnings quintile				
2	−65	1,778***	−0.13***	0.29***
3	−448***	3,106***	−0.17***	0.45***
4	−1,481***	4,162***	−0.29***	0.49***
5 = highest	−5,593***	6,988***	−0.46***	0.59***
Predicted initial earnings quintile				
2	−311**	1,306***	−0.07**	0.18***
3	−437**	2,887***	−0.03	0.40***
4	−887***	3,561***	−0.08**	0.42***
5 = highest	−3,219***	5,511***	−0.14***	0.52***

Notes: legend: * p < 0.10; ** p < 0.05; *** p < 0.01. Standard errors account for strata and clusters in sample survey design. Omitted categories are female, 25-34 year olds, illiterates/no schooling, rural area, metropolitan area, wage worker public, informal workers, agricultural workers, non-poor households, and lowest 20% quintile of initial earnings or predicted earnings.
Source: HIECPS, Feb 2008 to Feb 2009 (CAPMAS 2009).

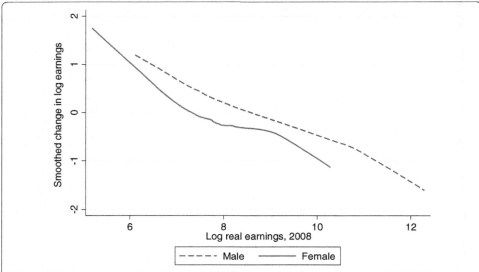

Figure 5 Change in log earnings based on initial log earnings by gender, Egypt 2008–2009. *Source*: HIECPS (Feb 2008 to Feb 2009 (CAPMAS 2009)). *Notes:* Locally weighted regression was used to determine the predicted change in log earnings based on log real earnings in 2008. Analysis was done separately by gender and then plotted on the same graph.

impression of whether a group (such as males) has had better average outcomes than another (women), is overturned when we compare the two groups conditional on the same initial earnings. This overturning effect generally holds for females, younger workers, those living in rural areas, or in regions with lower initial earnings, unpaid workers, informal workers, those working in agriculture and those living in poor households. While mean and median earnings changes for these groups were better than those of their counterparts, they performed worse on average than their counterparts who had similar initial earnings.

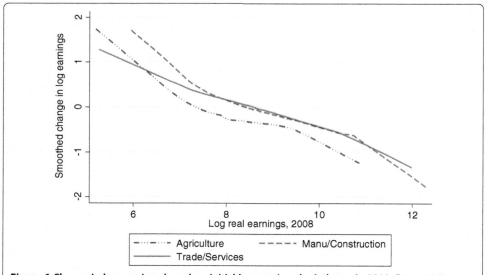

Figure 6 Change in log earnings based on initial log earnings by industry in 2008, Egypt 2008–2009. *Source*: HIECPS (Feb 2008 to Feb 2009 (CAPMAS 2009)). *Notes:* Locally weighted regression was used to determine the predicted change in log earnings based on log real earnings in 2008. Analysis was done separately by industry and then plotted on the same graph.

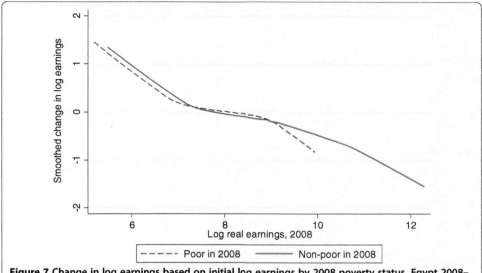

Figure 7 Change in log earnings based on initial log earnings by 2008 poverty status, Egypt 2008–2009. *Source:* HIECPS (Feb 2008 to Feb 2009 (CAPMAS 2009)). *Notes:* Locally weighted regression was used to determine the predicted change in log earnings based on log real earnings in 2008. Analysis was done separately by 2008 poverty status and then plotted on the same graph.

In short, it is very important to consider the impact of initial earnings when evaluating how certain types of individuals were able to succeed and advance during the period. This type of evaluation generally requires panel data.

5.5 The role of transitions across types of work

Next we examine the systematic earnings changes associated with moving to a different sector of employment or to a job with a different employer relationship. First, we assess how often these transitions take place.

Table 9a shows that just more than half (51 percent) of all panel workers are employed in trade and services in 2008. Ninety-two percent of these workers are employed there again in 2009, while five percent are in manufacturing or construction and three percent are in agriculture. Agriculture also retains the vast majority (88 percent) of its workers in 2009 while manufacturing and construction work appears a bit less stable, with the sector retaining just 78 percent of 2008 workers in 2009. Overall the flows result in a slight loss of employment in agriculture and manufacturing/construction and movements into trade and services, which now employ 53 percent of workers. Overall, 12 percent of panel members were in a different sector in 2009 than in 2008.

Table 9b demonstrates the strength of tie to public wage employment. Ninety-five percent of public wage workers in the panel remained in public wage employment in 2009 as compared to just 66 percent of those in private wage work, 69 percent of employers, 55 percent of the self-employed and 75 percent of the unpaid workers. Flows from private to public wage work were particularly plentiful, helping to explain the three percent increase in public wage employment and the corresponding three percent loss in private wage employment in 2009, even though flows into public employment came from all other types of employment.

Table 9 Employment transitions by type of work or worker, Egypt 2008 to 2009

a: Sector of work

	Sector in 2009		
Sector in 2008	Agriculture	Ind/Const	Trade/Services
Agriculture (31%)	87.8%	3.8%	8.4%
Industry/Construction (19%)	5.0%	78.2%	16.7%
Trade/Services (51%)	2.7%	5.0%	92.3%
Total	29%	18%	53%

b: Employer Relationship

	Employer Relationship in 2009				
Employer Relationship in 2008	Public Wage	Private Wage	Employer	Self-employed	Unpaid
Public Wage (33%)	94.9%	3.6%	0.8%	0.5%	0.1%
Private Wage (25%)	15.4%	66.0%	8.3%	8.1%	2.1%
Employer (15%)	2.8%	11.8%	69.3%	12.5%	3.5%
Self-employed (16%)	2.5%	11.4%	16.1%	55.3%	14.6%
Unpaid (10%)	2.2%	5.8%	3.5%	13.9%	74.7%
Total	36%	22%	16%	15%	11%

c: Formality

	Status in 2009	
Status in 2008	Informal	Formal
Informal (53%)	88.2%	11.8%
Formal (47%)	14.8%	85.2%
Total	53%	47%

Source: HIECPS, Feb 2008 to Feb 2009 (CAPMAS 2009).

The transient nature of self-employment is also apparent as just 55 percent of 2008 workers were self-employed in 2009. More than ten percent of these individuals ended up as private wage employees (11 percent), as employers (16 percent), and as unpaid workers (15 percent). While moving to employer status might be thought of as a successful outcome for a self-employed individual, other outcomes may be less certain. Movement to private wage employment may often occur by choice and may often be the result of business failure. Movement to unpaid worker status might result from more family members working in a successful household enterprise or it might be a result of failure of the business that the individual was running and falling back into another household enterprise. The earnings mobility outcomes may help us form opinions on these.

Tables 10a-b and 11 should be interpreted bearing in mind the mean (–950) and median (–446) earnings losses for the population of workers as a whole.

Those who left agricultural work were generally better able to stem the earnings losses. The median change and the percent experiencing positive earnings gains were higher for those who switched sectors, though the average decline in earnings for those who moved to trade/services was actually larger than those who stayed in agriculture. Meanwhile, those who moved into agricultural work were experiencing larger than average earnings losses. This evidence is consistent with what one might expect if there is significant labor market segmentation, with agriculture representing the least preferred free entry sector and the differential pay being offered to the same individual

Table 10 Mean and median earnings change by employment transition, Egypt 2008 to 2009

a: Sector of work

		Sector in 2009		
Sector in 2008		Agriculture	Ind/Const	Trade/Services
Agriculture	Mean	−852	−97	−921
	Median	−456	−115	−222
% positive		38%	48%	45%
	n obs	1,002	38	92
Industry/Construction	Mean	−1,342	−1,411	−154
	Median	−963	−641	−258
% positive		32%	37%	42%
	n obs	37	507	104
Trade/Services	Mean	−3,878	−966	−842
	Median	−1,148	−947	−349
% positive		39%	42%	44%
	n obs	54	87	1,559

b: Employer Relationship

		Employer Relationship in 2009				
Relationship in 2008		Public Wage	Private Wage	Employer	Self-employed	Unpaid
Public Wage	Mean	−614	−116			
	Median	−109	210			
% positive		47%	51%			
	n obs	1,053	39			
Private Wage	Mean	−640	−846	984	−178	−1,815
	Median	−188	−641	808	−235	−1,661
% positive		47%	37%	61%	46%	12%
	n obs	124	566	78	71	20
Employer	Mean		−2,956	−2,481	−3,441	
	Median		−2,364	−1,482	−1,744	
% positive			15%	32%	23%	
	n obs		61	390	68	
Self-employed	Mean		−3,388	19	−953	−1,116
	Median		−1,719	−205	−471	−603
% positive			22%	47%	38%	33%
	n obs		65	93	331	95
Unpaid	Mean		2,047		305	−277
	Median		1,644		245	−230
% positive			93%		59%	39%
	n obs		20		47	274

Notes: Cells with less than 20 observations not shown.
Source: HIECPS, Feb 2008 to Feb 2009 (CAPMAS 2009).

working in different sectors. However, a much more detailed analysis would be needed to assess this hypothesis more fully.

The earnings decline for those remaining in the industry/construction sector was large. Combined with the previous information of workers flowing out of this sector, a

Table 11 Formality

Status in 2008		Status in 2009	
		Informal	Formal
Informal	Mean	−865	−640
	Median	−479	−222
% positive		39%	46%
	n obs	1,690	212
Formal	Mean	−2,848	−765
	Median	−1,160	−267
% positive		29%	45%
	n obs	239	1,340

Source: HIECPS, Feb 2008 to Feb 2009 (CAPMAS 2009).

consistent picture emerges that this sector was under stress during the 2008 to 2009 period. The only group of individuals that started in industry/construction and ended with less than average earnings losses was the group that moved to trade/services. Correspondingly, those who started in trade/services suffered high median losses if they moved to industry/construction, but the mean earnings loss for this group and the percent experiencing positive gains were basically the same as the overall average. Thus, the data is less clearly consistent with what we would expect if there was segmentation across industry/construction and trade/services sectors. It does appear that the industry/construction sector was under strain. It is a bit surprising that those who transitioned from industry/construction to trade/services had such relatively positive earnings changes. This seems to be driven by those coming from construction or electrical utilities rather than manufacturing sectors, but the estimates are too variable to find the differences to be statistically significant.

Public wage workers who stayed on in public wage employment did better than average in stemming the loss in real earnings. This is surprising given their high initial earnings levels and our earlier results regarding high initial earnings. Those who moved from public to private wage employment did even better. This suggests that such moves were likely voluntary moves.

In fact, with the exception of movements into unpaid worker status, wage workers who moved to new work categories consistently had better earnings changes than those who stayed within their same worker category. Thus, a generalization might be to assume that most observed changes of wage workers were voluntary, while those moving to unpaid worker status were involuntary. It does not appear that this was a period of substantial labor shedding of wage workers, public or private. Instead, workers absorbed losses in their real wage.

In contrast to this, the employed and self-employed who moved to private wage experienced even worse mean and median changes than those who stayed in their respective categories, consistent with a notion of being involuntarily pushed out of business rather than finding a better job.

Those who started as employers took large losses whether they moved sectors or tried to ride out the storm remaining as an employer. The self-employed also had relatively large losses. This might seem to be surprising given that such individuals have the opportunity to immediately change their product prices in response to inflation

Table 12 Determinants of change in log earnings, Egypt 2008 to 2009

	(1)	(2)	(3)	(4)	(5)
Log earnings in 2008	−0.4655***	−0.5226***	−0.5352***	−0.5359***	
Predicted log earnings in 2008					−0.2818***
Male	0.4423***	0.3258***	0.2734***	0.2828***	0.1474***
Age	0.0510***	0.0423***	0.0412***	0.0408***	0.0235**
Age-squared	−0.0006***	−0.0005***	−0.0005***	−0.0005***	−0.0003**
Married	0.1082**	0.1461***	0.1441***	0.1475***	0.0798**
Illiterate/no formal schooling (omitted)					
Basic education/literacy	0.1130***	0.0417	0.0204	0.0214	0.0058
Completed Primary	0.1471***	0.0761**	0.0653*	0.0693*	0.039
Secondary education	0.2298***	0.1056***	0.0860***	0.0877***	0.0677**
University degree	0.4033***	0.2518***	0.2189***	0.2243***	0.1486***
Metropolitan (omitted)					
Lower Urban	0.0723	0.0673	0.0627	0.064	0.0882
Lower Rural	−0.0764*	−0.0501	−0.0515	−0.0613	−0.0146
Upper Urban	−0.0754	−0.0722	−0.0861	−0.0898	−0.0623
Upper Rural	−0.1771***	−0.1417***	−0.1183**	−0.1327**	−0.0999**
Working Housewife		−0.2626***	−0.1251*	−0.1387**	−0.0996
wage worker public (omitted)					
wage worker private		−0.0574**	−0.013	−0.0029	−0.0384
employer		0.0381	−0.0922	−0.0602	−0.1909***
self employed		−0.1214***	−0.0781	−0.0558	−0.0976
unpaid worker		−0.0447	0.2694***	0.2966***	0.3550***
Formal worker		0.0852***			
Agriculture (omitted)					
Manu/Const		0.0877**		0.0944***	0.060*
Trade/Services		0.0943**		0.0934**	0.068**
Poor in 2008		−0.0051	0.0053	0.0036	0.1438***
wage wkr public in 09 (omitted)					
wage wkr private in 09			−0.0225	−0.0336	−0.0482
employer in 09			0.3171***	0.2557***	0.1958***
self employed in 09			−0.0619	−0.092	−0.0675
unpaid worker in 09			−0.4984***	−0.5534***	−0.5460***
Informal-informal (omitted)					
Informal-formal			0.1049**	0.1210***	0.1135***
Formal-informal			−0.007	−0.0027	−0.0762*
Formal-formal			0.1470***	0.1559***	0.0517*
Agri - Agri (omitted)					
Agri - Manu/Const			0.2356***		
Agri - Trade/Services			0.1099		
Manu/Const - Agri			−0.1032		
Manu/Const - Manu/Const			0.1575***		
Manu/Const - Trade/Services			0.1642**		
Trade/Services - Agri			−0.1306		
Trade/Services - Manu/Const			0.1405**		

Table 12 Determinants of change in log earnings, Egypt 2008 to 2009 *(Continued)*

Trade/Services - Trade/Services			0.1548***		
Constant	2.3032***	3.0926***	3.1953***	3.2530***	1.6737***
n	3481	3481	3480	3481	3481
R-squared	0.2358	0.2728	0.3471	0.3411	0.1297

Notes: legend: * $p < 0.10$; ** $p < 0.05$; *** $p < 0.01$. Standard errors account for strata and clusters in sample survey design. Column (5) uses bootstrapped standard errors.
Source: HIECPS, Feb 2008 to Feb 2009 (CAPMAS 2009).

(and have their earnings rise) whereas workers may be locked into longer term contracts. This will be discussed more fully in Section 6.

Movements from formal to informal employment tended to result in very large losses. They were also quite numerous. This could signal labor shedding, where individuals are being forced to change jobs and losing out on pay. However, there was an inflow from informal to formal employment that was similar in size as the above outflow. This inflow did not result in earnings gains on par with the losses noted above. Therefore, it was not simply a case of individuals changing positions with similar earnings. An alternative explanation could be that employers under duress are opting out of the social pension system (and simultaneously giving workers reduced earnings). One might expect a certain flow from both of these causes in any time period. Without a baseline to know the typical flows and earnings changes from such transitions in Egypt, it is difficult to pinpoint an explanation.

Interestingly, those who moved from informal to formal sectors had earnings changes that were significantly but not so dramatically better than those who stayed informal. The changes were similar to those experienced by those who started and remained in the formal sector.

5.6 Multivariate analysis

We turn to multivariate analysis to better understand the determinants of earnings mobility. Table 12 presents a series of regressions that have the change in log earnings as the dependent variable. Results are presented using only exogenous base year characteristics and initial earnings (column 1) and then adding endogenous variables from the base year (column 2)[19]. Columns (3) and (4) include employment transition variables, with column (4) being the preferred specification (discussed below). In column (5), we replace initial log earnings with predicted initial log earnings and include all previous variables. In this specification, the effect of predicted initial log earnings is identified by fluctuations in log per capita consumption in the household in the base period.

Initial earnings are a powerful predictor of earnings change across all specifications. The coefficients imply that the predicted change in log earnings decreases by between 0.47 and 0.54 for each additional unit in reported log income. When using predicted initial log income, the coefficient drops to −0.28, which is still highly significant from an economic perspective. The coefficient is statistically significant at the one percent level for all specifications.

Another characteristic exhibiting a consistently important influence on predictions is gender. Males experience approximately 27 percent to 44 percent higher earnings changes than females, ceteris paribus, in columns (1)-(4)[20]. When using predicted initial earnings, this falls to about 15 percent higher, ceteris paribus, but remains both statistically significant and important in terms of economic loss. In contrast, re-running column (4) without including initial earnings, leads to a negative though statistically insignificant gender effect (see Table 13).

Higher education levels also seem to be associated with higher earnings changes when controlling for initial earnings. Focusing on column (4), those with secondary education and university education had statistically significant differences in earnings changes compared to those who were illiterate/had no schooling, with gains of approximately 8.8, and 22.4 percent respectively. If one does not control for initial earnings, the estimated differences by education level are neither individually nor jointly statistically significant.

Age is also statistically significant, with earnings changes increasing and then decreasing with age. In column (4) the turning point is 43 years of age, while in column (5) it is 39 years of age (not shown in the table). Being married raises predicted earnings change by approximately 15 percent in the preferred specification, although, in column (5), the point estimate is less than half the size and it is only statistically significant at the ten percent significance level. These effects were also considerably different when running regression analysis without initial earnings[21].

Using the preferred specification, the upper rural region had statistically lower earnings changes, ceteris paribus, than the Metropolitan region. Returning to Table 7, one may notice that the highest median pay in 2008 was in the Lower Urban region, followed by the Metropolitan region and the lowest pay was in Upper Rural region.

Looking at the employment transition variables, there are some surprising results. First, after controlling for other characteristics and initial earnings, the variables identifying transitions across industry in column (3) are not jointly statistically significant. The data did not reject the null hypothesis that only the initial sector of employment was needed for predicting earnings changes. This is surprising, but does allow a simpler form to be used as our preferred specification in column (4).

Using just initial industry characteristics we determine that those who started in agriculture experienced approximately nine percent lower earnings changes than others. The results are statistically significant. This result might seem surprising since the inflation was driven in part by rising food prices. One might assume that food producers would be able to increase their prices at least at the rate of inflation.

There are some potential explanations behind this unexpected result. We begin with some explanations that justify why farmers' gains from rising food prices might be less than expected for those unfamiliar with the Egyptian setting. First, for most of the small farmers, the agricultural production makes up only up to 40 percent of their incomes, and they simultaneously sell their labor to other farmers/enterprises. Since higher food prices only benefit farmers on the share they sell, and agricultural wages may be slow to adjust, particularly if the food price shocks come too late to adjust the production size, the overall gains may be less than expected. Second, many farmers in Egypt are net consumers of food. Egypt is a very large importer of grains (mostly wheat), oil, and sugar—three main items in the consumption basket. Meat production relies heavily on imported grains as well. Therefore, it's possible that the prices for the main consumption items and input costs were going up substantially faster than the production items. Finally, even assuming that farmers could benefit from higher prices, it did not seem

Table 13 Determinants of change in log earnings, with and without initial earnings

	(1)	(2)
	with initial earnings	without initial earnings
Log earnings in 2008	−0.5359***	
Male	0.2828***	−0.0076
Age	0.0408***	0.0022
Age-squared	−0.0005***	−0.0001
Married	0.1475***	0.0001
Illiterate/no formal schooling (omitted)		
Basic education/literacy	0.0214	−0.0308
Completed Primary	0.0693*	−0.0126
Secondary education	0.0877***	0.0203
University degree	0.2243***	0.0326
Metropolitan (omitted)		
Lower Urban	0.064	0.1136*
Lower Rural	−0.0613	0.0461
Upper Urban	−0.0898	−0.0238
Upper Rural	−0.1327**	−0.0368
Working Housewife	−0.1387**	−0.0457
wage worker public (omitted)		
wage worker private	−0.0029	−0.033
employer	−0.0602	−0.3161***
self employed	−0.0558	−0.0734
unpaid worker	0.2966***	0.4930***
wage wkr public in 09 (omitted)		
wage wkr private in 09	−0.0336	−0.0455
employer in 09	0.2557***	0.1889***
self employed in 09	−0.092	−0.0678
unpaid worker in 09	−0.5534***	−0.5493***
Informal-informal (omitted)		
Informal-formal	0.1210***	0.1174**
Formal-informal	−0.0027	−0.0812**
Formal-formal	0.1559***	0.0414
Agriculture (omitted)		
Manu/Const	0.0944***	0.0117
Trade/Services	0.0934**	0.0277
Poor in 2008	0.0036	0.2309***
Constant	3.2530***	−0.0816
n	3481	3481
R-squared	0.3411	0.1228

Notes: legend: * $p < 0.10$; ** $p < 0.05$; *** $p < 0.01$. Standard errors account for strata and clusters in sample survey design.
Source: HIECPS, Feb 2008 to Feb 2009 (CAPMAS 2009).

the case for most of the domestic prices on food items, which increase in a very different way from international prices, as shown in Figure 8.

These explanations are admittedly lacking. While they offer ideas on why the relative gains for those engaged in agriculture may be weaker than expected, they

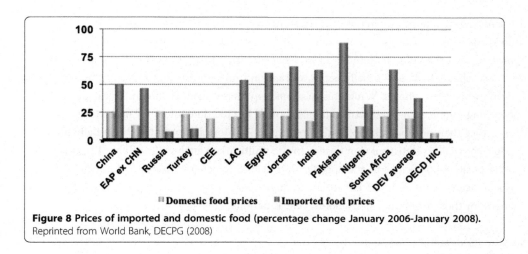

Figure 8 Prices of imported and domestic food (percentage change January 2006-January 2008).
Reprinted from World Bank, DECPG (2008)

do not explain why those in agriculture had outcomes that were actually worse than others.

An alternative explanation suggests that farmers faced rising input costs and suppressed gains in output prices. The rising input costs are primarily attributed to steeply rising fertilizer costs. On the other hand, a ban on rice exports caused the domestic price of rice to be lower than expected. These storylines are presented here as one possible explanation that warrants much further examination. We do not provide supplemental evidence other than to say this proposed explanation is somewhat consistent with the fact that the large earnings declines for those initially in agriculture are predominantly driven by changes for those initial employers or self-employed rather than for those who are working in agriculture as wage workers. Future work will allow us to offer more concrete evidence to support or dispute this storyline[22].

Those who ended up in the formal sector in 2009 (whether or not they were in the formal sector in 2008) had statistically significant changes in earnings, 12 to 16 percent greater than those who started informal and remained informal. Those who started in the formal sector and moved to informal sector did no worse than those who were informal throughout.

For employer relationship transitions, we did not include all possibilities as there were many cells with very few observations. Instead, we include category dummies in the base and final year. The data suggests that, ceteris paribus, there was no statistically significant advantage to where one came from, but that those who were employers in 2009 experienced significant higher earnings changes and those who were unpaid in 2009 had significantly lower earnings changes.

Overall, individuals from initially advantaged groups tended to suffer smaller losses in log earnings than their counterparts after we control for initial earnings. This result holds for such critical variables as gender, education, and region as well as for the married dummy variable and one's industry of employment in 2008. If we do not control for initial earnings, these relationships are often reversed or statistically insignificant. With regard to employment transitions, there is evidence that those ending in the better employer relationship positions or in the formal sector in 2009, tended to end up with a higher predicted change in earnings. An individual's transition across industries offers surprisingly little ability to help estimate his/her earnings change.

5.7 A review of changes by initial poverty status

Individuals from initially poor households fared as well or better than others. They do not appear to be more vulnerable to earnings declines during this period. Those initially from poor households had substantially better average and median earnings changes than those from non-poor households. While this relationship was reversed when conditioning on initial earnings alone, non-parametric analysis showed limited differences for individuals from poor rather than non-poor households (see Figure 7). More importantly, the initially poor variable showed no statistical significance in the multivariate analysis (see Table 12), except for the positive coefficient in the specification using predicted earnings (column 5). This was significant at the one percent level and suggested a 14 percent advantage in earnings changes for those from poor households, ceteris paribus.

5.8 A more detailed examination by gender

Table 14 offers separate regression analysis by gender. Some interesting differences emerge. First, while the importance of initial earnings is apparent for all three groups,

Table 14 Determinants of change in log earnings, by gender

	Male	Female
Log earnings in 2008	−0.4879***	−0.6533***
Age	0.0354***	0.0351
Age-squared	−0.0004***	−0.0004
Married	0.2429***	−0.1033*
Illiterate/no formal schooling (omitted)		
Basic education/literacy	0.0192	0.0206
Completed Primary	0.0515	0.1422
Secondary education	0.0747**	0.1005
University degree	0.2301***	0.2564***
Metropolitan (omitted)		
Lower Urban	0.0744	0.0793
Lower Rural	−0.0448	−0.0411
Upper Urban	−0.0384	−0.1535
Upper Rural	−0.1243**	−0.1631*
wage worker public (omitted)		
wage worker private	−0.0403	−0.1930*
employer	0.0024	−0.0382
self employed	−0.0206	−0.3898**
unpaid worker	−0.0503	−0.2502
Formal worker	0.0703**	0.2116**
Agriculture (omitted)		
Manu/Const	0.0337	0.1795
Trade/Services	0.0260	0.2113**
Poor in 2008	−0.0160	−0.0198
Constant	3.2490***	4.4566***
n	2439	1042
R-squared	0.2672	0.3311

Notes: legend: * p < 0.10; ** p < 0.05; *** p < 0.01. Standard errors account for strata and clusters in sample survey design. *Source:* HIECPS, Feb 2008 to Feb 2009 (CAPMAS 2009).

the impact is greater for women as compared to men. This could be due to a variety of reasons. For example, women may have a higher degree of transitory income as a general norm. Or, it could result from period-specific changes. Suppose, for example, successful women had a disproportionate decline in earnings because households had to spend more on food and had less left to spend on stock for the female run enterprises. Simultaneously, women with low earnings may have had disproportionate gains in earnings as they worked more aggressively in the labor market in an attempt to make up for inflation reducing the buying power associated with the male breadwinner's take home pay. We do not examine these points fully here, but leave them as open questions.

Additional differences exist between males and females. For example, while married men had 24 percent higher earnings gains than an otherwise similar non-married men, married women had 10 percent lower earnings than an otherwise similar non-married woman. However, the effect for females was not statistically significant. Additionally, females saw much greater differentials in earnings change experiences based on formal work status in 2008; employment type in 2008, specifically in comparison to public wage workers; and sector of employment in 2008, specifically non-agricultural versus agricultural workers.

While these differences are present, other aspects of the earnings change experience are quite similar across gender. Both groups were estimated to have earnings changes that increase and then decrease with age, with nearly identical turning points (at 43 years). Additionally, there were nearly identical gains for those with a University degree compared to those with no education. Other results across education levels were quite similar for males and females or were statistically insignificant. Results were also similar across gender when looking at changes experienced in different regions of Egypt.

6. Conclusions and areas of further research

Using panel data from February 2008 to February 2009, we observe changes in earnings experienced by workers in Egypt during a period of high inflation. In aggregate, the data shows that the labor market reacted to this rapid inflation by inducing a rapid decline in real earnings. There was no major reduction in employment levels, at least not for prime-aged workers. Average nominal earnings remained relatively unchanged. The mean and median changes in real earnings were almost universally negative across a wide spectrum of individual and regional characteristics.

At the individual level, however, the earnings change experience exhibited substantial heterogeneity, with 27 percent of the workers with employment in both periods reporting pay at least fifty percent higher or fifty percent lower than their reported 2008 earnings. Additionally, many individuals transitioned to new sectors of work or employer relationships during this period. Thus, for many individuals, this was a period of considerable fluidity and complexity compared to the rather simple aggregate story. As this is the first panel dataset in Egypt that captures such movements, we cannot determine the extent to which these earnings changes and employment transitions differ from what is typically found in a more stable economic period.

However, using this panel data and a descriptive regression approach, we are able to identify key covariates that have a significant association with earnings change. The descriptive regression approach cannot give us causal interpretations, but it does provide statistical determinants of earnings change. It gives circumstantial evidence that favors particular items as driving forces. It also leaves us with many new questions to explore in the future.

We found that initial earnings had a powerful negative association with earnings change. Those with higher earnings in 2008 had a greater average (and median) decline in earnings. This might be expected in a time period where inflation is driving the change in real earnings. Yet, the data also shows that those with higher reported log earnings in 2008 had a greater average decline in reported log earnings as well.

Such results may be driven by a spurious correlation resulting from classical measurement error. Thus, we re-computed the analysis using predicted earnings in place of initial earnings. The levels result was robust to this approach. The log result was not robust, although the coefficient was still negative. Thus, the data suggests that those with lower initial earnings experienced percentage declines that were, at worst, similar to those with higher initial earnings and there is some evidence that the percentage declines were lower for those with lower initial earnings.

The importance of controlling for initial earnings was evident when examining the relationship between earnings change and gender. On average, men experienced a much larger average decline in earnings than women. However, for men and women with the same initial earnings, women had a greater average fall in earnings.

For a number of other covariates, the story was similar. The disadvantaged groups—such as young workers, those living in rural areas or those living in low-earning regions—experienced smaller average declines in earnings than their advantaged counterparts. However, if individuals started with the same initial earnings, it was members of the disadvantaged group that experienced greater average declines. One exception to this was that those from poor households did not generally show themselves to be more vulnerable to earnings declines even after conditioning on initial earnings.

When controlling for a larger host of covariates, higher initial earnings remained negatively related to earnings change. This association is statistically significant and has large economic significance as well whether controlling for reported or predicted initial log earnings.

The inevitable question is, why? What is it about having high initial earnings in 2008 that causes individuals to fall further relative to similar individuals with lower initial earnings? Did these individuals possess some unobservable characteristics that are no longer being rewarded as well as before? Is it capturing a dynamic adjustment process where individuals with positive or negative shocks gradually return to their conditional mean? To begin to address these questions, we would need panel data with more than two periods. Thus, it remains an open question for future work.

One consequence of this negative relationship between earnings change and initial earnings is that individuals are often changing position in the earnings distribution. Thus, when assessing income inequality over time using cross-sectional data, one should recognize that there are likely different people in different earnings positions over time (see Fields and Sanchez-Puerta (2010) for a clear graphical example).

There is also more work to be done in understanding why women had worse earnings change experiences than men who started at the same initial earnings level. This result was robust to excluding women who were listed as working housewives. Yet, it is worth investigating whether these changes were brought on by lower investment in female businesses, firms offering lower pay or holding pay fixed for women or other possible reasons. Additionally, understanding why earnings changes were more responsive to initial earnings for women than men may help us better understand how initial earnings impact earnings change.

This influence of initial earnings leads to a situation where various groups might see themselves as disproportionately affected by the inflation shock and ensuing decline in earnings. For example, men might recognize the absolute value and even percentage value of their losses were greater than that of females. On the other hand, women might notice that their losses and percentage losses were far greater than men who started with the same initial earnings (and had otherwise similar characteristics as them). It is an open question whether such settings give rise to more social discontent than settings where aggregate differences and differences conditioning on those like oneself allows only one group to claim relative disadvantage. The absolute decline in earnings experienced by so many different types of individuals was undoubtedly a source of widespread social discontent in this period. But a hypothesis worth considering is that such discontent becomes even greater in situations where all groups could also consider themselves relatively worse off depending on whether they focus on aggregate effects or effects conditional on personal characteristics.

Finally, earnings changes for those initially engaged in agriculture were unexpected, given that the changes in inflation were driven in part by rising food prices. Those who started in agriculture had the biggest average decline in earnings, holding all else constant. A number of possible explanations have been raised. In our view the most plausible revolve around rising fertilizer costs with relatively stagnant farm-gate prices for at least some crops. A more complete explanation would require a detailed examination of the agricultural sector and is left for future work.

Endnotes

[1]Concurrent analysis of earnings mobility using this data has been undertaken by Silva as part of the World Bank investigation into informality. Earlier, Assad and Roushdy (2007) also used the panel data from the Egyptian labor market conditions surveys (ELMPS) conducted in 1998 and 2006 together with the 2005 HIECS to provide very detailed information on employment status, earnings, and poverty. The work was descriptive using transition matrices and focused on wage workers. Their results reveal that between 1998 and 2006 there was a notable improvement in labor-market conditions in Egypt. New jobs were created at a faster rate than the growth of the labor force, leading to a reduction in the unemployment rate. They also found an uneven increase in earnings where only few of the poor had benefited from these gains. However, both studies did not take into account the relationship between the initial earnings and earnings changes that is central to this paper.

[2]This statement is not meant to be a central thesis for what kept inflation from continuing to increase. The lack of adjustment of wages, itself, was likely driven by many underlying factors.

[3]An alternative hypothesis would be that they did raise prices but that demand for their product fell as buyers had less of their constant nominal earnings to spend on domestic services and products due to increased prices of the imported goods that they were buying.

[4]This process divides enterprise gains solely among residents engaged in a home enterprise. Such a division can lead to measurement error. Fortunately, more than half of those engaged in household enterprise work are the only ones in the household engaged in such activity (and thus do not need to split profit). In multiple person enterprises (often two person activities), there may be some concern in this regard.

[5]We also discard 9 observations in 2008 and 12 observations in 2009 that had zero earnings despite being listed as employed. These were primarily unpaid workers and we believe the values to be erroneous.

[6]We can reject the hypothesis that each dummy variable equals zero when testing them separately. Surprisingly, using a ten percent significance level, we cannot reject the joint hypothesis test that both of these dummy variables simultaneously equal zero.

[7]Such descriptive regressions do not attempt to eliminate or fix endogenous right hand side variables that can conflate causal interpretations of regression coefficients. This approach is useful in predicting *who* was affected by a given change, without explaining *why*. In other words, we may be able to say that individuals who transitioned from sector A to sector B experienced higher average earnings changes than those of similar age, education level, etc. who stayed in sector A. We cannot say that they earn more *because* they switched sectors or that anyone else who had made a similar switch would have enjoyed the same gain.

[8]Here, we ignore the fact that there is not a direct correspondence between earnings and consumption per capita.

[9]There may be some concern about marital status being considered exogenous. This will be discussed in the results section.

[10]The construction of the poverty lines is explained in The World Bank (2011).

[11]Cameron and Trivedi (2005) also offer a useful discussion of the lowess estimator. However, the previous paragraph paraphrases from the STATA manual, which also includes the basic formula for the tri-cube weighting scheme: $w_j =$ and $\Delta = 1.0001*\max(x_{i+} - x_i, x_i - x_{i-})$ where x_{i+} and x_{i-} are edges of the usable observations. As our bandwidth is 0.8, this is limited to be no more than 40% of the observations above and no more than 40% of the observations below the current observation when observations are lined up according to value of x. Put another way, an observation at the median level of x would use the middle 80% of the sample in its regression, while an observation at the upper extreme of x would use just the observations with the highest 40% of values of x. In our case x is initial earnings level. One negative feature of this approach is that it does not incorporate the probability weights in the underlying sample.

[12]In the case where we start with a negative coefficient, the attenuation bias will help mitigate the overall bias. For example, if the actual value is −0.50 rather than 0.50, we would find −0.55.

[13]Note: The measurement error, μ_{08}, will no longer be present in the predicted earnings from 2008, thus eliminating the spurious correlation. The new equation will be: $\Delta y_i + (\mu_{09,i} - \mu_{08,i}) = \beta_0 + \beta_1(yhat_{08,i}) + \varepsilon_i$. As the long as the measurement error in 2008, $\mu_{08,i}$ is not correlated with any of the variables used to predict initial earnings, which is a standard assumption of classical measurement error, it will not be present in our predicted earnings for 2008, here denoted by $yhat_{08,i}$.

[14]Employment participation rates were also increasing from 48% to 53% among those 18 to 24 year olds in 2008 and the rate for those 18 to 24 years old in 2009 was also

higher at 49%. These conclusions assume that those who lost their jobs were not more likely to be missing from the sample in 2009.

[15]Our data does not allow us to know if the individual is in the same job in both periods. We will also review changes in sectors and relationship with employer later in this paper.

[16]The difference in logs of (+ or -) 0.5 is a very rough approximation of a 50% change in earnings. Twenty seven percent of the weighted sample had reported earnings in 2009 that were 50% greater or less than reported 2008 earnings.

[17]In our data the variance of initial log earnings is roughly 0.68. Thus, if the variance of μ is .204 or greater, it would imply that the true coefficient is non-negative. Given a Normality assumption on our classical measurement error term and a standard deviation of $0.204^{0.5}$, this implies that 32 percent of respondents would be giving answers that were at least 45 percent above or below their true earnings level.

[18]See Figure 9 for the lowess model of the change in earnings after trimming the data of the lowest and top five percent of observations for each gender. Figure 10 shows the diagram using a local mean rather than local regression.

[19]As mentioned earlier, we take exogenous to mean characteristics that these 25 to 58 year olds brought to the labor market in 2008. One might reasonably question whether the married variable is exogenous. We ran this specification without the married variable and found results on all other coefficients and corresponding standard errors to be extremely similar to the model presented in Table 12.

[20]A more accurate approximation would be between 35 and 63 percent (Ex. $e^{0.30}$ - 1 = .35). However, we will follow convention and use the log approximation for all values in this paper.

[21]The age turning point was roughly 13 years old and being married had a zero coefficient.

[22]The authors would like to thank Ruslan Yemtsov, Julian Lampietti, and Maurice Saade for offering us some starting points in this area which we hope to follow in the future.

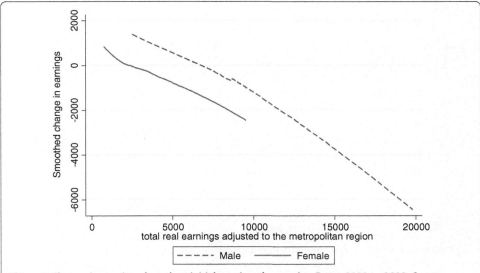

Figure 9 Change in earnings based on initial earnings by gender, Egypt 2008 to 2009. *Source:* HIECPS (Feb 2008 to Feb 2009 (CAPMAS 2009)). *Notes:* Locally weighted regression was used to determine the predicted change in earnings based on real earnings in 2008. Analysis was done separately by gender and then plotted on the same graph. The top and bottom 5 percent of initial earnings were excluded for each gender.

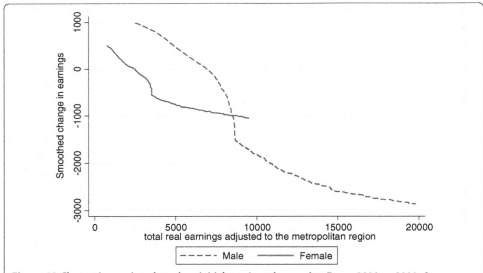

Figure 10 Change in earnings based on initial earnings, by gender, Egypt 2008 to 2009. *Source*: HIECPS (Feb 2008 to Feb 2009 (CAPMAS 2009)). *Notes*: Local mean constructed using tri-cube weight using *lowess* command with *mean* option. Top and bottom 5 percent of initial earnings are excluded for each gender.

Annex 1: measurement error simulation

In order to demonstrate how our lowess simulations are affected by classical measurement error, we conducted a simulation. For simplicity we treat the observed values of log 2008 earnings as true values. In order to create our simulated values of log 2008 reported earnings, we add a simulated measurement error realization to each

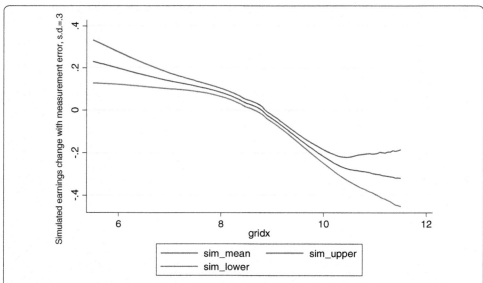

Figure 11 Simulated change in log earnings based on initial log earnings, Egypt 2008 to 2009. *Source*: Authors' compilation from HIECPS (Feb 2008 to Feb 2009 (CAPMAS 2009)). *Notes*: Simulated earnings values for 2008 and 2009 were both based on reported log 2008 earnings plus some random measurement error, which was drawn from a Normal distribution with mean zero and variance of 0.3. A change in earnings was then constructed directly from these simulated values. Finally, locally weighted regression was used to determine the predicted change in log earnings based on log real earnings in 2008. Upper and lower confidence intervals are shown as well.

observation. These realizations are drawn randomly from a Normal distribution with a mean of zero and a standard deviation of 0.3. This standard deviation is admittedly arbitrary, but we feel it offers a significant amount of measurement error. Under this distribution, 32 percent of the sample would receive a random measurement error term with a magnitude greater than approximately 30 percent of the value of their 'true' earnings level. Five percent of the sample would receive measurement error that was more than approximately 60 percent of their 'true' earnings level.

We then constructed a second set of values in the exact same manner and called them log 2009 reported earnings. We take the difference and run a lowess regression of the simulated difference on the simulated 2008 data. This simulation thus represents what the lowess graph would look like if individuals had no real change in earnings but a fairly significant amount of measurement error. The result, shown in Figure 11 below, is initially disturbing as it shares many feature with our observed lowess results of the change in earnings on initial earnings. It is distinctly downward sloping.

However, this level of measurement error definitely cannot explain the results observed in our data. Figure 12 graphs the simulation again, this time also graphing the lowess graph using the change in log reported earnings and log initial reported earnings observed in our dataset. The simulation was downward sloping but the magnitude of the changes is tiny compared to the magnitude using our observed data. Thus, we are reassured that our lowess results are not driven solely by classical measurement error. Others may not feel as confident in this conclusion if they feel measurement error has a much larger variance or is otherwise different from our maintained assumptions. In this sense, this validation approach is similar to the approach of Fields et al. (Fields et al. 2003a).

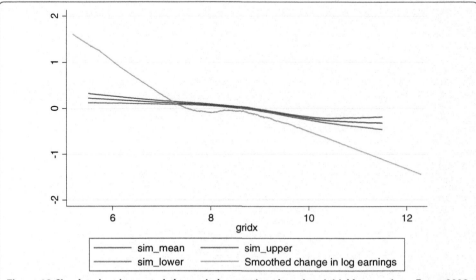

Figure 12 Simulated and reported change in log earnings based on initial log earnings, Egypt 2008 to 2009. *Source*: Authors' compilation from HIECPS (Feb 2008 to Feb 2009 (CAPMAS 2009)). *Note*: Simulated earnings values for 2008 and 2009 were both based on reported log 2008 earnings plus some random measurement error, which was drawn from a Normal distribution with mean zero and variance of 0.3. A change in earnings was then constructed directly from these simulated values. Finally, locally weighted regression was used to determine the predicted change in log earnings based on log real earnings in 2008. Upper and lower confidence intervals are shown as well.

Abbreviations
CAPMAS: Central Agency for Public Mobilization and Statistics; EGP: Egyptian Pound; HIECPS: Household Income, Expenditure and Consumption Panel Survey; HIECS: Household Income, Expenditure and Consumption Survey; LFSS: Labor Force Sample Survey; LPM: Linear Probability Model.

Competing interests
The IZA Journal of Labor & Development is committed to the IZA Guiding Principles of Research Integrity. The authors declare that they have observed these principles.

Acknowledgements
The authors would like to thank Rania Rouchdy, Ruslan Yemtsov, Joanna Silva, Julian Lampietti, Maurice Saade, Heba El-Laithy, Sherine El-Shawarbi, the Editor and an anonymous referee for their comments. We would also like to thank Nicholas Diebel, Mallimalika Gupta, Choon-Sung Lim, and Caleb Pomeroy for research assistant work related to this paper. Ideas expressed in this paper are those of the authors and do not reflect policies of their respective organizations. The usual disclaimers apply.
Responsible editor: David Lam

Author details
[1]Economics Department, Boston College, 140 Commonwealth Ave, Chestnut Hill, MA 02467, USA. [2]Faculty of Economics and Political Science, Cairo University, Cairo, Egypt. [3]World Bank, 1818 H Street NW, Washington, D.C 20433, USA.

References
Arabsheibani R (2000) Male–female Earnings Differentials in an Islamic Country: The Case of Highly Educated Egyptians. Educ Econ 8(2):129–138
Assaad R, Roushdy R (2007) Labor market trends and living standards in Egypt. In: Arab Republic of Egypt – Poverty Assessment Update, vol 1. The World Bank, Arab Republic of Egypt, pp 69–91
Beegle K, De Weerd J, Dercon S (2011) Migration and Economic Mobility in Tanzania: Evidence from a Tracking Survey. Rev Econ Stat 93(3):1010–1033
Belhaj-Hassine N (2012) Inequality of opportunity in Egypt. World Bank Econ Rev 26(2):265–295
Cameron AC, Trivedi PK (2005) Microeconometrics: Methods and applications. Cambridge University Press, Cambridge
CAPMAS (Central Agency for Public Mobilization and Statistics) (2009) Various issues. HIECS (Household Income, Expenditure and Consumption Surveys). CAPMAS, Cairo, Egypt
Cichello PL, Fields GS, Leibbrandt M (2005) Earnings and employment dynamics for Africans in post-apartheid South Africa: A panel study of KwaZulu-Natal. J Afr Econ 14(2):143–190
Cleveland WS (1979) Robust locally weighted regression and smoothing scatter plots. J Am Stat Assoc 74:829–836
Datt G, Olmsted J (2004) Induced wage effects of changes in food prices in Egypt. J Dev Stud 40(4):137–166
Fields GS (2008) A brief review of the literature on earnings mobility in developing countries. :, Working Papers n. 101, ILR School, Cornell University. http://digitalcommons.ilr.cornell.edu/workingpapers/101 (retrieved 07/05/2011)
Fields GS, Sanchez Puerta ML (2010) Earnings mobility in times of growth and decline: Argentina from 1996 to 2003. World Dev 38(6):870–880
Fields GS, Cichello PL, Freije S, Menéndez M, Newhouse D (2003a) For richer or for poorer? Evidence from Indonesia, South Africa, Spain, and Venezuela. J Econ Inequal 1(1):67–99
Fields GS, Cichello PL, Freije S, Menéndez M, Newhouse D (2003b) Household income dynamics: A four country story. J Dev Stud 40(2):30–54
Lundberg S (1985) The added worker effect. J Labor Econ 3(1):11–37
Roushdy R, Gadallah M (2011) Labor Market Adjustment to the World Financial Crisis: Evidence from Egypt. ERF Annual Conference paper, ERF17AC_054., http://www.erf.org.eg/cms.php?id=publication_details&publication_id=1363
Said M (2009) The Fall and Rise of Earnings and Inequality in Egypt: New Evidence from the Egypt Labor Market Panel Survey 2006. Ch. 2. In: Assaad R (ed) The Egyptian Labor Market Revisited. American University in Cairo Press, New York and Cairo, pp 53–81
Said M (2012) Wage Differentials during Economic Reform and Crisis: Evidence from Egypt and Jordan. Comp Econ Stud 54:65–101
Serneels P (2002) The added worker effect and intra household aspects of unemployment. CSAE Working Paper Series 2002–14. Centre for the Study of African Economies, University of Oxford
World Bank (2011) Poverty in Egypt 2008–2009: Withstanding the global economic crisis. The World Bank, Egypt
World Bank, DECPG (2008) Commodity Markets Review, Development Prospects Group. The World Bank, Washington, DC

2

Life skills, employability and training for disadvantaged youth: Evidence from a randomized evaluation design

Pablo Ibarraran[1]*, Laura Ripani[2], Bibiana Taboada[2], Juan Miguel Villa[3] and Brigida Garcia[4]

* Correspondence: pibarraran@iadb.org
[1] Inter-American Development Bank
(IDB), Washington, DC and IZA,
Bonn, Germany
Full list of author information is
available at the end of the article

Abstract

This paper presents an impact evaluation of a revamped version of the Dominican Republic's youth training program Juventud y Empleo. The paper analyzes the impact of the program on traditional labor market outcomes and on outcomes related to youth behavior and life style, expectations about the future and socio-emotional skills. In terms of labor market outcomes, the program has a positive impact on job formality for men of about 17 percent and there is also a seven percent increase in monthly earnings among those employed. However, there are no overall impacts on employment rates. Regarding non-labor market outcomes, the program reduces teenage pregnancy by five percentage points in the treatment group (about 45 percent), which is consistent with an overall increase in youth expectations about the future. The program also has a positive impact on non-cognitive skills as measured by three different scales. Scores improve between 0.08 and 0.16 standard deviations with the program. Although recent progress noted in the literature suggests that socio-emotional skills increase employability and quality of employment, the practical significance of the impacts is unclear, as there is only weak evidence that the life skills measures used are associated to better labor market performance. This is an area of growing interest and relevance that requires further research.

JEL codes: J24, J64, O15, O17.

Keywords: Impact evaluation; Dominican Republic; Youth training programs; Labor market outcomes; Employment; Life skills

1 Introduction

Youth training programs have been implemented in Latin America and the Caribbean (LAC) since the early 1990s. These programs target less-educated youth, a group that faces serious difficulties in achieving a successful insertion into the labor market, with the explicit aim of raising participants' job skills and matching them to suitable employers[1]. Drawing on lessons from evaluations of the Job Training Partnership Act in the United States and the Youth Training Scheme in Britain, these programs combine classroom training with a subsequent internship period of on-the-job work experience[2]. The training programs have two basic premises: first, that the lack of basic technical and life skills determine the poor labor market insertion of the targeted youth i.e. low wages, informality and underemployment, and second, that these courses are successful in enhancing those skills[3]. There is also an underlying assumption that the economy has or is creating vacancies to be filled by program graduates[4].

A salient characteristic of these programs is their emphasis on socio-emotional skills[5], which have gained increasing importance in most of these projects (Ibarrarán and Rosas 2009; Gonzalez et al. 2011). Until recently, however, job training programs have included socio-emotional skills components in an *ad hoc* manner, based on scant qualitative evidence and without focusing too much on measuring these skills or the results of training in improving them. Recent evidence on the importance of non-cognitive skills both from econometric and qualitative analyses of determinants of success in the labor market show that employers value certain behaviors and attitudes that are linked to high-productivity workers (Heckman et al. 2006; Urzua 2009; Fazio 2011).

While conceptually socio-emotional skills are well defined, it has been difficult to measure and analyze them empirically. Recent literature has explored alternative measurements (Brunello and Schlotter 2011; Felfe et al. 2011), mostly for developed countries. However, there is a knowledge gap on how to measure socio-emotional skills in the LAC region and about the importance of such skills in explaining the labor market outcomes of youth, particularly disadvantaged youth. Furthermore, from a policy perspective, it is important to know whether and how socio-emotional skills can be acquired by young people in Latin America and the Caribbean.

One of the most innovative youth-training programs in LAC is the Dominican Republic's Youth and Employment Program, *Juventud y Empleo* (JE). JE was first designed in 1999 and is the first program of its type to have an experimental evaluation from its inception. This evaluation design has enabled program managers to learn from the implementation of the program and to use the evaluation findings to improve subsequent phases, in a virtuous cycle of evaluation and feedback. This cycle includes rigorous quantitative as well as qualitative evidence. In this way, the program has been modified to test new hypotheses.

While previous evaluations of this program have focused almost exclusively on the labor market impacts—namely, employment rate, labor earnings and quality of employment, which we also report on—this paper also takes a closer look at the mechanisms by which training is supposed to improve participants' labor market performance, specifically, by increasing the non-cognitive and socio-emotional skills with which they join the labor force. We also examine other important outcomes that can be attributed to training, such as the teenage pregnancy rate. Given the high teenage pregnancy rates in the Dominican Republic and the negative labor-market consequences of teenage pregnancy, this is an important outcome from a theoretical and a practical standpoint. Dominican teenagers receive little instruction in sex education. In the country, about 17 percent of females aged 15–19 years old already have children (Oficina Nacional de Estadística ONE 2008).

Evidence from the LAC region confirms the negative effects of teenage pregnancy on various socio-economic variables. In Mexico, in the short run, teenage pregnancy reduces years of schooling, school attendance and hours of work, while it increases marriage rates. In the long run, teenage pregnancy results in a loss in years of education and in lower income. It also contributes to a higher probability of being married and divorced (Acero-Gomez and Campos-Vazquez 2011).

Our analysis is based on a sample of applicants for the cohort of trainees that participated in a version of the JE program that was modified as a result of the first impact evaluation. The cohort under study applied to receive training during 2008. We show that labor market impacts are mixed, with a negligible impact on overall employment and a substantial impact on job quality for men. We find positive impacts in terms of perceptions and expectations about the future, in particular for young women who simultaneously reduce their pregnancy rates considerably. We also document a positive impact of training on alternative measures of life skills, particularly leadership skills, conflict resolution, self-organization and persistency of effort. These skills, in particular persistency of effort, have been analyzed and the findings show that they improve labor market outcomes in developed countries (Heckman et al. 2006). The impact of those soft skills on labor market performance in developing countries is a rich area for future research.

The paper is organized as follows. After this introduction, Section 2 provides the specifics of the program, as well as a description of its previous evaluation. Section 3 describes the basic design features of this evaluation and the data collected. Section 4 presents the results, followed by conclusions in Section 5.

2 The juventud y empleo program

2.1 Description of the intervention

The *JE* program is a Dominican active labor market program (ALMP) that aims to improve the labor market entry of youth between 16 and 29 years of age who did not complete high school. It has been in operation since 2001 and was the first job training program in Latin America to incorporate a randomized evaluation component when the project was designed.

The program offers a wide range of job training courses such as administrative assistant, baker, hair stylist, clerk, auto mechanic, bartender, and so on. The Ministry of Labor outsources the provision of training services to private training institutions (*Centros Operadores del Sistema*, COS) that are registered and approved by the national training institution (*Instituto Nacional de Formación Técnico Profesional*, INFOTEP). Courses of 225 hours are conducted in the COS facilities and split into two parts: 75 hours of basic or life skills training, and 150 hours of technical or vocational training. Basic skills training is meant to strengthen trainees' self- esteem and work habits, while vocational training is meant to address the technical training needs of local employers. Training at the COS is followed by an internship in a private sector firm, which should be contacted by the COS in order to develop training programs tailored to the firm´s labor demand. Young people are identified by the COS according to their preferred vocation and the availability of the desired course. Once they reach 35 potential participants, the COS sends the names and identification numbers to the program coordinating unit (PCU), which randomly selects those who are offered the training course.

2.2 Previous evaluations

The first impact evaluation of this program (Card et al. 2011) was based on a sample of applicants of the second cohort of the JE program who applied to receive training in early 2004. Baseline data were collected from applicants prior to random assignment through registration forms completed at the COS. A follow-up survey was administered from May to July 2005; some 10 to 14 months after most trainees had finished their initial coursework. Simple comparisons between trainees in the follow-up survey and members of the control group show little impact on employment, although there is some evidence of a modest impact on wages and formality for men. Unfortunately, however, the randomized design of the JE evaluation was potentially compromised by the failure to include in the follow-up survey people who were originally assigned to receive training but failed to show up or attended only briefly.

Moreover, as is often the case in voluntary programs even under a well-implemented random assignment, compliance was not perfect: some of the lottery winners (intended to be treated) did not participate in the training either because they did not show up or they dropped out at some point. Some who were selected for the control group ended up taking the training as replacements of drop-outs and no-shows or for some other reason.

Card et al. (2011) addressed the problem caused by the failure to follow up on no-shows through selection correction models and by showing with the baseline data that the characteristics of no-shows were similar to those of the replacements. They also excluded the reassigned controls from alternative specifications and the results held. The estimated impacts on employment are all fairly close to zero, and there are no statistically significant differences by gender, age, education, or geographic location. The estimated impacts on monthly earnings are fairly similar for men and women, and for younger and older workers, but they show interesting patterns by education and geographic location. If one compares better-educated applicants in Santo Domingo to all others the results are striking: this subgroup accounts for virtually all of the observed positive impact on monthly earnings[6].

The only other impact evaluation with randomized design of a similar training program in Latin America –the Colombian *Jóvenes en Acción* program– was done by Attanasio et al. (2011). They conclude that the program, which was contemporary to JE and had the same components, raised earnings and employment, especially for women. Women offered training earned 18% more and had a 0.05 higher probability of employment than those not offered training, mainly in formal sector jobs[7].

3 Evaluation design

This second evaluation focuses on a modified version of the program and its evaluation design. While the core of the project –two-stage training followed by an internship– is maintained and the evaluation is still based on random assignment, there are some important changes:

- COS are supposed to work closer to the firms that provide the internship in order to develop tailored courses to train people for real vacancies[8].
- The life skills section of the training was revamped as firms argued that what they valued most from training were the general job-readiness and life skills rather than the technical training[9].
- Random assignment was done on a larger sample for each course (20 treatments, 15 controls).
- Follow-up was improved in terms of sample size, survey instruments and quality controls of the field work.

Table 1 Classification of participants by assignment and treatment status

	Selected in the lottery, $Z_i = 1$	Not selected in the lottery, $Z_i = 0$
Participated in the program, $D_i = 1$	"Complier" Beneficiaries	Replacements/Always Takers
Did not participate in the program, $D_i = 0$	No-shows, dropouts/Never Takers	"Complier" Control group

Source: Authors.

Random assignment was applied on a group of potential participants identified by the COS that applied to the program and met the eligibility criteria[10]. The program received the information from the COS and verified that none of the applicants had been registered before. For each course, the COS submitted data on 35 eligible and interested young people, and the program managers at the PCU randomly selected and then divided them into two groups. The first one is formed by 20 young people who were offered the program. The second group is composed by the remaining 15 young people, who were assigned to the control group.

If young people offered the program did not respond or dropped out before the tenth day of ongoing classes, the COS could replace up to five slots with members of the control group. The replacements were supposed to be randomly selected by the PCU within the control group, and the PCU provided the names directly to the COS. However, in practice, the COS experienced some degree of discretion in selecting the replacements, which might have led to selection bias. This is why we focus on the original random assignment to estimate the impact of the program, where there were no concerns about selection bias.

Despite having an ideal initial configuration of the treatment and control groups due to successful randomization, there was imperfect compliance due to (non-random) decisions by COS and participants[11]. Introducing a general notation, let Z_i represent the random assignment of each young person i where $Z_i = 1$ are those randomly assigned to the treatment group and $Z_i = 0$ are those randomly assigned to the control group. Similarly, let D_i represent the final treatment status were $D_i = 1$ are those who attended the course and $D_i = 0$ those who did not do so. Table 1 clarifies the setting.

During the registration process, the program identified 10,309 applicants who met the selection criteria, with the distribution presented in Table 2, according to the administrative data.

Note that the number of never-takers equals the number of always-takers because the PCU tried to maintain the number of participants per course.

3.1 Identification strategy

Follow-up data were collected on a representative sample of all those who participated in the lottery and, thus, is suitable for the estimation of the impact of the program on those who won the lottery —to whom a course was randomly offered—. This is the Intention to Treat Effect (ITT) that estimates the impact of offering the JE program,

Table 2 Classification of treatment groups

	Selected in the lottery, $Z_i = 1$	Not selected in the lottery, $Z_i = 0$	Total
Participated in the program, $D_i = 1$	4,937	977	5,914
Did not participate in the program, $D_i = 0$	977	3,418	4,395
TOTAL	5,914	4,395	10,309

Source: Administrative data.

regardless of what happened after the random assignment. That is, some young people may have finally decided not to attend the courses or dropped out during the first week of classes, while some of those assigned to the control group may have ended up receiving the treatment.

Because the ITT yields the causal effect of Z_i, its estimation includes all the group of young people that participated in the random assignment, including those for whom $D_i \neq Z_i$, the pairs $D_i = 1 \mid Z_i = 0$ and $D_i = 0 \mid Z_i = 1$, formed by those who took the course although they were randomly assigned to the control group and those who did not show up or dropped out although they belonged to the treatment group, respectively[12]. Therefore, one may expect that the effect of offering JE becomes smaller to the extent that the proportion of those with $D_i \neq Z_i$ increases[13].

Under certain conditions, it is also possible to estimate the impact of the program on the compliers, i.e. those who took the course because they were selected in the lottery[14]. Without loss of generality, in this paper we largely discuss the ITT estimates computed with standard ordinary least squares[15].

3.2 Baseline data

The baseline data were collected at the registration stage at each COS. They were available for all those eligible and interested to participate in the program, a total of 10,309 young people. Table 3 shows some characteristics from the baseline survey and

Table 3 Basic characteristics at baseline

Characteristic	$Z_i = 1$	$Z_i = 0$	Difference (Z_i)	
	(a)	(b)	(a) - (b)	t
Age	22.03	21.99	0.04	0.59
Gender (male = 1)	0.37	0.38	−0.01	−1.35
Marital status (married = 1)	0.24	0.24	0.00	−0.03
Number of children	0.71	0.70	0.01	0.42
Attend school (currently)	0.23	0.23	0.01	0.76
Incomplete elementary	0.20	0.20	0.00	−0.3
Complete elementary	0.05	0.05	0.00	−0.2
Incomplete high school	0.55	0.58	−0.03	1.09
Complete high school	0.04	0.03	0.00	0.79
More than high school	0.00	0.00	0.00	0.02
Missing education	0.04	0.04	0.00	−0.65
No data on education	0.11	0.12	−0.01	−1.19
Fraction with prior work experience	0.20	0.22	−0.02	1.37
Currently employed	0.04	0.04	0.00	0.15
Currently salaried worker	0.02	0.02	0.00	−0.23
Currently unemployed	0.53	0.52	0.00	0.28
ICV Score (0 to 100)*	62.81	62.93	−0.12	−0.59
Urban areas	0.89	0.89	0.00	−0.47
Lives in Santo Domingo	0.24	0.24	0.00	0.27
Receives remittances	0.11	0.11	0.00	−0.31
Observations	5,914	4,395		

Source: JE baseline data and administrative records.
Note: Means, differences and t-statistics are calculated by linear regression with robust standard errors.
***p < 0.01, **p < 0.05, *p < 0.1.

a t-statistic for equality of means between the Z_i groups as an evidence of randomness. Most participants –62 percent—are women, and nearly all of those reporting some education have not completed high school. Ninety percent of participants live in urban areas and about a quarter live in Santo Domingo. The average age is 22 years. About 22 percent of individuals were attending school at the time of the baseline. As shown in the table's last column, random assignment was well implemented as all of the characteristics are balanced.

It is interesting to note that only 4 percent of young people declared being employed at the baseline prior to the beginning of the courses, and that 52 percent of them were unemployed, meaning that 44 percent were inactive. This may be due to the requirements of the selection process, which demanded that they be inactive or unemployed, and may also be an expression of the Ashenfelter's dip (Ashenfelter 1978), i.e. that both groups received a shock that increased unemployment levels right before the program started. According to the National Labor Force Survey (known as ENFT, *Encuesta Nacional de Fuerza de Trabajo*), in 2008 the employment rate in the Dominican Republic for young people 16 to 29 years old with less than complete high school education was 43 percent.

3.3 Follow-up survey

After the completion of the courses, a follow-up household survey was carried out between November 2010 and February 2011 (18 to 24 months after graduation) on a random sample of 5,000 out of the 10,309 young people who had initially registered[16]. This sample has 3,250 individuals from the treatment group and 1,750 from the control group.

The questionnaire for the follow-up household survey was put together by an interdisciplinary team from the Ministry of Labor of the Dominican Republic, the Inter-American Development Bank and the World Bank. It includes 15 modules that collect data on household composition and socioeconomic characteristics, labor force participation[17], labor history, assets, time use, JE courses and internship, consumption, health status, risk aversion, future expectations, pregnancy history, dwelling materials and basic skills, including non-cognitive skills and self-esteem.

About 80 percent of the sample were located at their households for the follow up survey, with virtually no difference between those selected and those not selected in the lottery (in the case of $Z_i = 1$ and $Z_i = 0$, 80.8 and 80.4 percent were interviewed, respectively). This compares favorably to the first evaluation of JE, where the attrition rate was larger and unbalanced between beneficiaries and members of the comparison group (the attrition rates were 35 and 45 percent, respectively).

We verified the similarity of the interviewed treatment and control groups. We also compared the basic characteristics of those that were interviewed and those that were not. Additional file 1: Table S1 compares the sample of those intended to be interviewed and those finally interviewed. The original and the realized samples have similar characteristics at baseline. Nonetheless, comparing the original and realized groups on the same random assignment (Z_i) there is a small imbalance in the poverty indicator (ICV) for the control group, but the differences are close to zero. Regarding the treatment group (column (*a*) - (*c*)), the most notable differences emerged in school attendance and location in urban areas, for which disparities are statistically significant but very small. Hence, we assume that attrition was random and that it affected equally both those selected and those not selected in the lottery.

Table 4 Notification from COS by lottery results

Were you notified to start the course?

	$Z_i = 0$		$Z_i = 1$	
Yes	615	47.0%	2,335	92.9%
No	693	53.0%	178	7.1%
Total	1,308		2,513	

Source: Follow-up survey and administrative data.

The follow-up survey includes questions to confirm whether the respondent actually participated in the program. This is important because the COS enjoyed some degree of control over who took the course that is not reflected on the PCU administrative data. Also, in the process of replacing no-shows and dropouts some members of the $Z_i = 0$ group were contacted as replacements and, even if some of them may have declined to participate, they are still classified as control group compliers.

During the follow-up survey, enumerators did not have information on the classification of the youth into the treatment or control groups according to the administrative data. Young people were asked if the COS contacted them after the registration to notify them that they had been selected and to inform them the date and time when the course would start. Table 4 presents the answers to this question, showing that a large fraction of those who were not selected in the lottery were contacted by the COS in order to participate in the program[18].

Table 5 further explores the composition of the realized treatment and control groups according to administrative data and information from the follow-up survey.

According to administrative records, about 22 percent of the randomly assigned control group ($Z_i = 0$) and 85 percent of the treatment group ($Z_i = 1$) were contacted by the COS and accepted the course. Nonetheless, according to the follow-up survey, 37 percent of those not selected by the lottery ($Z_i = 0$) reported being contacted by the COS and accepting to participate in the program. Moreover, 23 percent of the control group ($Z_i = 0$) reported having taken the course and even completing an internship of three or more weeks. These figures show that compliance was low (in particular for the $Z_i = 0$ group). The lottery, however, did have a strong impact on the probability of participating and thus constitutes a very strong instrument[19].

In this paper, the D_i variable is defined based on information from the follow-up survey[20]. Individuals for whom $D_i = 1$ are those who reported having been contacted by the COS to begin the course and having accepted to start it[21]. Alternative measures of $D_i = 1$ were also used in order to determine if there were any differences between those who started the program, those who completed the classroom training, and those who

Table 5 Final composition of the treatment and control groups

		Administrative data		Follow-up survey: accepted the course		Follow-up survey: completed course and internship	
		$Z_i = 0$	$Z_i = 1$	$Z_i = 0$	$Z_i = 1$	$Z_i = 0$	$Z_i = 1$
D_i	0	1,098	389	883	380	1,088	799
	1	309	2,240	524	2,249	319	1,830
TOTAL		1,407	2,629	1,407	2,629	1,407	2,629

Source: Follow-up survey and administrative data.

also completed the internship[22]. The analyses using alternative definitions of Di are robust.

4 Results

The outcomes explored in this paper can be classified into the following three categories:

- Labor market outcomes
- Outcomes related to youth behavior and life style, perceptions and expectations
- Measurements of socio-emotional skills.

We estimate the impact of the program on all of these outcomes for the complete sample and for various subgroups defined by gender, age, education, region and course[23]. In addition, in order to interpret the results, we look at the relationship between the non-cognitive measures and labor market outcomes.

4.1 Labor market outcomes

Selected labor market outcomes in the follow-up survey by random assignment status are presented in Tables 6 and 7. In terms of employment rate, Table 6 shows that there are only minor differences between $Z_i = 0$ and $Z_i = 1$: employment is 62.5 and 61.6 percent respectively.

Table 6 Employment characteristics in the follow-up survey

Outcome	$Z_i = 0$	$Z_i = 1$
Employed	62.5%	61.6%
Agriculture and mining	1.95%	1.49%
Industry	9.60%	8.29%
Services	88.5%	90.2%
Duration of current job (months)	16.21	15.48
Permanent Job	42.2%	41.7%
Employed at large firms[a]	12.7%	13.2%
Salaried workers	35.2%	36.4%
Unpaid workers	2.92%	2.75%
Self-employed workers	20.8%	19.5%
Workers w/ labor risk insurance	9.97%	11.08%
Workers with health insurance	17.4%	18.0%
Workers with written contract	12.7%	13.8%
Weekly worked days	5.12	5.08
Weekly worked hours	38.83	38.25
Wants to work more hours	43.4%	42.9%
Wants to change current job	50.4%	48.9%
Workers seeking another job	17.7%	19.1%
Monthly wage (Dominican peso)[b]	2464.1	2535.5
Hourly wage (Dominican peso)[b]	18.38	18.26

Source: Follow-up survey.
Note: Outcomes are unconditional on employment status.
[a]Large firms are those that employ 51 or more employees.
[b]One US dollar = 35 Dominican pesos.

Table 7 Labor force participation status in the follow-up survey

Outcome	$Z_i = 0$	$Z_i = 1$
All		
Employed	62.2%	61.7%
Unemployed	21.2%	23.4%
Inactive	16.6%	14.9%
Male		
Employed	80.2%	76.6%
Unemployed	15.0%	18.5%
Inactive	4.9%	4.8%
Female		
Employed	51.0%	53.1%
Unemployed	25.0%	26.2%
Inactive	24.0%	20.7%

Source: Follow-up survey.

Labor force participation is examined in Table 7. Female inactivity is larger for individuals assigned to the control group, while the opposite is true for employment and unemployment. Male inactivity and employment are higher for individuals assigned to the control group, while unemployment is higher for individuals assigned to the treatment group.

Figures 1 and 2 below show the employment history of individuals assigned to the treatment and control groups in the overall sample and in Santo Domingo. Taking into account the findings from the previous evaluation, program operators expected to find larger impacts in Santo Domingo because of its labor market dynamics. As expected, there were no differences in the months before the program started, particularly in the two to three months before registration took place. There were negative differences while trainees were taking the courses, and there was a catch-up after the courses. Overall, there were no impacts on employment, and in Santo Domingo there seems to be a positive difference in the months closer to the follow-up survey.

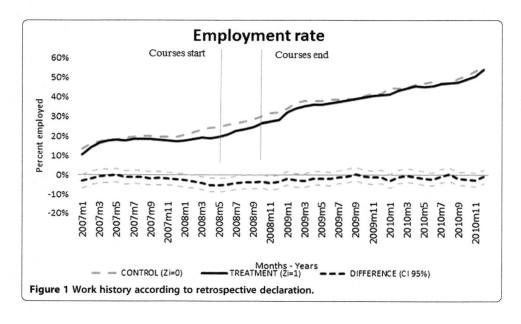

Figure 1 Work history according to retrospective declaration.

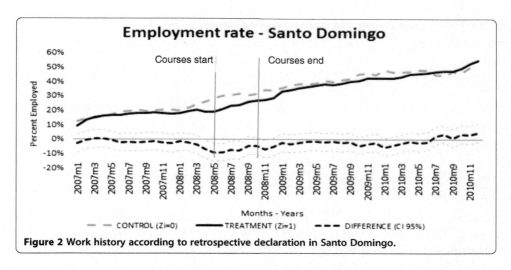

Figure 2 Work history according to retrospective declaration in Santo Domingo.

Table 8 shows the ITT estimates for the standard labor market outcomes. Although the program has no statistically significant impact on employment, for men it has statistically significant impacts on formality, measured as employer provided health insurance or as having a written contract. Males assigned to the treatment group are four percentage points more likely to get a job in the formal sector than males assigned to the control group. This represents an impact of 17 percent over the control group average[24]. As shown in the last column, the results are particularly strong for males in Santo Domingo.

There is no impact on monthly earnings for the complete sample. However estimates for monthly earnings conditional on being employed show that the program does have a positive statistically significant impact. Among those employed, individuals assigned to the treatment group have monthly earnings seven percent higher than individuals assigned to the control group. This holds for women in general, and for men in Santo Domingo.

There also seems to be a relation with the duration of unemployment, which is longer for males assigned to the treatment group than for males assigned to the control group. This could reflect the fact that males assigned to the treatment group are searching for better quality jobs even if these are harder to find, or that they have higher reservation wages. This would also be consistent with the last result reported in the table: hours seeking for a job in the last working day. Here, the average time reported by individuals assigned to the treatment group reflects a 60 percent increase compared to the control group mean.

4.2 Risky behavior and pregnancy, perceptions and expectations

An important element of the life skills component is to enable young people to plan and think about their future in a more serious and organized manner. By giving them elements to increase their self-esteem and develop their personal abilities to compete in the labor market, young people can become more optimistic about their future and realize the importance of making the adequate decisions today, which may influence their risky behaviors. Hence, a first step in the success of the life skills component is raising young people's expectations about their future, as this should encourage them to engage in positive behaviors (which become more "profitable") and prevent them from undertaking negative ones (which become more "costly").

Table 8 ITT estimation on selected labor market outcomes

Intention to treat effect	(1)	(2)	(3)	(1)	(1)	(2)
Outcomes	All	Women	Men	Santo Domingo	SD women	SD men
Employed	−0.0127	0.0069	−0.0244	0.0035	0.0317	−0.0285
	(0.0178)	(0.0237)	(0.0234)	(0.0334)	(0.0436)	(0.0418)
$Z_i = 0$ Mean	0.625	0.516	0.797	0.599	0.519	0.752
Employed with health insurance	0.0124	0.0024	0.0423*	0.0244	−0.0048	0.1079**
	(0.0127)	(0.0147)	(0.0235)	(0.0209)	(0.0253)	(0.0411)
$Z_i = 0$ Mean	0.169	0.128	0.235	0.166	0.146	0.206
Employed with written contract	0.0183*	0.0111	0.0430**	0.0161	−0.0063	0.0893**
	(0.0107)	(0.0128)	(0.0203)	(0.0189)	(0.0246)	(0.0358)
$Z_i = 0$ Mean	0.123	0.0924	0.171	0.127	0.108	0.163
Monthly earnings	192.5509	249.2847	284.2723	393.8667	380.8441	591.6433
	(170.2102)	(163.3309)	(298.4813)	(358.8349)	(325.2659)	(652.0422)
$Z_i = 0$ Mean	2946	1932	4558	3074	2309	4527
Ln monthly earnings	0.0866**	0.1425**	0.0931	0.1682**	0.1605	0.2190*
	(0.0436)	(0.0644)	(0.0586)	(0.0736)	(0.1085)	(0.1185)
$Z_i = 0$ Mean	8.223	7.999	8.441	8.306	8.167	8.479
Labor force participation	0.0109	0.0153	0.0136	0.0143	0.0191	0.0165
	(0.0128)	(0.0192)	(0.0129)	(0.0222)	(0.0321)	(0.0256)
$Z_i = 0$ Mean	0.837	0.771	0.942	0.846	0.799	0.936
Duration (weeks) of unemployment	2.6994**	2.0906	3.4542**	0.7825	1.4161	−0.9038
	(1.1297)	(1.5952)	(1.5079)	(2.0976)	(2.8280)	(2.5909)
$Z_i = 0$ Mean	8.883	11.24	5.143	11.75	12.98	9.402
Hours job-seeking in last working day	0.0620**	0.0475	0.0901**	0.1035**	0.1100**	0.1175
	(0.0247)	(0.0293)	(0.0448)	(0.0484)	(0.0459)	(0.1068)
$Z_i = 0$ Mean	0.104	0.0944	0.119	0.113	0.0794	0.177
Observations	3,761	2,350	1,411	1,197	797	400

Note: Robust standard errors clustered at the course level in parentheses.
COS fixed effects included in the estimation.
***p < 0.01, **p < 0.05, *p < 0.1.
One US dollar = 35 Dominican pesos.

Table 9 presents, for all females in the sample regardless of their marital status, the impact of the program on pregnancy at the time of the follow-up survey. The estimates indicate that the program had a statistically significant negative impact on the probability of being pregnant. Females in the treatment group were on average two percentage points less likely to be pregnant than females in the control group. It is worth noting that this effect was driven by the group of females between 16 and 19 years old. Hence, the program was effective in reducing teenage pregnancy, which as discussed in the introduction is related to their future labor market outcomes. ITT estimates for other risky behaviors such as consumption of alcohol, cigarettes, drugs and lottery were also computed. However, while the individuals assigned to the treatment group seemed to spend on average less money on consumption of these goods than the individuals assigned to the control group, the differences were not statistically significant.

Table 9 ITT estimation on pregnancy

Intention to treat effect Outcomes	(1) All women	(2) Age 16-19	(3) Age 20-24	(4) Age > 24	(5) Incomplete elementary	(6) Incomplete high school
Pregnant	−0.0226**	−0.0492*	−0.0157	0.0053	−0.0478	−0.0195
	(0.0110)	(0.0292)	(0.0182)	(0.0160)	(0.0298)	(0.0147)
Zi = 0 Mean	0.0810	0.115	0.0811	0.0472	0.118	0.0785
Observations	2,350	599	1,098	653	467	1,331

Note: Robust standard errors clustered at the course level in parentheses.
COS fixed effects included in the estimation.
***p < 0.01, **p < 0.05, *p < 0.1.

Results for perceptions and expectations are presented in Table 10. The project has a positive impact in improving youth perceptions about their current situation and their expectations regarding the future[25]. On average, individuals assigned to the treatment group are more likely to consider having a very good health than those in the control group, and are more likely to have higher expectations about their future in topics related to their education level, neighborhood, owning a business, having the desired job, completing professional aspirations, having a better life in 20 years, offering their children a better life, and having a wealthier position and more social recognition in 10 years[26]. These impacts are stronger for females and younger individuals. In other words, it is women and adolescents that seem to get more optimistic when assigned to the program. Estimates for expectations of negative situations such as getting HIV-AIDS, dying violently or being involved in criminal activities were also estimated. However, there was no statistically significant impact on expectations related to negative situations. This may be consistent with training increasing the optimism and overconfidence bias (Thaler and Sunstein 2009) by overstating the likelihood of positive outcomes in the future. Not observing changes in the estimation of negative outcomes is consistent with the fact that training emphasized positive emotional skills (and not so much the costs and dangers of risky behavior), and also that people do not like to think of themselves in negative situations.

Raising expectations is valuable not only as a channel to discourage negative (risky, unproductive) behaviors and results, but as a channel to encourage positive (healthy, productive) ones. In this regard, the observed increase in positive expectations may not only be related to the observed changes in risky behaviors, in this case, particularly, to teenage pregnancy, but also to the observed increase in productive behaviors, such as those related to entering the labor market. As shown in the previous section, individuals in the treatment group on average devote more time to search for a job than individuals in the control group. They also tend to remain unemployed longer before finding a job, perhaps because they are more demanding in terms of job quality and reservation wages. Thus, these results could be related to their more positive perceptions of themselves and optimistic expectations about the future.

In fact, this is the whole point about changing youth expectations: to trigger desirable behavioral changes that may lead to better socio-economic results, including labor market ones. To the extent that raising positive perceptions and expectations translates into healthier and more productive behaviors, which in turn lead to better social and employment conditions, there is a reason for encouraging such changes in youth. On

Table 10 ITT estimation on expectations

Intention to treat effect	(1)	(2)	(3)	(4)	(5)	(6)
Outcomes	All	Women	Men	Age 16-19	Age 20-24	Age >24
Considers having very good health (%)	0.0386**	0.0382**	0.0533*	0.0321	0.0646***	0.0085
	(0.0151)	(0.0181)	(0.0272)	(0.0291)	(0.0245)	(0.0288)
$Z_i = 0$ Mean	0.287	0.222	0.392	0.315	0.291	0.244
Expectations: Having a better education level	0.0577*	0.1021***	−0.0023	0.1063*	0.0809*	−0.0441
	(0.0299)	(0.0389)	(0.0444)	(0.0558)	(0.0427)	(0.0646)
$Z_i = 0$ Mean	4.180	4.175	4.189	4.236	4.143	4.186
Expectations: Living in a better neighborhood	0.0477	0.1077**	−0.0515	0.1045*	0.0359	0.0582
	(0.0330)	(0.0426)	(0.0523)	(0.0619)	(0.0475)	(0.0760)
$Z_i = 0$ Mean	3.898	3.886	3.918	3.840	3.932	3.904
Expectations: Owning a business	0.0553	0.0968**	−0.0085	0.1699**	0.0271	0.0295
	(0.0384)	(0.0483)	(0.0637)	(0.0832)	(0.0541)	(0.0781)
$Z_i = 0$ Mean	3.759	3.728	3.809	3.609	3.813	3.842
Expectations: Completing professional aspirations	0.0684**	0.0911***	0.0353	0.1543***	0.0582	−0.0163
	(0.0276)	(0.0331)	(0.0461)	(0.0513)	(0.0410)	(0.0601)
$Z_i = 0$ Mean	4.250	4.262	4.231	4.199	4.267	4.282
Expectations: Having a better life in 20 years	0.0543**	0.0590*	0.0565	0.1811***	0.0057	0.0230
	(0.0249)	(0.0317)	(0.0419)	(0.0518)	(0.0316)	(0.0573)
$Z_i = 0$ Mean	4.455	4.471	4.429	4.386	4.502	4.443
Expectations: Children having a better life	0.0360	0.0426	0.0124	0.1224**	−0.0017	0.0387
	(0.0238)	(0.0298)	(0.0396)	(0.0481)	(0.0338)	(0.0487)
$Z_i = 0$ Mean	4.523	4.544	4.489	4.472	4.543	4.546
Expectations: Wealth position in 10 years	0.0677**	0.1057***	0.0049	0.0731	0.0272	0.1742***
	(0.0278)	(0.0353)	(0.0472)	(0.0532)	(0.0392)	(0.0633)
$Z_i = 0$ Mean	3.932	3.943	3.915	3.950	3.974	3.821
Observations	3,761	2,350	1,411	1,068	1,814	879

Note: Robust standard errors clustered at the course level in parentheses.
COS fixed effects included in the estimation.
***p < 0.01, **p < 0.05, *p < 0.1.
Expectations are measured in a 1 (very unlikely) to 5 (very likely) scale.

the contrary, if none of the latter does happen, then there would not be a point for increasing expectation per se, at least from a labor market insertion perspective[27].

4.3 Life skills

A contribution of this paper is to present empirical evidence on the impacts of training on life skills. For this purpose, the Social and Personal Competencies Scale, CPS for its Spanish acronym (*Escala de Competencias Personales y Sociales*) was developed in July 2010 by a team of experts to evaluate the life skills component of the program. The CPS is a non-cognitive test that measures the effectiveness of the life skills module of the program in developing positive attitudes and values. The test measures six basic competencies: leadership, behavior in situations of conflict, self-esteem, abilities to relate with others, order, and empathy and communication skills. It produces a general score and a specific score for each of these dimensions. A higher score in the scale is associated with a higher level of development in the social and personal competencies.

We also use the Rosenberg and Grit scales, which are standard and proven methodologies in psychology to measure personality traits and socio-emotional competence. The Rosenberg Scale is a professional instrument used in clinical practice to measure self-esteem levels[28]. The test is composed of 10 questions that should take between one to three minutes to answer. A higher score on the scale is associated with a higher level of self-esteem (Brea 2010). The Grit Scale focuses on determination and strength of mind[29]. It measures persistency of effort, enthusiasm about long term goals, consistency of interests, and ambition. The instrument consists of 13 questions that can be completed in one to four minutes. Higher scores on the Grit Scale are associated with higher levels of determination and motivation during long periods of time despite failure or adversity (Brea 2010).

Scores for our sample were all estimated as described in Brea (2010). Results are presented in terms of standard deviations in order to ease interpretation. As shown in Table 11, the program has a positive and statistically significant impact in most

Table 11 ITT estimation on the CPS scale

Intention to treat effect Outcomes ((Xi-Xc)/σc)	(1) All	(2) Women	(3) Men	(4) Age 16-19	(5) Incomplete high school	(6) Santo Domingo
Total CPS Score	0.1025***	0.0888**	0.1364**	0.1960***	0.1095**	0.2584***
	(0.0364)	(0.0442)	(0.0670)	(0.0636)	(0.0465)	(0.0609)
CPS: Leadership	0.0862**	0.0552	0.1425**	0.1585**	0.0751	0.1651***
	(0.0357)	(0.0441)	(0.0607)	(0.0637)	(0.0464)	(0.0617)
CPS: Behavior in situations of conflict	0.1049***	0.1017**	0.1128*	0.2414***	0.1023**	0.2693***
	(0.0368)	(0.0461)	(0.0643)	(0.0670)	(0.0478)	(0.0639)
CPS: Self-esteem	0.0719**	0.0444	0.1265**	0.1590**	0.0542	0.1612**
	(0.0358)	(0.0449)	(0.0612)	(0.0650)	(0.0442)	(0.0640)
CPS: Abilities to relate with others	0.0510	0.0459	0.0579	0.1133*	0.0309	0.1633**
	(0.0369)	(0.0457)	(0.0633)	(0.0647)	(0.0455)	(0.0644)
CPS: Empathy and communication skills	0.0525	0.0533	0.0768	0.0588	0.1169***	0.1558***
	(0.0337)	(0.0433)	(0.0613)	(0.0644)	(0.0450)	(0.0543)
CPS: Order and self-organization	0.0966***	0.0875**	0.1124*	0.1758***	0.0702	0.2412***
	(0.0354)	(0.0424)	(0.0606)	(0.0595)	(0.0441)	(0.0607)
Rosenberg's Scale	0.0183	−0.0417	0.1087*	0.0734	0.0637	0.0083
	(0.0364)	(0.0439)	(0.0608)	(0.0667)	(0.0462)	(0.0629)
Total Grit Scale	0.0750**	0.1019**	0.0208	0.1451**	0.1042**	0.1133**
	(0.0373)	(0.0446)	(0.0642)	(0.0661)	(0.0476)	(0.0560)
Grit: Persistency of effort	0.0757**	0.0996**	0.0209	0.1837***	0.1202***	0.1357**
	(0.0355)	(0.0421)	(0.0622)	(0.0644)	(0.0434)	(0.0578)
Grit: Ambition	0.0686*	0.0791*	0.0241	0.1611**	0.1224***	0.0878
	(0.0351)	(0.0428)	(0.0642)	(0.0623)	(0.0430)	(0.0591)
Observations	3,761	2,350	1,411	1,068	2,129	1,197

Note: Robust standard errors clustered at the course level in parentheses.
COS fixed effects included in the estimation.
***p < 0.01, **p < 0.05, *p < 0.1.

CPS measures. On average, the total CPS score of individuals assigned to the treatment group is 0.11 standard deviations higher than the score of individuals assigned to the control group. Impacts of similar magnitudes hold for CPS scores on leadership, behavior in situations of conflict, self-esteem, and order and self-organization. There are no overall impacts on the CPS scores on abilities to relate with others and empathy and communication skills. For most of the indicators these results hold for both males and females, but the impact on males tends to be larger. By groups, the impact concentrates on the youngest individuals, on the better educated –incomplete high school is the highest education level to be eligible for the program– and in Santo Domingo. While the program does not have an impact on the Rosenberg Scale for the complete sample, it increases the Rosenberg Scale of males in about 0.11 standard deviations. Looking at the impacts on the Grit Scale, the estimates show that the program has a positive and statistically significant effect in the total scale and in the sub-scales for persistency of effort and ambition. On average, the total Grit Scale of individuals assigned to the treatment group is 0.08 standard deviations higher than the score of individuals assigned to the control group. The impact on the subscales mentioned above is comparable in magnitude. As in the results for the CPS scale, impacts on the total Grit Scale and the different subscales concentrate and are stronger on the youngest individuals, the ones with higher educational attainment, and on those living in Santo Domingo. However, there is a sharp contrast on the results by gender, as in this case the impacts are only statistically significant for females.

While there is a statistically significant impact on several of the measures of non-cognitive development analyzed above, it is hard to determine the practical significance of these results. Literature on the relationship between non-cognitive skills and professional success is relatively new and it is still uncertain which specific competencies positively relate to participation in the labor market. In addition, there is also little evidence on the magnitude of the changes in non-cognitive abilities that are required to generate observable changes on the levels of youth employability.

However, in the literature on cognitive and non-cognitive skills development there is some indication that our results are moving on the desired direction. While the existing studies are not directly comparable to ours as they analyze different populations and interventions, they at least give us an idea of the potential of the program in terms of the magnitude of the effects measured in standard deviations. Evidence on the development of cognitive skills is largely available in the education sector literature. In general, successful interventions in primary education have an impact of close to 0.4 standard deviations per year in educational attainment[30]. Evidence on the development of non-cognitive skills is much more limited, but a recent study by Felfe et al. (2011) shows that participation in sports clubs by children aged three to 10 years old in Germany has an overall positive impact of 0.13 standard deviations in non-cognitive skills. Therefore, taking into account that the life skills component of the program only lasted 75 hours and had impacts of around 0.1 standard deviations in several measures of non-cognitive development 18–24 months after the end of the courses, it seems to be the case that the effect of the program on non-cognitive abilities is sizable[31].

Given that there is a robust statistically significant impact of the program on non-cognitive skills as measured by three different instruments, and taking into account that there is only limited empirical evidence on the role of non-cognitive development and labor market outcomes, we carried out an exercise to further explore the relation between each of the scales used in this paper to measure life skills and the probability of being employed. We estimate standard regressions in which the dependent variable is the employment status of the individual and the explanatory variable of interest is each of the above scales for the control group[32]. The regressions include a set of additional covariates to control for gender, age, education, experience, and whether the individual is currently attending school. Table 12 presents the results from this exercise which are rather disappointing: there does not seem to be any meaningful association between having higher levels of life skills, as measured by our instruments, and employment[33,34].

5 Conclusions

Juventud y Empleo is a labor training program for disadvantaged youth in the Dominican Republic. It is one of the first programs of its type in Latin America to

Table 12 OLS estimation on employment and the CPS scale (control group)

OLS estimations Dependent variable: employed	(1) All	(2) Women	(3) Men	(4) Age 16-19	(5) Incomplete high school	(6) Santo Domingo
Total CPS Score	0.0076	0.0146	−0.0052	0.0013	0.0049	−0.0051
	(0.0134)	(0.0189)	(0.0195)	(0.0268)	(0.0193)	(0.0234)
CPS: Leadership	−0.0044	0.0054	−0.0266	−0.0052	−0.0073	−0.0233
	(0.0133)	(0.0186)	(0.0195)	(0.0260)	(0.0192)	(0.0244)
CPS: Behavior in situations of conflict	−0.0089	−0.0170	−0.0035	−0.0185	−0.0076	−0.0322
	(0.0134)	(0.0189)	(0.0198)	(0.0271)	(0.0193)	(0.0231)
CPS: Self-esteem	0.0172	0.0157	0.0245	−0.0046	0.0247	0.0057
	(0.0133)	(0.0186)	(0.0206)	(0.0275)	(0.0197)	(0.0244)
CPS: Abilities to relate with others	0.0167	0.0181	0.0117	0.0240	0.0146	0.0131
	(0.0137)	(0.0189)	(0.0209)	(0.0276)	(0.0198)	(0.0237)
CPS: Order and self-organization	0.0066	0.0143	−0.0103	0.0137	0.0109	0.0123
	(0.0135)	(0.0188)	(0.0201)	(0.0267)	(0.0197)	(0.0225)
Rosenberg's Scale	0.0069	0.0171	−0.0046	0.0027	0.0160	0.0196
	(0.0136)	(0.0195)	(0.0190)	(0.0253)	(0.0185)	(0.0237)
Total Grit Scale	0.0046	0.0043	0.0040	−0.0145	−0.0223	−0.0101
	(0.0136)	(0.0191)	(0.0201)	(0.0260)	(0.0182)	(0.0247)
Grit: Persistency of effort	0.0196	0.0256	0.0095	−0.0003	−0.0172	−0.0020
	(0.0137)	(0.0190)	(0.0207)	(0.0261)	(0.0185)	(0.0248)
Grit: Ambition	−0.0118	−0.0112	−0.0084	−0.0416*	−0.0406**	−0.0282
	(0.0136)	(0.0189)	(0.0210)	(0.0250)	(0.0187)	(0.0250)
Mean dependent variable	0.625	0.516	0.797	0.588	0.630	0.599
Observations	1,286	790	496	381	717	409

Note: Robust standard errors clustered at the course level in parentheses.
COS fixed effects included in the estimation.
***$p < 0.01$, **$p < 0.05$, *$p < 0.1$.

incorporate a randomized design that allows the implementation of rigorous impact evaluations, which provide feedback to the program in its different phases. The first impact evaluation of JE showed limited impacts on employment and wages, which lead to changes in the program that focused on working closer with the private sector and providing a stronger life skills component, which were identified by employers as the most valuable component of the project. This evaluation looks at data from the first cohort since the program was re-launched, and evaluates the impact of the program both on traditional labor market outcomes and on outcomes related to youth behavior and life style, expectations about the future and socio-emotional skills.

While the design and implementation of this evaluation incorporated the lessons from the first JE evaluation experience, there were still certain flaws that could have been prevented and that should be taken into account in future evaluations of the JE program and other training programs. Mainly, the compliance with the randomization protocol should have been stricter and should have limited the possibilities for COS to include individuals from the control group in the program. A potential solution for this difficulty could have been randomizing the pool of eligible potential participants into three groups: treatment, control and waitlist. In this way, the COS would have only been allowed to contact individuals in the waitlist group, keeping the control group completely clean. This would have also contributed to making administrative data more transparent and likely more consistent with the follow up survey.

Despite the adverse economic conditions under which the cohort under study participated and graduated from JE, there are positive impacts on quality of employment for males. On average, males in the treatment group are four percentage points more likely to have employer provided health insurance than individuals in the control group. The program also has a positive effect on monthly earnings among those employed. On average, employed individuals in the treatment group have monthly earnings that are seven percent higher than employed individuals in the control group. Both of these results are even stronger for Santo Domingo, were the impacts reach 11 and 24 percentage points, respectively. The program, however, has no statistically significant impact on overall employment. Here, it should be noted that an important caveat of this type of evaluations is their partial equilibrium approach. While the evaluation can assert that the program has some positive impacts on the quality of the jobs that participants get, particularly men, it does not inform on whether these good jobs are incremental or if they correspond to crowding-out by program participants. Hence, it is possible that the positive impacts may be overstated[35].

Regarding outcomes related to youth behavior, expectations and non-cognitive skills, the results from this evaluation are somewhat positive. The program is effective in reducing pregnancy, especially in teenagers. Females aged 16–19 in the treatment group are on average five percentage points less likely to be pregnant at the moment of the follow up survey. This corresponds to a 45 percent drop in comparison to the average pregnancy rate for the same age group in the control group.

The reduction in the pregnancy rate is consistent with the positive impact of the program in terms of youth expectations about their future, which could be leading to positive changes in youth behavior. On average, individuals in the treatment group, and especially females and younger individuals, have higher expectations about their future in terms of having a better life in 20 years, living in a better neighborhood, owning a business, and moving up in the wealth ladder.

This evaluation also shows positive impacts of JE in different measures of non-cognitive skills. Using the CPS, Rosenberg and Grit scales, estimations show a consistent improvement in scores, ranging between 8 and 16 percent of a standard deviation. It is hard to interpret the practical significance of these results as evidence on this topic is very limited. Further analyses carried out in this paper show no correlation between some of these measures and employment. These results should encourage further research on the relationship between non-cognitive skills and labor market performance in order to understand the mechanisms through which life skills training can contribute to youth insertion into the labor market. Research on the instruments used to measure such skills is also needed.

Overall, is it worth spending scarce resources in this program (or in this type of programs)? The average cost of this program was about US$700, of which US$200 were transfers to participants as stipend for transportation and meals. Assuming no opportunity costs of participants during the training and if the impacts on income are maintained at 8%, the cost —without transfers- would be recovered in about 50 months (the average income of the control group was about US$130)[36]. We also documented impacts in reducing teenage pregnancy, which clearly has a positive value in terms of health and labor market perspectives of those youngsters. The program reduced one pregnancy for every twenty teenage female participants, so the cost of preventing one teenage pregnancy would be in the range of US$10,000-US$66,000[37]. Also, if in the long run more non-cognitive skills and more positive expectations result in better labor market outcomes or life paths, the benefits would increase accordingly. However, in the short-run, these programs are clearly not a big win. But then again, development practitioners are well aware that big wins are extremely rare. In any case, while policymakers continue to face social pressure to deal with the ongoing problem of youth unemployment and program managers will claim that the newest version of the project will certainly yield positive results, it is necessary to continue evaluating and learning from the implementation of these projects.

Endnotes

[1]See Heckman et al. (1999) for a general overview of training programs, and Betcherman and Dar (2004) for a recent summary that includes some evaluations of developing country training programs.

[2]The Job Training Partnership Act program is described extensively by Heckman et al. (1999). Dolton, Makepeace and Treble (1994) describe the Youth Training Scheme.

[3]For a recent assessment of these programs, see Gonzalez et al. (2011).

[4]As implemented in LAC, these programs place a heavy emphasis on the private sector, both as a provider of training and as a demander of trainees. Private training firms compete for public funds with proposals that need to be backed by commitments from local employers to offer internships.

[5]While cognitive skills are related to the ability to learn and the intellectual coefficient, socio-emotional or non-cognitive skills (also known as personality traits or life skills) are related to behaviors and attitudes, and are also referred to as to "soft skills".

[6]While interesting it is important to note that these findings must be interpreted cautiously, since the sub-sample of largest impact was determined after the fact, rather than based on an ex ante analysis plan.

[7]The study on Colombia reports a modest and statistically insignificant effect on overall employment (including unpaid work), but a large and statistically significant effect on formal sector employment.

[8]While the role of the private sector as driver of demand was envisioned since the design of the original program, in practice internships were provided without any real prospect of employment. This in part was due to the lag between the moment when training courses were developed by COS and private firms and the moment when graduates where actually ready for the internship, which was determined by how courses were selected, in term-specific public bids. In the new program, course selection would be done throughout the year, in order to respond better to private sector demand.

[9]A complementary evaluation based on another cohort of trainees led by the World Bank analyzed the impact of providing only life skills versus the traditional training, and their preliminary findings suggest that there is no valued added of the technical training (Martinez 2011). A qualitative analysis by Fazio (2011) presents additional evidence that firms value more the life skills component than the technical training.

[10]The eligibility criteria are that participants should be 16 to 29 years old; living in poor neighborhoods; not attending school; with incomplete high school or less; unemployed, underemployed or inactive; and hold an identity card.

[11]However, there are no reasons to believe that this imperfect compliance was due to defiers; that is, to individuals who did exactly the opposite of what was indicated to them by the lottery, regardless of its result. Given that program participants were selected from a pool of applicants who had registered voluntarily to participate in the course, it does not seem likely that some of these individuals would have declined the course when winning the lottery and managed to enter the course when losing it. Such situation would have been like having some individuals wanting to boycott the program, which to our knowledge never occurred. On the contrary, the program seemed to be positively accepted and perceived at the local and national level.

[12]See Angrist and Pischke (2009); and Duflo et al. (2008).

[13]If the program has a positive impact and we compare $Z_i = 1$ with $Z_i = 0$ but less than 100 percent of the former took the percent of the former took the course and more than 0 percent of the latter participated in the program, then the comparison yields an underestimation of the "true" program impacts. This is why under imperfect compliance of the random assignment the ITT leads to the dilution of the impact of the program.

[14]Although we can estimate the size of the compliers (as the difference in the participation rate among those that won and those that lost the lottery), we cannot

identify them individually. The impact on this group is known as the Local Average Treatment Effect (LATE), which yields a larger impact than the ITT since it assumes that any difference in the average outcome between the $Z_i = 1$ group and the $Z_i = 0$ group is due to the larger fraction of the former that participated in the training. Thus, the estimation of the LATE for JE compliers yields the impact of the program on those who were treated because they won the lottery; otherwise they would not have been recruited to attend the courses. In the instrumental variables jargon, the lottery is an instrument, unrelated with the outcome but related to participation in the program (it increases the probability of participation by about fifty percentage points).

[15]We also estimate the LATE using Two Stage Least Squares (2SLS): the estimates are simply the OLS reduced form scaled up by the difference in the participation rate between those with $Z_i = 1$ and $Z_i = 0$ (the first stage of the 2SLS). Given that standard errors are adjusted accordingly, statistical significance does not change. Results for LATE estimations are shown in the Additional file 1.

[16]The sample size was set at 5,000 to detect an 8 percent increase in income with a power of 0.8 and an attrition of 30 percent of the sample with the *sampsi* Stata command.

[17]Most of the questions that measure labor market outcomes are based on the ENFT that is carried out twice a year by the Central Bank of the Dominican Republic. Some questions were modified and adapted to the JE evaluation and youth population; the basic indicators of labor force participation are generated following the ENFT and allow performing an external validation of our data.

[18]The fact that such a large fraction of the individuals with $Z_i = 0$ were contacted to begin the course is partly explained by the rule that allowed COS to contact up to 33 percent (5 out of 15) of controls as replacements for no-shows or dropouts. However, even after accounting for this, a proportion of 47 percent seems considerably large and reflects that non-compliance was high and that in practice COS were not rigorous in the application of the randomization protocol. While they did contact almost everyone that won the lottery, they also contacted nearly half of the people that didn't. Given that the decision about who in the control group to contact (apart from the 33% for replacements) was probably not random, this non-compliance might have generated a bias in the selection of individuals into the program. For this reason, most of the analyses in this paper are based on ITT estimates.

[19]When looking at baseline characteristics among the different complier and non-complier groups there does not seem to be any statistically significant differences. Only the number of children seems to be statistically different (at a 10% level) before the program between these groups, with the never-taker group having a larger amount of children on average. Additional file 1: Table S2 presents this information.

[20]Given that the follow-up survey shows a larger "always taker" group than the administrative data, it was decided to define D_i based on the latter in order to be more conservative. Also, taking into consideration that COS may have had incentives to under report such group as it reveals their own non-compliance with the randomization protocol, the information from the follow-up survey was found to be more reliable.

[21]Another filter was introduced. We wanted to make sure that those that were not contacted by the COS did not manage to participate in the program by other methods. Hence, we include in the $D_i = 1$ group those that report having taken the course, despite the fact that they were never contacted to begin the courses. Approximately 30 individuals from the control group with these characteristics were accepted by the COS to take the course and complete the internship.

[22]A decomposition of the initial $D_i = 1$ group by level of participation in the program is presented in Additional file 1: Figure S1.

[23]The estimation for the different subpopulations compares individuals from the treatment and control groups within each specific subpopulation. So, for example, the ITT coefficients of Santo Domingo compare individuals from the treatment group in Santo Domingo with individuals from the control group in Santo Domingo. This applies even to the type of course subpopulations, as there are individuals both in the treatment and the control groups for each type of course.

[24]This is consistent with the results from the first evaluation of the program, and with evaluations of similar programs that report impacts on the probability of getting formal employment (Attanasio et al. (2011), Ibarrarán and Rosas (2009)).

[25]The control group mean reveals that Dominican youth are very optimistic to begin with. Hence, improvements in the treatment group are with respect to a very high starting point.

[26]In this context in which youth have not even completed high school, expectations of a better education level refer to going back to school or continuing to take training courses of the sort of the JE program.

[27]Hence, if one were to carry out a cost-benefit analysis, specifically, of the raising perceptions and expectations "component" of the JE program, it would be necessary to assume or measure a quantitative relation between: i) the changes in the "expectation scales" and the changes in some selected behaviors; and ii) the changes in these selected behaviors and the changes in labor market outcomes. Then it should be possible to compare the costs of providing the "component" to the benefits of obtaining the corresponding changes in labor market outcomes. In a way, it would be like doing a general cost-benefit analysis of the program, but weighting it up by the fraction attributable to this "component".

[28]The Rosenberg Scale was first presented in 1965 and later revised in 1989, and it has been validated in 53 countries and translated into 28 languages. See Rosenberg (1989).

[29]The Grit Scale was created in 2007 and later revised in 2009. See Duckworth et al. (2007).

[30]See Hill et al. (2007) for a guide on interpreting effect sizes in research.

[31]It is possible that some of the effects on life skills are due to the internship and not only to the life skills training component. This is an important area for future research, as the interaction between life skills and training may have important policy implications in terms of which elements of the training package are more effective.

[32]We use only the individuals assigned to the control group. The objective of limiting the sample is to avoid the endogeneity that would arise when using the entire sample,

as individuals assigned to the treatment could have both higher scores in the non-cognitive scales and higher levels of employment.

[33]We also tried using additional dependent variables, such as formality and earnings, and did not find any impacts. Similarly, we excluded some of the control variables and obtained equivalent results.

[34]As with perceptions and expectations, life skills are not a program objective by themselves, but a channel through which it should be possible to increase youth employability. As a result, they have an economic value to the extent that they are associated with improvements in labor market outcomes. The regressions here presented show that such relationship between like skills and employment needs to be further studied; not only to understand it in itself, but to enable the completion of cost-benefit analyses related to non-cognitive skills training activities.

[35]See Hirshleifer et al. (2014) for a recent discussion on this issue.

[36]These computations use the ITT estimates reported in the paper. One could also do the analysis based on the LATE or Treatment-on-the-treated estimates shown in the Additional file 1, which basically double the impacts, thus reducing the time required to recover the costs in half. However, given that the interpretation of LATE is local, referring only to those that take the course because they won the lottery, we prefer to be conservative and use the standard intention-to-treat estimates for cost/benefit considerations.

[37]The lower number is computed based on the need to train twenty female teenagers in order to prevent one pregnancy, with a cost (excluding transfers) of US $500 per trainee. The upper bound is based on the actual composition of trainees, in which only 16% of trainees were teenage females. If the LATE estimates shown in the Additional file 1 are taken at face value, the cost-range would be about half (US$5,000-US$33,000).

Additional file

Additional file 1: Figure S1. Program Participation Stages. Table S1. Original and realized for the follow-up survey. Table S2. Characteristics of the Complier and Non-Complier Groups. Table S3. LATE estimation on selected labor market outcomes. Table S4. LATE estimation on pregnancy. Table S5. LATE estimation on expectations. Table S6. LATE estimation on the CPS Scale.

Competing interests
The IZA Journal of Labor & Development is committed to the IZA Guiding Principles of Research Integrity. The authors declare that they have observed these principles.

Acknowledgements
This project is a collaborative effort involving many people. First, we want to recognize the work and commitment to the evaluation agenda of the program of José Luis Polanco, director of the project coordinating unit (PCU) at the Ministry of Labor in the Dominican Republic. He and his team have taken the evaluation very seriously posing the relevant questions and taking action to improve the project based on the evaluation findings. We are especially thankful for the collaboration of Douglas Hasbun from the PCU. Additionally, we have benefited from the inputs with key staff at the Ministry of Labor, in particular Deyanira Matrillé from the Labor Market's Observatory, Sarah Pimentel from the National Employment Service, and María de Lourdes Cabrera, the Ministry's General Director for Employment. We also recognize the ongoing support of the Minister of Labor Francisco Dominguez and of the Director of the INFOTEP, the national training institute, without whom the implementation of the program and the rigorous evaluation would not have been possible. This document is part of a broad evaluation agenda in which Paloma Acevedo and Carlos Asenjo from the World Bank and Sebastián Martinez from the IDB have played a key role. We acknowledge excellent comments and suggestions from Guilherme Sedlacek, Norbert Schady, an anonymous peer reviewer for the IDB WP series, and from seminar participants at the 2011 IZA conference in Labor and Development,

and at the Inter-American Development Bank - 3ie International Conference on Impact Evaluation. The views expressed in this paper are those of the authors and should not be attributed to the Inter-American Development Bank.
Responsible editor: David Lam

Author details
[1]Inter-American Development Bank (IDB), Washington, DC and IZA, Bonn, Germany. [2]Inter-American Development Bank (IDB), Washington, DC, USA. [3]University of Manchester, Manchester, England. [4]Professor at the Universidad Autónoma de Santo Domingo, Santo Domingo, Dominican Republic.

References
Acero-Gomez E, Campos-Vazquez R (2011) "Teenage Pregnancy in Mexico: Evolution and Consequences". Paper for the World Bank Report "Teenage Pregnancy in Latin America", Washington, DC
Angrist J, Pischke J (2009) Mostly Harmless Econometrics: An Empiricist's Companion. Princeton University Press, Princeton NJ
Ashenfelter O (1978) Estimating the Effect of Training Programs on Earnings. Rev Econ Stat 60:47–50
Attanasio O, Kugler A, Meghir C (2011) Subsidizing Vocational Training for Disadvantaged Youth in Colombia: Evidence from a Randomized Trial. Am Econ J 3(3):188–220
Betcherman GK, Dar A (2004) "Impacts of Active Labour Market Programs: New Evidence from Evaluations with Particular Attention to Developing and Transition Countries.". World Bank Social Protection Discussion Paper 0402, Washington, DC
Brea M (2010) "Interpretación de las Escalas CPS, Rosenberg y Grit y Propuestas de Revisión para Mejorar la Confiabilidad." (Document prepared for the World Bank). Ther World Bank, Washington, DC
Brunello G, Schlotter M (2011) "Non Cognitive Skills and Personality Traits: Labour Market Relevance and their Development in Education and Training Systems." IZA Discussion paper 5743. The Institute for the Study of Labor (IZA), Bonn, Germany, p 5743
Card D, Ibarrarán P, Regalia F, Rosas-Shady D, Soares Y (2011) The Labor Market Impacts of Youth Training in the Dominican Republic. J Labor Econ 29(2):267–300
Dolton PJ, Makepeace GH, Treble JG (1994) "The Youth Training Scheme and the School-to-Work Transition," Oxford Economic Papers, Oxford University Press, 46(4):629–657
Duckworth AL, Peterson C, Matthews MD, Kelly DR (2007) Grit: Perseverance and Passion for Long-Term Goals. J Pers Soc Psychol 92(6):1087–1101
Duflo E, Glennerster R, Kremer M (2008) "Using Randomization in Development Economics Research: A Toolkit". In: Paul Schultz T, John A, Strauss A (eds) Handbook of Development Economics," Elsevier, vol 4, 1st edn
Fazio MV (2011) "Análisis de la percepción de los empleadores acerca de las pasantías y las perspectivas de inserción laboral en esas empresas." BID. Nota Técnica IDB-TN-240. Banco Interamericano de Desarrollo, Washington, DC
Felfe C, Lechner M, Steinmayr A (2011) "Sports and Child Development." IZA Discussion paper 6105. Institute for the Study of Labor (IZA), Bonn, Germany
Gonzalez C, Ripani L, Rosas D (2011) Mejorando las Oportunidades de Inserción Laboral de Jóvenes en América Latina. BID. Nota Técnica,
Heckman J, Lalonde RJ, Smith J (1999) The Economics and Econometrics of Active Labor Market Programs. In: Ashenfelter O, Card D (eds) Handbook of Labor Economics, vol 3A. Elsevier, New York, pp 1865–2097
Heckman J, Stixrud J, Urzua S (2006) The Effects of Cognitive and Noncognitive Abilities on Labor Market Outcomes and Social Behavior. J Labor Econ 24(3):411–482
Hill CJ, Bloom HS, Black AR, Lipsey MW (2007) "Empirical Benchmarks for Interpreting Effect Sizes in Research". MDRC Working Papers on Research Methodology. MDRC, New York, NY
Hirshleifer S, McKenzie D, Almeida R, Ridao-Cano C (2014) "The Impact of Vocational Training for the Unemployed. Experimental Evidence from Turkey," World Bank. Policy Research Working Paper 6807. The World Bank, Washington, DC
Ibarrarán P, Rosas D (2009) Evaluating the Impact of Job Training Programs in Latin America: Evidence from IDB Funded Operations. J Dev Effect 2(1):195–216
Martinez S (2011) "Impacts of the Dominican Republic Youth Employment Program: Hard Skills or Soft Skills", Mimeo. http://siteresources.worldbank.org/INTLM/Resources/390041-1141141801867/2275364-1313438221557/PJE_DR_PPT.pdf
Oficina Nacional de Estadística (ONE) (2008) "Madres Adolescentes en República Dominicana".
Rosenberg M (1989) "Society and the Adolescent Self-Image." Revised Edition. Wesleya University Press, Middletown, C.T
Thaler R, Sunstein CR (2009) Nudge: Improving decisions about health, wealth and happiness. Penguin, New York
Urzua S (2009) Transición Escuela-Trabajo El Rol de las Habilidades y el Sistema Educativo. Report for the Inter-American Development Bank. Inter-American Development Bank, Washington, DC

3

Are migrants discriminated against in Chinese urban labour markets?

Jason Gagnon[1], Theodora Xenogiani[2] and Chunbing Xing[3]*

*Correspondence:
xingchb@bnu.edu.cn
[1] OECD Development Centre, Paris
Cedex 16, France
Full list of author information is
available at the end of the article

Abstract

We use a nationally representative survey to investigate the incidence of discrimination against internal migrant workers in urban China, considering both migrants from rural areas (rural migrants) and those from other urban areas (urban migrants). We find that both rural and urban migrants are discriminated out of jobs with formal labour contracts. Results also suggest that urban migrants are compensated for working in the informal sector by earning higher wages. There is evidence however of wage discrimination against rural *hukou* status. A semi-parametric method suggests a larger discrimination against migrants in the upper half of the wage distribution. Discrimination against migrants seems not to decrease as their duration of stay in the urban labour market increases.

JEL codes: J7; J51; O15; N35

Keywords: China; Discrimination; Labour market; Wages; Internal migration

1 Introduction

Institutional reform, a wide and increasing rural-urban income gap[1] and the easing of internal migration restrictions, have contributed to attracting millions of workers to the fast-growing urban centres of China since the early 1980s (Cai 2000). Between 1990 and 2005 more than 100 million individuals migrated from rural to urban areas (MGI 2009) and the stock of internal migrants was estimated at 150 million in 2009 (Meng and Zhang 2010).[2] According to the 1% Chinese population survey, rural migrant workers accounted for more than 20% of the labour force in the urban labour market in 2005. Previous analyses shed little doubt as to whether this influx of labour helped fill labour shortages and spur economic growth (Liang 2001; Song and Zhang 2003). The literature is more divided as to the welfare of these migrant workers.

Research on China shows that internal migrants disproportionately take up informal sector jobs, earn less and are less likely to be covered by a social safety net (see for instance the China Labor Bulletin (2008)). The situation is exacerbated by the residence registration system (*hukou*), which largely determines one's access to local public goods and services. The *hukou* system has generated a dualistic labour market in which migrants can be discriminated on income but also on the type of jobs they have access to. To draw inference on the existence and extent of discrimination, however, researchers need to consider the fact that migrant workers have different characteristics than urban residents, such as lower education levels. To what extent their disproportional presence in the informal sector and lower income are due to lower human capital level is an empirical question that has generated a lot of attention. At present, there seems to be no consensus on the extent of discrimination against migrant workers in the Chinese urban labour market.

The literature investigating discrimination against rural migrants mainly focuses on wages. Such an approach is incomplete, since other benefits are associated with one's *hukou* status. These benefits not only include those provided by employers and pensions, but also local public services (education, medical services, and housing), the access to which depends heavily on having a good job. While employer-provided non-wage benefits can be empirically accounted for to some extent, it is hard to monetarize the value associated with local public services. One way to deal with this issue is to look at the distribution of formal and informal jobs, since they often determine access to non-wage benefits in one's job.

This paper investigates the incidence of discrimination against internal migrants in urban China using the 2005 Chinese Population Survey, a large nationally representative dataset. It questions whether their disproportionate presence in the informal labour market is due to discrimination or to their lower human capital levels. Counterfactual empirical results show that if migrants (both rural and urban) were treated as urban residents (based on observable characteristics), there would be more with formal sector jobs. An Oaxaca-Blinder decomposition (OB, Blinder 1973; Oaxaca 1973) based on a linear probability model of having an informal sector job suggests that a sizable share of the gap between migrant workers and urban residents cannot be explained by the differences in their observable characteristics, suggesting discrimination out of the formal sector against migrant workers.

The paper then turns to the income gap. An OB decomposition, based on a standard OLS wage regression for each group, suggests that most of the income gap between rural migrants and urban residents can be explained by differences in observed characteristics, which is consistent with recent studies. However, it would be misleading to draw the conclusion that rural migrants are not discriminated against in the urban labour market. First, the typical type of job each group holds is different. Even at similar income levels, urban residents are more likely to have jobs in the formal sector than migrant workers, which are more stable and associated with better social security coverage and many benefits that are hard to monetarize. Second, discrimination might vary across the income distribution. This cannot be captured by a simple OB decomposition, which only decomposes the income gaps in means.

We therefore do two additional exercises. First, we exploit the fact that the *hukou* system has two components. One is the agricultural and non-agricultural division (or rural vs. urban), and the other is the specific location in which a *hukou* is registered. We introduce urban migrants into the analysis as a new reference group for rural migrants, as they have an urban *hukou* but are not registered in the location in which they are working. We find that urban migrants, on average, earn more than both urban residents and rural migrants. Since urban migrants differ from urban residents only in migrant status, we interpret any unexplained components of the decomposition as a premium associated with migration. This premium can also be interpreted as compensation for the loss of *hukou*-related benefits. This is consistent with the fact that urban migrants give up various benefits associated with a local *hukou* registration, which must be compensated for when they migrate. Incomes must therefore be higher for urban migrants as long as they have the freedom to choose the location in which they work. Urban migrants are a more appropriate group to study income discrimination against rural migrants, because urban local benefits have been monetarized for urban migrants at least to some extent.[3]

As urban migrants and rural migrants differ only in *hukou* status, we interpret the unexplained component of the decomposition as discrimination against rural *hukou* status. By comparing urban migrants with both rural migrants and urban residents, results suggest that the presumed absence of income discrimination against rural migrants is in fact the net effect of a discrimination against a rural *hukou* status and a premium accrued by both rural and urban migrants in the labour market.

Second, we deepen the decomposition analysis using the semi-parametric approach proposed by DiNardo *et al.* (1996) to explain the income gap along its entire distribution. Results suggest that discrimination against migrant workers occurs in the upper half of the income distribution.

We also take into account duration in the urban labour market. When the groups of migrants are divided according to whether they have spent more or less than 5 years in a location other than the one in which their *hukou* is registered, duration does not matter in alleviating discrimination against migrant workers.

This paper contributes to the literature in the following ways. First, it uses a dataset which has advantages in identifying a nationally representative migrant sample. Second, it applies an OB method to decompose the gap between migrant and non-migrant groups in the likelihood of working in the formal or informal sector. It is worth mentioning that the Brown *et al.* (1980) method takes sectoral distribution into consideration in its decomposition analysis. However, if the income gap between different sectors is small, taking the sectoral distribution into consideration will not change the results of the simple OB decomposition of the income gaps.[4] Given the fact that the formal/informal dimension is important in its own right, we perform a simple OB decomposition to investigate the gap in formal/informal sector distributions between migrants and non-migrants. Third, it applies a non-parametric analysis of the wage distribution, rather than investigating differences in means. Fourth, it considers an additional group of individuals, namely migrants with urban (or non-agricultural) *hukou* status. This group makes up a large share of the work force in the Chinese urban labour market, but is neglected in many studies. Adding this group into the analysis helps better identify discrimination along the two dimensions of the *hukou* system: local vs. non-local and rural vs. urban (or agricultural vs. non-agricultural).

The paper is organised as follows. Section 2 provides a short discussion of the institutional context and a literature review of migrant labour outcomes in the Chinese urban labour market. Section 3 describes the 2005 1% population survey microdataset used in this paper. Section 4 presents and discusses the model specification and Section 5 reports empirical results, where rural migrants are compared not only with urban residents but also with urban migrants, both in terms of wages and the sectors in which they work. Section 6 discusses policy implications and concludes.

2   The *hukou* system and the Chinese urban labour market

The institutional framework in which the Chinese urban labour market operates has been covered extensively, with particular attention being placed on the residential registration (*hukou*) system see (Cai 2000; Deng and Gustafsson 2006; Zhao 2005). This system was originally designed in the 1950s to control migration within the country by registering household members in designated rural or urban locations. In practice, one's *hukou* status is categorized by both socio-economic eligibility (agricultural vs. non-agricultural) and registered residential location (local vs. non-local) Chan and Buckingham (2008). The first classification determines entitlement to state subsidized food grain and other prerogatives. The second classification defines one's rights to many benefits (access to health care, public education, housing, and better access to jobs) in a specific locality. *Hukou* status is determined by birth, following the status held by one's parents. To migrate permanently, one needs to change registration location.

The lack of access to social benefits in one's job is likely to contribute to an important decrease in welfare; a report by the China Labor Bulletin (2008), for instance, reported that the current wage gap between urban and rural regions would increase from 3- to 6-fold in real terms, if the benefits accrued from social security were considered. Due to significant differences in employment opportunities and welfare and benefit entitlements, there is a strong incentive for rural residents to change their *hukou* registration from agricultural to non-agricultural, which requires approval from the state. Both the process and the number of such moves are tightly controlled by the government. Temporary migrants who cannot change registration location also need official approval to move. To migrate without authorization, people are vulnerable to round-ups and deportation, and cannot access many other local rights.

Despite the system, growth in the manufacturing (export) sector in China over the last twenty years has attracted a significant number of migrant workers to fast-growing urban centres. Policy makers both of the central and local governments have since faced a significant challenge in integrating new arrivals. *hukou* policies have become increasingly flexible since the 1980s. A major change was the decentralisation of the system's management, with many local governments obtaining full managerial power to determine their own policies towards migrants. It has also become easier for workers and households to transfer their registrations to other locations (in particular to small and medium-sized cities), and temporary residence permits are being granted more often. Notably, it has become possible for people to migrate and obtain a job without a valid permit. This paper focuses on migrants who have not changed their *hukou* status, since those that have changed it cannot be identified in the Chinese Population Survey. This group is nevertheless, very small.

Deliberate discrimination of migrants in cities remained legal until very recently, with the aim of reducing competition in urban centres (Cai 2000) and avoiding the creation of slums common in big countries urbanising in a relatively short period of time. Migrants are less likely to access good jobs and earn less on average than non-migrants (Zhao 2005). Local public services remain either inaccessible or expensive for them. Although rural migrants (those with an agricultural *hukou* status) may stay for long periods in urban areas, most are not covered by the urban social security system nor entitled to various other social and economic benefits. It is also worth mentioning that most of these benefits are determined by the specific location in which the *hukou* is registered, meaning that migrants from other urban areas also face such problems.

Earlier studies on China using OB decompositions or related methods find some evidence of discrimination against rural migrants in the urban labour market. For instance, Meng and Zhang (2001) find that 51% of the wage gap between urban residents and migrants is due to unexplained factors, while Dinh and Maurer-Fazio (2004) find 25%, Wang (2005) 43% and Deng (2007) 60%. These findings are challenged by more recent studies. Using the 2002 China Household Income Project data, both Démurger *et al*. (2009) and Messinis (2013) find that the main source of disparity between urban residents and rural migrants is related to pre-market variables (education opportunities) rather than those directly related to the performance in the labour market. Using the 2005 China Urban Labor Survey (CULS),[5] Lee (2012) finds that there is only a small amount of discrimination between migrant and urban workers in terms of wages. However, when total labour remuneration is taken into account, the extent of the discrimination against migrant workers is larger. It is still difficult to put a monetary value on many of the *hukou*-related benefits, which include access to local public schools, medical services, and secure and decent jobs. Existing studies do not take into consideration these benefits. They also use data from different regions at different times and ultimately derive different conclusions, making any comparison a difficult task (Zhao 2005).

In comparison to existing literature, this paper uses a national dataset with better coverage of migrants at a similar moment in time. It also investigates differences beyond wages, looking at differences in the probability of having an informal job. Finally it investigates differences not only at the mean but across the whole wage distribution.

3   Data and summary statistics

Data used in this analysis come from a one-fifth random draw of the 2005 1% population survey, which is administered by the Chinese National Bureau of Statistics (NBS). The sample size of around 2.3 million individuals covers 31 provinces, municipalities, and autonomous regions, and is representative of mainland China. The sample studied in this analysis includes individuals aged from 16 to 60 and who are not currently in school. Employers, household workers, and observations with no or zero declared income are also not considered.

The 2005 Chinese Population Survey has advantages for studying migrant labour market outcomes relative to household surveys. An ordinary household survey may be less likely to obtain a representative sample of migrants due to the floating nature of migrants and due to its inherent sampling process. For example, surveys that base their sampling frame on neighbourhoods and communities may under-represent migrants who arrived recently and do not live in registered housing and those who live at the construction site collectively. Census data does not suffer from such problems, since it aims at covering the entire population. It therefore provides a good coverage of the migrant population within China - including the floating population.

This paper focuses solely on individuals working in urban areas. The area in which an individual is currently residing or working is classified into three categories in the survey: city, town, and village. In this analysis, city and town are defined as urban areas and villages are defined as rural areas. These definitions are consistent with those used by the NBS to produce rural and urban statistics.[6]

Two questions in the questionnaire are used to identify migrants in the urban labour market: (1) In which location is your *hukou* registered? and (2) How long ago did you leave this location? Migrants are defined as those who have left their registered *hukou* location for more than six months. Another question asks the type of *hukou* (agricultural or non-agricultural) and helps divide migrants further into two categories. As individuals with an agricultural *hukou* usually come from rural areas, we refer to this group as rural migrants. Similarly, we refer to migrants with non-agricultural *hukou* as urban migrants as most of them come from other urban areas, and refer to residents who have local urban *hukou* as urban residents.

In addition, the questionnaire asks the reason for migrating. Most migrants said they had moved for work, and this is especially true for rural migrants (the share is approximately 61%). We restrict our sample to those who migrated for work or business-related reasons. The definitions of informal employment are based on an individual's declared employment status and the availability of a formal labour contract, consistent with the standard ILO guidelines (ILO 1993, 2003). The possible answers as to one's employment status include the following: employee, employer (who employs other persons), self-employed (who are neither employed by others nor do they employ others) and household worker. Only employees and the self-employed are retained for the analysis.

Those declaring themselves to be self-employed are categorised as being part of the informal sector. Employees were then further divided depending on their declared contract status, which had the following possible answers: fixed term contract, no fixed term contract (long term contract) and no contract. Individuals answering that they do not have a contract are considered to have informal sector jobs, while those answering that they have a contract, regardless of whether it is fixed or not, are considered to have formal sector jobs. Although it is required by law that the employees and employers sign a contract, many employees do not have contracts due to lack of inspection and poor enforcement.[7] These two definitions of informal employment (self-employment and the absence of a formal labour contract) are mutually exclusive. They provide a certain degree of heterogeneity within the informal sector, yet both are characterised by the lack of social security coverage.

Income data is captured using income earned in the previous month. In cases where income was not earned monthly, respondents were asked to calculate a monthly income. To calculate the hourly income, we divide the monthly income by monthly working hours, calculated as hours worked last week × 4. Educational level was divided into four levels, following ISCED standards: (1) primary and below, (2) junior middle, (3) senior middle, and (4) college and above.

Summary statistics are reported in Table 1. There are 219712 urban residents, 94621 rural migrants, and 22214 urban migrants in our analysis, accounting for 65%, 28%, and 7% of the whole sample, respectively. Compared to migrant workers, urban residents are older, primarily married and relatively highly educated. Self-employed workers are typically older than the other groups, less educated, and male, while showing higher incomes than workers without a formal contract.

In terms of wages, urban migrants earn the most of the three groups, followed by urban residents and rural migrants, who earn about half of the hourly wage of urban migrants. Rural migrants are the most likely not to have a formal labour contract, with a share of about 48%, followed by urban migrants (34%) and finally urban residents (30%). Both

Table 1 Summary statistics

	Total (1)	Formal contract (2)	Self-employed (3)	Without contract (4)
A. urban residents				
Age	38.0	38.3	39.1	37.2
Education levels (%)				
Primary and below	5.7	3.8	14.6	6.0
Junior middle school	30.1	24.1	52.6	33.0
Senior middle school	33.9	35.7	28.5	32.4
College and above	30.3	36.4	4.3	28.6
Female (%)	41.8	41.4	37.1	44.4
Not married (%)	12.0	11.5	6.7	15.2
Left the *hukou* within 0.5–5 years	-	-	-	-
Monthly income (Yuan)	1133.1	1286.5	857.9	940.2
Hourly income (Yuan)	6.6	7.6	4.3	5.4
No unemployment insurance (%)	55.4	36.0	94.1	78.3
No pension (%)	37.3	19.1	78.5	56.9
No medical insurance (%)	36.3	18.9	81.7	52.6
Obs.	219712	128509	25832	65371
B. rural migrants				
Age	30.2	28.8	35.7	29.2
Education levels (%)				
Primary and below	19.6	12.6	30.4	20.8
Junior middle school	62.5	62.9	57.2	64.2
Senior middle school	15.9	21.3	11.6	13.6
College and above	1.9	3.2	0.7	1.4
Female (%)	41.4	45.2	29.3	43.1
Not married (%)	36.5	43.4	8.5	41.7
Left the *hukou* within 0.5–5 years	73.1	73.9	60.4	77.1
Monthly income (Yuan)	997.9	1144.7	994.0	892.2
Hourly income (Yuan)	4.8	5.7	4.6	4.2
No unemployment insurance (%)	92.9	82.8	99.5	97.9
No pension (%)	85.8	66.8	97.7	95.3
No medical insurance (%)	82.5	62.2	94.9	92.7
Obs.	94621	32947	16536	45138
C. urban migrants				
Age	31.8	31.3	36.6	30.5
Education levels (%)				
Primary and below	4.6	2.4	9.8	5.5
Junior middle school	29.4	20.3	45.7	36.4
Senior middle school	36.5	36.7	33.6	37.3
College and above	29.5	40.6	10.8	20.7
Female (%)	41.1	40.2	35.2	45.0
Not married (%)	36.7	39.4	10.7	43.9
Left the *hukou* within 0.5–5 years	70.3	69.5	62.7	74.7
Monthly income (Yuan)	1688.5	2090.2	1351.6	1218.0
Hourly income (Yuan)	9.3	11.9	6.8	6.5
No unemployment insurance (%)	71.8	53.7	94.4	89.7
No pension (%)	57.0	34.5	80.6	81.2
No medical insurance (%)	59.6	37.5	85.4	82.5
Obs.	22214	11482	3272	7460

Source: 1% population survey of China (2005).

rural and urban migrants are more likely to be self-employed than urban residents, and self-employed workers have higher incomes than workers without a formal contract.

The data also show that more urban residents have formal labour contracts, relative to migrants. It is also evident from the data that migrants are less covered by social security benefits, since they generally have informal sector jobs that do not include unemployment insurance, pension benefits, or medical coverage.

4 OB and DFL decompositions

The methodology for this paper is based on two decomposition models, one based on the probability of having an informal sector job and the other on incomes.

We first investigate differences between the three groups in the probability of having an informal sector job. Three multinomial logit models are estimated, one for each group (rural migrants, urban residents, and urban migrants), with the dependent variable being a categorical variable representing each type of job, and a set of control variables. Types of job are defined as: $j = formal\ jobs$, $self\text{-}employment$, and $jobs\ without\ a\ formal\ labour$ $contract$, with the latter two representing the informal sector. The results of these models are used to calculate counterfactual shares of each employment sector for each migrant group as if they were treated as another group.

Because the OB decomposition method requires two groups instead of three, a linear probability model (LPM) is then estimated to identify the main factors associated with having an informal sector job:

$$Prob^g(inf = 1|X) = X_i^g \beta^g \tag{1}$$

where inf is a binary variable that equals one if an individual has a job in the informal sector. Superscript $g = (ur; rm; um)$ refers to urban residents, rural migrants and urban migrants. X_i^g is a vector of control variables, including education, age, age squared, marital status, gender, and provincial dummies.

We then compute OB decompositions for the gaps in formal-informal sector distributions between different groups g based on the results derived from $\overline{Prob}^g(inf = 1) = \overline{X}^g \hat{\beta}^g$, with $\overline{Prob}^g(inf = 1)$ and $\overline{X}$ referring to sample means, and $\hat{\beta}^g$ representing the OLS estimates of β^g. The OB model comparing urban residents and rural migrants, for instance, would be as follows:

$$\overline{Prob}^u(inf = 1) - \overline{Prob}^m(inf = 1) = \left(\overline{X}^u - \overline{X}^m\right)\hat{\beta}^u + \left(\hat{\beta}^u - \hat{\beta}^m\right)\overline{X}^m \tag{2}$$

The second term on the right-hand side, $\left(\overline{X}^u - \overline{X}^m\right)\hat{\beta}^u$, represents the gap in probability due to individual characteristics (such as human capital) in the absence of discrimination. The term $\left(\hat{\beta}^u - \hat{\beta}^m\right)\overline{X}^m$, measures the relative gap in probability due to unexplained factors. Discrimination, according to the OB literature, is assumed to be the unexplained difference in the regression coefficients.[8]

We then turn to income gaps. The OB decomposition method is also applied to decompose the income gaps between different groups, replacing $\overline{Prob}^g(inf = 1)$ by income levels $\overline{W}$. In addition, we decompose the income gaps in the whole distribution. The income distribution for different groups g is modelled as follows:

$$\theta^g(W) = \int f^g(W|X)\phi^g(X)dX \tag{3}$$

where $\theta^g(W)$ is the distribution of income for group g, $f^g(W|X)$ is the conditional distribution, and $\phi^g(X)$ is the distribution of X for group g. To decompose the difference in income distributions between rural migrants and urban residents, for example, we need to construct a counterfactual distribution:[9]

$$\theta^{cf}(W) = \int f^u(W|X)\phi^m(X)dX \qquad (4)$$

which is a combination of the characteristics of the migrants and the wage structure for urban residents. We define a real-valued functional, $v(\theta(.))$, that can be thought of as a set of rules mapping different distributions $\theta(.)$ to different real numbers. The $v(.)$ can be a rule calculating various statistical measures of $\theta(.)$, such as variance, Theil indices, and percentiles. The change in the distribution $v(.)$ can be divided into two parts:

$$v\left(\theta^u\right) - v\left(\theta^m\right) = \left[v\left(\theta^u\right) - v\left(\theta^{cf}\right)\right] + \left[v\left(\theta^{cf}\right) - v\left(\theta^m\right)\right] \qquad (5)$$

We can then decompose any functional of the distribution into explained and unexplained parts. This exercise would be identical to the OB decomposition if we considered the difference in means.

DiNardo *et al.* (1996) point out that the counterfactual distribution in equation (5) can be constructed through a re-weighting method by doing the following. First, run a probit model with both rural migrants and urban residents with the dependent variable being an indicator for urban residents (yes=1/no=0) and the same set of control variables as before. Second, calculate a weighted variable $\hat{\rho} = (1 - \hat{p})/\hat{p}$ based on the probability of being an urban resident ($\hat{p}$) from the results of the probit model. Third, estimate the distribution function using the observations of urban residents and the weighted variable $\hat{\rho}$.

The weighted variable plays a fundamental role. Since rural migrants are less educated, observations of urban residents with lower education levels will be given more weight so that we can get closer to the characteristic distribution of rural migrants. The probability of a less educated individual being an urban resident ($\hat{p}$) is relatively lower and the weight assigned is therefore relatively higher.

An alternative approach to construct the counterfactual distribution is based on quantile regressions (*the QR approach*). This paper uses the DFL approach as it is computationally faster.[10]

5 Empirical results

5.1 Discrimination out of formal sector jobs

Table 2 presents the estimated coefficients associated with the probability of having an informal sector job for each group using a multinomial logit model. Education has a consistently significant impact on the type of job one has, with highly educated workers having a lower probability of working in informal sectors. Table 3 presents a counterfactual exercise providing the distribution of each group by type of job as if they had similar coefficients as their counterparts. Using the coefficients estimated for urban residents (as reported in the first two columns, Table 2), more rural migrants would have formal labour contracts (from 35% to 47%), the share of those without contracts would decrease by about the same amount while the share of the self-employed would largely remain unchanged. Urban migrants also seem to face discrimination out of the formal sector, but to a lesser extent than rural migrants. If urban migrants were treated as urban residents,

Table 2 Marginal effects of multinomial logit regressions

	Urban residents		Rural migrants		Urban migrants	
	Self-employed	Without contract	Self-employed	Without contract	Self-employed	Without contract
Age	-0.007	-0.100***	0.143***	-0.022***	0.140***	-0.078***
	(0.007)	(0.005)	(0.009)	(0.006)	(0.020)	(0.013)
Age2	-0.000	0.001***	-0.002***	0.000***	-0.002***	0.001***
	(0.000)	(0.000)	(0.000)	(0.000)	(0.000)	(0.000)
Female	-0.225***	0.114***	-0.543***	-0.143***	-0.111**	0.109***
	(0.015)	(0.010)	(0.023)	(0.015)	(0.046)	(0.032)
Junior middle school	-0.537***	-0.098***	-0.563***	-0.497***	-0.463***	-0.342***
	(0.026)	(0.024)	(0.027)	(0.022)	(0.094)	(0.085)
Senior middle school	-1.509***	-0.521***	-1.037***	-0.971***	-1.180***	-0.923***
	(0.027)	(0.024)	(0.037)	(0.027)	(0.095)	(0.084)
College and above	-3.449***	-0.694***	-1.847***	-1.412***	-2.234***	-1.600***
	(0.039)	(0.024)	(0.104)	(0.055)	(0.105)	(0.087)
Unmarried	-0.475***	0.121***	-1.103***	0.059**	-0.780***	0.203***
	(0.035)	(0.020)	(0.042)	(0.024)	(0.081)	(0.047)
N	219712		94621		22214	

Notes: *, **, and *** represent significance levels of 10%, 5%, and 1%, respectively.
Samples include individuals aged 16–60 years and who are out of school.
Observations of migrants who migrated for reasons not related to employment were dropped.
The base category in the multinomial logit is formal employment.
Regional dummies are included in the regressions but not reported.
Standard errors are reported below coefficients.
Source: 1% population survey of China (2005).

Table 3 Sectoral Distributions based on Multinomial Logit Regression Results

	Actual distributions (%)			Predicted distributions (%)					
				As urban residents		As rural migrants		As urban migrants	
	Urban residents	Rural migrants	Urban migrants	Rural migrants	Urban migrants	Urban residents	Urban migrants	Urban residents	Rural migrants
Formal contract	58	35	52	47	57	38	44	47	39
Self-employed	12	17	15	17	11	26	16	22	18
Without contract	30	48	34	36	32	36	40	30	43
Total	100	100	100	100	100	100	100	100	100

Notes: The sample includes those aged 16–60 years old and who are out of school.
Observations with no or zero income declared were dropped.
Source: 1% population survey of China (2005).

there would be more of them in the formal sector (57% rather than 52%), and fewer in self-employment (11% rather than 15%). If instead urban migrants had the same coefficients as rural migrants, there would be fewer urban migrants in the formal sector (from 52% to 44%) and more workers without formal labour contracts (from 34% to 40%), indicating potential discrimination against rural *hukou* status.

To further investigate the incidence of discrimination in the type of job one has, the probability of having an informal sector job is estimated using a linear probability model, and the decomposition results are reported in Table 4. The results in panel A are calculated based on the counterfactual probability $\bar{X}^m \hat{\beta}^u$, while those in panel B based on $\bar{X}^u \hat{\beta}^m$. In the first three columns of panel A, the total sample is divided by formal and informal jobs, the latter including self-employment and jobs without formal labour contracts. First, the gap in the share of workers having an informal sector job between rural migrants and urban residents is large. The share of rural migrants having an informal sector job is 34 percentage points higher than that of urban residents. The OB decomposition result shows that only 17% of the difference can be explained by differences in observed characteristics, while 83% is unexplained. Using different counterfactual probabilities (panel B) gives similar results (14% explained and 86% unexplained).

The difference in the probability of having an informal sector job between urban migrants and urban residents is smaller than it is for rural migrants (17% vs. 34%). However, 83% of the difference is also unexplained despite the fact that urban migrants enjoy the highest average income level. Thus, the results suggest significant discrimination against both types of migrants out of formal sector jobs. Observed characteristics explain a relatively larger share (around 50%) of the probability of having an informal sector job when rural migrants are compared to urban migrants. However, half of the difference is nevertheless due to unexplained factors and we interpret this as evidence of some discrimination against rural *hukou* status.

Using the same method, we also decompose the gaps in the probability of being self-employed (columns 4–6) *or* without a formal contract (columns 7–9), the results also indicate discrimination against both rural and urban migrant workers out of formal sector jobs.

5.2   Income discrimination against rural migrants, revisited
5.2.1   OB decomposition results
We then run straightforward OLS income regressions on the determinants of hourly incomes by type of job (formal work, self-employment and without a formal labour contract) for each type of worker (urban residents, rural migrants, urban migrants). Controls include age, age squared, four levels of education, marital status and gender and the results are presented in Table 5.[11]

There are significant differences in the coefficients of each group. The returns to education, for example, are generally higher for urban residents than for rural migrants (see panels A and B). As for urban migrants (panel C), the returns to education are lower than those for urban residents, but higher than those for rural migrants. Within each group in panels A, B, and C, the returns to education are the highest for formal contract jobs, followed by the jobs without contracts, and then the self-employed. Incomes also differ according to gender, marital status, and age. Earnings for women are significantly lower than those of men. The gap is larger for the self-employed than for the formally

Table 4 Oaxaca-Blinder decomposition of the gap in the average probability of having an informal sector job

A: W=1	Self-employed and without a contract			Self-employed			Without a contract		
	coef.	s.e.	%	coef.	s.e.	%	coef.	s.e.	%
Rural migrants vs. urban residents									
Difference	0.337	0.002		0.087	0.001		0.250	0.002	
Explained	0.059	0.001	17	0.035	0.001	41	0.023	0.001	9
Unexplained	0.279	0.002	83	0.051	0.001	59	0.227	0.002	91
Urban migrants vs. urban residents									
Difference	0.166	0.003		0.057	0.002		0.109	0.003	
Explained	0.028	0.001	17	-0.005	0.001	-9	0.034	0.001	31
Unexplained	0.138	0.003	83	0.062	0.002	109	0.075	0.003	69
Urban migrants vs. rural migrants									
Difference	-0.171	0.004		-0.030	0.002		-0.141	0.003	
Explained	-0.087	0.003	51	-0.006	0.003	20	-0.081	0.003	57
Unexplained	-0.085	0.005	49	-0.024	0.003	80	-0.061	0.005	43
Non-recent migrants									
Difference	-0.191	0.006		-0.072	0.005		-0.119	0.006	
Explained	-0.100	0.006	52	-0.048	0.005	66	-0.052	0.006	44
Unexplained	-0.092	0.008	48	-0.024	0.007	34	-0.067	0.008	56
Recent migrants									
Difference	-0.162	0.004		-0.015	0.003		-0.147	0.004	
Explained	-0.079	0.004	49	0.007	0.003	-46	-0.086	0.004	59
Unexplained	-0.082	0.006	51	-0.022	0.004	146	-0.060	0.006	41
B: W=0	coef.	s.e.	%	coef.	s.e.	%	coef.	s.e.	%
Rural migrants vs. urban residents									
Difference	0.337	0.002		0.087	0.001		0.250	0.002	
Explained	0.047	0.004	14	-0.093	0.003	-107	0.140	0.004	56
Unexplained	0.291	0.004	86	0.180	0.003	207	0.111	0.004	44
Urban migrants vs. urban residents									
Difference	0.166	0.003		0.057	0.002		0.109	0.003	
Explained	-0.034	0.004	-21	-0.067	0.002	-117	0.033	0.003	30
Unexplained	0.200	0.005	121	0.124	0.003	217	0.076	0.004	70
Urban migrants vs. rural migrants									
Difference	-0.171	0.004		-0.030	0.002		-0.141	0.003	
Explained	-0.098	0.004	57	-0.028	0.003	94	-0.070	0.004	50
Unexplained	-0.073	0.005	43	-0.002	0.003	6	-0.071	0.005	50
Non-recent migrants									
Difference	-0.191	0.006		-0.072	0.005		-0.119	0.006	
Explained	-0.086	0.007	45	-0.048	0.005	67	-0.038	0.006	32
Unexplained	-0.105	0.009	55	-0.024	0.007	33	-0.081	0.008	68
Recent migrants									
Difference	-0.162	0.004		-0.015	0.003		-0.147	0.004	
Explained	-0.105	0.005	65	-0.021	0.003	138	-0.085	0.005	58
Unexplained	-0.056	0.006	35	0.006	0.004	-38	-0.062	0.006	42

The decomposition results are based on a linear probability model.

The sample includes individuals aged 16–60 years and who are out of school.

Observations with no or zero income declared were dropped.

Results in panel A (W=1) are calculated based on the counterfactual $\bar{X}^m \hat{\beta}^u$, and those in panel B (W=0) based on $\bar{X}^u \hat{\beta}^m$.

Source: 1% population survey of China (2005).

Table 5 OLS income regression results: dependent variable=log (hourly income)

	Formal contract	Self-employed	Without a contract
A: Urban residents			
Age	0.034***	0.017***	0.020***
	(0.002)	(0.004)	(0.002)
Age2	-0.000***	-0.000***	-0.000***
	(0.000)	(0.000)	(0.000)
Female	-0.161***	-0.259***	-0.189***
	(0.003)	(0.008)	(0.004)
Junior middle school	0.372***	0.121***	0.213***
	(0.009)	(0.013)	(0.010)
Senior middle school	0.650***	0.233***	0.483***
	(0.009)	(0.014)	(0.010)
College and above	1.070***	0.573***	1.021***
	(0.009)	(0.023)	(0.010)
Unmarried	-0.009	-0.065***	-0.075***
	(0.007)	(0.019)	(0.008)
R-squared	0.349	0.127	0.368
N	128509	25832	65371
B: Rural migrants			
Age	0.039***	0.021***	0.037***
	(0.002)	(0.004)	(0.002)
Age2	-0.001***	-0.000***	-0.001***
	(0.000)	(0.000)	(0.000)
Female	-0.181***	-0.293***	-0.194***
	(0.006)	(0.011)	(0.004)
Junior middle school	0.195***	0.170***	0.160***
	(0.009)	(0.012)	(0.006)
Senior middle school	0.441***	0.279***	0.349***
	(0.011)	(0.017)	(0.008)
College and above	0.948***	0.527***	0.746***
	(0.018)	(0.058)	(0.019)
Unmarried	-0.022**	-0.025	-0.049***
	(0.010)	(0.022)	(0.007)
R-squared	0.213	0.127	0.195
N	32947	16536	45138
C: Urban migrants			
Age	0.077***	0.006	0.049***
	(0.005)	(0.012)	(0.005)
Age2	-0.001***	-0.000	-0.001***
	(0.000)	(0.000)	(0.000)
Female	-0.187***	-0.229***	-0.162***
	(0.012)	(0.028)	(0.013)
Junior middle school	0.252***	0.189***	0.177***
	(0.040)	(0.047)	(0.030)
Senior middle school	0.532***	0.348***	0.419***
	(0.040)	(0.049)	(0.030)
College and above	1.089***	0.687***	0.916***
	(0.040)	(0.059)	(0.032)
Unmarried	0.025	0.157***	-0.003
	(0.017)	(0.051)	(0.020)
R-squared	0.382	0.175	0.340
N	11482	3272	7460

Notes: *, **, and *** represent significance levels of 10%, 5%, and 1%, respectively.
Samples include those aged 16–60 years old and who are out of school.
Observations with no or zero income declared were dropped.
Province dummies and a constant are included in the regressions but not reported.
Standard errors are reported in brackets.
Source: 1% population survey of China (2005).

employed and workers without a formal labour contract, but there are only small differences in coefficients among urban residents, rural migrants, and urban migrants along gender lines.

Using these results, an OB decomposition is computed between rural migrants and urban residents. The results are shown in the first three columns of Table 6. If the type of

Table 6 Oaxaca-Blinder decomposition of income gaps

		Urban residents vs. rural migrants			Rural migrants vs. urban migrants			Urban residents vs. urban migrants		
A: W=1		coef.	s.e.	%	coef.	s.e.	%	coef.	s.e.	%
Total difference	Difference	0.238	0.002		-0.488	0.006		-0.250	0.006	
	Explained	0.232	0.003	97	-0.255	0.005	52	-0.078	0.003	31
	Unexplained	0.006	0.003	3	-0.233	0.006	48	-0.172	0.005	69
Formal employment	Difference	0.252	0.004		-0.604	0.008		-0.351	0.008	
	Explained	0.220	0.004	87	-0.351	0.008	58	-0.141	0.005	40
	Unexplained	0.033	0.005	13	-0.252	0.009	42	-0.210	0.007	60
Self employed	Difference	-0.096	0.007		-0.236	0.015		-0.333	0.015	
	Explained	-0.096	0.006	100	-0.032	0.009	14	-0.110	0.007	33
	Unexplained	0.000	0.008	0	-0.204	0.016	86	-0.222	0.014	67
No contract	Difference	0.153	0.004		-0.302	0.008		-0.149	0.008	
	Explained	0.212	0.004	139	-0.150	0.006	50	-0.003	0.006	2
	Unexplained	-0.060	0.005	-39	-0.152	0.008	50	-0.146	0.007	98
Recent migrants	Difference	0.267	0.003		-0.475	0.007		-0.208	0.007	
	Explained	0.257	0.003	96	-0.253	0.005	53	-0.060	0.004	29
	Unexplained	0.010	0.003	4	-0.222	0.007	47	-0.148	0.005	71
Non recent migrants	Difference	0.160	0.004		-0.510	0.011		-0.350	0.011	
	Explained	0.163	0.003	102	-0.246	0.009	48	-0.120	0.006	34
	Unexplained	-0.003	0.004	-2	-0.264	0.012	52	-0.230	0.009	66
B: W=0		coef.	s.e.	%	coef.	s.e.	%	coef.	s.e.	%
Total difference	Difference	0.238	0.002		-0.488	0.006		-0.250	0.006	
	Explained	0.168	0.005	71	-0.317	0.007	65	-0.157	0.006	63
	Unexplained	0.070	0.005	29	-0.171	0.007	35	-0.094	0.006	37
Formal employment	Difference	0.252	0.004		-0.604	0.008		-0.351	0.008	
	Explained	0.228	0.008	90	-0.414	0.010	69	-0.211	0.009	60
	Unexplained	0.025	0.008	10	-0.190	0.011	31	-0.140	0.009	40
Self employed	Difference	-0.096	0.007		-0.236	0.015		-0.333	0.015	
	Explained	-0.059	0.006	62	-0.053	0.015	22	-0.141	0.010	42
	Unexplained	-0.037	0.009	38	-0.184	0.019	78	-0.192	0.015	58
No contract	Difference	0.153	0.004		-0.302	0.008		-0.149	0.008	
	Explained	0.111	0.007	73	-0.185	0.009	61	-0.102	0.009	69
	Unexplained	0.042	0.007	27	-0.117	0.010	39	-0.047	0.010	31
Recent migrants	Difference	0.267	0.003		-0.475	0.007		-0.208	0.007	
	Explained	0.175	0.005	66	-0.324	0.008	68	-0.135	0.007	65
	Unexplained	0.092	0.006	34	-0.151	0.008	32	-0.073	0.007	35
Non recent migrants	Difference	0.160	0.004		-0.510	0.011		-0.350	0.011	
	Explained	0.117	0.009	73	-0.289	0.012	57	-0.232	0.011	66
	Unexplained	0.044	0.010	27	-0.221	0.014	43	-0.118	0.012	34

Notes: Results are based on the income regressions of Tables 5.
Samples include those aged 16–60 years old and who are out of school.
Observations with no or zero income declared were dropped.
Results in panel A (W=1) are calculated based on the counterfactual $\bar{X}^m \hat{\beta}^u$, and those in panel B (W=0) based on $\bar{X}^u \hat{\beta}^m$.
Source: 1% population survey of China (2005).

employment sector is not taken into account, nearly all of the income gap (97%) between rural migrants and urban residents can be attributed to differences in observed individual characteristics. If we use an alternative counterfactual income ($\bar{X}^u\hat{\beta}^m$), the explained share will decrease, but still as high as 70%. Running separate OB decompositions for each sector does not alter the results by much. According to these OB decompositions, the gap between rural migrants and urban residents is mainly due to differences in human capital.

The results may again be the net effect of a premium accrued from migration and discrimination associated with a rural *hukou* status. Urban migrants with urban *hukou* status are used to disentangle the two effects.

The middle three columns of Table 6 report OB decomposition results for the income gap between rural and urban migrants, two groups that differ only in rural/urban *hukou* status. The general results indicate that 52% of the income gap between these two groups can be explained by observed differences in their individual characteristics and 48% remains unexplained. We also find some heterogeneity across sectors. In the formal sector, observed differences in characteristics can explain 58% of the income gap whereas in the group without formal contracts the share of explained gap is only 50%. Amongst the self-employed workers, only 14% of the gap in this group can be explained by observable individual characteristics, suggesting discrimination against rural *hukou* status. These patterns remain if alternative counterfactual incomes are used (see panel B, Table 6).

Urban migrants are then measured up against urban residents to evaluate discrimination associated with being a migrant (not registered locally) but with a non-agricultural *hukou* status. Since urban migrants earn more than urban residents, the OB decomposition in the last three columns of Table 6 suggests that migrants do indeed gain a premium. The decomposition exercise shows that 69% of the income difference is unexplained, on average, between urban migrants and urban residents. But this result is sensitive to the choice of the counterfactual income (it becomes 37% in panel B, Table 6). Moreover, decomposition results broken down by sector show that the unexplained shares are 60%, 67% and 98% for workers in the formal sector, the self-employed, and workers with no formal labour contract respectively. These unexplained shares become smaller in panel B, but it is still safe to draw the conclusion that if urban migrants were treated the same as urban residents, their incomes would decrease but would still be higher than those of urban residents with the same observable characteristics.

There may be two reasons for this result. First, urban migrants are positively selected in terms of unobservable characteristics. Second, urban migrants ask for compensation for giving up secure jobs. Suppose an urban worker is considering a move to another city. She must find a better job, otherwise she will not migrate. So compared to those who do not migrate with identical characteristics, she must have a higher income to compensate for the *hukou* related benefits she gives up.

To investigate the effect of *hukou* status on discrimination more deeply, we look across the income distribution to see if the effect differs at different points. Panel A of Figure 1 shows the actual income distributions of rural migrants and urban residents and the counterfactual distribution supposing rural migrants were paid as if they were urban residents. To obtain the counterfactual distribution, we first run a probit model including both rural migrants and urban residents with the dependent variable equalling 1 if the individual is an urban resident. The predicted weights $\hat{\rho} = (1 - \hat{p})/\hat{p}$ are then applied to

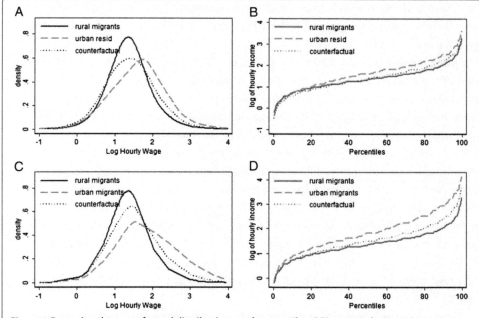

Figure 1 Factual and counterfactual distributions and percentiles, DFL approach. A: rural migrants vs. urban residents (densities). **B:** rural migrants vs. urban residents (percentiles). **C:** rural migrants vs. urban migrants (densities). **D:** rural migrants vs. urban migrants (percentiles).

the urban resident sample. The results indicate that even if rural migrants were paid like urban residents according to their observable characteristics, their average income level would not increase significantly. This is consistent with the OB decomposition results. However, their income dispersion would increase. This means that rural migrants in the upper half of the income distribution would earn higher incomes, while those at the lower half would earn less. This pattern is also clear in panel B of Figure 1, where the actual and counterfactual percentiles are reported. For the middle level percentiles, the actual and counterfactual income levels for rural migrants are not significantly different.

We also compare rural migrants with urban migrants (rather than urban residents) using the DFL approach to construct counterfactual distributions. Results, shown in Panel C and D of Figure 1, indicate that if rural migrants were paid like urban migrants, their income distribution would move further to the right, but remain lower than the distribution of urban migrants. This effect is larger for individuals in the upper half of the income distribution.

In conclusion, there seems to be some, although not overwhelming support for discrimination against those with rural *hukou* status, while there seems to be more support for a premium garnered by being a migrant.

5.3   Does migration duration matter?

The Harris and Todaro (1970) framework suggests that migrants may first enter the informal labour market, accumulating experience before obtaining an opportunity for a formal sector job. The income premium earned by migrants observed above likely varies according to the amount of time migrants have spent in the urban labour market. In order to evaluate this labour market assimilation effect, we separate migrant samples according to their duration in the urban labour market and then investigate the differences in the distribution by job type and income, as in the exercises presented earlier. To define the two groups, we use a cutoff of 5 years in the urban labour market.[12]

Descriptive statistics are presented in Table 1. For both rural and urban migrants, the duration of their migration episode is important. More than 70% of migrants (rural and urban) have less than 5 years of local urban living experience. Both rural and urban self-employed migrants tend to have resided longer in the host labour market, while workers with no formal labour contract tend to be more recent arrivals.

The first two columns in Table 7 present the distribution by job type for both recent and non-recent rural migrants. Job type changes significantly as urban area experience increases, but most changes happen within the informal sector. The share of rural migrants in the formal sector remains almost unchanged. On the other hand, the share of self-employed migrants increases from 14% to 26%. The pattern for urban migrants is similar to that of rural migrants. Despite the increase in urban area experience, the probability of an urban migrant having a formal sector job only increases slightly (by 2 percentage points). The share of self-employed migrants, however, increases from 13% to 18%.

Table 8 reports results from a multinomial logit model based on job type for both recent and non-recent migrants, showing that the probability of being self-employed increases as people age. It is therefore expected that if recent migrants (both rural and urban) are treated as non-recent migrants, a greater number of them will be self-employed, but the share of formal sector employment will remain relatively unchanged. The results suggest that although migration duration matters for the type of jobs held by migrants, it plays a minor role in helping migrants obtain a formal sector job. In addition, the OB decomposition based on a linear probability model in Table 4 suggests that the discrimination against rural migrants does not decrease with duration in an urban area. We reach this conclusion by comparing rural and urban migrants with the same amount of urban area experience, and the results indicate that the unexplained part of the gap (both in terms of absolute difference and in relative share) does not decrease.

We also look at the determinants of income for rural and urban migrants depending on duration, and the results are reported in Table 9. For recent migrants, incomes increase relatively more quickly and the gap between women and men is lower. These results combined with those in Table 5 are used to perform OB decompositions. The results in Table 6 indicate that most of the income gap between both recent and non-recent migrants and

Table 7 Sectoral distribution of migrants based on multinomial logit model (by migration duration)

	Rural migrants			Urban migrants		
	Actual distribution		Predicted distribution	Actual distribution		Predicted distribution
	Non-recent	Recent	Recent as non-recent	Non-recent	Recent	Recent as non-recent
Formal contract	34	35	36	53	51	54
Self-employed	26	14	18	18	13	15
Without contract	41	50	46	29	36	32
Total	100	100	100	100	100	100

Samples include individuals aged 16–60 years and who are out of school.
Observations of migrants who migrated for reasons not related to employment were dropped.
Source: 1% population survey of China (2005).

Table 8 Marginal effects of multinomial logit results (by migration duration)

Rural migrants	Non-recent		Recent	
	Self-employed	No contract	Self-employed	No contract
Age	0.129***	-0.013	0.127***	-0.028***
	(0.018)	(0.014)	(0.011)	(0.007)
Age2	-0.001***	0.000	-0.001***	0.000***
	(0.000)	(0.000)	(0.000)	(0.000)
Female	-0.382***	-0.079**	-0.612***	-0.169***
	(0.039)	(0.032)	(0.028)	(0.018)
Junior middle school	-0.486***	-0.413***	-0.590***	-0.526***
	(0.044)	(0.039)	(0.035)	(0.027)
Senior middle school	-1.000***	-0.903***	-1.057***	-0.988***
	(0.059)	(0.050)	(0.048)	(0.033)
College and above	-2.325***	-1.351***	-1.615***	-1.428***
	(0.197)	(0.107)	(0.123)	(0.065)
Unmarried	-0.701***	0.286***	-1.211***	-0.020
	(0.079)	(0.051)	(0.050)	(0.028)
N	25482		69139	

Urban migrants	Non-recent		Recent	
	Self-employed	No contract	Self-employed	No contract
Age	0.124***	-0.036	0.156***	-0.081***
	(0.036)	(0.028)	(0.025)	(0.015)
Age2	-0.001***	0.000	-0.002***	0.001***
	(0.000)	(0.000)	(0.000)	(0.000)
Female	-0.084	0.086	-0.123**	0.113***
	(0.078)	(0.062)	(0.057)	(0.037)
Junior middle school	-0.314**	-0.269*	-0.569***	-0.413***
	(0.144)	(0.139)	(0.124)	(0.108)
Senior middle school	-1.024***	-0.759***	-1.287***	-1.032***
	(0.147)	(0.139)	(0.125)	(0.108)
College and above	-2.089***	-1.394***	-2.346***	-1.724***
	(0.169)	(0.145)	(0.137)	(0.110)
Unmarried	-0.455***	0.314***	-0.884***	0.154***
	(0.145)	(0.088)	(0.097)	(0.055)
N	6608		15606	

Notes: *, **, and *** represent significance levels of 10%, 5%, and 1%, respectively.
Samples include individuals aged 16–60 years and who are out of school.
Migrants that migrated for reasons not related to employment were dropped.
The base category in the multinomial logit is formal employment.
Regional dummies are included in the regressions but not reported.
Standard errors are reported in brackets.
Source: 1% population survey of China (2005).

urban residents is still due to observable characteristics. By comparing rural and urban migrants, the unexplained part of the income gap between the two groups does not decrease as duration in an urban area increases.

These results regarding duration spent in an urban area indicate that discrimination, both for job type and income, does not decrease as duration in urban areas for migrants increases.

6 Conclusions

In this paper, a nationally representative sample of individuals is used to investigate whether migrants are discriminated in terms of income and out of jobs with formal labour

Table 9 OLS income regression results by migration duration: dependent variable=log (hourly income)

	Rural migrants		Urban migrants	
	Non-recent	Recent	Non-recent	Recent
Age	0.021***	0.034***	0.033***	0.065***
	(0.003)	(0.002)	(0.008)	(0.004)
Age2	-0.000***	-0.000***	-0.000***	-0.001***
	(0.000)	(0.000)	(0.000)	(0.000)
Female	-0.283***	-0.167***	-0.237***	-0.168***
	(0.008)	(0.004)	(0.018)	(0.010)
Junior middle school	0.180***	0.184***	0.208***	0.229***
	(0.009)	(0.005)	(0.038)	(0.027)
Senior middle school	0.406***	0.404***	0.462***	0.511***
	(0.012)	(0.007)	(0.038)	(0.027)
College and above	0.955***	0.863***	1.094***	1.072***
	(0.028)	(0.014)	(0.039)	(0.028)
Unmarried	-0.076***	-0.012*	-0.035	0.047***
	(0.013)	(0.006)	(0.026)	(0.015)
R-squared	0.206	0.181	0.394	0.379
N	25482	69139	6608	15606

Notes: *, **, and *** represent significance levels of 10%, 5%, and 1%, respectively.
The dependent variable is the log of hourly income.
Samples include those aged 16–60 years old and who are out of school.
Observations with no or zero income declared were dropped.
Province dummies and a constant are included in the regressions but not reported.
Standard errors are reported in brackets.
Source: 1% population survey of China (2005).

contracts in the urban labour market in China. It contributes to the existing literature in several important ways. First, as opposed to other papers investigating discrimination in China, the data are nationally representative and provide a better coverage of rural and urban migrants. Second, it distinguishes between rural and urban migrants in order to independently identify discrimination against rural *hukou* status and discrimination against non-local *hukou* status. Third, it breaks down jobs according to whether they include formal labour contracts, and differentiates between those without a formal labour contract and self-employed workers.

An OB decomposition of the fitted probability of having an informal sector job shows that migrants (both rural and urban) are discriminated against for jobs with formal labour contracts. The extent of discrimination is larger for rural migrants indicating further discrimination against those with rural *hukou* status.

A comparison of rural migrants and urban residents shows that nearly all of the income gap can be explained by differences in individual characteristics, suggesting that discrimination is almost negligible. A comparison between rural migrants and urban migrants, isolating the migration effect but not the rural/urban *hukou* status effect, shows that 40% of the income gap is unexplained by observed characteristics. By comparing instead urban migrants with urban residents, this time isolating the *hukou* effect (agricultural/non-agricultural), we find evidence of discrimination in income. Since urban migrants earn the most of all groups, we therefore presume that the absence of discrimination from the comparison between rural migrants and urban residents is a net effect of discrimination against rural *hukou* status and a premium accrued generally by migrating.

There are limitations in the approach taken in this paper. The first is in the choice of the appropriate reference group. Although this paper takes a step forward by using urban migrants as an additional reference group, there may be unobservable characteristics between rural migrants and urban migrants. Moreover, while self-selection into the labour force could be dealt with in this paper, another source of endogeneity may stem from choice of sector. In fact, the results of our OB decompositions for urban migrants suggests that the self-employed may indeed be self-selected.

The policy implications of our results suggest that, since rural migrants enjoy a premium as migrants yet face discrimination at the same time, the reason they may be worse off when compared to urban residents is due to their lower levels of human capital. Increasing the education levels of rural migrants and providing them with training and relevant urban labour market skills will help increase their earning opportunities. As both rural and urban migrants face discrimination in access to jobs with formal labour contracts, reforming the labour market, notably removing barriers to accessing public goods, may help migrants access better jobs.

This study suggests evidence of discrimination in the urban labour market against those with rural *hukou* status. In addition, migrants without social security coverage face high costs for health services. In terms of schooling and childcare, many migrants leave their children home in the rural parts of China, in effect putting more pressure on household members left-behind and adding to the already existing social strain caused by migration. Hence it is important to ensure that migrants have access to basic social services, even in cases where they are employed informally.

Endnotes

[1] The ratio in 2007, for instance, was 3.3 to 1 (China Statistical Yearbook, National Bureau of Statistics of China 2008).

[2] This number is only slightly below the number of total international migrants in the world, which in 2005 was estimated at 191 million (United Nations 2009).

[3] This analysis depends on the assumption that people with different *hukou* registrations have the same (unobserved) ability. However, people with local *hukou* have higher innate ability (this may be true, for example, for those who obtained *hukou* through special achievement). In this case, the income gap would be a lower estimate for the true *hukou* premium. It might also be true that people born with local *hukou* status have lower ability or less entrepreneurial spirit compared to migrants without local *hukou* status. These possibilities need to be taken into consideration when interpreting results.

[4] The major difference between the formal and informal sector comes from non-wage benefits, which are hard to quantify. For example, formal jobs are more secure, offer better conditions and benefits which may not be reflected in the wage. Workers may even be willing to accept a lower wage to have a formal sector job. These aspects cannot be dealt with using the Brown *et al.* (1980) method. We also decompose the income gaps using the Brown method and the results are similar to those obtained using the regular OB decomposition.

[5] The China Urban Labor Survey covers only five cities: Shanghai, Wuhan, Shenyang, Fuzhou, and Xian, all of which are provincial capitals.

[6] Cities (*shiqu*) refer to the city proper of regions of different administrative levels. Prefecture-level cities or higher level cities directly controlled by the central government usually govern surrounding counties, including rural areas. In cases of county level cities, city proper refers to the areas where the county government is located and some nearby neighbourhoods. Towns (zhen) refer to where the town level government is

located. Zhen is a level of administrative government approved by higher level government. In Chinese statistics, urban (or *chengzhen*) refers to city and town. Villages (xiangcun) refer to rural areas.

[7] The contracts should have the following terms: the term (length) of the contract; tasks; working time and vacations allocated; compensation; social security (such as unemployment insurance; pension; medical insurance; and housing). Some employers (usually in the private sector) do not sign contracts mainly to circumvent the need to pay insurance for employees.

[8] We also calculate the OB decomposition using an alternative counterfactual income $\bar{X}^u \hat{\beta}^m$, the gap can then be decomposed into: $\left(\bar{X}^u - \bar{X}^m \right) \hat{\beta}^m + \left(\hat{\beta}^u - \hat{\beta}^m \right) \bar{X}^u$.

[9] Similarly, we can construct an alternative counterfactual distribution for the decomposition: $\theta^{cf1}(W) = \int f^u(W|X) \phi^m(X) dX$.

[10] By running quantile regressions at different quantiles using data of urban residents, we obtain a detailed description of its conditional distribution. The estimated skill price structure (conditional distribution) can then be applied to data (skill distribution) of rural migrants by multiplying the quantile coefficient matrix of urban residents by the data matrix of rural migrants. This approach estimates the conditional distribution explicitly, with some risk of imposing strong restrictions on its structure. No effort is needed to estimate the composition change parametrically. Chernozhukov *et al.* 2013 show that the quantile approach and DFL reweighting approach are equally valid under correct specifications. We choose DFL because it is computationally fast. We also tried to use the QR approach to construct the counterfactual distributions. They produce similar results.

[11] We also do exercises controlling for industry and occupation dummies, and both the regression results and the decomposition results are similar to those without controlling for industry and occupation.

[12] We also use a 3-year cutoff as a robustness check, and the results are similar.

Competing interests
The IZA Journal of Labor and Development is committed to the IZA Guiding Principles of Research Integrity. The authors declare that they have observed these principles.

Acknowledgements
The authors thank an anonymous referee and Jackline Wahba (the Editor) for their helpful comments. The authors also would like to thank and acknowledge the useful feedback and comments received during the 10–11 July 2008 experts' meeting on migration and development in Paris as well as those received from participants of the Development Centre's internal seminar series in October 2008. Chunbing Xing acknowledges the financial support from the National Natural Science Foundation of China (No. 71103019).
Responsible editor: Jackline Wahba

Author details
[1]OECD Development Centre, Paris Cedex 16, France. [2]OECD Directorate for Employment, Labour and Social Affairs, Paris Cedex 16, France. [3]Beijing Normal University, Beijing, China.

References
Blinder A (1973) Income discrimination: reduced form and structural estimates. J Hum Resour 8(4):436–455
Brown RS, Moon M, Zoloth BS (1980) Incorporating occupational attainment in studies of male-female earnings differentials. J Human Resour 15(1):3–28
Cai F (2000) The invisible hand and visible feet: internal migration in China. World Econ China 5:24–31
Chan KW, Buckingham W (2008) Is China abolishing the Hukou system? China Quarterly 195:582–606
Chernozhukov V, Fernandez-Val I, Melly B (2013) Inference on counterfactual distributions. Econometrica 81(6):2205–2268
China Labor Bulletin (2008) Incomes in China. www.china-labor.org.hk
Démurger S, Gurgand M, Li S, Yue X (2009) Migrants as second-class workers in urban China? A Decomposition Analysis. J Comp Econ 37(4):610–628
Deng Q (2007) Earnings differential between urban residents and rural migrants: evidence from Oaxaca-Blinder and quantile regression decompositions. Chin J Population Sci 2:8–16. (in Chinese)
Deng Q, Gustafsson B (2006) China's Lesser Known Migrants. IZA, Bonn. IZA Discussion Paper No. 2152
DiNardo J, Fortin N, Lemieux T (1996) Labor market institutions and the distribution of wages, 1973–1992: a semi-parametric approach. Econometrica 64(5):1001–1044

Dinh N, Maurer-Fazio M (2004) Differential rewards to, and contributions of, education in urban China's segmented labor markets. Pac Econ, Rev 9(3):173–189

Harris J, Todaro M (1970) Migration, unemployment, and development: a two-sector analysis. Am Econ Rev 60:126–142

ILO (1993) Resolution concerning statistics of employment in the informal sector, adopted by the Fifteenth International Conference of Labour Statisticians In: Fifteenth International Conference of Labour Statisticians, Geneva, 19-28 January 1993. Report of the Conference (Geneva, ILO)

ILO (2003) Guidelines concerning a statistical definition of informal employment, endorsed by the Seventeenth International Conference of Labour Statisticians (November-December 2003) In: Seventeenth International Conference of Labour Statisticians, Geneva, 24 November-3 December. Report of the Conference (Geneva, doc. ICLS/17/2003/R.)

Lee L (2012) Decomposing income differentials between migrant workers and urban workers in urban China's labor markets. China Econ Rev 23(2):461–470

Liang Z (2001) The age of migration in China. Popul Dev, Rev 27(3):499–524

Meng X, Zhang D (2010) Labor market impact of large scale internal migration on Chinese urban 'Native' workers. IZA, Bonn. IZA Discussion Paper No. 5288

Meng X, Zhang J (2001) The two-tier labor market in urban China: occupational segregation and income differentials between urban residents and rural migrants in Shanghai. J Comp Econ 29(3):485–504

Messinis G (2013) Returns to education and rural migrant income differentials in China: IV quantile treatment effects. China Econ Rev 26:39–55

MGI (2009) Preparing for China's urban billion. McKinsey Global Institute, March. http://www.mckinsey.com/insights/urbanization/preparing_for_urban_billion_in_china

National Bureau of Statistics Of China (2008) China statistical yearbook. China Statistics Press, Beijing

Oaxaca R (1973) Male-female income differentials in urban labor markets. Int Econ, Rev 14(3):693–709

Song S, Zhang H (2003) Rural-urban migration and urbanization in China: evidence from time-series and cross-section analyses. China Econ Rev Elsevier 14(4):386–400

United Nations (2009) International migration report 2006: a global assessment. Department of Economic and Social Affairs, New York

Wang M (2005) Employment opportunities and income gaps in the urban labor market: a study of the employment and incomes of migrant laborers. Soc Sci China 5:36–46. (in Chinese)

Zhao Z (2005) Migration, labor market flexibility, and income determination in China: a review. Dev Econ 43:285–315

4

Mandatory costs by firm size thresholds: firm location, growth and death in Sri Lanka

Babatunde O Abidoye[1], Peter F Orazem[2*] and Milan Vodopivec[3]

* Correspondence: pfo@iastate.edu
[2]IZA and Department of Economics, Iowa State University, Ames, IA 50010, USA
Full list of author information is available at the end of the article

Abstract

Sri Lanka's Termination of Employment of Workmen Act (TEWA) requires that firms with 15 or more workers justify layoffs and provide generous severance pay to displaced workers, with smaller firms being exempted. Although formally subject to TEWA, firms in Export Promotion Zones (EPZs) do not face the same constraints as nonEPZ firms due to size incentives and lax labor law enforcement in that sector. In EPZ, 77% of firms have more than 15 employees while 76% of nonEPZ firms are smaller than 15 employees. Panel data on all formal sector firms between 1995 and 2003 shows that 80% of the size gap is from sorting of large firms into the EPZ. In addition, EPZ firms grow faster and are less likely to die than comparably sized nonEPZ firms. Despite its intent, TEWA lowered employment.

JEL code: J30

Keywords: Firing cost; Employment protection; Firm entry; Firm growth; Threshold; Export promotion zone; Sri Lanka

1 Introduction

As part of its effort to protect workers from job loss, Sri Lanka adopted the Termination of Employment of Workman Act (TEWA) in 1971. The act aimed to limit unemployment by raising the cost of layoffs. It required that each layoff of a covered worker, whether the layoff involved a single employee or a mass layoff, must be approved by the government. Until 2003, the government also determined on a case-by-case basis the level of severance pay that the firm was required to pay to the laid off workers.

Since its introduction, critics have argued that the TEWA's non-transparent, discretionary, and costly regulations discourage employment growth, hinder reallocation of labor from inefficient firms to more profitable sectors, slow the introduction of new technologies, and increase unemployment. There is at least a *prima facie* case that the TEWA policy has affected the size distribution of firms in Sri Lanka compared to that in 15 other developing countries reported by Leidholm and Mead (1987). Sixty-eight percent of Sri Lankan firms had 10 or fewer employees, in the top third of small firm shares in the Leidholm-Mead compilation.[1] Only 12% of Sri Lanka firms had over 49 workers which would have given it the second smallest large firm share in the Leidholm-Mead listing. However, Sri Lanka's firms in Export Promotion Zones (EPZ) have a remarkably different size distribution: only 17% of the firms have 10 or fewer workers and 57% have more than 49. Of all the countries for which we have size-distribution information, Sri Lanka's EPZ firms have the smallest fraction of workers in firms with fewer than 10 workers and the largest fraction of workers in firms with over 49 workers. Meanwhile, the reason the overall size distribution in Sri Lanka is weighted more heavily toward small firms is that the nonEPZ firms are so unusually small.

Micro-econometric analyses have shown that employment protection policies can have negative consequences for workers. Heckman and Pages (2000) show that in Latin America, more stringent job security laws are associated with lower employment and higher unemployment, particularly among young workers. Similarly, Besley and Burgess (2004) find that labor regulations in India had important adverse effects on output and employment. Expanding on that study, Ahsan and Pages (2009) report that regulations concerned with labor disputes and job security hurt covered workers. Bassanini and Duval (2006) find that changes in tax and labor policies explain about half of the 1982–2003 changes in unemployment among OECD countries. Other studies using macro-economic data have also found negative efficiency effects of severance pay including Nickell and Layard (1999), Haffner et al. (2001), and the OECD (1999). Nevertheless, these negative findings from labor market regulations are not universal, particularly those based on cross-section analysis (Baker et al. 2005).[2]

This paper adds to this literature by identifying the impacts of the Sri Lanka TEWA on firm employment and growth. We exploit two sources of variation in the way firms are treated to identify the policy's effects. First, the law only applies to firms with more than 14 workers, and so smaller firms need not comply. Second, firms in EPZ do not face the same constraints imposed by the TEWA. These sharp differences in policies applied to firms of different size create several strategic options. Firms that anticipate growing beyond 14 workers will try to sort into the EPZ to avoid the constraints imposed by the law. The cost of growing beyond 14 workers may discourage nonEPZ firms from growing. Furthermore, the costs imposed by the TEWA may be large enough to drive covered firms out of business. Panel data on the cohort of all firms registering for business in Sri Lanka between 1995 and 2002 is used to provide evidence for all three possibilities.

Consistent with our theoretical predictions, we find that the potential TEWA costs result in substantially lower firm size in the nonEPZ sector, with the differential incentives to add workers inside and outside the EPZ clearly limiting growth for firms well below the threshold. EPZ firms have a 26 percentage point larger growth probability below the 14 worker employment threshold and a 14 percentage point growth advantage above the threshold. In addition, evidence is consistent with the view that the cost of adding a 15th worker implies a larger marginal cost of expansion for all nonEPZ firms below the threshold compared to nonEPZ firms already above the threshold, and so nonEPZ firms above the threshold have more rapid employment growth than nonEPZ firms below the threshold. NonEPZ firms already above the threshold are 21 percentage points more likely to add employees than are nonEPZ firms below the threshold. Finally, the results show that the biggest and most significant differences in survival probability (about 10 percentage point) is the higher exit rate of nonEPZ firms relative to EPZ firms.

The paper is organized as follows. Section 2 provides an institutional background, highlighting the intentions of the TEWA at its introduction, and its provisions and procedures. It also gives a description of EPZ and nonEPZ firms and description of the data. Section 3 presents the model highlighting firm entry and exit decisions. Section 4 describes the empirical section focusing on the need for analysis by firm. Section 5 presents the empirical results based on the estimation of the multinomial model of employment growth of firms. Section 6 concludes with a summary and policy recommendations.

2 Institutional background and data descriptions
2.1 Termination of Employment of Workmen Act
The TEWA was enacted at a time when Sri Lanka was pursuing isolationist economic policies including an import-substitution industrialization policy, stringent exchange controls, price controls on many commodities, and a program of nationalization of a wide-range of establishments (Ranaraja 2005).[3] The TEWA applies to all firms employing 15 or more workers. For covered private firms, all terminations for any reason other than discipline are regulated by the TEWA, including redundancies arising from organizational restructuring and financial or economic constraints, temporary lay-offs, terminations as a result of the business closure, and even incompetence.[4] A worker qualifies as long as he or she worked at least 180 days in the 12 month period preceding the termination.

The TEWA requires that covered employers must seek the consent of the Commissioner General of Labor (CGL) before they are allowed to dismiss workers, even if it concerns a single worker. The CGL may refuse to sanction the layoff or, if permission is granted, the employer will be required to pay severance in an amount determined by the CGL. Over the sample period, the procedure by which the severance is determined was not specified in law but was subject to a lengthy and seemingly arbitrary deliberation. In December 2003, the TEWA switched to a formula-based severance payment that is uniformly applied to all firms. While that amendment eliminated the ad hoc determination of the level of severance pay, the other elements of the policy, including the need for prior approval of layoffs, are still in place.

In dealing with termination applications by employers or complaints by workers, the CGL has the power of a District Court to conduct inquiries, such as summoning and compelling the attendance of witnesses, production of records, and recording testimony. The employer must satisfy the CGL that terminating the identified group of workers is in the best interest of the employer. While the evaluation is going on, the workers continue to be paid wages and other benefits until the CGL makes a decision, even where there is no work to be done. The final order of the CGL does not take into consideration the wages paid by the employer during the inquiry period. Data for 2003 confirm that the TEWA procedure is a very lengthy one - the average processing time of employer applications was 9.8 months, and it exceeded one year in more than 25 percent of cases (World Bank 2007).

Severance pay was quite generous. During 2002–03, the severance averaged nearly 2 times the monthly salary per year of service, and the multiple could rise as high as 6 times the monthly salary. Judged by international standards, this level of TEWA severance is extremely high. Using 2002 data, a year for which we have some data on individual compensation, we can infer the relationship between generosity of payments and years of service with the firm. A Sri Lankan worker with 20 years of service received an average severance package equal to 29 months of wages. In contrast, the average severance was 16 months of wages in other Asian countries, 12 months in Latin America, 7 months in Africa, 6 months in the OECD, and 4 months in transition countries. Sri Lankan workers with shorter duration of prior service were also awarded much more generous level of severance pay than workers in other countries. Since the switch to the fixed severance formula in December 2003, the program has become even more generous (World Bank 2007).

The high turnover costs imposed by the TEWA have led to a relatively small number of applications for separations by employers. Between 2000 and 2003, of more than 80 thousand covered firms, annual filings for the right to initiate a separation varied from 71 to 105 applications (World Bank 2007). Less than half of these cases were concluded by the order of the commissioner because they were settled "voluntarily", whether because the firm withdrew the application or induced the worker to retire voluntarily with retirement packages that ranged from 6 to 45 months of wages. As is apparent, it is difficult for firms to avoid the costs of the TEWA. Inflexible labor regulations were one of the five most commonly cited business challenges reported by urban firms in Sri Lanka[5].

Firms in EPZ were reported to be given a preferential treatment that allowed them to limit or avoid the costs of the TEWA. Because EPZ firms were technically subject to the same regulations, the extent of the lax enforcement is difficult to quantify, but any preferential treatment should be apparent when comparing EPZ firm personnel decisions relative to those of nonEPZ firms. In addition, EPZ firms were eligible for many Board of Investments (BOI) incentives that rewarded firm growth. The size distribution of firms inside and outside the EPZ is summarized in Table 1. Large firms are atypically located in EPZ. Only 22.5% of EPZ firms have fewer than 14 workers compared to 75.6% of nonEPZ firms! In contrast, the EPZ firms are over 3 times more likely than nonEPZ firms to have grown beyond the threshold employment level. It certainly appears that the incentives to grow must differ between the two groups of firms.

Table 1 also shows that there are apparent differences in the probability that firms increase or decrease their workforce. NonEPZ firms are much more likely than EPZ firms to reduce or maintain their current employment level, regardless of size. EPZ firms are

Table 1 Distribution of Sri Lanka firms by initial size, change in employment over the years, and EPZ status (%), 1995 – 2003

EPZ firms	Percent of sample	Shrink	Stay	Grow	Total
Less than 14 workers	22.5	29.3	26.7	44.0	100.0
14 workers	1.1	45.8	13.6	40.7	100.0
More than 14 workers	76.4	45.4	2.2	52.4	100.0
Total EPZ workers = 5,441					
Non EPZ firms	**Percent of sample**	**Shrink**	**Stay**	**Grow**	**Total**
Less than 14 workers	75.6	37.2	40.8	22.0	100.0
14 workers	1.2	53.9	13.2	32.9	100.0
More than 14 workers	23.2	55.8	5.1	39.1	100.0
Total nonEPZ workers = 320,866					

Source: Authors' calculations based on the universe of all formal sector firms in Sri Lanka, 1995–2003.
EPZ: Export Promotion Zone.

much more likely to add to their employment base. The largest contrast in probability of employment growth is below the threshold: the smallest EPZ firms are twice as likely to increase employment compared to nonEPZ firms. If it is true that the cost of hiring is lower for EPZ firms, then the pattern of employment growth and decline would differ between EPZ and non-EPZ firms.

In Figure 1, we illustrate the probability of firm employment growth and decline in EPZ and nonEPZ firms around the 14–15 employee threshold. Immediately we see that EPZ firms are more likely to grow and nonEPZ firms are more likely to shrink at all firm sizes, an outcome that will prove consistent with the theory. NonEPZ firms are modestly more likely to both shrink and grow above the threshold, compared to nonEPZ firms below the threshold. In other settings, small firms are the most likely to both grow and shrink and so we would expect these lines to slope downward absent any constraints on firm choice (Evans 1987; Cabral 1995; Arkolakis 2013). The patterns for EPZ firms are harder to discern due to relatively small numbers at each firm size. It appears that EPZ firms are also more likely to grow above the threshold but there is no obvious change in the probability of firm shrinkage around the threshold.

At 14 workers where the 15th worker would trigger compliance with the TEWA, for EPZ firms the probability of employment growth decreases and the probability of firm employment decline increases. NonEPZ firms have the same pattern but the difference is only a few percentage points. The lack of massing at 14 employees outside the EPZ may seem surprising. However, firms wanting to avoid the TEWA would be expected to remain below 15 employees, but their constrained optimum employment choice may not be exactly at 14 workers. As a result, the TEWA would be expected to create higher probability of firms shrinking above the threshold and lower probability of firms growing below the threshold, a result that is supported by the patterns in Figure 1. Moreover, data measurement errors (see above) may also contribute to less pronounced differences in observed behavior at the threshold.

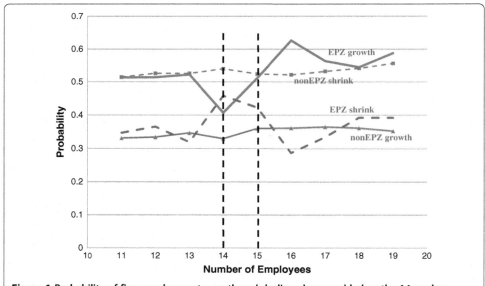

Figure 1 Probability of firm employment growth and decline above and below the 14 worker threshold, by firm size and EPZ status, 1995–2003 averages.

To further isolate the effect of the TEWA, we need to remove the effects of firm observed and unobserved productivity attributes from the analysis. In addition, the TEWA effect will be spread across firm decisions to expand, remain at current size, or shrink in the face of external shocks. That will require a more structured analysis of the data.

2.2 Data description

To test for differences in firm location, growth and decline between EPZ and nonEPZ sectors, we make use of a unique panel data set that includes annual employment data for 80,560 firms in Sri Lanka over the 1995–2003 periods. The period coincides with a consistent set of restrictions on layoffs. Those policies were relaxed modestly at the end of 2003. The data are compiled by the Sri Lanka Employees' Provident Fund (EPF) on all private sector firms and workers paying contributions to the fund. All registered firms regardless of size are required to pay contributions for their workers. The data are maintained by the Central Bank of Sri Lanka.

The data are quite limited, however. Apart from the number of workers employed during the year, the only other information contained in the database is the firm's name and region: each firm is designated as having a base in one of 24 regions. The name allows us to identify which firms belong to an EPZ. The Sri Lankan Board of Investment provided us a list of names for firms that operate in EPZs. We matched these names with 1,124 firms in the EPF list, and these firms comprise our EPZ group.

The EPF data are not free of problems. The data set only contains workers for whom the firm paid contributions during the year. If for whatever reason such contributions are not paid, the true number of workers in the firm will deviate from the number reported to the EPF. The most frequent reason for such discrepancies is the presence of financial difficulties that prevent a firm from paying contributions in the current year. Even delayed payments are not used to correct the data retrospectively. Therefore, these employment numbers will only reflect the contemporaneously reported number of workers for whom the firm is making an EPF contribution. The frequency or magnitude of this measurement error is not known.

Also, the nature of the data does not allow us to differentiate between quits and layoffs and so we assume that any net loss of workers is due to layoffs. This seems reasonable, as workers who quit will presumably be replaced, resulting in no employment loss. We will discuss further in the empirical section on how we exploit the nature of the data to understand firm size decision.

The data also provide information on firms in different years. We make use of the longitudinal nature of the data to specifically identify cohorts of firms and follow their evolution over time. Thus firms that do not make contributions in 1995 but started paying contribution in 1996 are considered to be one cohort and are followed until 2003. The same is done for subsequent years. The identification of different cohorts in the data has the advantage of reducing heterogeneity and provides for a simple test of selection to explain firm size distribution and location in EPZ or nonEPZ region.

As the summary data in Table 1 reveal, there are substantial differences in average firm size and growth patterns consistent with differences in the marginal cost of hiring across the EPZ and nonEPZ regions. To evaluate the strength of that correlation more formally, we next propose a theoretical model to understand firm entry and exit decision.

3 Firm entry decisions: How much of the gap in size distribution between EPZ and nonEPZ firms is due to sorting by firm size at entry?

3.1 Theory

Firms face two interrelated decisions at the time of entry designated by subscript 0: whether to locate in an EPZ zone and how much labor (L_0) and capital (K_0) to employ. We assume that there is a fixed entry cost, F_0^{EPZ}, that firms incur from attaining EPZ status. These costs would include all official and under-the-table costs of applying for and attaining EPZ status plus any additional business expenses associated with location or entry[6]. In exchange, the firm receives benefits from alleged lax enforcement of the TEWA and preferential tax treatment and exemption from export duties applied to worker output. That distinction sets up the comparison between EPZ and nonEPZ firms for the empirical work.

We summarize the distinction with a parameter δk that measures the cost of compliance with the TEWA net of any benefits from being in the EPZ. The superscript k denotes the cost of compliance in E: EPZ or N: nonEPZ. The measure of δk is a positive or negative proportional markup over the wage. If the firm is nonEPZ, the $\delta k \geq 0$, with a positive markup if the firm has more than 14 employees so that it faces possible severance and related firing costs that are proportional to the wage. If the firm is in the EPZ, we expect $\delta^E \leq \delta^N$ because of lax enforcement of TEWA requirements, and δ^E may even be negative if the firm receives tax benefits and/or subsidies tied to firm size.

All firms, EPZ or nonEPZ, have to pay market wages, w_0 and so the hourly labor cost per worker is $w_0(1 + \delta^K)$. All nonEPZ firms with $L_0 < 15$ face $\delta^N = 0$ and pay w_0 per hour for labor, while all nonEPZ firms with $L_0 \geq 15$ pay $w_0(1 + \delta^N)$ per hour; $\delta^N > 0$. All EPZ firms pay $w_0(1 + \delta^N) \leq w0(1 + \delta N)$ when compared with equally sized nonEPZ firms.

Assuming the firm's production function takes the Cobb-Douglas form

$$Q_0 = A\tau_0 L_0^{\alpha_L} K_0^{\alpha_K} \tag{1}$$

The variable τ_0 is a permanent exogenous technology shock to labor productivity that takes an initial value of unity. The production parameters are defined by $A > 0, 0 < \alpha_L < 1$, and $0 < \alpha_K < 1$. Setting output price at unity and cost of capital as r, the firm's initial optimum input levels L_0^* and K_0^* are set by the first-order conditions:

$$\alpha_L A\tau_0 L_0^{\alpha_L-1} K_0^{\alpha_K} = w_0(1 + \delta^k) \tag{2A}$$

$$\alpha_K A\tau_0 L_0^{\alpha_L} K_0^{\alpha_K-1} = r \tag{2B}$$

An entering firm will decide on whether to enter the EPZ by comparing anticipated profits with and without EPZ status. For firms with $L_0^* < 15$, profits are higher in the nonEPZ state if $\delta^E > 0$, or if $\delta^E < 0$ and $\left|\frac{w_0\delta^E L_0^*}{r}\right| < F_0^{EPZ}$ where the term on the left of the inequality is the discounted value of the stream of anticipated EPZ subsidies. The cost advantage for small firms locating in the nonEPZ sector is that they are exempt from TEWA costs and also avoid paying F_0^{EPZ}. For firms with $L_0^* \geq 15$, it is optimal to get EPZ status when $F_0^{EPZ} < \frac{\delta^N w_0 L_0^*}{r}$, where the term on the right is the discounted value of the stream of anticipated TEWA payments in perpetuity. Consequently, it is possible for a firm planning to have 15 or more employees to select the nonEPZ sector. Presuming firms face the same market wages, capital costs, potential EPZ benefits, and potential TEWA costs, the firms most likely to sort into the EPZ sector have the largest initial employment levels, L_0^*.

This simple model shows that small firms will tend to sort into nonEPZ and large firms into EPZ at the time of entry, conditional on prevailing wages, capital costs and technology. That suggests that empirical analysis of the size distribution of firms must compare firms facing the same prices and technologies at the time of entry. Moreover, empirical studies have consistently shown that firm growth rates and death rates are initially both slow with firm age and so we need to standardize firm age to generate accurate transition probabilities (Evans 1987; Cabral 1995; Arkolakis 2013). These arguments dictate our use of cohorts of newly born firms for our analysis.

3.2 Evidence of the impact of sorting on the gap in firm size between EPZ and nonEPZ

Table 2 provides summary information on the size distribution of firms in EPZ and nonEPZ regions for successive entry cohorts from 1996 through 2002. Recall that the overall percentage of firms with at least 15 employees is 76% in the EPZ and 23% in the nonEPZ (see Table 1). The proportion of EPZ firms already above 14 workers at entry varies between 53% and 70% with an average of 62%. It is apparent that the EPZ firms quickly add workers with the fraction above 15 workers rising 2.5% per year averaged across the cohorts. If 76% is taken as the final percentage of firms employing over 15 workers, sorting of large firms into EPZ is responsible for about 80% of the EPZ size distribution.

In the nonEPZ sector, only 9% of the firms in a cohort start with at least 15 employees, and the fraction actually decrease through the first few years. By 2003, 8% of these seven firm entry cohorts had 15 or more workers. It is apparent that the nonEPZ firms do not grow as readily as the EPZ firms. While we cannot argue with certainty that the proximate cause is the TEWA, the results are consistent with the predicted impact of the TEWA on firm entry decisions.

There is a 53 percentage point gap between the worker distribution of EPZ and nonEPZ firms in the population as shown in Table 1. The average gap at entry between large EPZ and nonEPZ firms is also 53 percentage points as shown in Table 2. However, the population measure excludes firms that have died, while the cohort estimates

Table 2 Distribution of EPZ and non EPZ firms at entry (1996) and the end of sample (2003)

	% large at entry, EPZ	% large in 2003, EPZ	% large at entry, non EPZ	% large in 2003, non EPZ	% of large firms at entry that is EPZ	% of large firms in 2003 that is EPZ	% of firms in EPZ at entry
1996	55	71	11	9	6	10	1
1997	67	72	12	10	7	9	1
1998	62	68	10	8	9	12	2
1999	65	67	8	7	10	11	1
2000	70	76	11	10	9	10	1
2001	53	65	8	7	8	10	1
2002	60	65	8	8	9	11	1
Average	62	69	9	8	8	10	1

Source: Authors' calculations based n the universe of all formal sector firms in Sri Lanka, 1995–2003.
EPZ: Export Promotion Zone.

at entry include all firms. It is possible that the fraction of firms with over 15 employees will grow because small firms add workers over time, or it may be that the fraction increases because small firms are more likely to die. As we will see, sorting at entry is an important source of the difference between EPZ and nonEPZ firm size distributions, but differential growth and death rates also play a role.

4 Can the TEWA affect firm employment growth and death?
4.1 Theory

When firms commit to their initial capital stock and decide whether or not to enter the EPZ, they do not know the future path of prices and technology. Having committed to a capital stock and a location, their response to these changing economic circumstances is limited to labor adjustments in the short run. At some future time, t, the condition setting their short-run employment level will be

$$\alpha_L A \tau_t L_t^{\alpha_L - 1} K_0^{*\alpha_K} \geq w_t \left(1 + \delta^k\right) \tag{3A}$$

The firm's optimal labor allocation is conditioned on the initial capital investment at entry. It is also affected by the evolution of technology, τ_t, and wages, w_t.[7]

We let technology evolve according to:

$$\ln(\tau_t) = \ln(\tau_{t-1}) + \bar{\eta}_0 + \eta_t; \; \eta_t \sim N\left(0, \sigma_\eta^2\right) \tag{3B}$$

The variable $\bar{\eta}_0$ is the trend growth in technology known by all firms at the time of entry, but η_t is an unforeseeable but permanent technology innovation that the firm cannot control. This specification for τ_t presumes that the firm's labor productivity is a random walk process about the trend. We assume similarly that market wages (w_t) evolve according to a random walk process with a known drift[8] so that

$$\ln(w_t) = \ln(w_{t-1}) + \bar{\omega}_0 + \omega_t; \; \omega_t \sim N\left(0, \sigma_\omega^2\right) \tag{3C}$$

The variable $\bar{\omega}_0$ is the trend growth in wages known by all firms at the time of entry, but ω_t is an unforeseeable but permanent innovation in wages that the firm cannot control.

We can model the changes in the firm's employment decisions by applying 3A-C to two successive years and solving for the change in desired labor. From here on, we define the notional firm input demand that would hold at an interior solution in period t as L_t^* and K_t^*. The form of the decision depends on whether the firm comes under the TEWA policy. We examine several cases that will illustrate the range of possible responses to the TEWA system. Recall that we are assuming that EPZ firms are exempt from all TEWA requirements in forming these responses, an assumption that we will test with the data.

4.1.1 Case 1: Firm is exempt from TEWA with $\delta^N = 0$ and $\delta^E \leq 0$ in both periods with $L_{t-1}^* < 15$ and $L_t^* < 15$

Assuming interior solutions, the change in desired labor is governed by $\ln\left(\frac{L_t}{L_{t-1}}\right) = \frac{\eta_t - \omega_t}{(1 - \alpha_L)}$.

The firm is not constrained by the severance policy and adjusts labor upward with positive labor productivity shocks and negative wage shocks. If EPZ firms receive favorable subsidies so that $\delta^E < 0$, comparable adverse shocks are less likely to cause the left hand side of

(3A) to fall below the right-hand side for EPZ firms compared to nonEPZ firms. As a consequence, below the threshold, nonEPZ firms are more likely to shrink or less likely to expand compared to EPZ firms.

4.1.2 Case 2: Firm is covered by TEWA so $\delta^N > \delta^E \gtreqless 0$ in both periods because $L^*_{t-1} \geq 15$ and $L^*_t \leq 15$

Assuming interior solutions, the change in desired labor is also governed by $\ln\left(\frac{L_t}{L_{t-1}}\right) = \frac{\eta_t - \omega_t}{(1-\alpha_L)}$ and so optimal labor demand responds as with the exempt firms in Case 1. However, even at their optimum labor allocations, the nonEPZ firms face a constant disadvantage of having higher labor costs and more distorted capital labor ratios compared to their EPZ competitors. As before, comparable adverse shocks are more likely to lead to violations of the first order condition (3A) for nonEPZ firms than EPZ firms. In addition, even if they are at their optimum labor allocation, nonEPZ firm profit levels will be lower than that of comparably sized EPZ firms because of their higher labor costs. As a result, above the threshold, nonEPZ firms are more likely to shrink and less likely to expand compared to equally sized EPZ firms.

4.1.3 Case 3: Firm has $L^*_{t-1} \geq 15$ and considers remaining below the threshold in period t even though $L^*_t \leq 15$ if the firm is exempt from the TEWA

In this case, assume first that employment in *t-1* is fixed by the interior solution of 3A-C such that $L^*_{t-1} < 15$. However, in the next period, the firm's optimal staffing would move it into the covered region:

$$\alpha_L A \tau_t L_t^{\alpha_L - 1} K_0^{*\alpha_K} = w_t \rightarrow L^*_t \geq 15$$

$$\alpha_L A \tau_t L_t^{*\alpha_L - 1} K_0^{*\alpha_K} < w_t\left(1 + \delta^k L^*_t\right); \, \forall L^*_t \geq 15; \, \delta > 0$$

This is the case where the firm would want to expand beyond 14 employees if it faced the market wage alone. However, in moving beyond 14 employees, the firm has to pay for the TEWA severance system for all L^*_t workers, leading to an even larger increase in the marginal cost of adding any workers beyond 14. As a consequence, the firm will set their staffing at some second-best level $L_t < 15$ and where the marginal product $\alpha_L A \tau_t L_t^{\alpha_L - 1} K_0^{*\alpha_K} > w_t$.[9] Because $\delta^N > \delta^E$, it is more likely that nonEPZ firms will decide not to expand beyond 14 workers compared to EPZ firms.

4.2 Empirical framework

The discussion illustrates that the TEWA can alter the incentives for nonEPZ firms to expand or shrink compared to similarly sized EPZ firms. Both above and below the threshold, the combination of special tax and subsidy treatments from the EPZ and the costs of compliance with the TEWA create conditions that increase the likelihood that nonEPZ firms will shrink or fail to grow compared to their EPZ counterparts. At the threshold, nonEPZ firms are more likely to face additional labor costs that cause them to remain below the threshold. As we show in this section, these predictions can be tested with longitudinal data on cohorts of firms entering business at the same time.

The use of a common startup date is important for two reasons. First, all firms will be exposed to the same information on wages, technology and macroeconomic conditions, greatly simplifying the specification of common shocks. Second, a sample of the universe of all starting firms avoids the selection bias that would exist had we been constrained to a sample of surviving firms in which the weakest would have been already eliminated.

The empirical section described below can be viewed in the difference-in-differences framework, using firms at or above the severance threshold as the treatment group, and those with fewer than 14 workers and those in EPZs as control groups. The first control group follows naturally from the design of the TEWA system, because the regulations do not apply to firms employing less than 15 workers. The second control group is formed based on the assumption that enforcement is ineffective in EPZs, allowing firms to escape paying separation costs as dictated by TEWA.

4.2.1 Measuring the TEWA effect on probability of firm growth

We begin by applying an interior solution to (3A) which defines the firm's notional demand in period t as

$$(\alpha_L - 1)\ln L_t^* = \ln\left(\frac{w_t(1 + \delta^k)}{\alpha_L A \tau_t K_0^{*\alpha_K}}\right) \tag{4A}$$

The first order condition for notional employment in period $t + 1$ is

$$(\alpha_L - 1)\ln L_{t+1}^* = \ln\left(\frac{w_{t+1}(1 + \delta^k)}{\alpha_L A \tau_{t+1} K_0^{*\alpha_K}}\right) = (\alpha_L - 1)\ln L_t^* + \omega_{t+1} - \eta_{t+1} \tag{4B}$$

where we apply (4A), (3B) and (3C). Rearranging, we have that the change in notional employment from t to $t + 1$ is

$$\ln\left(\frac{L_{t+1}^*}{L_t^*}\right) = \frac{\bar{\eta}_0 + \eta_{t+1} - \bar{\omega}_0 - \omega_{t+1}}{(1 - \alpha_L)} \tag{5}$$

which means that if firm employment evolves without frictions, the change in notional employment will be a random walk with drift. Employment increases with trend growth and unexpected innovations in technology and decreases with expected wage increases and positive wage shocks. Importantly, the firm-specific Hicksian productivity factor A is differenced away, and so labor demand or supply shifts related to firm-specific unobservable productivity, firm location, or industry are held constant in the frictionless solution. However, the constraints on maximization caused by the TEWA will mean that actual firm employment growth will deviate from the frictionless outcome. The greater frictions in the nonEPZ sector should be apparent when we compare employment changes in those firms with the less constrained employment growth in the EPZ sector above, at and below the threshold.

This simple model does not take into account the stylized facts about firm growth by firm age and size. Our assessment of the literature suggests that these tendencies are unlikely to cause faster growth in the EPZ sector. First, as noted above, firm growth rates tend to decrease with firm age (Evans 1987; Cabral 1995; Arkolakis 2013). This will not bias comparisons across EPZ and nonEPZ firms, but it will induce a downward trend in longitudinal firm growth rates within the sectors. Potentially of greater concern is a second stylized result that exporting firms tend to grow faster than non-exporting firms which could bias the comparison across the EPZ and nonEPZ firms. However, extensive reviews of the empirical literature by Wagner (2007), Wagner (2012) and Singh (2010) suggest that the productivity advantage to exporting firms is driven by the sorting of more efficient firms into the export sector, similar to our own finding that larger firms enter the EPZ sector while smaller firms enter the nonEPZ sector. In contrast, there is no consistent evidence that the act of exporting raises firm growth rates. Again, these past findings suggest that the comparison across EPZ and nonEPZ sectors will not be biased by the act of exporting after controlling for the initial conditions at time of entry. In fact, evidence suggests that the highest firm growth rates among exporting firms are concentrated among the very small firms, while larger firms have growth rates near zero (Arkolakis 2013). If true, the bias would actually go against finding faster growth rates in the EPZ sector as firm size increases.

Actual employment changes for the *ith* firm are modeled as an approximation to the firm's notional employment changes as

$$\ln\left(\frac{L_{it+1}}{L_{it}}\right) = \beta_0 + \beta_{EPZ}EPZ_i + \beta_{L^-}E_{it}^{L^-} + \beta_{L^+}E_{it}^{L^+} + \left\{\gamma_{L^-}E_{it}^{L^-} + \gamma_{L^+}E_{it}^{L^+}\right\} * EPZ_i$$
$$+ \frac{\bar{\eta}_{i0} - \bar{\omega}_{i0}}{(1-\alpha_L)} + \frac{\eta_{it+1} - \omega_{it+1}}{(1-\alpha_L)} \tag{6}$$

This specification adds terms to (5) that allow differential responses to the wage and technology shocks depending on whether the firm is inside or outside the EPZ and whether its employment level lies above or below the threshold. The constant β_0 corresponds to the base case which is set to be the anticipated employment change at a firm with $L_{it} = 14$ in a nonEPZ region. The other possible employment levels in period t are indicated by a dummy variable $E_{it}^{L^-}$ when employment is below 14 and $E_{it}^{L^+}$ when employment is above 14. The corresponding coefficients differentiate between employment growth effects below the threshold (β_{L^-}) and above the threshold (β_{L^+}). The dummy variable EPZ_i indicates that the firm is in an export promotion zone. Given the other parameters, the coefficient β_{EPZ} measures the difference in employment growth between EPZ and nonEPZ firms at the threshold $L_{it} = 14$. The γ_{L^-} capture additional differences in employment growth between EPZ and nonEPZ below the threshold and γ_{L^+} measures additional differences between the sectors above the threshold. If EPZ firms face fewer frictions in employment adjustments because of partial or full immunity from the TEWA or other benefits associated with EPZ status, γ_{L^-} and γ_{L^+} will be positive and significant. The γ_{L^-} and γ_{L^+} may differ from one another if there are different relative regulatory costs between EPZ and nonEPZ sectors above and below the threshold.

Our last requirement to estimate (6) is to operationalize the random walk and drift terms. The wage and technology trend terms are firm-specific and reflect information known at the time of entry. We approximate these terms by $\frac{\bar{\eta}_{i0} - \bar{\omega}_{i0}}{(1-\alpha_L)} = \phi_L \ln(L_{i0}) + \phi_0$ where the initial employment level reflects the firm's anticipated input needs based on what the firm knew at the time of entry and the second term is a cohort-specific term reflecting common expectations of the drift terms held by all firms entering at the same time. The second term requires that we control for a common fixed effect for all firms in the entry cohort. Inclusion of these terms helps to control for nonrandom sorting into firm size groups across firms and across entry cohorts.

The random walk terms are *i.i.d.* errors when we estimate one period employment changes. We let $\epsilon_{it}^{\Lambda} = \frac{\eta_{it+1} - \omega_{it+1}}{(1-\alpha_L)}$ be the composite error term in the employment change relationship. If ϵ_{it}^{Λ} is distributed extreme value, then (6) can be posed as a multinomial logit specification. If we further define the term $\Delta\Lambda_{t+1}$ as a trichotomous variable and define the right-hand side terms excluding ϵ_{it} as $Z'_{it}B^{\Lambda}$, the estimable variant of (6) that will yield the parameters of interest is

$$\Delta\Lambda_{t+1} = 1 \text{ if } \ln\left(\frac{L_{it+1}}{L_{it}}\right) - Z'_{it}B^{\Lambda} < \epsilon_{it}^{\Lambda}$$

$$\Delta\Lambda_{t+1} = 2 \text{ if } \ln\left(\frac{L_{it+1}}{L_{it}}\right) - Z'_{it}B^{\Lambda} = \epsilon_{it}^{\Lambda} \quad\quad\quad (7)$$

$$\Delta\Lambda_{t+1} = 3 \text{ if } \ln\left(\frac{L_{it+1}}{L_{it}}\right) - Z'_{it}B^{\Lambda} > \epsilon_{it}^{\Lambda}$$

Table 3 summarizes the identification and interpretation of the coefficients. The first column shows the parameters describing firm growth for EPZ firms below, at and above the threshold. The second column shows the corresponding parameter estimates for nonEPZ firms. The first differences of the nonEPZ estimates allow us to identify β_{L^-} and β_{L^+}. The double difference allows us to identify γ_{L^-} and γ_{L^+}. $\beta_{L^-} > 0$ indicates faster growth than the base case for nonEPZ firms below 14 workers. Similarly, $\beta_{L^+} > 0$ indicates faster employment growth than the base case for nonEPZ firms above 14 workers. $\beta_{EPZ} + \gamma_{L^-} > 0$ indicates that EPZ firms are growing faster than nonEPZ firms below 14 workers and $\beta_{EPZ} + \gamma_{L^+} > 0$ indicates that EPZ firms are growing faster than nonEPZ firms above 14 workers. The coefficient β_{EPZ} tells us if EPZ firms grow faster than nonEPZ firms at the threshold. These coefficient estimates form the basis of our hypothesis tests.

4.2.2 Measuring the TEWA effect on probability of Firm Death

Even with perfect foresight, firms will not completely avoid the TEWA costs by sorting into or out of the EPZ. NonEPZ firms face a labor cost disadvantage every period because $\delta^N \geq \delta^E$ both above and below the threshold. Because nonEPZ firms will pay an artificially high labor cost per hour, they will pick an inefficiently high ratio of capital per worker. The higher input costs than their EPZ competitors also leave them more

Table 3 Parameters controlling the probability of employment growth by type of firms

Employment in period *t*	Type of firm		
	EPZ	Non EPZ	Difference
Firm employment growth effects below the threshold			
$E_{it}^{L^-} = 1 : L_{it-1} \leq 13$	$\beta_{L^-} + \beta_{EPZ} + \gamma_{L^-}$	β_{L^-}	$\beta_{EPZ} + \gamma_{L^-}$
$L_{it} = 14$	β_{EPZ}	reference	β_{EPZ}
Difference	$\beta_{L^-} + \gamma_{L^-}$	β_{L^-}	γ_{L^-}
Firm employment growth effects above the threshold			
$E_{it}^{L^+} = 1 : L_{it} \geq 15$	$\beta_{L^+} + \beta_{EPZ} + \gamma_{L^+}$	β_{L^+}	$\beta_{EPZ} + \gamma_{L^+}$
$L_{it} = 14$	β_{EPZ}	reference	β_{EPZ}
Difference	$\beta_{L^+} + \gamma_{L^+}$	β_{L^+}	γ_{L^+}

EPZ: Export Promotion Zone.

exposed to adverse wage or technology shocks, increasing the probability that nonEPZ firms will shrink or fail.

We can test the hypothesized greater likelihood of firm death for nonEPZ firms using a similar specification as in (7) but with an alternative dependent variable. The details of the parameterizations follow exactly from the previous section except that the expected signs are opposite those for firm growth. We denote the composite error term as $\epsilon_{it}^{Y} = \frac{\eta_{it+1} - \omega_{it+1}}{(1-\alpha_L)}$ which we assume is distributed extreme value. Then, we can derive a binomial logit specification for firm deaths which are indicated by unit values of the dichotomous variable ΔY_{T+1}. Denoting the terms on the right-hand side of (7) excluding the error as $Z_{it}'B^{Y}$, we can define firm deaths by

$$
\Delta Y_{t+1} = 1 \text{ if } \ln\left(\frac{L_{it+1}}{L_{it}}\right) - Z_{it}'B^{Y} \leq \epsilon_{it}^{Y}
$$
$$
\Delta Y_{t+1} = 0 \text{ if } \ln\left(\frac{L_{it+1}}{L_{it}}\right) - Z_{it}'B^{Y} > \epsilon_{it}^{Y}
$$

(8)

where a firm death occurs when the notional reduction in staffing from year t to $t+1$ is sufficiently large that it is more profitable for the firm to exit than to remain in operation with reduced staffing. If the additional costs faced by nonEPZ firms are sufficiently large compared to EPZ firms, then we would find negative values for β_{EPZ}, γ_{L^-} and γ_{L^+}.

5 Can the TEWA affect firm employment growth and death?

In Table 4 and Table 5, we present the results of our estimation of the firm employment growth and firm death equations, estimated over the pooled firm entry cohorts from 1996 through 2002. These firms are followed annually until 2003, and so their growth and decline is tracked from one to seven years after entry. Constant terms for cohort year of birth are used to correct for the common information on macroeconomic conditions that shape anticipated price, wage and technology trends at the time of entry. The firm's initial employment level is used as a proxy for firm-specific information on technologies and wages that shaped the initial profit maximizing employment level. These parameters are estimated, but not reported[10].

For ease of interpretation, all estimated coefficients are converted into their implied transition probabilities. Therefore, all results reported in Table 4 and Table 5 reflect the marginal effects by EPZ or nonEPZ status of the prior year's employment level on the probability of employment growth, decline, or firm death. We report the reduced form coefficients in the upper panel and the lower panel presents the values of the hypotheses tests and the test statistics.

5.1 Employment growth and decline inside and outside the EPZ

The reduced form parameters give the average annual probability of employment growth relative to the reference firm which is a nonEPZ firm with 14 employees in year t. Smaller EPZ firms are 9 percentage points more likely to add workers than the reference firm. In contrast, smaller nonEPZ firms are nearly 17 percentage points less likely to add workers than a reference firm! Therefore, the differential incentives to add workers inside and outside the EPZ clearly limit growth for firms well below the threshold. As indicated in the theory section, there is no reason to believe that the

Table 4 Reduced form and structural estimates of the probability of employment growth conditional on prior employment level inside and outside Enterprise Protection Zones as per equation (6) using Probit model with cluster robust standard errors

Reduced form parameters: $EPZ_i = 1$	Marginal effect[a]
$L_{it} \leq 13$, $E_{it}^{L^-} = 1$: $\beta_{L^-} + \beta_{EPZ} + \gamma_{L^-}$	0.089** (0.023)
$L_{it} = 14$: β_{EPZ}	0.123 (0.079)
$L_{it} \geq 15$, $E_{it}^{L^+} = 1$: $\beta_{L^+} + \beta_{EPZ} + \gamma_{L^+}$	0.190** (0.019)
Reduced form parameters: $EPZ_i = 0$	
$L_{it} \leq 13$, $E_{it}^{L^-} = 1$: β_{L^-}	−0.166** (0.015)
$L_{it} = 14$: reference	−
$L_{it} \geq 15$, $E_{it}^{L^+} = 0$: β_{L^+}	0.048** (0.013)
Structural estimates	
Hypothesis: Relative to nonEPZ firms of like size and vintage...	Marginal effect[b]
$\beta_{EPZ} > 0$: EPZ firms grow faster at the threshold	0.123** (224.1)
$\beta_{EPZ} + \gamma_{L^-} > 0$: EPZ firms grow faster below the threshold	0.255** (160.7)
$\beta_{EPZ} + \gamma_{L^+} > 0$: EPZ firms grow faster above the threshold	0.142** (2952)
Hypothesis: Relative to same sector firms below the threshold...	
$\beta_{L^+} - \beta_{L^-} > 0$: nonEPZ firms grow faster above the threshold	0.214** (21.2)
$(\beta_{L^+} + \gamma_{L^+}) - (\beta_{L^-} + \gamma_{L^-}) > 0$: EPZ firms grow faster above the threshold	0.101** (41.5)
Hypothesis: Relative to EPZ firms at the threshold....	
$\gamma_{L^-} = 0$: EPZ firms grow at a different rate below the threshold	0.133* (3.5)
$\gamma_{L^+} = 0$: EPZ firms grow at a different rate above the threshold	0.020 (0.01)

Log-likelihood value of −94817.0 with 79% of the observation predicted correctly.
[a]Marginal effect reported with attached standard error in parenthesis.
[b]Marginal effect reported with attached Chi-square statistic in parentheses. Critical value is 3.84 at the .05 significance level.
*significance at the 0.1 level. **significance at the .05 level.
EPZ: Export Promotion Zone.

constrained optimal employment level for a firm facing a substantial added cost of employing 15 workers would be 14 workers. This finding suggests that potential TEWA costs result in substantially lower firm size in the nonEPZ sector, even for firms well below the 14 firm threshold.

Above the threshold, EPZ firms are 19 percentage points more likely to add workers than the reference nonEPZ firm with 14 workers. In contrast, nonEPZ firms already above the threshold are 5 percentage points more likely to add workers than the reference firm. Because firm adding a 15th worker face additional costs on all 15 workers, we would expect a larger marginal cost to expansion for firms at the threshold compared to those already above the threshold.

Turning to the structural estimates, EPZ firms at the threshold are 12 percentage points more likely to add workers than the reference nonEPZ firm at the threshold, a difference that easily meets any standard significance criteria. The hypothesis that EPZ firms grow faster than comparably sized nonEPZ firms in the same entry cohort either above or below the threshold also passes any standard significance criteria. These effects are not small: 26 percentage point larger growth probability for firms below the threshold and a 14 percentage point growth advantage for firms above the threshold. This is overwhelming support of the hypothesis that firms in the EPZ grow faster than firms with identical initial size and year of entry in the nonEPZ sector.

Table 5 Reduced form and structural estimates of the probability of firm death conditional on prior employment level inside and outside Enterprise Protection Zones as per equation (7) using Probit model with cluster robust standard errors

Reduced form parameters: $EPZ_i = 1$	Marginal effect[a]
$L_{it} \leq 13$, $E_{it}^{L^-} = 1$: $\beta_{L^-} + \beta_{EPZ} + \gamma_{L^-}$	−0.073** (0.011)
$L_{it} = 14$: β_{EPZ}	−0.032 (0.062)
$L_{it} \geq 15$, $E_{it}^{L^+} = 1$: $\beta_{L^+} + \beta_{EPZ} + \gamma_{L^+}$	−0.093** (0.009)
Reduced form parameters: $EPZ_i = 0$	
$L_{it} \leq 13$, $E_{it}^{L^-} = 1$: β_{L^-}	0.023** (0.011)
$L_{it} = 14$: reference	–
$L_{it} \geq 15$, $E_{it}^{L^+} = 0$: β_{L^+}	0.004 (0.012)
Structural estimates	
Hypothesis: Relative to nonEPZ firms of like size and vintage...	**Marginal effect[b]**
$\beta_{EPZ} < 0$: EPZ firms survive more readily at the threshold	−0.032** (66.4)
$\beta_{EPZ} + \gamma_{L^-} < 0$: EPZ firms survive more readily below the threshold	−0.096** (72.6)
$\beta_{EPZ} + \gamma_{L^+} < 0$: EPZ firms survive more readily above the threshold	−0.096** (30.1)
Hypothesis: Relative to firms in the same sector below the threshold...	
$\beta_{L^+} - \beta_{L^-} < 0$: nonEPZ firms survive more readily above the threshold	−0.022 (1.22)
$(\beta_{L^+} + \gamma_{L^+}) - (\beta_{L^-} + \gamma_{L^-}) < 0$: EPZ firms survive more readily above the threshold	−0.020 (0.266)
Hypothesis: Relative to EPZ firms at the threshold....	
$\gamma_{L^-} = 0$: EPZ firms below the threshold have a different survival rate	−0.064 (1.22)
$\gamma_{L^+} = 0$: EPZ firms above the threshold have a different survival rate	−0.065 (1.66)

Log-likelihood value of −77956.7 with 85% of the observation predicted correctly.
[a]Marginal effect reported with attached standard error in parenthesis.
[b]Marginal effect reported with attached Chi-square statistic in parentheses. Critical value is 3.84 at the .05 significance level.
*significance at the 0.1 level. **significance at the .05 level.
EPZ: Export Promotion Zone.

The TEWA costs tend to keep nonEPZ firms small. NonEPZ firms below the threshold are 17 percentage points less likely to grow than are firms at the threshold, defying the tendency for firm growth rates to decrease with firm size. In contrast, EPZ firms below the threshold are more likely to add workers, consistent with the unconstrained pattern of firm growth by size found elsewhere. nonEPZ firms that manage to cross the threshold are 5% more likely to grow than the firms at the threshold who face very large marginal costs of the 15th worker, and are 21 percentage points more likely to add employees than are nonEPZ firms below the threshold. In contrast, there are no significant differences between employment growth probabilities of EPZ firms at or above the threshold. The differences in growth probability between EPZ above and below the threshold are only marginally significant. In short, growth rates for EPZ firms are quite similar to the unconstrained random walk with drift, while the pattern for nonEPZ firms is very different from the typical pattern of the fastest growth rates concentrated among the smallest firms.

5.1.1 Firm death inside and outside the EPZ
Table 5 reports the marginal probabilities of firm exit by current firm size and sector. EPZ firms below and above the threshold are 7 and 9 percentage points less likely to

exit in a given year compared to comparably sized nonEPZ firms of the same vintage. At the threshold, EPZ firms are 3 percentage points less likely to exit but the estimate is not precise. NonEPZ firms below the threshold are the most likely to die at a 2 percentage point elevated exit rate per year. NonEPZ firms above the threshold have the same exit probability as firms at the threshold.

The structural hypothesis tests demonstrate a higher risk of death for almost all nonEPZ firms, regardless of size. The one-tailed test that EPZ firms are more likely to survive than nonEPZ firms at the threshold is not definitive. However, firms below the threshold have a 10 percentage point higher probability of death than comparably sized EPZ frims. For firms above the threshold, again there is a 10 percentage point higher probability of exit for nonEPZ firms. All of these estimates easily passes critical values. Greater exposure to the TEWA expenses and other disadvantages of nonEPZ firms relative to EPZ firms of comparable initial size and vintage increases significantly the likelihood that nonEPZ firms will fail.

For both EPZ and nonEPZ sectors, there is a small advantage of size – about a two percentage point lower risk of death per year relative to smaller firms in the same sector. However, the difference is only statistically significant for the nonEPZ sector. In addition, we cannot reject the null hypothesis of a uniform firm survival probability above and below the threshold in the EPZ sector. Therefore, survival probability does not change significantly by firm size in the EPZ, but small nonEPZ firms do face a higher probability of failure compared to other nonEPZ firms. However, the biggest and most significant differences in survival probability is the higher exit rate in nonEPZ relative to EPZ firms of equal initial size and vintage.

5.1.2 Placebo tests
We reestimated the model of firm employment growth used in Table 4 but using alternate artificial threshold sizes of $L_{it} = 20$ and $L_{it} = 30$. For these placebo regressions, we limit the sample to firms above 14 workers to take out the effect of the actual threhold. The results are reported in Table 6 with the Table 4 results repeated in the first column. The results in column 1 are very different from those in the last two columns. Probability of firm growth in the nonEPZ sector below the threshold are now not significantly different from the probability at the placibo threshold (at the threshold of 20) or positive (at the threshold of 30) rather than negative. The differences in growth rates for nonEPZ firms above and below the threshold are now only 4–5 percentage points compared to the 21 percentage points using the true thresholds. However, the EPZ firms continue to have a growth advantage over their nonEPZ counterparts consistent with the expected lower cost of employment expansion in the EPZ sector at all employment levels. In addition, EPZ firms grow at equal rates above and below the placebo thresholds which is consistent with the expected growth pattern for the EPZ sector for firms above the true threshold. In short, the EPZ firms continue to act as expected with the placebo thresholds while the nonEPZ firms look markedly different from their behavior about the true thresholds. These findings buttress the validity of the findings in Table 4.

6 Conclusion
Numerous studies have explained the effect of labor market restriction on unemployment, employment growth and wage inequality in OECD countries. This study extends

Table 6 Reduced form and structural estimates of the probability of employment growth conditional on prior employment level inside and outside Enterprise Protection Zones as per equation (6) using Probit model with cluster robust standard errors

Reduced form parameters: $EPZ_i = 1$	$T = 14^a$ from Table 4	Placebo 1: $T = 20^a$ Sample excludes $L_{it} < 15$	Placebo 2: $T = 30^a$ Sample excludes $L_{it} < 15$
$L_{it} \leq T{-}1,\ E_{it}^{L^-} = 1:\ \beta_{L^-} + \beta_{EPZ} + \gamma_{L^-}$	0.09** (0.02)	0.23*** (0.05)	0.25*** (0.03)
$L_{it} = T:\ \beta_{EPZ}$	0.12* (0.08)	0.31*** (0.10)	0.36*** (0.10)
$L_{it} \geq T+1,\ E_{it}^{L^+} = 1:\ \beta_{L^+} + \beta_{EPZ} + \gamma_{L^+}$	0.19** (0.02)	0.20*** (0.01)	0.22*** (0.01)
Reduced form parameters: $EPZ_i = 0$			
$L_{it} \leq T{-}1,\ E_{it}^{L^-} = 1:\ \beta_{L^-}$	-0.17** (0.02)	0.01 (0.01)	0.04*** (0.01)
$L_{it} = T:$ reference	–	–	–
$L_{it} \geq T+1,\ E_{it}^{L^+} = 0:\ \beta_{L^+}$	0.048** (0.01)	0.049*** (0.01)	0.08*** (0.01)
Structural estimates			
Hypothesis: Relative to nonEPZ firms of like size and vintage[b]			
$\beta_{EPZ} > 0$: EPZ firms grow faster at the threshold	0.123** (224)	0.31** (5.7)	0.36** (18)
$\beta_{EPZ} + \gamma_{L^-} > 0$: EPZ firms grow faster below the threshold	0.255** (161)	0.219** (21.63)	0.21** (49.4)
$\beta_{EPZ} + \gamma_{L^+} > 0$: EPZ firms grow faster above the threshold	0.142** (2952)	0.15** (131)	0.14** (101)
Hypothesis: Relative to same sector firms below the threshold[b]			
$\beta_{L^+} - \beta_{L^-} > 0$: nonEPZ firms grow faster above the threshold	0.214** (21)	0.048** (22.6)	0.04** (17.65)
$(\beta_{L^+} + \gamma_{L^+}) - (\beta_{L^-} + \gamma_{L^-}) > 0$: EPZ firms grow faster above the threshold	0.101** (42)	-0.03 (42)	-0.03 (0.60)
Hypothesis: Relative to EPZ firms at the threshold[b]			
$\gamma_{L^-} = 0$: EPZ firms grow at a different rate below the threshold	0.133* (3.5)	−0.08 (3.5)	−0.15 (0.14)
$\gamma_{L^+} = 0$: EPZ firms grow at a different rate above the threshold	0.020 (0.01)	−0.15 (0.01)	−0.22 (0.43)

[a]Marginal effect reproted with attached standard error in parenthesis.
[b]Marginal effect reported with attached Chi-square statistic in parentheses. Critical value is 3.84 at the .05 significance level.
*significance at the 0.1 level, **significance at the .05 level, ***significance at the .01 level.
EPZ: Export Promotion Zone.

this inquiry to the case of employment protection in a developing country context, namely the TEWA in Sri Lanka. The program imposes severance costs on firms with 15 or more workers in Sri Lanka, but not on smaller firms or firms in export promotion zones (EPZ).

We find that the size distribution of firms differs dramatically across the EPZ and nonEPZ sectors, with 76% of nonEPZ firms having less than 15 workers while 77% of EPZ firms have at least 15 employees. Using panel data on employment in the universe of formal sector firms in Sri Lanka from 1995 to 2003, we found evidence that 62% of EPZ firms open for business with at least 15 employees compared to only 9% of nonEPZ firms. That implies that disproportionate sorting of large firms into EPZ explains about 80% of the gap in firm size distribution across EPZ and nonEPZ sectors. Moreover, EPZ firms above the threshold are 14 percentage points more likely to add workers than are comparably sized nonEPZ firms, while EPZ firms below the threshold have an astounding 26 percentage point higher probability of growing relative to their nonEPZ counterparts. While the large firm share of nonEPZ firms rises over time, even that turns out to be due to poor outcomes in the nonEPZ sector. Small nonEPZ firms are slightly more likely to exit than nonEPZ firms which lowers the small firm share of all nonEPZ firms over time. In fact, small and large nonEPZ firms are 10 percentage points more likely to die than are their EPZ counterparts of like size and vintage.

The totality of the evidence suggests that the TEWA restrictions on firing that were supposed to increase employment stability had exactly the opposite result. By imposing a tax on firm growth, the system causes nonEPZ firms to inefficiently limit employment, increasing the odds that the firm will fail. While large firms atypically sort into the EPZ and avoid the regulatory expenses, a significant number of firms are caught by the regulatory costs. Results suggest that these firms would hire more workers and be more likely to succeed if nonEPZ and EPZ firms operated under the same, more liberal rules regarding the costs of hiring and firing.

Endnotes

[1] Sri Lanka data were compiled from the universe of formal sector firms in Sri Lanka described later in the paper.

[2] Freeman (2008) presents a review of both theoretical and empirical effects of labor market institutions. Addison and Teixeira (2001) review findings regarding the effects of employment protection legislation.

[3] The rationale for the policy, as stated in the Industrial Policy of Ceylon (1971), was that "....the [Government] is pledged to the establishment of a socialist society. This commitment calls for major changes in industrial policy to eliminate some of the social and economic consequences of the policy followed in the past few years [such as] the concentration of monopoly power in the hands of a few investors, leading to gross inequalities in the distribution of income and the entrenchment of privileged groups in society ... [and] the heavy reliance of local industry on imported raw material, components and technology. . . .".

[4] Incompetence is not considered a disciplinary matter. Even in the case of disciplinary layoffs due to misconduct or poor discipline, the employer must inform the worker in writing of the reasons for such termination before the second day after such termination, failing which, the worker is entitled to seek redress under the TEWA on the basis that the termination of his services was not for disciplinary reasons.

[5] The others were an unreliable supply of electricity; uncertain government policy; macroeconomic instability; and the high cost of obtaining external financing (World Bank 2005).

[6] We should note that we have no evidence that the application for EPZ status is anything but above board. We are just trying to be complete in allowing for supra-normal application costs.

[7] The technology shock could also include innovations in the real price of output. To economize on terms, we fix the output price at unity and let all changes in the value of labor time work their way through productivity shocks.

[8] Ashenfelter and Card (1982) showed that wages evolve according to an AR(1) process with first-order coefficient insignificantly different from 1, and so the random walk assumption is not a radical departure from reality.

[9] In the Cobb-Douglas formulation used here, and with the restriction that capital is fixed, the second best solution is to set employment at 14. A more general specification could result in the second best employment level at less than 14.

[10]In practice, our main parameters of interest were not sensitive to the inclusion or exclusion of these cohort and firm-specific entry conditions.

Competing interests
The IZA Journal of Labor & Development is committed to the IZA Guiding Principles of Research Integrity. The authors declare that they have observed these principles.

Acknowledgements
The authors wish to thank the Central Bank of Sri Lanka for providing data and to Ramani Gunatilaka for providing useful comments to earlier drafts of the paper.
Responsible editor: David Lam

Author details
[1]Department of Agricultural Economics, Extension and Rural Development, University of Pretoria, Pretoria 0002, South Africa. [2]IZA and Department of Economics, Iowa State University, Ames, IA 50010, USA. [3]IZA, International School for Social and Business Studies, Celje, Slovenia and University of Primorska, Faculty of Management, Koper, Slovenia.

References
Addison JT, Teixeira P (2001) "The Economics of Employment Protection". In: IZA Discussion Paper no. 381. Institute for the Study of Labor, Bonn, Germany
Ahsan A, Pages C (2009) Are All Labor Regulations Equal? Evidence from Indian Manufacturing. J Comp Econ 37(1):62–75
Arkolakis C (2013) A Unified Theory of Firm Selection and Growth. Yale University Working Paper, New Haven, CT
Ashenfelter O, Card D (1982) Time Series Representations of Economic Variables and Alternative Models for the Labour Market. Review Econ Stud 49(1):761–781
Baker D, Glyn A, Howell D, Schmitt J (2005) "Labor Market Institutions and Unemployment: A Critical Assessment of the Cross-Country Evidence". In Fighting Unemployment: The Limits of Free Market Orthodoxy, ed. David R. Howell. Oxford University Press, Oxford
Bassanini A, Duval R (2006) "Employment Patterns In OECD Countries: Reassessing the Role of Policies and Institutions". In: OECD Economics Department Working Paper No. 486
Besley T, Burgess R (2004) Can Labor Regulation Hinder Economic Performance? Evidence from India. Q J Econ 119(1):91–134
Cabral L (1995) Sunk Costs, Firm Size and Firm Growth. J Ind Econ 43(2):161–172
Evans DS (1987) The Relationship Between Firm Growth, Size, and Age: Estimates for 100 Manufacturing Industries. J Ind Econ 35(4):567–581
Freeman RB (2008) Labor Market Institutions around the World. In: Blyton P, Bacon N, Fiorito J, Heery E (eds) The SAGE Handbook of Industrial Relations. SAGE Publications Ltd., London
Haffner R, Nickell S, Nicoletti G, Scarpetta S, Zoega G (2001) "European Integration, Liberalization and Labour Market Performance". In: Bertola G, Boeri T, Nicoletti G (eds) Welfare and Employment in a United Europe. The MIT Press, Cambridge, MA
Heckman JJ, Pages C (2000) The Cost of Job Security Regulation: Evidence from Latin American Labor Markets. Economia 1(1):109–154
Leidholm C, Mead D (1987) "Small-Scale Industries in Developing Countries: Empirical Evidence and Policy Implications". In: International Development Paper 9. Agricultural Economics Department, Michigan State University,
Nickell S, Layard R (1999) "Labor Market Institutions and Economic Performance". In: Ashenfelter O, Card D (eds) Handbook of Labor Economics, vol 3, chapter 46, 1st edn. Elsevier, Amsterdam pp 3029–3084
OECD (1999) OECD Employment Outlook 1999. OECD, Paris
Ranaraja S (2005) "The Functioning of the Termination of Employment Act Of 1971". In: World Bank, HDNSP, processed
Singh T (2010) Does international trade cause economic growth? A survey. World Econ 33(11):1517–1564
Wagner J (2007) Exports and productivity: A survey of the evidence from firm-level data. World Econ 30(1):60–82
Wagner J (2012) International trade and firm performance: a survey of empirical studies since 2006. Rev World Econ 148(2):235–267
World Bank (2005) "Sri Lanka: Improving The Rural And Urban Investment Climate". In: World Bank, Poverty Reduction and Economic Management Network, South Asia Region
World Bank (2007) "Sri Lanka: Strengthening Social Protection". In: World Bank, Human Development Unit, South Asia Region, Report No. 38197-LK

5

Court-ship, *kinship* and *business*: a study on the interaction between the formal and the informal institutions and its effect on entrepreneurship

Tanika Chakraborty[1]*, Anirban Mukherjee[2] and Sarani Saha[1]

*Correspondence: tanika@iitk.ac.in
[1] Indian Institute of Technology, Kanpur, India
Full list of author information is available at the end of the article

Abstract

In this paper we theoretically and empirically examine how the interaction between the formal court system and the informal loan network affects a household's decision to start a business. We find that when the formal court system is weak, expansion of informal credit network leads to the proliferation of business. However, with a sufficiently strong court system, expansion of the credit network has a negative effect on business prospects. This result is explained by the contradictions between formal laws and norms used by informal networks.

JEL codes: K12; L26; O17

Keywords: Informal network; Court; Formal institution; Entrepreneurship

1 Introduction

Effective contract enforcement is the key to the process of economic development. A contract can be enforced by the formal legal court or by informal community courts, for instance *panchayats* in South Asia. In less developed societies both types of institutions co-exist, often coming in each others way. These conflicts are well documented in the context of the marriage market and common property management (Chowdhry 2004; Keremane et al. 2006; Madsen 1991; Nagraj 2010; Yadav 2009). However, till date there has not been any study that analyzes and estimates the effect of such interactions on economic decision making. In this paper we look at the effect of the interaction between the informal loan network and formal court system on the decision to run a business using both analytical and quantitative methods. We find that the informal network helps in business proliferation when the formal court system is weak. However, when the formal court system improves sufficiently, business might fall in areas with strong informal networks.

Our paper is related to a vast body of literature that studies the effect of institutions on economic development. There is a consensus among economists that better institutions encourage capital accumulation and subsequent growth (Acemoglu et al. 2001, 2002; Rajan and Zingales 1998). However, the existing empirical literature on the effectiveness of formal institutions mostly look at the institutions of property rights which prevent the elites from expropriating. One exception is Acemoglu and Johnson (2003), who distinguish between the effects of property rights institutions and contracting institutions on growth. Using a cross country data set, they find that while good property rights institutions have a positive effect on growth, the effect of contracting institutions is not robust. This result is counter intuitive, and one possible reason could be that their data, which only measures the quality of formal contracting institutions, fails to account for the role of informal network based institutions, ubiquitous in many developing countries. Evidence shows that in the absence of effective formal courts of law, business often thrives under the informal institutions (Biggs and Shah 2006; McMillan and Woodruff 1999). In a related paper, Harriss-White (2010) finds that in absence of effective formal institutions, Indian SMEs are largely regulated by what she calls "social regulation." This is nothing but informal institutions working through community networks and reputation mechanisms. The caste system prevailing in India can also be seen as a grand framework of contract enforcement using the reputation mechanism (Freitas 2006). The key to the success of such reputation based mechanisms is information about one's past action (therefore reputation) flowing in the community network (Ghosh and Ray 1996; Rosenthal and Landau 1979; Kandori 1992). Many credit institutions in less developed countries, such as ROSCA in East Asia (Besley et al. 1993) and Grameen Bank in Bangladesh (Ghatak 1991), crucially depend on such information flow within communities. The use of community level information for enforcing contracts was also ubiquitous in medieval Europe (Greif et al. 1994; Greif 1993; Slivinski and Sussman 2009).

Besides the general literature on institutions and its impact on economic growth, this paper is also related to the role of networks in credit provisioning. Network membership, which is often characterized by caste or ethnicity, may work both in positive and negative ways. A number of studies found in the African context that community membership can increase the probability of getting a loan if one's own community controls the supply of loans (Biggs and Srivastava 2002; Fafchamps 2000,2003, Fisman 2003; Gajigo and Foltz 2010). On the other hand, it may decrease the probability of getting loans if the credit granting authority has any negative bias towards the credit applicants ethnicity. This result has been confirmed by various studies in the context of the United States (Blanchflower et al. 2003; Fairlie and Robb 2007).

However, most of the literature on institutions look at formal and informal institutions as separate phases of development – the informal system getting replaced by the formal ones in due course of development (La Porta and Shleifer 2014). At best, some authors have adopted a dual sector approach – making formal and informal two parallel sets of rules without interfering with one another (Straub 2005). But in reality, formal and informal institutions interact and mutually constitute each other. Evidence suggests that social capital affects formal economic behavior like financial decisions. Luigi et al. (2004) find that in Italy people are more likely to use formal checks, invest less in cash and more in stocks, have higher access to institutional credit and make less use of informal credit in areas of high social capital. The effect of social capital is stronger in areas with weaker legal enforcements. In a similar line of research, Karlan (2005) uses an experimental approach to find the effect of social capital on financial decisions. The interaction between formal institutions and informal norms also plays a role in the management of common property resources. For example, Sandner (2003) looked at the interaction between formal institutions and norms of the Kuna community in Central America for preservation of marine resources. He shows that erosion of norms and insufficient development of formal institutions can lead to over exploitation of marine resources.

The interaction between formal and informal institutions is particularly important in less developed countries. In these countries *de facto practices* are quite different from *de jure rules* – and these differences are often shaped by the interaction between formal and informal institutions. The only theoretical exposition of such interactions that we have come across is Dixit (2004) where he argues that the development of the formal may have a detrimental effect on the informal mechanisms. The informal system relies heavily on the reputation mechanism, where someone with a reputation of cheating does not get a job within his/her community. People using formal contracts however do not care about reputation – punishment under formal contracting is direct and enforced by a third party (fine, imprisonment). Hence one can always cheat someone using the informal contract and then find their next employment with another employer using a formal contract.

On the empirical front there has been much less research on this issue. One of the few papers related to relevance of institutions in affecting business decisions is Chemin (2012). He finds that reforms in the civil court procedure leads to lower breaches of contract, higher access to capital and building of new capacity in India. However, what Chemin finds is an average effect of more efficient courts. His research does not answer whether the effect is different for areas with different initial conditions in terms of informal institutions (such as the presence of *caste panchayat*). We claim that the effect of better legislation on business decisions will critically depend on these initial conditions. Another closely related paper is Klapper et al. (2006). Their study, based on 34 Eastern and Western European countries, find that higher requirements to comply with formal bureaucratic regulation prevents new businesses from entering the industry by increasing entry cost.

The main contention of our paper is that formal and informal institutions might come in the way of each other, producing undesired results in places where traditional, community based dispute resolving systems are widespread. We define a business in terms of a contract where a contractor agrees to supply certain inputs to an entrepreneur. The quality of the input cannot be verified beforehand or by any third party, creating a possible moral hazard problem. The only way to punish a cheater contractor is to fire him and deny him any future employment opportunity. Hence, we have a structure similar to Shapiro and Stiglitz (1984) and Greif (1993), where the only way to prevent cheating is to pay the cheater contractor an honesty-inducing price for his input so that he finds that cheating pays off is less than the honesty pay-off.

The entrepreneurs can come from a traditional producer community or someone coming from outside the community. The latter group can only enter the market if the formal contracting institutions are of sufficiently good quality. For entrepreneurs belonging to the traditional community, the community norm requires them to boycott a contractor who cheated any community member. This makes the cost of cheating someone very high for the contractor, depressing the honesty inducing price of his input supplies.

We argue that in the presence of an effective formal system, the capacity to punish declines in the informal system. This is precisely because a strong formal system allows entrepreneurs from outside the community to enter the market who do not abide by the community norm of not hiring a past cheater. This makes it easy for a cheater contractor (who cheated a community member in the past) to find employment with an entrepreneur who does not belong to the community. This increases the honesty inducing price for the input, pushing the entrepreneurs with small capital stock out of the market.

Our theoretical model suggests that in areas with strong networks, an honesty inducing input price is low, accommodating small entrepreneurs in the system. But as formal systems improve (and consequently the input price rises), these areas are the worst hit as facing the rising input prices, the entrepreneurs are forced to quit the market.

We use the India Human Development Survey (IHDS) 2004-2005 to test our theoretical predictions. In accordance with the theoretical predictions, our empirical evidence suggests that business is affected by the interplay of formal institutions and informal norms. Specifically, when formal institutions are strong enough, we find that the probability of doing business is lower in the presence of a large informal network. Given the cross-sectional nature of the data, we should be careful in interpreting our results as causal.

However, this inference does not suggest the preservation of the informal institutions by limiting the power of the formal courts. It rather emphasizes the possibility of jeopardizing the expansion of business by imposing a rapid expansion of the formal contracting system. There is no point in denying that improvement in formal contracting enhances efficiency and social mobility by allowing contractors without any family/community connection to enter the market. However, the preexistence of a strong informal institutional framework, captured by large community networks, makes the rapid institutional switch socially costly as it may exclude people from participating in the market. Most importantly, the exclusion comes from the high cost of accessing the formal institutions. Given the efficiency property of formal institutions, the most logical implication of our research is to reduce the cost of formal contracting.

The rest of the paper is organized as follows. Section 2 presents the analytical model, Section 3 outlines the empirical framework, Section 4 summarizes the data used to test the implications of our model, Section 5 reports the empirical findings and, finally, Section 6 concludes.

2　Model

2.1　Agents: contractors and entrepreneurs

There is a pool of potential entrepreneurs who produce a good G. For producing the good G, they need an input X, which is supplied by a set of contractors who come from a traditional X producing community C. The entrepreneurs however may come from both the traditional community (C) and outside community (NC). The production of the input requires high skill, but only a fraction of the community C has the skill – we call them High type contractors. The rest of the contractors, who we call Low type, do not have the necessary skill to supply the input. Therefore, if a low type is chosen, the entrepreneur makes zero profit. Whether a contractor is High type is common knowledge within the C community but not outside. So when a contractor from C community asks for work, a typical NC entrepreneur cannot tell whether the contractor has the appropriate skill. This however is common knowledge for a C entrepreneur For an NC entrepreneur, the first problem is that of adverse selection – to be able to distinguish between the High and the Low type.

However, there is a second level problem as well – the problem of moral hazard. Even after a High type contractor is selected, he may supply bad quality input as it saves effort for the contractor. Note that using a bad quality input for producing G is better than hiring a Low type contractor. A Low type contractor is a fraud who does not have the skill to produce the input even of bad quality. Hence, from an entrepreneur's perspective, a High type supplying bad quality input yields a better outcome than hiring a Low type contractor who cannot supply any input. We write the condition as follows:

$$0 < \kappa < \pi^B < \pi^G, \tag{1}$$

where κ is the reservation income of the entrepreneur. π^j is his income by hiring the high type contractor, where the contractor supplies quality j input ($j = B, G$). If the entrepreneur hires the Low type contractor, he gets 0 profit, which is less than his reservation pay-off. Hence, while choosing a contractor faces two types of problems, the first one is a typical problem of adverse selection, and the second one is of moral hazard.

Before proceeding further let us discuss why both the moral hazard and adverse selection problems are necessary for the formulation of our model.

The moral hazard and the adverse selection problems bring out the role that two types of institutions – formal and informal – play. Let us first take the case of the moral hazard problem where a contractor can shirk. The only punishment for cheating is not hiring a cheater again. For entrepreneurs belonging to the entrepreneurial caste, if one entrepreneur is cheated, all entrepreneurs belonging to the caste boycott the cheater contractor. This makes the punishment cost of cheating a caste entrepreneur more than cheating a non-caste member. The informal institutions in this case take the form of information flow within the community. This information advantage allows the caste entrepreneurs to impose the punishment on a cheating contractor. This is not possible in the case of non-caste entrepreneurs due to the lack of credible information. Instead, the non-caste members who cannot go to informal institutions solve the moral hazard problem simply by paying a higher honesty-inducing wage than their caste member counterpart. Note that this analysis does not require modeling of formal institutions.

The adverse selection problem, on the other hand, arises in the model because, ex-ante, it is not possible to distinguish between the Low and the High type. Here comes the role of formal institutions. The formal institutions of contract enforcement are essentially third party enforcement (court, police etc). They solve this problem by punishing a Low type contractor who poses as the High type contractor. The higher is the quality of the formal institutions, the higher is the probability of catching and punishing a Low type mimicking a High type. Therefore, the quality of formal institutions enters our analysis through the channel of the adverse selection problem, making the adverse selection problem crucial to our theory. Both the moral hazard and adverse selection problems are important in our analysis because they are solved by the informal and formal institutions respectively.

The entrepreneurs can be characterized in two dimensions: community identity and endowment. An entrepreneur i is endowed with business skill, or capital, θ_i, and the endowment is distributed according to the distribution ϕ. An entrepreneur i's output y_i is positively related to his endowment. There is another dimension of any entrepreneur – either he belongs to a traditional business community (C) or does not belong to that community (NC). However, the distributions for θ are the same for C and NC type entrepreneurs. The main difference between C and NC types is in terms of accessing informal institutions. Only C type entrepreneurs can access the informal network for adjudicating any dispute with the contractors. However, both C and NC type entrepreneurs can access the formal court. Note that the quality of an input (good or bad) cannot be verified by the court. Hence, the court is only useful if a Low type contractor misrepresented himself as a High type and took money for supplying the input.

The entrepreneur faces two levels of problems. Finding a High type is the first level of the problem. In the second level, the entrepreneur has to ensure that the High type is not behaving opportunistically – i.e., not supplying bad input after being hired.

2.2 Institutions

Let us now elaborate the role of institutions in solving the problems faced by the entrepreneurs. There are two types of contracting institutions available in the economy. One is formal courts characterized by third party enforcement and the second is informal networks characterized by reputation based mechanisms. In what follows, we discuss the different roles played by the formal versus informal institutions in solving the problem of asymmetric information faced by the entrepreneurs.

2.3 Adverse selection problem: the role of court

We have already mentioned that there are two types of problems that an entrepreneur faces: Low type posing as High type, and after recruitment, high type supplying bad quality input. From the entrepreneur's point of view, a low type contractor (who can only supply zero input) is worse than hiring a high type who supplies bad quality. There are two ways of catching and punishing a Low type.

The informal network of C members possesses the information regarding its member's skillfulness, i.e., everybody in the community knows which member in the community does not have the necessary training to produce X. Hence, no Low type contractor is hired by a C type entrepreneur. In other words, belonging to the community network solves the problem of adverse selection for a C entrepreneur. But NC entrepreneurs cannot access this information about the true type of the contractor, ex-ante. Instead, the NC entrepreneurs can sign a formal contract with a potential contractor, and if he turns out to be the Low type, they can file a lawsuit against the Low type posing as High and get the Low type punished with probability σ, where, σ is the quality of the formal court. Hence, with a sufficiently strong formal court, Low type community members will not pose as a High type member. In general, mimicking the High type is not worthwhile for the Low type if

$$\sigma(P - M) + (1 - \sigma)(P) < 0, \tag{2}$$

where P is the price that the low type gets by posing as the High type, and M is the penalty he pays if he gets caught. The reservation pay-off of the Low type is 0. The condition tells us that there will be no Low type posing as High type if

$$\sigma > \frac{P}{M} = \sigma^* \tag{3}$$

For $\sigma < \sigma^*$ the quality of formal institutions is so bad that Low types can mimic High types and get away with it. This makes the NC type entrepreneurs find that it is not worthwhile to join the market. For low enough *sigma*, all Low types mimic as high types, and given that C type entrepreneurs already know who is Low type, there is a very high probability that NC type entrepreneurs are matched with Low type. This leads to our first theorem:

Theorem 2.1. *For a sufficiently high quality of formal institutions (σ^*), Low types do not find it worthwhile to mimic the High type, and as a result, NC entrepreneurs enter the market.*

2.4 The moral hazard problem

Unlike adverse selection, the moral hazard problem however cannot be solved by any third party as the quality of the input is not verifiable by the third party. Only the entrepreneur can find out the quality of the input, and the punishment she can inflict is not hiring a cheater contractor for subsequent periods. The monetary value of the punishment can be measured by a wage that a contractor loses if he is fired. We follow the efficiency wage theory framework proposed by Shapiro and Stiglitz (1984) and Greif (1993) for analyzing the solution to the moral hazard problem.

We start with the case where ($\sigma < \sigma^*$), and only C type entrepreneurs operate. C entrepreneurs solve the adverse selection problem of selecting the High type through the information network. Hence, they face the moral hazard problem only – the problem of ensuring that High type supplies good quality input. The entrepreneur can solve the problem by offering a payment to the contractor so that the cheating pay-off is less than the honesty pay-off. This section is modeled after Greif (1993).

The contractor supplies one unit of the input to the entrepreneur and gets a payment ρ. If he supplies bad quality input, he saves some cost η but at the end of the period gets fired. However, there is an exogenous probability of terminating the contract given by q. In that case, if the contractor is honest, he is hired again. For characterizing the honesty inducing equilibrium, we define the following expressions:

The pay-off for an honest agent is given by

$$V_h = \rho + \beta(1-q)V_h + qV_h^u \tag{4}$$

This shows that the lifetime payoff of an honest contractor can be divided in to current and future pay-offs. In the current period an honest agent gets factor payment ρ. In the next period, however, she might get fired for an exogenous reason with probability q and continue to get V_h^u – the lifetime pay off of an honest unemployed agent. On the other hand, the agent may stay in the job with probability $1 - q$ and continue to earn an honest employed agent's pay-off – V_h. The future pay offs are discounted by the discount rate β.

By cheating, an agent gets a one time pay-off η in the current period. However, this one time payment comes at the cost of losing his job at the end of the current period. From the next period onwards he gets the pay-off of an unemployed cheater. An unemployed cheater can be rehired with probability p_c in the next period and get V_h. With probability $(1 - p_c)$ a cheater is not re-hired, and he gets reservation wage ($\overline{\omega}$). The pay-off for an unemployed cheater, V_c^u, is summarized by the following equation:

$$V_c^u = \beta p_c V_h + \beta(1 - p_c)\left(\overline{\omega} + V_c^u\right) \tag{5}$$

An honest agent can also lose her job for exogenous reasons. However, she may be rehired with probability p_h in the next period and get V_h. On the other hand, with probability $(1 - p_h)$ she may remain unemployed and get $\left(\overline{\omega} + V_h^u\right)$ – reservation pay-off plus life time utility of an honest unemployed agent.

$$V_h^u = \beta p_h V_h + \beta(1 - p_h)\left(\overline{\omega} + V_h^u\right) \tag{6}$$

The payment to a contractor (ρ) that prevents her from cheating must satisfy the condition

$$V_h \geq \eta + V_c^u \tag{7}$$

It is easy to understand that no entrepreneur has any incentive to pay a ρ more than the minimum honesty-inducing payment.

Theorem 2.2. *A contractor's honesty inducing payment is rising in the probability of rehiring a cheater agent.*

We provide the formal proof in the appendix. But the intuition of this theorem is quite straight forward. The only punishment an entrepreneur can inflict is firing the agent, which involves the monetary cost of the forgone payment. If the cheater agents can easily be rehired, the cost of losing the current job is low. In that case the input price (that he misses because of getting fired) needs to be big enough to prevent one from cheating. So we have $\rho^* = \rho(p_c), \rho' > 0$. We assume that community members will not appoint a contractor who has cheated another community member, i.e., in the environment where all the entrepreneurs are type C, we get $p_c = 0$. This is possible due to the flow of information within the community of a C type entrepreneur. However, an NC type contractor cannot access any such information. Hence, she cannot distinguish between an agent who cheated in the past and the one who did not. For her $p_c = p_h > 0$, this leads to the next corollary:

Corollary 2.3. *The honesty inducing payment for the contractors hired by NC entrepreneurs is higher than that for the ones hired by the C entrepreneurs.*

2.5   The interaction effect

First we analyze how the improvements in the formal court system affects the C type entrepreneurs. The improvements in the formal court system do not directly affect C type entrepreneurs. It affects the C type by facilitating the entry of the NC type. NC type entrepreneurs can only enter the market if the formal institutions are good enough to solve the adverse selection problem. Hence, a good court allows the NC entrepreneurs to enter the market. Once in the market, the NC entrepreneurs solve the moral hazard problem the same way the C entrepreneurs solve the problem, i.e., paying the honesty-inducing price. But the entry of NC entrepreneurs will have an indirect impact on the C entrepreneurs as the equilibrium price for the input will go up, reducing the profit margin of the existing C entrepreneurs. This determines the number of C entrepreneurs. Who are the C entrepreneurs running businesses? The entrepreneurs with endowment θ_i will be in business such that

$$\pi_i(\theta_i) \geq \rho^*, \tag{8}$$

where ρ^* is the equilibrium price for the input. Solving (8) for equality, we get the lowest endowment entrepreneur that can be in the business $\widetilde{\theta} = \theta(\rho^*)$, where $\widetilde{\theta}$ is rising in ρ^*. From this we get our next proposition

Theorem 2.4. *The cut-off endowment level of the entrepreneurs is a function of the input price, and the cut-off goes up as the input price goes up*

If the equilibrium input price (ρ^*) goes up, only the entrepreneurs with sufficiently high endowment can stay in the market. As the input price goes up following the entry of the NC type entrepreneurs, the cut-off endowment level goes up. Let us now look at the volume of business following the entry of the NC entrepreneurs. Entry of the NC entrepreneurs increases the number of NC business, but it decreases the number of the C entrepreneurs as the cut-off endowment level gets revised upwards. Hence, theoretically, the net effect is ambiguous, making the empirical investigation important.

Suppose the number of possible community entrepreneurs is M_c. In period 0 we do not have any NC entrepreneur in the market. So the number of businesses is equal to the probability that a potential C entrepreneur will start a business times M_C. Suppose in period 0 the cut off endowment level was θ_0. Hence the total number of businesses is given by

$$B_0 = M_C \times (1 - \Phi(\theta_0)) \tag{9}$$

In period 1, NC entrepreneurs enter, and as a result, input price goes up, moving the cut-off endowment level to $\theta_1 > \theta_0$ for both C and NC entrepreneurs as they both face the same input price. Hence, while new entrants (NC entrepreneurs) add to the volume of business, the quitting community entrepreneurs reduce it, making the net effect ambiguous. Assume that the pool of potential NC entrepreneurs is M_N. The volume of NC businesses is given by

$$B_1^N = M_N \times (1 - \Phi(\theta_1)) \tag{10}$$

The number of community businesses in period 1 is given by

$$B_1^C = M_C \times (1 - \Phi(\theta_1)) \tag{11}$$

Hence, total business in period 1 is given by

$$B_1 = M_N \times (1 - \Phi(\theta_1)) + M_C \times (1 - \Phi(\theta_1)) \tag{12}$$

The change in business is given by

$$B_1 - B_0 = M_N (1 - \Phi(\theta_1)) - M_C (\Phi(\theta_1) - \Phi(\theta_0)) \tag{13}$$

From this we get $B_0 \lessgtr B_1$ according to

$$\frac{M_N}{M_C} \gtrless \frac{(\Phi(\theta_1) - \Phi(\theta_0)}{(1 - \Phi(\theta_1))} \tag{14}$$

Theoretically we do not have any clear cut answer as to whether entry of NC entrepreneurs will lead to an increase or decrease in the number of businesses. This depends on the relative size of the pool of C and NC entrepreneurs and the shape of the endowment distribution. The larger is the value of M_C compared to M_N, the more likely it is that with the improvement in the formal institutions (and consequently entry of the NC entrepreneurs), total number of businesses will fall. This will happen when the new entry will not be sufficient to cover for the exit of the community entrepreneurs. In other words, the entrants come from the upper tail of the endowment distribution, while the quitters come from the lower tail. Hence, total business will shrink if the lower tail is denser than the upper tail. This should be the case for a less developed country characterized by inequality, where the number of people belonging to the upper wealth percentile is less than that in the lower percentile.

Next we review the interaction effect between the formal and the informal institutions and its effect on the volume of business. In the previous sections we have assumed that there is one homogeneous community network where the probability of rehiring a cheater is zero. We now extend this set up by introducing heterogeneity in terms of community network. We assume that there are n districts, and each district j is characterized by network size v_j. We further assume that the probability of rehiring a cheater is a falling function of the network size

$$p_c^j = g(v_j), \tag{15}$$

where $g' < 0$. This assumption implies that in a district characterized by big network, a large number of people know about one's cheating history, and the cheater finds it difficult to get a job. Let us now elaborate how the improvements in the formal court system affects districts with different degrees of networks differently.

In other words, we examine the role of interaction between the existing informal network mechanism and the formal institutions in determining the volume of business. In period 0, the larger the network, lower is the probability for a cheater contractor to be rehired, and lower is the input price. Hence, in a district characterized by a larger network, the cutoff endowment level for the C entrepreneurs is lower than that in a district with a smaller network. This means

$$\theta_0 = \theta(v), \tag{16}$$

where v represents the size of the network and $\theta'(v) < 0$. This means that the value of θ_0 is low in high network districts. Given that θ_1 is determined by the cut-off level of the NC entrepreneurs, which has nothing to do with the existing network size, the expression $(\Phi(\theta_1) - \Phi(\theta_0))$ is rising in the network size. Since the size of the quitting businesses is rising in $(\Phi(\theta_1) - \Phi(\theta_0))$, we get the following theorem

Theorem 2.5. *If formal institutions improve, sufficiently allowing the NC entrepreneurs to set up business, the reduction in the community businesses will be higher in high network districts than that in the low network districts. If the negative impact of the quitting C entrepreneurs is strong enough, this will lead to greater reduction in the total volume of business in the districts with higher networks.*

We next turn to the empirical section to test the implications of our model using data from India.

3 Empirical specification

Empirically, a way to test the theoretical predictions would be to estimate a regression of the probability of doing business on the the interaction between formal and informal institutions using panel data. A panel setting would enable us to estimate the effect of introducing formal institutions in an economy with pre-existing informal institutions. However, in the absence of any longitudinal information, we only provide suggestive evidence on our theoretical predictions. Specifically, we compare districts with varying degrees of informal and formal institutions using cross sectional data. In particular, we estimate the following specification:

$$P(SE)_{id} = \beta_0 + \beta_1 IN_d * FC_d + \beta_2 IN_d + \beta_3 FC_d + X_{id} + \epsilon_{id}, \quad (17)$$

where $P(SE)_{id}$ reflects the probability with which a household i in district d chooses to be self-employed over being wage employed. IN_d is a proxy for the quality of informal institutions in district d. FC_d is a proxy for the quality of formal institutions in district d. The interaction between IN_d and FC_d is our main variable of interest. According to theoretical predictions of our model, a positive β_2 would imply that a higher proportion of households choose to do business when the informal network is large, which thereby helps to facilitate information flow within the network. Additionally, β_1 captures the impact of formal institutions on the relationship between informal institutions and self-employment. Specifically, a negative β_1 would imply that when the quality of formal institutions increasess businesses would exit from areas with a greater prevalence of informal institutions. Similarly, β_3 captures the independent effect of the quality of formal institutions on probability of self employment. A positive β_3 implies that as the quality of formal institution improves, businesses would flourish as it enables some new entrepreneurs to enter the market.

Note however that informal and formal institutions might evolve endogenously at the district level. One way to deal with this could be to use historical data to capture the introduction of the formal court system.[1] However, we cannot adopt this approach due to the paucity of such data. Instead, we try to control for a range of household and district level controls captured in X_{id}. Specifically, we include religion, caste, education, amount of loan taken, any caste-group membership at the household level and availability of formal loans at the district level.

4 Data

We use data from the India Human Development Survey (IHDS) for this study. The IHDS is a nationally representative survey of 41,554 households interviewed in 2004 and 2005 (Desai et al. 2009). Surveyed households are distributed across 382 of India's 602 districts. Our study covers households which are either self-employed, wage employed or unemployed. This leads to a sample size of 34,521 households across 373 districts in our study. For our dependent variable we use the information on employment status of different members of a household to create a household level variable of self-employment status. We define a household to be self employed if at least one member in the household owns a business in the non-agricultural sector. A household is defined to be wage-employed if at least one member is wage-employed, and no one is self-employed. A household is defined to be unemployed if no one in the household is employed.[2]

Our main variables of interest are informal and formal institutional quality. In equation 17, we proxy informal institutions, IN_d, by the fraction of households in a district d that takes loans from informal sources, viz., friends, relatives and community credit groups.[3] In general, an informal loan network not only captures the extent of loans available in a district, but it also reflects the close association between members of the network. A larger size of the informal network facilitates flow of information within the network and helps in enforcing the reputation mechanism.

The quality of formal institutions is captured by the perceived quality of formal courts of law. We measure FC_d as the fraction of households in a district d which perceives the judiciary to be strong.[4] Specifically, the survey asks households to rank different institutions on a scale of one to three, where three signifies the least confidence in a particular institution, and one signifies the highest confidence. We consider the perceived court quality to be strong when a household's ranking of court efficiency is one.

Table 1 provides the summary of our estimation sample. About 23% of our full sample is self employed. However, when we disaggregate by sector, we find a much higher prevalence of self employment in the urban sector – about 29% of the sample is self-employed in urban as opposed to 19% in the rural sector. This has implications for the importance of the relationship between self-employment and institutional quality, which we revisit in Section 5.1. When we look at the prevalence of informal networks, we find that about 12% of the full sample has borrowed from informal sources. Moreover, the extent of informality is not very different between urban and rural sectors. With respect to the quality of formal courts, 53% of our full sample perceive the court to be efficient. Once again, the difference in perception is small between urban and rural sectors. The availability of formal loans is higher in rural areas, possibly reflecting the higher prevalence of government rural banks providing agricultural loans. However, as expected, the average size of loans is much higher in urban regions. Table 1 additionally reports the means for the other control variables that we use in our empirical specification.

Table 1 Summary

	All	Rural	Urban
Fraction Self Employed	0.232	0.195	0.289
	(0.422)	(0.396)	(0.454)
Mean District Population	815.026	808.634	826.557
	(438.6)	(349)	(565)
Informal Network(IN)	0.124	0.131	0.112
	(0.113)	(0.111)	(0.126)
Perceived Court Quality(FC)	0.533	0.545	0.512
	(0.192)	(0.193)	(0.214)
Formal Loan Availability	0.153	0.166	0.131
	(0.099)	(0.103)	(0.103)
Loan Amount	44381.67	32719.12	73513.91
	(212311)	(108359)	(356614)
Size Caste Network	0.133	0.147	0.106
	(0.194)	(0.213)	(0.172)
Hindu	0.807	0.824	0.776
	(0.394)	(0.381)	(0.416)
Brahmin	0.058	0.041	0.089
	(0.234)	(0.198)	(0.285)
HH Fraction literate	0.791	0.729	0.901
	(0.407	(0.444)	(0.298)
HH Caste Association	0.133	0.148	0.106
	(0.339)	(0.355)	(0.308)
Observations	41554	26734	14820

5 Results

Table 2 reports the results from a linear estimation of equation 1. The outcome variable reflects the probability of a household being self-employed compared to being wage employed. Column 1 includes a measure of informality at the district level (II_d), an indicator for strong institutions(SI_d), and an interaction between the two. Since our variables of interest vary only at the district level, we report clustered standard errors at the district level in all specifications.

The results in column 1 indicate a nonlinear relationship between the degree of informality and self employment. The coefficient on informal networks by itself suggests that a greater extent of informality in a district predicts a higher probability of self-employment. However, this relationship depends on the strength of formal institutions. Specifically, the negative coefficient on the interaction term implies a nonlinear relationship. This can be seen from the following equation.

$$\frac{\partial Pr(SE)}{\partial II_d} = -\beta_1 SI_d + \beta_2 \tag{18}$$

Our result implies $\frac{\partial Pr(SE)}{\partial II_d} \gtreqless 0$, according to $SI_d \lesseqgtr \overline{SI_d} = \frac{\beta_1}{\beta_2}$. This means that greater informal networks positively affect the probability of starting a business as long as the quality of the formal court is below a certain threshold. However as the formal institutions become sufficiently strong, a higher number of business would quit in areas with larger informal networks.

Table 2 Probability of self employment vs wage employment

	(1)	(2)	(3)	(4)	(5)
IN*FC	-0.633**	-0.675***	-0.792***	-0.667**	-0.630**
	(0.249)	(0.255)	(0.290)	(0.260)	(0.268)
Informal Network(IN)	0.355**	0.384**	0.344**	0.334**	0.315*
	(0.148)	(0.152)	(0.172)	(0.156)	(0.162)
Formal Court(FC)	0.031	0.043	0.095*	0.084	0.082
	(0.035)	(0.036)	(0.053)	(0.053)	(0.053)
Formal Loan Availability		-0.083	-0.072	-0.136*	-0.144**
		(0.052)	(0.067)	(0.071)	(0.07)
Loan Amount			0.001**	0.001**	0.001**
			(0.001)	(0.001)	(0.001)
Caste Association					0.027*
					(0.014)
Hindu				-0.079***	-0.079***
				(0.012)	(0.012)
High Caste				0.0671**	0.069***
				(0.023)	(0.023)
Education				0.144***	0.144***
				(0.009)	(0.009)
Constant	0.213***	0.218***	0.207***	0.170***	0.167***
	(0.019)	(0.019)	(0.031)	(0.033)	(0.033)
Observations	34,521	34,521	14,185	14,159	14,156
R-squared	0.001	0.002	0.007	0.033	0.034

Source: IHDS 2004–2005, own calculations.
Notes: Linear probability models. Standard errors in parentheses, adjusted for clustering at village level.
*** significant at 1%; ** significant at 5%; * significant at 10%.

More specifically the coefficients can be interpreted in the following way. In column 1, the estimates imply that the threshold level of formal institutions is given by 0.54 (β_2/β_1). Hence, districts where more than 54% of the households perceive the judiciary to be strong are above the threshold level of formal institutions. Now consider two districts within this group – one with a low prevalence of informal networks (D_{LI}) and another with a high prevalence of informal networks (D_{HI}). Then our coefficients imply that the probability of self employment is lower in D_{HI} compared to D_{LI}.[5] Specifically, if 60% of households perceive the court to be efficient, then a one unit difference in the extent of informal networks between D_{HI} and D_{LI} leads to a 10 percentage point lower probability of self employment in D_{HI} compared to D_{LI} districts.

Conversely, now consider the situation where the level of formal institutions is less than the threshold level of 0.5. Consider the same two districts, D_{HI} and D_{LI}. Here our coefficients imply that the the probability of self employment is higher in D_{HI} compared to D_{LI}. Specifically, if only 40% of the households in a district perceive the court to be strong, a one unit higher level of informal networks leads to a 10 percentage point higher likelihood of doing business.

Next we add a number of control variables to the above basic specification. It is possible that districts with greater availability of informal loans also have a higher availability of any loan so that 'IN' simply captures the extent of the total loan availability in the district instead of the extent of informality. Hence, we control for the availability of formal loans in the district in column 2. The coefficients indicate similar effects of informality.

Column 3 includes a proxy for the credit worthiness of a household indicated by the maximum amount of loan taken. Results remain unchanged here as well. The coefficient on the control variable suggests the obvious that if a household has taken a larger amount of loan, it is more likely to start a business.

Column 4 controls for other household level characteristics like religion, caste and an indicator whether a household has any literate member. The results are in the same spirit as before. The coefficients on *High Caste* and *Education* are as expected. More educated households and traditionally higher castes are more likely to be self employed. *Hindu* households, on the contrary, are less likely to self employed compared to households from other religious backgrounds.

Finally, in column 5 we also control for household participation in a caste network since that might increase both a household's probability of getting a loan and starting a business. Results remain the same as before. Moreover, as expected, household participation in a caste network increases the probability of self-employment.

To further verify that our results are not sensitive to varied specifications, we carry out the following robustness check. In Table 3 we include unemployment in the reference category. We now compare the probability of self employment with wage employment and unemployment. The results remain unaffected by the inclusion of unemployment in the reference category. The coefficients on the interaction term and informal institutions show similar nonlinear effects of informal networks on business decision, depending on the extent of formal institutions.

5.1 Heterogeneity analysis

In Table 1 we observe that the incidence of self-employment is much higher in urban areas compared to rural areas. Hence, in Table 4, we estimate the relationship separately

Table 3 Probability of self employment vs wage employment & unemployment

	(1)	(2)	(3)	(4)	(5)
IN*FC	-0.596**	-0.630***	-0.798***	-0.688***	-0.652**
	(0.230)	(0.237)	(0.275)	(0.251)	(0.260)
Informal Network(IN)	0.355***	0.379***	0.354**	0.350**	0.333**
	(0.137)	(0.141)	(0.164)	(0.151)	(0.157)
Formal Court(FC)	0.031	0.041	0.102*	0.092*	0.091*
	(0.033)	(0.035)	(0.052)	(0.051)	(0.052)
Formal Loan Availability		-0.071	-0.081	-0.143**	-0.151**
		(0.051)	(0.066)	(0.071)	(0.069)
Loan Amount			0.001**	0.001***	0.001***
			(0.001)	(0.001)	(0.001)
Caste Association					0.028**
					(0.014)
Hindu				-0.071***	-0.071***
				(0.012)	(0.012)
High Caste				0.059***	0.061***
				(0.022)	(0.022)
Education				0.139***	0.139***
				(0.009)	(0.009)
Constant	0.196***	0.201***	0.195***	0.155***	0.152***
	(0.018)	(0.019)	(0.031)	(0.032)	(0.033)
Observations	36,837	14,737	14,708	14,704	
R-squared	0.002	0.007	0.031	0.031	

Source: IHDS 2004–2005, own calculations.
Notes: Linear probability models. Standard errors in parentheses, adjusted for clustering at village level.
***significant at 1%; **significant at 5%; *significant at 10%.

for rural and urban regions.[6] The results discussed in Table 2 are primarily driven by the urban region. Informality by itself or its interaction with formal institutions doesn't play a significant role in predicting self employment for the rural region. It is possible that the link between informality and self employment is more relevant for the urban region which is characterized by a higher prevalence of self-employment.

In general, it should be easier to start a new business in the presence of a large informal network because it facilitates the flow of information and provides easy access to loans. However, according to our theoretical predictions, the presence of a large informal network would also lead to a greater exodus of businesses when the quality of formal institutions crosses a threshold. To re-examine these possibilities we conduct a heterogeneity analysis by estimating our model separately for the extent of association of households in various caste organizations. In districts where a large fraction of households participate in caste networks, there would be a greater flow of information within the network. Consequently, it would be easier to enforce contracts using the informal system of the reputation mechanism and facilitate business opportunities. We define a district to have a strong caste network if a larger share of households in a district participate in caste organizations.[7] Table 5 reports the results from this analysis. A one percentage point increase in the size of informal networks leads to a 0.52 percentage point higher probability of doing business in districts with large caste networks. In comparison, a one percentage point increase in the size of informal networks leads to a 0.32 percentage point higher probability of doing business in districts with small caste networks. Additionally, the coefficient

Table 4 Probability of self employment vs wage employment: Rural & Urban

	(1)	(2)
	Rural	Urban
IN*FC	-0.339	-0.849***
	(0.292)	(0.300)
Informal Network(IN)	0.121	0.421**
	(0.184)	(0.179)
Formal Court(FC)	0.056	0.128
	(0.055)	(0.084)
Formal Loan Availability	-0.173**	-0.072
	(0.067)	(0.123)
Loan Amount	0.003***	0.001***
	(0.001)	(0.001)
Caste Association	0.019	0.075**
	(0.0139)	(0.0292)
Hindu	-0.085***	-0.04**
	(0.016)	(0.02)
High Caste	0.091***	0.02
	(0.033)	(0.034)
Education	0.126***	0.130***
	(0.009)	(0.022)
Constant	0.185***	0.161***
	(0.036)	(0.051)
Observations	9,622	4,534
R-squared	0.037	0.017

Source: IHDS 2004–2005, own calculations.
Notes: Linear probability models. Standard errors in parentheses, adjusted for clustering at village level.
*** significant at 1%; **significant at 5%; *significant at 10%.

on the interaction term shows that the fall in business opportunities is higher in districts with large caste networks when the quality of the formal court is above a threshold.

Finally, we also investigate how a greater influx of NC entrepreneurs affects our baseline relationship. Specifically, we look at the extent of migration into and out of a district as it determines the composition of the pool of entrepreneurs within a district. A higher number of out-of-community entrepreneurs is likely to be present in high-migration compared to low-migration districts.[8] Analogously, a higher number of low-endowment community entrepreneurs will operate in low migration districts. In this situation when the formal institutions become sufficiently strong, there would be a greater exit of low-endowment entrepreneurs from the low-migration districts. In other words, since high-migration districts would have a larger number of high-endowment out-of-community entrepreneurs to begin with, the interaction between informal network and formal courts will have a much weaker effect than the low-migration districts, which are populated by low-endowment entrepreneurs. Therefore, we conduct a heterogeneity analysis separately for districts with high and low migration in the urban region as presented in Table 6. We define a district to have high migration if the fraction of migrants in that district is greater than the median. In accordance with our theoretical predictions, the informal network and its interaction with the formal court matters for self-employment in districts with low-migration, possibly due to a greater prevalence of community entrepreneurs. We do not find any significant relationship for the districts with high-migration.

Table 5 Heterogeneity analysis: network size

	(1)	(2)
	Large Network	Small Network
IN*FC	-1.040***	-0.643**
	(0.376)	(0.317)
Informal Network(IN)	0.528**	0.314*
	(0.218)	(0.166)
Formal Court(FC)	0.135*	0.105
	(0.078)	(0.069)
Formal Loan Availability	-0.029	-0.138
	(0.091)	(0.102)
Loan Amount	0.001*	0.001**
	(0.000)	(0.000)
Caste Association	0.052**	0.158*
	(0.024)	(0.092)
Hindu	-0.041*	-0.045*
	(0.024)	(0.025)
High Caste	0.057	-0.008
	(0.042)	(0.037)
Education	0.129***	0.127***
	(0.032)	(0.029)
Constant	0.164***	0.176***
	(0.056)	(0.051)
Observations	2,323	2,211
R-squared	0.017	0.016

Source: IHDS 2004–2005, own calculations.
Notes: Linear probability models. Standard errors in parentheses, adjusted for clustering at village level.
***significant at 1%; **significant at 5%; *significant at 10%.

6　Conclusion

The relation between the informal and formal institutions of contract enforcement is usually seen as substitutional – the former being replaced by the latter in the course of economic development. The experiences of developing countries, however, show that these two type of institutions co-exist. Understanding the nature of their interaction therefore becomes crucial for designing optimal institutions. In this paper we model the interaction between these two types of institutions and its effect on the prospect of running a business. We test the implications of the model using household level data for India.

The informal institutions of contract enforcement, which works on a reputation based mechanism, are critical for the operations of micro-entrepreneurs who cannot access costly formal institutions for enforcing the contracts. Unlike the formal institutions which depend on the legal system for enforcing contracts, the informal institutions punish a cheater by denying him any future employment. However, such mechanisms are limited to certain communities where members abide by the community norm of not employing one who has cheated someone from that community. The system gets weaker if entrepreneurs start violating this norm. The rise of formal institutions allows non-community members to enter the market who do not follow such norms. This, in our analysis, significantly weakens the effectiveness of the informal institutions.

Our theoretical result shows that as long as the quality of formal institutions is below a threshold level, strong informal networks help in business proliferation. However, when the formal institutions get sufficiently strong, they come in the way of the informal ones

Table 6 Heterogeneity analysis: migration

	(1)	(2)
	High Migration	Low Migration
IN*FC	-0.701	-0.809**
	(0.647)	(0.369)
Informal Network(IN)	0.311	0.491*
	(0.318)	(0.263)
Formal Court(FC)	0.152	0.045
	(0.120)	(0.108)
Formal Loan Availability	-0.085	-0.002
	(0.169)	(0.174)
Loan Amount	0.001***	0.001***
	(0.000)	(0.000)
Caste Association	0.078**	0.072
	(0.037)	(0.044)
Hindu	-0.049*	-0.025
	(0.026)	(0.03)
High Caste	-0.002	0.053
	(0.042)	(0.06)
Education	0.125***	0.141***
	(0.029)	(0.036)
Constant	0.160**	0.169**
	(0.071)	(0.078)
Observations	2,786	1,748
R-squared	0.017	0.023

Source: IHDS 2004–2005, own calculations.
Notes: Linear probability models. Standard errors in parentheses, adjusted for clustering at village level.
*** significant at 1%; **significant at 5%; *significant at 10%.

(following the mechanism we detailed above) and increase the cost of running businesses. This affects the poorer entrepreneurs more adversely than their more well off counterparts because it is the small capitalists who find running business using the formal mechanism not profitable enough. We test our theoretical predictions using IHDS data and find support for our theoretical results. We plan to extend our analysis in the future by constructing a panel using administrative data on court quality. Additionally, future waves of IHDS data would allow us to observe the evolution of informal institutions over time. This will help us to provide more convincing evidence.

The main result of our paper apparently warns against the possible backlash of strengthening the formal institutions in a less developed country that is characterized by strong informal institutions. Our position, however, does not endorse maintenance of informal mechanisms. Instead, we emphasize that informal institutions, even though inefficient, are crucial for the micro-entrepreneurs to run their businesses. The implications of our paper are two fold: first, strong formal and strong informal institutions create a negative impact on the probability of doing business; more importantly, such negative impacts typically force the capital poor section of the entrepreneurs to quit the market. Hence, even if the strengthening of formal institutions may lead to efficient outcomes in the long run, it increases inequality in the short run. The main contribution of our paper is to emphasizing this trade off which is often neglected in the institutions-entrepreneurship literature. The policy implication should lead to a better designing of formal institutions so that the exclusion of micro-entrepreneurs can be prevented.

Endnotes

[1] One such study is done by Kranton and Swamy (1999) who conduct a descriptive analysis of the effect of court systems on agricultural credit markets using historical data from British India.

[2] We also define a separate category as agricultural household if at least one member owns agricultural land or is employed in agriculture and no one is self-employed or wage-employed. However, we did not include this reference category in our analysis because they form a very small fraction of the total number of households.

[3] All our district level estimates are computed as a fraction of the total number of households in a district.

[4] Note that the formal court quality measure might suffer from measurement error problems as it is based on household perception, implying that our estimates form a lower bound. We plan to collect administrative data related to court quality to construct a more precise measure.

[5] For $SI_d = 0.6, P(SE) = \beta_0 + \beta_1 II_d * 0.6 + \beta_2 II_d$.

[6] These results are robust to all the specifications reported in Table 2. However, we only report the specification with full set of controls.

[7] Moreover since the baseline relationship is driven primarily by the urban sector, we restrict this analysis to the urban sector.

[8] Out-of-community entrepreneurs represent the NC entrepreneurs in our theoretical model.

Appendix

$$V_h \left[1 - \beta(1 - q)\right] = \rho^* + qV_h^u \tag{19}$$

$$V_h^u = \beta p_h V_h + \beta(1 - p_h)\left(\overline{w} + V_h^u\right) \tag{20}$$

$$V_c^u = \beta p_c V_h + \beta(1 - p_c)\left(\overline{w} + V_c^u\right) \tag{21}$$

$$V_h \geq \eta + V_c^u \tag{22}$$

Define $T = \frac{1}{1-\beta(1-q)}$. So we have

$$V_h = T\rho^* + TqV_h^u \tag{23}$$

Substituting this in equation (8), we get

$$V_h^u = \beta p_h \left[\rho^* T + TqV_h^u\right] + \beta(1 - p_h) V_h^u + \beta(1 - p_h)\overline{w} \tag{24}$$

$$V_h^u \left[1 - \beta p_h Tq - \beta(1 - p_h)\right] = \beta p_h \rho T + \beta(1 - p_h)\overline{w} \tag{25}$$

From the last equation, we get

$$V_h^u = \frac{T\rho\beta p_h}{\left[1 - \beta p_h Tq - \beta(1 - p_h)\right]} + \frac{\beta(1 - p_h)}{\left[1 - \beta p_h Tq - \beta(1 - p_h)\right]}\overline{w} \tag{26}$$

We can then write the previous expression as

$$V_h^u = \rho T_{1h} + T_{2h}\overline{w} \tag{27}$$

From equation (9) we get

$$V_c^u(1 - \beta(1 - p_c)) = \beta p_c V_h + \beta(1 - p_c)\overline{w} \tag{28}$$

The above expression can be written as

$$V_c^u = T_{1c}V_h + T_{2c}\overline{w}, \tag{29}$$

where $T_{1c} = \frac{\beta p_c}{1-\beta(1-p_c)}$ and $T_{2c} = \frac{\beta(1-p_c)}{1-\beta(1-p_c)}$. The honesty-inducing condition tells us

$$V_h - V_c^u \geq \eta \tag{30}$$

Substituting from the previous expressions, we find

$$V_h - (T_{1c}V_h + T_{2c}\overline{w}) \geq \eta \tag{31}$$

From equations (11) and (15), we find

$$T\rho^* + Tq\left[\rho T_{1h} + T_{2h}\overline{w}\right] \geq \frac{\eta}{1-T_{1c}} + \frac{T_{2c}}{1-T_{1c}}\overline{w} \tag{32}$$

From this we get

$$\rho T[1 + TqT_{1h}] \geq \frac{\eta}{1-T_{1c}} + \frac{T_{2c}}{1-T_{1c}}\overline{w} - TqT_{2h}\overline{w} \tag{33}$$

This leads to the condition

$$\rho \geq \frac{1}{T\left[1 + TqT_{1h}\right]} \times \left[\frac{\eta}{1-T_{1c}} + \frac{T_{2c}}{1-T_{1c}}\overline{w} - TqT_{2h}\overline{w}\right] \tag{34}$$

Recall that

$$\frac{1}{1-T_{1c}} = 1 + \frac{\beta}{1-\beta}p_c \tag{35}$$

and

$$\frac{T_{2c}}{1-T_{1c}} = \frac{\beta(1-p_c)}{1-\beta} \tag{36}$$

Hence, we find,

$$\frac{\partial \rho^*}{\partial p_c} = \frac{1}{T\left[1 + TqT_{1h}\right]} \times (\eta - \overline{w})\frac{\beta}{1-\beta} \tag{37}$$

This expression is positive as long as $\eta - \overline{w} > 0$, which tells us that the one time cheating payoff is more than the reservation payoff. This has to be the case because the industry payoff is more than the reservation wage, and the one time cheating payoff is more than the industry payoff.

Competing interests
The IZA Journal of Labor & Development is committed to the IZA Guiding Principles of Research Integrity. The authors declare that they have observed these principles.

Acknowledgements
'We thank the seminar participants at Delhi School of Economics, IIT Kanpur, ISI-Calcutta, Indian School of Business, University of Hannover and conference participants at IZA/World Bank Conference on Employment and Development 2014 and CEA 2014 for their useful comments and suggestions. We are also thankful to an anonymous referee for the valuable feedback. We gratefully acknowledge the funding received from ICSSR and IDRC for this project.

Responsible editor: David Lam

Author details
[1]Indian Institute of Technology, Kanpur, India. [2]University of Calcutta, Calcutta, India.

References
Acemoglu D, Johnson S (2003) Unbundling Institutions. Technical report, National Bureau of Economic Research
Acemoglu D, Johnson S, Robinson J (2001) The colonial origins of comparative development. Am Econ Rev 91(5):1369–1401

Acemoglu D, Johnson S, Robinson J (2002) Reversal of fortune:geography and institutions in the making of the modern world income distribution. Q J Econ 117(4):1231–1294

Besley T, Coate S, Loury G (1993) The economics of rotating savings and credit associations. Am Econ Rev 83(4):792–810

Biggs T, Shah MK (2006) African smes, networks, and manufacturing performance. J Bank Finance 30(11):3043–3066

Biggs RMT, Srivastava P (2002) Ethnic networks and access to credit: Evidence from the manufacturing sector in kenya. J Econ Behav Organ 49:473–486

Blanchflower DG, Levine PB, Zimmerman DJ (2003) Discrimination in the small-business credit market. Rev Economics Stat 85(4):930–943

Chowdhry P (2004) Caste panchayats and the policing of marriage in haryana: Enforcing kinship and territorial exogamy. Contrib Indian Sociol 38(1-2):1–42

Chemin M (2012) Does court speed shape economic activity? evidence from a court reform in india. J Law Economics and Organization 28(3):460–485

Dixit A (2004) Lawlessness and economics: alternative modes of governance. Princeton University Press

Fafchamps M (2000) Ethnicity and credit in african manufacturing. J Dev Economics 61(1):205–235

Fafchamps M (2003) Ethnicity and networks in african trade. Contrib Econ Anal Policy 2(1):14

Fairlie RW, Robb AM (2007) Why are black-owned businesses less successful than white-owned businesses? the role of families, inheritances, and business human capital. J Labor Econ 25(2):289–323

Fisman RJ (2003) Ethnic ties and the provision of credit: Relationship-level evidence from african firms. B.E. J Econ Anal Policy advances.3(1):4

Freitas K (2006) The indian caste system as a means of contract enforcement. Nortwestern University. unpublished manuscript

Gajigo O, Foltz JD (2010) Ethnic Networks and Enterprise Credit: The Serahules of The Gambia. Working Paper

Ghatak M (1991) Group lending, local information and peer selection. J Dev Econ 60(1):27–50

Ghosh P, Ray D (1996) Cooperation in community interaction without information flows. Rev Econ Stud 63(3):491–519

Greif A, Milgrom P, Weingast B (1994) Coordination, commitment, and enforcement: The case of the merchant guild. J Pol Econ 102(August):745–776

Greif A (1993) Contract enforceability and economic institutions in early trade: The maghribi traders' coalition. Am Econ Rev 83(3):525–548

Harriss-White B (2010) Globalization, the financial crisis and petty production in indias socially regulated informal economy. Glob Labour J 1(1):152–177

Kandori M (1992) Social norms and community enforcement. Rev Econ Stud 59(1):63–80

Karlan D (2005) Using experimental economics to measure social capital and predict financial decisions. Am Econ Rev 95(5):526–556

Keremane GB, McKay J, Narayanamoorthy A (2006) The decline of innovative local self-governance institutions for water management the case of pani panchayats. Int J Rural Manag 2(1):107–122

Klapper L, Laeven L, Rajan R (2006) Entry regulation as a barrier to entrepreneurship. J Financ Econ 82(3):591–629

Kranton RE, Swamy AV (1999) The hazards of piecemeal reform: British civil courts and the credit market in colonial india. J Dev Econ 58(1):1–24

La Porta R, Shleifer A (2014) Informality and development. J Econ Perspect 28(3):109–26

Luigi S, Sapienza P, Zingales L (2004) The role of social capital in financial development. Am Econ Rev 94(3):526–556

Madsen ST (1991) Clan, kinship, and panchayat justice among the jats of western uttar pradesh. Anthropos 86:351–365

McMillan J, Woodruff C (1999) Interfirm relationships and informal credit in vietnam. Q J Econ 114(4):1285–1320. doi:10.1162/003355399556278

Nagraj V (2010) Local and customary forums : Adapting and innovating rules of formal law. Indian J Gender Stud 17(3):429–450

Rajan R, Zingales L (1998) Financial dependence and growth. Am Econ Rev 88(5):559–586

Rosenthal R, Landau H (1979) A game theoretic analysis of bargaining with reputation. J Math Psychol 20:235–255

Sandner V (2003) Myths and laws: changing institutions of indigenous marine resource management in Central America. Springer

Shapiro C, Stiglitz JE (1984) Equilibrium unemployment as a worker discipline device. The American Economic Review

Slivinski A, Sussman N (2009) Taxation mechanisms and growth, in medieval paris. In: Geneva, European Economic History Association Conference

Straub S (2005) Informal sector: The credit market channel. J Dev Econ 78(2):299–321

Yadav B (2009) Khap panchayats: Stealing freedom? Econ Pol Wkly 44(52):16–19

6

The effect of children on female labor force participation in urban Iran

Ebrahim Azimi

Correspondence: eaa20@sfu.ca
Department of Economics, Simon
Fraser University, 8888 University
Drive, Burnaby, British Columbia,
Canada

Abstract

This paper estimates the effect of having children on labor force participation of mothers in urban Iranian areas. I exploit sex composition of children as an exogenous source of variation in family size to account for endogeneity of fertility. Using information from the Iranian Household Income and Expenditure Survey (HIES) over three samples, namely, households with one and more, two and more, and three and more children, I find no significant effect of fertility on female labor force participation in Iran.

JEL codes: J13, J22

Keywords: Female labor force participation; Fertility; Children sex composition; Son preference; Instrumental variables

1 Introduction

In economic literature, children are often considered a barrier to female labor force participation (FLFP). In the last three decades, fertility in Iran has dropped sharply from an average of seven births per woman in 1984 to less than two births in 2005. Although fertility in Iran has experienced one of the fastest declines in modern human history, no considerable rise in FLFP in Iran is documented (Aghajanian 1995; Abbasi-Shavazi et al. 2009; Majbouri 2010). Using household-level information, this paper investigates the effect of children on FLFP of mothers in urban Iran.

The association between fertility and FLFP is extensively documented in theoretical models of work and family. While it is difficult to empirically estimate the endogenous effect of fertility on FLFP (Schultz 1981; Goldin 1995), several studies estimate its causal effect by exploiting an exogenous variation in family size. For example, Rosenzweig and Wolpin (1980) and Bronars and Grogger (1994) use twinning at the first birth. Angrist and Evans (1998) use an instrumental variables (IV) strategy based on the sex composition of siblings in families with two or more children. Agüero and Marks (2008) exploit random assignment of infertility as an exogenous variation in family size. Using the Iranian Household Income and Expenditure Survey (HIES), this paper contributes new evidence on the effect of fertility on FLFP by using an IV strategy.

I follow Angrist and Evans (1998) strategy to construct IV estimates of the effect of fertility on FLFP based on sex composition of children. While in the US, parents are more likely to have a third child if their first two children are of the same sex, in Iran, as parents prefer sons to daughters, the presence of daughters in their previous children acts as a positive shock to fertility. To show this relationship and investigate the effect of children on FLFP, I construct three samples: one with families with one and more children (1^+), another with two and more children (2^+), and the third with three and more children (3^+). In all these samples, families with more daughters than sons are more likely to have another child. In other words, presence of more girls relative to boys results in an increased likelihood of having another child. Considering this relationship, I construct an IV based on the sex composition of previous children to investigate the effect of fertility on FLFP by using dummies for the gender of the first child, the first two children, and the first three children in the samples of 1^+, 2^+, and 3^+, respectively. As sex-selective abortion and infanticide are rare in Iran, I consider sex composition among children as essentially random. To support this claim, I follow Almond and Edlund (2008) by observing that sex ratio does not vary significantly with birth order parity and sex composition of the previous children.

To the best of my knowledge, this is the first estimation of the effect of fertility on FLFP in Iran. While most empirical estimations of the effect of fertility on FLFP find a negative impact, which in most cases is less negative than its ordinary least squares (OLS) counterparts, I find no significant effect of children on the labor force participation of Iranian mothers in urban areas. This result is similar to Agüero and Marks (2008), who find an insignificant effect of fertility on FLFP in six Latin American countries.

The rest of this paper is organized as follows. In the next section, I present the data. In section "Sex composition of children and fertility", I describe the methodology and explain how fertility in Iran is influenced by the sex composition of previous children. Section "Estimation results" presents the results, and section "Conclusion" concludes.

2 Data and descriptive statistics

I use data from the HIES (1994–2003). This survey is conducted annually by the Statistical Center of Iran. For each member of a family, this survey contains information on demographic characteristics such as geographic location, age, gender, education, relationship with the householder, marriage status, employment status, occupation, and income. It also contains information on family expenditures, housing characteristics, and ownership of assets and amenities.

The number of households in the HIES ranged from 17,500 in 1998 to 36,500 in 1995. To ensure that the insignificant effect of fertility on FLFP is not a result of insufficient data, I use 10 rounds of the HIES data (1994–2003), all of which follow the same definition for labor force participation.

The following restrictions are applied to the sample. 1) Polygamous families are excluded from the sample; otherwise, it would have been impossible to match the children to the women. 2) I exclude all cases wherein two or more families share a common residence. Given that household identification, which is based on residential address, is the only way to distinguish families, I am unable to distinguish children of families that share the same residence. 3) Similar to most household surveys, the HIES does not track children according to their households. To match the children with their respective mothers, I restrict the sample to women aged between 20–35 years whose oldest child is younger than 18 years. Few women younger than 19 have two or more children, and women older than 35 are likely to have children who have already migrated from the family. By restricting the sample, I ensure that the family's oldest child is still living with the parents and has not migrated from the family on account of marriage, higher education, or work.

Additional file 1: Table S1 compares the selected sample with the overall sample of women for some measures of fertility and FLFP. The three samples of women include: (1) women aged between 20–35 years; (2) women aged between 36–50 years; and (3) women aged between 20–35 years with two or more children and whose oldest child is younger than 18. I highlight three features of fertility and FLFP in Iran from 1990–2004 in this table. First, we observe a declining trend in the number of children; second, depending on the year of the interview, a low FLFP rate of 10–14 percent in urban areas for the selected sample is observed. The rigidity of FLFP in this period is an important feature that has been addressed in the literature (Majbouri 2010). Third, fertility and FLFP are comparable for all three categories.

Trends in fertility and FLFP are depicted in Figures 1 and 2, respectively, for three subsamples of women from the HIES data.

While fertility shows a sharp decline during this period, based on economic theory, we expect an increase in FLFP. However, we observe no such increase over the period in Figure 2. The objective of this paper is to investigate whether and to what extent fertility impacts FLFP in urban Iran. I continue this discussion in section "Estimation results", where I present the results.

Table 1 reports the summary statistics for each sample of the 20 to 35-year-old mothers in the three samples of 1^+, 2^+, and 3^+.

3 Sex composition of children and fertility

Similar to Angrist and Evans (1998), I use the following two-stage least squares (2SLS) regression model of FLFP:

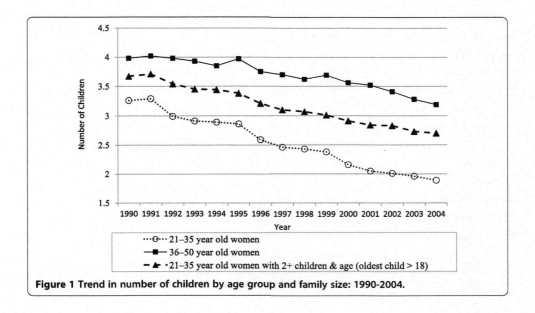

Figure 1 Trend in number of children by age group and family size: 1990-2004.

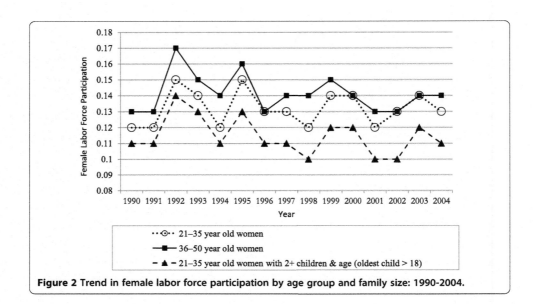

Figure 2 Trend in female labor force participation by age group and family size: 1990-2004.

$$x_i = \alpha_0.w_i + \alpha_1.z_i + \varepsilon_i \tag{1}$$

$$y_i = \beta_0.w_i + \beta_1.\hat{x}_\ell + \eta_i \tag{2}$$

Here, x_i is a measure of fertility for woman i; y_i is an indicator of FLFP; w_i includes socioeconomic characteristics of i; and z_i denotes the instrumental variable based on the sex composition of the children. The instrumental variable is an indicator for the sex composition of the children. The theoretical framework underlying the effect of son preference on fertility is captured by the quality–quantity model of fertility developed

Table 1 Summary statistics: women aged 21–35 years

	1+ sample		2+ sample		3+ sample	
	Mean	St. dev.	Mean	St. dev.	Mean	St. dev.
FLFP	0.129	(0.335)	0.116	(0.320)	0.0978	(0.297)
Number of children	2.627	(1.431)	3.110	(1.279)	3.917	(1.131)
Three-and-more-children indicator	0.447	(0.497)	0.579	(0.494)	1	(0)
Four-and-more-children indicator	0.235	(0.424)	0.305	(0.460)	0.526	(0.499)
Firstborn son indicator	0.514	(0.500)	0.509	(0.500)	0.497	(0.500)
Second-born son indicator	0.510	(0.500)	0.510	(0.500)	0.502	(0.500)
Two-son indicator	0.260	(0.439)	0.260	(0.439)	0.255	(0.436)
Two-daughter indicator	0.241	(0.428)	0.241	(0.428)	0.257	(0.437)
Age	28.88	(3.967)	29.69	(3.685)	30.53	(3.376)
Age at first birth	19.98	(3.462)	19.25	(3.096)	18.49	(2.745)
Years of schooling	6.715	(4.267)	6.023	(4.076)	4.810	(3.727)
Presence of relatives in the family	0.0893	(0.285)	0.0896	(0.286)	0.0962	(0.295)
Incidence of zero in nonlabor income	0.812	(0.391)	0.809	(0.393)	0.807	(0.394)
Logarithm of nonlabor income	2.581	(5.426)	2.616	(5.449)	2.622	(5.427)
Observations	56845		43868		25399	

Note: I report the mean of each variable with the standard deviation in parentheses.
The variable "age at first birth" is measured by assuming that matching of the women with their respected children is perfect. Therefore, this variable is measured by error.

by Becker and Lewis (1974). Based on this model, in the current study, parents derive utility from quantity and quality of children. The sex composition of children in this model is viewed as a source of utility related to the quality of children. If parents are not satisfied with the sex composition of children, they will be more likely to expand their family to draw utility from quantity of children or from a more desired composition of children. Therefore, having more children is a response to dissatisfaction from the sex composition of the children.

Based on the above framework and similar to Ben-Porath and Welch (1976), I analyze the effect of the sex composition of children on fertility among Iranian families. Table 2 reports how the firstborn's sex influences the number of children. In the 1^+ sample, the difference by the first child's sex suggests that families with a firstborn daughter are one percentage point more likely to have a second child. This is consistent with the preference for a son among Iranian parents. Similarly, in the 2^+ and 3^+ samples, the presence of a firstborn son reduces the likelihood of a third and a fourth child. Thus, the firstborn's sex is a plausible instrumental variable for number of children.

Similarly, among families with two or more children, the difference by the firstborn's sex suggests that those with a firstborn daughter are 2.4 percentage points more likely to have a third child (Table 3). This finding is also consistent with the fact that Iranian parents have a marked son preference, especially for the first birth.

Similar to the case of the firstborn daughter, the second daughter also increases the likelihood of having a third child. The effect, however, is smaller than that of the firstborn girl. Parents of a second daughter are 1.7 percentage points more likely to have a third child. Further, while parents with two sons are 1.2 percentage points less likely to have a third child, parents with two girls are 4.5 percentage points more likely to have a third child. This also shows that parents of a mix of male and female children are 2.4 percentage points less likely to have a third child relative to parents of same-sex children.

There are three points worth mentioning about Table 3. First, all the evidence demonstrates a marked preference for sons among Iranian families; while sons reduce the likelihood of a third child, daughters increase it. Second, the effect of two daughters is larger compared to other combinations. Third, this table shows that the sex composition of children has a strong explanatory power on fertility

Table 2 Fraction of families who had a second child depending on the sex of the first child

	1^+ sample		2^+ sample		3^+ sample	
	Fraction of sample	Fraction that had a 2nd child	Fraction of sample	Fraction that had a third child	Fraction of sample	Fraction that had a 4th child
(1) firstborn son	51.3%	0.790	51.0%	0.603	50.6%	0.559
		(0.002)		(0.003)		(0.004)
(2) firstborn daughter	48.7%	0.799	49.0%	0.627	49.4%	0.583
		(0.002)		(0.003)		(0.004)
Difference (1)-(2)		−0.009***		−0.024***		−0.024***
		(0.003)		(0.004)		(0.005)

Note: Standard errors are reported in parentheses.
***significant at the 1% level.

Table 3 Fraction of families who had another child depending on the sex composition of previous children: 2⁺ sample

	Fraction of sample	Fraction that had a third child
(1) firstborn son	51.0%	0.603 (0.003)
(2) firstborn daughter	49.0%	0.627 (0.003)
Difference: (1)-(2)		−0.024*** (0.004)
(1) second-born son	51.1%	0.607 (0.003)
(2) second-born daughter	48.9%	0.624 (0.003)
Difference: (1)-(2)		-0.017*** (0.004)
(1) two sons	26.2%	0.607 (0.004)
(2) not (two sons)	73.8%	0.618 (0.002)
Difference: (1)-(2)		-0.012*** (0.005)
(1) two daughters	24.0%	0.649 (0.004)
(2) not (two daughters)	76.0%	0.604 (0.002)
Difference: (1)-(2)		0.045*** (0.005)
(1) mixed sex	50.2%	0.627 (0.003)
(2) same sex	49.8%	0.603 (0.003)
Difference: (1)-(2)		0.024*** (0.004)

Note: Standard errors are reported in parentheses.
***significant at the 1% level.

decisions in Iranian families. Based on these results, I use an indicator of two daughters as an instrumental variable to estimate the effect of a third child on FLFP in the 2⁺ sample.

Similarly, Table 4 reports the relation between sex composition of children and probability of having a fourth child in families with at least three children. Based on this table, I use the indicator of having at least two sons as an instrument to investigate the effect of a fourth child on FLFP in the 3⁺ sample.

Random assignment of sex composition makes it very likely that these IV estimates of the effect of fertility on FLFP have a causal interpretation. Selective abortion and infanticide are quite rare in Iran because both have been illegal since the 1979 Islamic Revolution, except in very specific cases where the mother is in serious danger or the baby is expected to born with a severe disease (Hoodfar 1996; Mehryar et al. 2007). Thus, we treat the gender composition of children as essentially random.

One empirical test for random assignment of the sex composition of children is to compare the sex ratio by birth order and sex of previous children (Almond and Edlund 2008). For the general human population, sex ratio, defined as the proportion of males to females, is about 1.05, with the exception of during and after wartime, where it was documented to be slightly higher. Otherwise, a higher-than-normal sex ratio is a sign of sex-selective abortion. In such cases, the sex ratio will depend on previous children's sex composition. For example, due to the availability of prenatal sex determination, a two-child family that already has a daughter and prefers sons is more likely to abort a girl fetus relative to a boy fetus. Table 5 reports sex ratio by birth order and previous children's sex composition. No significant inflated sex ratio is evident from this table. Although the sex ratio is slightly larger than 1.05 for the third child, there is no significant difference between the sex ratios of families with two sons and families with two daughters. Thus, the sex composition of children can be treated as random.

Table 4 Fraction of families who had a fourth child depending on parity and sex composition of previous children

	Fraction of sample	Fraction that had a 4th child
(1) 3 sons	13.6%	0.560
		(0.007)
(2) other combinations	86.4%	0.573
		(0.003)
Difference: (1)-(2)		−0.013**
		(0.007)
(1) 3 daughters	12.7%	0.557
		(0.007)
(2) other mixes	87.3%	0.573
		(0.003)
Difference: (1)-(2)		−0.015**
		(0.008)
(1) same sex	25.8%	0.594
		(0.005)
(2) mixed sex	74.2%	0.563
		(0.003)
Difference: (1)-(2)		0.031***
		(0.006)
(1) 2 sons, 1 daughter	38.0%	0.548
		(0.004)
(2) other compositions	62.0%	0.585
		(0.003)
Difference: (1)-(2)		−0.036***
		(0.005)
(1) 1 son, 2 daughters	36.2%	0.578
		(0.004)
(2) other compositions	63.8%	0.567
		(0.003)
Difference: (1)-(2)		0.011**
		(0.005)

Note: Standard errors are reported in parentheses.
***significant at the 1% level, **significant at the 5% level.

Table 5 Sex ratio by parity and sex composition of previous children

Birth order	Previous children	Observations	Sex ratio	95% confidence interval	
				Lower bound	Upper bound
First		132,599	1.055	1.044	1.066
Second	girl	51,689	1.032	1.015	1.050
	boy	53,920	1.049	1.031	1.066
Third	girl, girl	17,356	1.082	1.051	1.115
	girl, boy	33,703	1.067	1.044	1.090
	boy, boy	17,685	1.080	1.048	1.112

The results of the 1996 and 2006 Iranian Censuses in Additional file 1: Table S2 support the randomness of sex composition in Iran.

An alternative test for random assignment of child sex composition is to compare demographic characteristics of families by the sex composition of children (Angrist and Evans 1998). If sex composition is random, there is no significant difference between demographic characteristics of families by this composition, as the insignificant differences in Table 6 suggest.

The random assignment of sex composition of children makes it very likely that the reduced form regressions of fertility and FLFP have a causal interpretation. Section "Estimation results" reports this estimation, and the results confirm that the three dummies of firstborn son, two daughters, and two sons and more are plausible instrumental variables for investigating the effect of fertility on FLFP in the 1^+, 2^+, and 3^+ samples, respectively. I use number of children and indicators of having more than two and three children as the measures of fertility for the 1^+, 2^+, and 3^+ samples, respectively.

4 Estimation results

In this section, I estimate the effect of having more children on FLFP using the 2SLS regression model of FLFP shown in equations (1) and (2). As explained earlier, I estimate the model for three subsamples of women. I use number of children, an indicator denoting that a woman has more than 2 children, and an indicator denoting that a woman has more than three children as measures of fertility for the samples 1^+, 2^+, and 3^+, respectively. The respective instrumental variables are indicators of a firstborn son, two daughters, and two or more sons.

All the specifications include indicators of age, namely, $I(25 \leq age \leq 29)$, $I(30 \leq age \leq 35)$; indicators of schooling, namely, $I(1 \leq schooling \leq 5)$, $I(6 \leq schooling \leq 8)$, $I(9 \leq schooling \leq 12)$, $I(13 \leq schooling)$; age at first birth[1]; log(nonlabor income); and year effects.

Table 7 reports the results of the OLS and IV estimates of the effect of children on FLFP for all three samples as well as the results of the first-stage estimates.

All three samples confirm the strong association between fertility and child sex composition. The F-statistics of a test for weak instrument hypothesis based on Stock and Yogo (2005) strongly rejects the null hypothesis of a weak instrument. The IV estimates suggest no significant effect of fertility on FLFP, while the OLS estimates report negative effects. Although the OLS estimates are small, they are significant. Most studies of

Table 6 Difference in mean for demographics by sex composition of children

	A firstborn son	Two daughters	Two or more sons
Age	−0.012	0.030	−0.020
	(0.026)	(0.034)	(0.036)
Literacy	−0.002	−0.004	0.006
	(0.003)	(0.005)	(0.006)
Education	−0.013	−0.050	0.051
	(0.035)	(0.044)	(0.044)
Husband's years of education	−0.004	−0.042	0.081
	(0.038)	(0.049)	(0.053)
Sample	1^+ sample	2^+ sample	3^+ sample

Note: Standard errors are reported in parentheses.

Table 7 OLS and 2SLS estimates of the effect of fertility on FLFP in urban Iran

	1^+ sample		2^+ sample		3^+ sample	
	OLS	2SLS	OLS	2SLS	OLS	2SLS
First-stage results: fertility equation						
A firstborn son		−0.106***				
		(0.009)				
Two daughters				0.042***		
				(0.004)		
Two or more sons						−0.044***
						(0.005)
Estimation results: FLFP equation						
Number of children	−0.008***	0.005				
	(0.001)	(0.026)				
More than 2 children			−0.011***	−0.033		
			(0.004)	(0.060)		
More than 3 children					−0.009**	−0.019
					(0.004)	(0.068)
Observations	56,845	56,845	43,868	43,868	25,399	25,399
1st stage R-squared		0.562		0.344		0.226
2nd stage R-squared	0.183	0.183	0.152	0.151	0.084	0.083
IV F-statistics		149.253		149.430		89.917

Note: All the specifications include indicators of age: $I(25 \leq age \leq 29)$, $I(30 \leq age \leq 35)$; indicators of schooling: $I(1 \leq schooling \leq 5)$, $I(6 \leq schooling \leq 8)$, $I(9 \leq schooling \leq 12)$, $I(schooling \leq 13)$; age at first birth; log(nonlabor income); and year effects. Standard errors are reported in parentheses. ***significant at the 1% level, **significant at the 5% level.

the causal effect of fertility on FLFP find a negative effect, which is usually smaller than the OLS estimates but is still significant. For example, using the firstborn's sex as an instrumental variable; Chun and Oh (2002) find that an additional child reduces the labor force participation of Korean mothers by 27%. Angrist and Evans (1998) estimate the effect of a third child on women's income to be −0.12. On the other hand, Agüero and Marks (2008) find no evidence that fertility has a causal effect on FLFP.

Although the insignificant effect of fertility on FLFP is consistent with the aggregate trend of FLFP for urban Iranian families (see Figures 1 and 2), the result is nevertheless surprising.

My finding suggests that children at the extensive margin are not a barrier for the female labor supply. However, one possibility is that fertility influences labor supply of women at the intensive margin. That is, women may change their work hours in response to having a larger family. Unfortunately, information on hours of work are not available in the HIES. Therefore, it is not feasible to estimate the effect of children on female labor supply at the intensive margin. Even if this is a plausible explanation, the rigidity of FLFP at low levels is still surprising.

The low rate of FLFP in Iran and its rigidity over the last three decades have been referred to as a puzzle in development literature (Majbouri 2010). It is more surprising to know that this rigidity was concurrent with a sharp decline in fertility, as mentioned earlier, and a considerable increase in the education of women. For example, according to the Statistical Center of Iran, the female-to-male student ratio in Iranian public and private colleges has increased from less than 0.4 in 1990 to about 1.2 in 2005.

With the sharp decline in fertility and considerable increase in women's education in Iran, we expect an increase in FLFP. However, FLFP has remained low at 10–14 percent. While investigating the reasons behind the low rate and rigidity of FLFP is outside the scope of this paper, I state a few potential reasons: Many observers believe that religion is the main reason for the low representation of women in the labor market (Sharabi 1988). They emphasize the common problem of low FLFP throughout the Middle East and attribute it to the influence of traditional and religious norms. The suggested mechanism is that traditional norms result in discrimination against women in the labor market, by restricting both labor supply and labor demand for women. This explanation, however, does not seem plausible as countries like Bangladesh and Indonesia are predominantly Muslim but have high rates of FLFP.

Using cross-country data, Ross (2008) shows that the effect of Islam disappears as he controls for oil and gas income, and he concludes that oil, not Islam, is responsible for low rates of FLFP in Iran and other Middle Eastern countries. Majbouri (2015) challenges this argument by proposing a mechanism through which oil and gas income along with traditional institutions account for the rigidity of FLFP. He explains that oil and gas income acts as rent and strengthens traditional norms and the religion's influence among Muslim countries with access to oil income.

5 Conclusion

Rigidity of FLFP in urban Iran in the last three decades has been a consensus in development literature. It is more surprising to know that it has been simultaneous with the period in which fertility has sharply declined and women's education has considerably increased (Majbouri 2010). I investigate the causal effect of fertility on FLFP to shed light on a part of this puzzle.

Following Angrist and Evans (1998), I exploit the random assignment of sex composition of children as an instrument to investigate the causal effect of fertility on FLFP among Iranian families in urban areas. As Iranian parents prefer to have sons relative to daughters, I show that the presence of sons reduces the likelihood of having more children in Iranian families. Based on this information, I exploit the sex composition of children to investigate the effect of fertility on FLFP.

While most estimates of the causal effect of fertility on FLFP report negative effects, I find no evidence that the presence of more children is a barrier for mothers to work. This finding is similar to that of Agüero and Marks (2008) and consistent with the aggregate trend in FLFP in urban Iran. Oil and gas income along with traditional institutions in Iran are considered to account for the rigidity of FLFP (Majbouri 2015).

Endnote

[1] As explained in section "Data and descriptive statistics", I restrict the sample according to the ages of the women and their oldest child to match the women with their respective children. If the match is not close to perfect, the estimate of the variable "age at first birth" will be erroneous, resulting in a bias in estimates. In my result, however, excluding this variable does not change the main finding of the paper; that is, fertility continues to have an insignificant effect on FLFP.

Additional file

Additional file 1: Table S1. Fertility and FLFP in Iran during 1990–2004. **Table S2.** Under-18 population by gender and sex ratio in Iran.

Competing interests
The IZA Journal of Labor & Development is committed to the IZA Guiding Principles of Research Integrity. The author declares that he has observed these principles.

Acknowledgements
The research presented in this paper is part of my PhD dissertation at Simon Fraser University. I thank Simon Woodcock and Krishna Pendakur for their support and advice. I also thank Jane Friesen, Brian Krauth, Andrew McGee, Hitoshi Shigeoka, Fernando Aragon, Chris Muris, Mehdi Majbouri, all the participants of the labor and family session at the Canadian Economic Association conference 2010 at University of Ottawa, and participants at the 2011 HAND forum at Massachusetts Institute of Technology, the editor (David Lam), and the anonymous referee for helpful comments. All remaining mistakes are mine.
Responsible editor: David Lam

References
Abbasi-Shavazi MJ, McDonald P, Hosseini-Chavoshi M (2009) The fertility transition in Iran. Revolution and Reproduction. Springer, Dordrecht
Aghajanian A (1995) A new direction in population policy and family planning in the Islamic Republic of Iran. Asia-Pacific Popul J United Nations 10(1):3–20
Agüero JM, Marks MS (2008) Motherhood and female labor force participation: evidence from infertility shocks. The American Economic Review, pp 500–504
Almond D, Edlund L (2008) Son-biased sex ratios in the 2000 United States Census. Proc Natl Acad Sci 105(15):5681–5682
Angrist JD, Evans WN (1998) Children and their parents' labor supply: evidence from exogenous variation in family size. Am Econ Rev 88(3):450–477
Becker GS, Lewis HG (1974) Interaction between quantity and quality of children. In Economics of the family: Marriage, children, and human capital. UMI, pp 81–90
Ben-Porath Y, Welch F (1976) Do sex preferences really matter? The Quarterly Journal of Economics, pp 285–307
Bronars SG, Grogger J (1994) The economic consequences of unwed motherhood: using twin births as a natural experiment. Am Econ Rev 84(5):1141–1156
Chun H, Oh J (2002) An instrumental variable estimate of the effect of fertility on the labour force participation of married women. Applied Economics Letters 9(10):631-634
Goldin C (1995) Career and family: College women look to the past (No. w5188). National Bureau of Economic Research
Hoodfar H (1996) Bargaining with fundamentalism: women and the politics of population control in Iran. Reprod Health Matters 4(8):30–40
Majbouri M (2010) Against the wind: labor force participation of women and economic instability in Iran. Available at SSRN 2419323
Majbouri M (2015) Oil, patriarchy, and female labor force participation, Working paper
Mehryar AH, Ahmad-Nia S, Kazemipour S (2007) Reproductive health in Iran: pragmatic achievements, unmet needs, and ethical challenges in a theocratic system. Stud Fam Plann 38(4):352–361
Rosenzweig MR, Wolpin KI (1980) Testing the quantity-quality fertility model: the use of twins as a natural experiment. Econometrica J Econ Soc 48(1):227–240
Ross ML (2008) Oil, Islam, and women. American Political Science Review 102(01):107-123
Schultz TP (1981) Economics of population. Perspectives on Economics Series
Sharabi H (1988) Neopatriarchy: a theory of distorted change in arab society. Oxford University Press, New York
Stock JH, Yogo M (2005) Testing for weak instruments in linear IV regression. Identification and inference for econometric models: Essays in honor of Thomas Rothenberg

7

Do benefit recipients change their labor supply after receiving the cash transfer? Evidence from the Peruvian *Juntos* program

Fernando Fernandez[1]* and Victor Saldarriaga[2]

*Correspondence:
fjfernandez@iadb.org
[1] Inter-American Development
Bank, 1300 New York Avenue NW,
Washington, D.C. 20577 USA
Full list of author information is
available at the end of the article

Abstract

We investigate the short-term labor supply responses to a Conditional Cash Transfers program in Peru. Rather than comparing treated and non-treated households, we examine how benefit recipients change their labor supply after receiving the cash transfer. Our empirical strategy exploits exogenous variation in the distance between the program's payment schedule and interview dates from the Peruvian National Household Survey. Results suggest that cash recipients reduce their labor supply by 6–10 hours in the week following the payment date. This reduction in hours of work is larger for married women and for mothers with children aged 5 or less. In addition, results are robust to different specifications, changes in the sample and a placebo test.

JEL codes: I38, J22
Keywords: Conditional cash transfers; Labor supply; Juntos; Peru

1 Introduction

Around the world, Conditional Cash Transfer programs (henceforth, CCTs) are considered powerful means to reduce poverty. By providing monetary transfers to families conditional on a set of fulfillments, such as school attendance and health care of children, the objective of CCTs is twofold. The first is alleviation of current poverty through periodical stipends; allowing families to increase overall consumption. The second goal is to reduce future poverty by increasing human capital of children, which is achieved by means of program conditionalities.

During recent years, CCTs have received a great attention from policymakers and academics, since significant reductions in poverty levels have been observed after their implementation. Furthermore, these programs have been catalogued as one of the main models of safety-nets in developing economies. After the success of programs such as *Bolsa Escola* in Brazil and *PROGRESA* in Mexico "virtually every country in Latin America has such a program" (Fiszbein and Schady 2009).

Most of the existing literature on the effects of CCTs has focused on scholastic achievement, health and nutritional outcomes of children. However, less attention has been paid to the indirect effects that cash transfers could have on adults' behavior. More specifically, little is known about the effects of CCTs on adult labor supply. While cash transfers are necessary to accomplish improvements in consumption, education and health, they can also generate incentives to reduce work intensity among adults, since this payment can be thought of as a pure *income* effect.

Recent experimental evidence has shown small effects of CCTs on labor supply of adults from beneficiary households (Parker and Skoufias 2000; Maluccio and Flores 2005; Skoufias and Di Maro 2008; Galasso 2006; Foguel and Paes de Barros 2010). This literature relies on comparisons between beneficiaries and non-beneficiaries to estimate the so-called average treatment effect of CCTs on labor supply. Nevertheless, there is no evidence on the immediate labor supply response to cash benefits.

This article deviates from the previous literature in two subtle but important ways. On the one hand, this study represents the first attempt to analyze the transitory effects of welfare programs, namely CCTs, on labor supply. That is, we do *not* aim to estimate the average treatment effect of CCTs on labor supply. Instead, we are interested in exploring whether benefit recipients change their labor supply after they receive the cash transfer. On the other hand, we adopt a novel empirical strategy which exploits exogenous variation in the difference between the program's pay dates and interview dates of a household survey. The combination of pay dates and interview dates allows us to compare beneficiaries' labor supply before and after receiving the cash transfer. We think of these deviations as representing our contribution to the literature on the labor supply responses to cash transfers.

There are several reasons why analyzing immediate labor supply responses to cash transfers can be of particular interest. First, cash recipients are independent workers and the available evidence suggests that such workers do not behave according to life-cycle models of labor supply but instead they work "one day at a time" (Camerer et al. 1997; Fehr and Goette 2007; Goette et al. 2004). Moreover, these studies argue that independent workers (who are free to choose when and how much to work) are better described as having income targets: once they reach their income target they stop working. Second, beneficiaries of CCTs are, by construction, credit constrained. These restrictions may prevent households to smooth consumption and leisure and, therefore, both variables may react to the timing of cash transfers. Indeed, empirical studies have shown that consumption of welfare recipients jumps up after the pay date and then declines (Shapiro 2005; Mastrobuoni and Weinberg 2009). Third, benefit recipients of CCTs live in rural areas where access to markets is quite limited. In such locations, every time beneficiaries are paid, they must incur in transportation costs (money but also time). Therefore, these short-term responses are relevant for the design of CCTs. In particular, the time that beneficiaries spend picking up the money is an opportunity cost that policy makers should take into account when choosing among alternative payment methods (bank deposits versus cash-in-hand) and frequencies (monthly versus bimonthly).

We find that cash recipients (female household heads) hours of work are reduced by 6 hours in the week following the pay date. This reduction is rather large, since it implies a decline of roughly 20% of their weekly hours of work. Moreover, this decrease in hours of work is larger for married women and mothers with children aged 5 or less. However, no significant effects are found for labor force participation, nor for the probability of working for paid activities. We do not find significant effects of cash transfers on the labor supply of recipients' partners (when we restrict the sample to married recipients).

The document is structured as follows. Related literature is reviewed in Section 2. In Section 3, we describe the program, named *Juntos* and its mechanics. Section 4 presents the econometric set-up and describes the data. Section 5 presents the results and additional robustness checks. In Section 6 we discuss our results and make comparisons with respect to previous empirical findings. Section 7 concludes.

2 Literature review

2.1 Theoretical considerations

Research on labor supply responses to welfare programs has long been a subject of interest for economists, especially in developed economies where the expansion of benefit transfer programs to low-income population was initiated during the 1960s. Since then, researchers and policy-makers have been concerned on how welfare programs affect working incentives of beneficiaries as well as the indirect (unintended) effects these transfers may generate on non-targeted population living in localities covered by the program.

For instance, the effect of welfare programs on labor supply has been widely studied. The most prominent programs are Aid to Families with Dependent Children (AFDC), the Earned Income Tax Credit (EITC), and more recently the Food Stamp Program in the U.S. along with the Working Families Tax Credit in the U.K. (see Moffitt 2002 for an extended review and discussion). The discussion of how welfare participation affects labor supply of adults can be divided according to (i) the predicted effects of the canonical model of labor supply, (ii) program conditions, and (iii) models of household labor supply.

The potential effects of benefit transfers can be explained based on the basic static model of labor supply. In this model, individuals maximize between consumption and leisure facing a budget constraint, which is composed by labor (wage) and non-labor (initial wealth and monetary or in-kind transfers) income. In this study, we focus on the particular role CCTs can play in determining working incentives[1].

As pointed out by Alzúa et al. (2013), CCTs have four potential channels through which adult labor supply could be affected. First, cash transfers represent an increment in non-labor income. Given that no conditions are imposed with regard to labor effort of beneficiaries, this lump-sum transfer is a pure income effect, and therefore, both employment and working hours are expected to decline. Second, program conditions can also alter working behavior of adults. For instance, most of the conditions attached to cash transfer programs imply school enrolment and a maximum number of days accepted for children to be absent from school. This increase in school attendance of children allows parents to augment labor participation and working hours as well, for they avoid allocating time in childcare. Third, if child labor is crucial in determining households' budget constraint, increasing school attendance would also affect adult labor supply. Fourth, cash transfers can also affect local markets, and thereby, have an indirect impact on non-beneficiaries. Using a sample from the Mexican *PROGRESA* program, Angelucci and De Giorgi (2009) find that consumption of ineligible households increases in villages where the program was randomly implemented. Alternatively, qualitative studies (Segovia 2001, for example) have described the appearance of fairs ever since CCTs arrived to different localities[2].

Another important consideration is whether welfare programs impose arbitrary restrictions on adult labor supply in order to circumvent working disincentives. Despite the initial unconditional intent related to working effort, some developed countries have indexed program benefits according to the labor supply behavior of beneficiaries. For instance, the Temporary Assistance for Needy Families (TANF) program in the U.S. (formerly known as the AFDC) initially imposes that at least 20% of TANF recipients in each State participate in work or work-related activities for a minimum of 20 hours per week. These activities include regular employment, subsidized employment, commuting, on the job training, and 12 months of vocational training for young beneficiaries aiming to participate in the labor force. Alternatively, the EITC program, also in the U.S., consists in a refundable tax credit for low- and medium-income families which increases according to a standard range of annually labor income and the number of qualifying children in the family[3]. These types of cash transfers, both conditional on minimum working hours or increasing with earned income, act like a contract rigidity, not allowing individuals to make optimal allocation of working hours. Thus, especially in the case of the EITC where the benefit is attached to labor income, the response on individual working effort would depend on which of the two possible effects - substitution or income - prevail. Empirical findings suggest that it is participation (entry) rather than hours of work which responds to the EITC[4].

Unlike these "tied welfare benefits", CCTs in Latin American do not restrict eligibility on labor force participation[5]. This lack of restrictions implies that the *looseness* of the budget constraint due to the welfare benefit introduces a pure income effect, hence, encouraging beneficiaries to demand more leisure. Further, if those individuals barely ineligibles (say because of being just above the poverty line) reduce their working effort in order to narrow down total income and "cheat" the system to become eligibles, then the net effect of CCTs on labor supply would depend not only on the amount of reduced working hours of the ever-eligibles and the formerly ineligibles, but also on the behavior of the latter group once they have been selected as program beneficiaries and the transfer has been received (e.g., they can return to their initial - optimal - working effort)[6].

An open question is who in the family actually reduces his working effort. Since cash is usually transferred to a particular household member (i.e., housewives), it is worth taking into consideration how welfare is distributed among family members. For this reason, theoretical considerations of models of household labor supply can also add useful insights. In this line, aside from the potential effects of CCTs on individual adult labor supply, there exists an open debate on whether families pool their welfare resources. According to this hypothesis, family members act as if they are maximizing a single utility function. Two separate models have been developed associated to this "unitary" behavior: the "agreement" (Samuelson 1956) and the "dominant family member" frameworks (Becker 1981).

Maximizing a single utility function implies that, regardless of who receives the welfare income, each of the family members would benefit from the monetary transfer through an intra-family allocation process. In contrast to this "common will" frame, individual cooperative utility models of intra-family bargaining processes (Manser and Brown 1980; McElroy and Horney 1981; and Lundberg and Pollak 1993) as well as non cooperative bargaining models (Lundberg and Pollak 1994) have also been postulated. In these models, income is administered by a single agent within the family (for example, the mother) and thus allocation of resources on consumption and leisure could differ across household members.

Recent empirical evidence suggests that single cooperative utility functions prevail in the family bargaining process. Regarding welfare benefits, Lundberg et al. (1997) test the hypothesis of whether families pool their resources exploiting a U.K. policy change which dictated that child allowances were to be transferred exclusively to wives (mothers). The authors find evidence that this policy change induced women to spend more resources on women's and children's clothing relative to men's clothing. In spite of labor supply, Bertrand et al. (2003) suggest that drops in prime-age men's labor supply are stronger than that of prime-age women when the South African pension benefits are received by women. In a recent study, Ardington et al. (2009) discuss that pension benefits could, in the case of perfect resource sharing within the family, reduce hours of work and participation of adults, or in the case of imperfect credit markets, social pensions can be used as a credit support for job seekers.

2.2 Empirical evidence from Latin American countries

To the best of our knowledge, seven empirical studies have been carried out addressing the potential effects of CCTs on adult labor supply in Latin American countries. Identification strategies of most of these studies are based on the fact of random treatment (most of them at the village level) of the CCTs across the targeted population.

Parker and Skoufias (2000) exploit the experimental design of the Mexican *PROGRESA* program (currently known as *Oportunidades*), which randomly assigned treated and control villages, to address the question of whether CCTs alter labor participation and overall leisure time of adults. The authors find no significant effects of program participation on participation rates in the labor force. Instead, they do find that women are more likely to reduce hours allocated to leisure mainly because of program commitments such as taking children to schools, health centers and participating in community work.

In a later study, Skoufias and Di Maro (2008) evaluate the effects of *PROGRESA* on outcomes measuring adult labor supply. Alike Parker and Skoufias (2000) their identification strategy relies on a difference-in-differences estimation procedure comparing eligible adults living in treated villages (beneficiaries) versus eligible adults living in non treated low-income Mexican villages. The authors do not find statistically significant effects of program participation on the probability of being employed. Moreover, given random assignment of program deployment across villages, the authors find that cross-sectional estimates of CCTs on working hours of adults living in treated villages are not statistically different from working hours of adults living in (randomly) untreated villages.

Using a similar estimation methodology for the Nicaraguan *Red de Protección Social (RPS)* program, Maluccio and Flores (2005) find that program participation reduces men's (but not women's) working effort by 5.5 hours. Maluccio (2010) analyzes the effect of *RPS* on the overall household labor supply; that is, the sum of each member's labor intensity. The author finds a negative small but statistically significant effect of the program on household hours of work, especially in agricultural activities, and argues that this reduction can be explained based on the fact that these activities are perhaps associated to lower marginal rates of return. In contrast, Foguel and Paes de Barros (2010) find no statistically significant effects of six Brazilian programs (*Bolsa Escola, Bolsa Alimentação, Bolsa Família*, among others) on adult labor supply, neither on the extensive nor the intensive margins.

Galasso (2006) uses propensity score matching and regression discontinuity methods for evaluating the impact of *Chile Solidario* on adult labor supply. Although positive impacts are found for the take-up of labor market programs, such as re-insertion and training programs, the author finds no increments on the share of beneficiaries who are employed, nor on the share of beneficiaries who have a stable employment. However, increases in participation rates in the labor force are observed only for rural areas.

Finally, Alzúa et al. (2013) find negative but small - if not inexistent - effects of three different programs from Latin American countries (*RPS* in Nicaragua, *PROGRESA* in Mexico, and *Programa de Asignación Familiar* in Honduras) on adult labor force participation and the probability of migrating from agricultural to other working activities. However, they do find a reduction of about 4.7 to 6.3 weekly hours worked in the case of Nicaraguan *RPS* and a positive and significant effect of Mexican *PROGRESA* program on male wages.

Most of the aforementioned studies rely on the experimental design of the different programs evaluated, and most of them (with the exception of Galasso 2006 and Skoufias and Di Maro 2008) fail to control for the possibility of reallocation of working effort of ineligibles in communities or villages regarding program deployment, as pointed out by Angelucci and De Giorgi (2009). Not taking into account this potential effect may introduce negative bias (in absolute terms) to the parameters of interest assuming that ineligibles are more prone to increase their labor intensity given the increase in the demand for consumable goods and agricultural productive assets in days nearby the transfer schedules. Because this potential increase in the demand of a particular set of goods may increase real wages of ineligibles (introducing a substitution effect), previous empirical findings based on double-difference comparisons are likely to understate the labor supply responses to CCTs.

Unlike previous studies we adopt a different approach to measure labor force variations as a response to welfare income. In particular, we are interested in exploring whether working behavior changes in days near *Juntos* pay dates. Although this analysis does not allow us to identify average treatment effects of program participation on working effort of adults, it is useful for reconciling theoretical aspects of the canonical labor supply model with empirical evidence. The advantage of examining short-term effects of cash transfers on labor supply of adults is that: (i) it is possible to disentangle *income* effects from general equilibrium effects often observed in the long run, and (ii) capture effects of transfers itself and no other effects such as labor supply responses of parents to a reduction in child labor introduced by the program.

3 The program and its mechanics

3.1 Background

The Peruvian *Juntos* program was implemented on April 2005 after a period of political upheaval and relatively economic stagnation experimented at the beginning of the new century during government transition. By 2002, with the new economic reforms brought up by the former president Alejandro Toledo, the country's economy began to recover reaching growth rates above 5% by the mid-2000s. Together, the economic expansion and the implementation of welfare programs focusing on poverty alleviation and job creation lead to a significant increase of mean per capita income (from US$ 2,450 by 2005 to US$ 4,050 PPP by the end of year 2010) and, more strikingly, a sharp reduction of roughly 50% of the overall poverty rate which went from 54% in the mid-2000s to 27% by the end of the last decade.

Particularly, *Juntos* periodically transfers a stipend to families living in poverty and extreme poverty conditions, and in return, families must meet certain requirements including schooling and health care. The program was created with the aim of strengthening government presence in remote areas of the country and providing eligible families with a set of health, nutritional, educational, and identity services, for enhancing health and nutritional status of pregnant women and their babies, nursing women, and infants, as well as fostering human capital accumulation of children under age 14.

Juntos is still the most remarkable amid the social welfare programs in Peru, which has generated the greatest impacts on poverty alleviation and human capital accumulation of children. This can be noticed through the great expansion of the program since it began to operate. By 2005, almost 22,500 households living in 26 municipalities benefited from this program, whereas in 2012 *Juntos* was deployed in almost 1,011 municipalities, representing roughly 55.2% of the national territory and benefiting 649,553 households living in poverty and extreme poverty conditions. Recently, Perova and Vakis (2012) found that *Juntos* increased overall household income by 43% and was responsible of a 16% and 30% decrease in poverty and extreme poverty rates, respectively, in municipalities where *Juntos* was initially deployed[7].

In terms of investments, public expenditures generated by *Juntos* went from US$ 45 million in 2005 to US$ 177 million in 2007. In this latter year, there was a noticeable expansion of the program along the Peruvian territory, covering almost 612 more municipalities and more than 400,000 households relative to the 2005 wave. By the end of 2012, public expenditures associated to *Juntos* were calculated to be almost US$ 225 million. This figure represents roughly 18% of the Peruvian expenditures in safety-net programs.

3.2 Eligibility

Juntos is a means tested program. As Perova and Vakis (2012) clearly describe, selection of the beneficiary households consists in three steps. The first one is related to selection of eligible municipalities. This selection is based on five criteria: (i) exposure to violence during the late 1980s and early 1990s terrorism era; (ii) poverty level, measured as the proportion of population with unsatisfied needs; (iii) poverty gap; (iv) level of under five chronic malnutrition; and (v) presence of extreme income poverty.

The second step consists in a census of all households in eligible districts collected by the Instituto Nacional de Estadística e Informática (INEI). A proxy means formula was used to determine household eligibility, based on poverty. Only households with the presence of children under age 14 or pregnant women were selected. The algorithm for defining eligibility of households is based on a Logit model, which estimates the probability of a household living in poverty conditional on a set of observable characteristics.

Finally, the third stage consists in community validation. This was done in community assemblies, carried out by local authorities and representatives of the Ministry of Education and Ministry of Health with the aim of minimizing inclusion and exclusion errors. In general, final selection depends on community validation, and once the household is selected, the housewife (household recipient) must sign a letter in which the household is committed to meet the co-responsibilities, and a health center or post is selected in order for the beneficiaries to make their periodical medical checkups.

Once the household is enrolled in the program, transfers are given to the female head of the household according to the payment schedule defined by the program's administration. According to the Peruvian National Household Survey (ENAHO, for its Spanish acronym), almost 99% of female heads reported to be receiving the transfer on a monthly basis.

3.3 Components

Initially, the monthly amount was 100 Nuevos Soles (Peruvian local currency). This amount is roughly equivalent to US\$ 37 (in current dollars). Since 2010, however, the amount was doubled (200 Nuevos Soles) but beneficiaries would receive the cash transfer every two months so that the level of the annual amount remained unchanged (1200 Nuevos Soles). This change was introduced because of the low rate of money withdrawal from bank accounts given the long distances beneficiaries must travel in order to pick up the money. In our context, the monthly transfer was quite generous, representing over 50% of beneficiaries' monthly per capita household expenditures.

Pay dates are defined at the village level which implies that some municipalities have more than one payment date. *Juntos* sets a particular day in every village so we have some within-municipality variation in payment dates. However, within a district, all payments occur on the same week. This feature of the program does not represent a major problem to our strategy as it will be shown in Section 5.

Once they receive the cash, beneficiaries are free to choose how they spend the money. However, all beneficiaries must meet the following conditions: (i) children of ages 6–14 years attend at least 85% school classes; (ii) children of ages 0–59 months get fully immunized and visit health centers where their growth is measured and vitamins are provided; (iii) children of ages 3–36 months get nutrition supplements; (iv) pregnant women visit health clinics for prenatal care; (v) nursing women visit health centers for postnatal care; (vi) parents attend health clinics to receive information about nutrition, health and hygiene; (vii) parents without ID (identification) attend the program Mi Nombre (*My Name*). *Juntos* was initially intended as a program of temporary assistance to families, with a duration of 4 years, conditional on households escaping from poverty. Yet, impoverished households can renew their participation for 4 more years with a benefit reduction of 20%.

In 2009 there were two payment methods through which beneficiaries can receive the cash transfer. The main way to receive the cash was to go to the local branch of the Peruvian National Bank and withdraw the money (54% of the beneficiaries in our sample). The second way was to go to the main square of the village on the day of payment and wait for an armored van which contained the money. The difference between these methods is that the former allows the beneficiary to go to the bank at some other day while the latter does not. Moreover, the armored van constitutes a deliver mechanism in which beneficiaries do not spend much time in going to withdraw the money. Finally, both systems are mutually exclusive at the village level so beneficiaries do not choose the way they get the money.

4 Methodology

4.1 Econometric model

Differences between Juntos pay dates and ENAHO's interview dates within a given municipality constitute the basis of our empirical strategy. In particular, we will explore whether labor supply is reduced in the days near the pay dates. What we do in practice is to compare beneficiaries, within the same municipality, who are interviewed just after the payment to those who are not. Given that most households members are engaged in agricultural and highly-flexible occupations (i.e., independent workers), it is likely to observe that individuals reduce their working effort in days following the cash receipt.

Though we exploit within-municipality variation in interview dates of ENAHO, our measure of temporal distance is constructed as the difference between pay dates and the week previous to the survey. This week prior to the interview day is called the "reference week". When interviewers survey households, they usually ask household members whether they have done specific activities during the last seven days. For instance, when asking about labor force participation, interviewers ask the following question: "during the last week, from [day 1] to [interview day], did you have any job?". Given the way the survey is conducted, all outcomes related to labor supply of surveyed members correspond to the seven days prior to the interview day (i.e., the reference week).

For the empirical analysis, we construct four dummy variables according to the distance between the pay day and the reference week. Specifically, the first dummy variable is equal to one if the pay date takes place, at least, two weeks before the reference week, and zero otherwise. Similarly, the second dummy takes the value of one when the pay date occurs one week before the reference week, and zero otherwise. The third dummy variable is equal to one if the pay date happens some day during the reference week, and zero otherwise. Finally, the fourth dummy variable takes the value of one when the pay date takes place after the reference week, and zero if not[8].

We divide the temporal distance between pay dates and interview dates in terms of weeks for two reasons. First, as pointed earlier, within a given municipality there exists a probability to observe more than one pay date. This is because administrative records on pay dates are available at the village level, which is the smallest geopolitical unit in Peru. Yet, ENAHO dataset contains geographical identifiers only at the municipality level (which may contain more than one village). This data limitation forces us to collapse administrative records containing payment dates by village at the municipality level in order to merge them with the ENAHO dataset. When doing so, almost all villages (99.8% in our sample) within a given municipality are observed to have pay dates during the same week. Second, it has been observed that not all beneficiaries withdraw the money on the very same pay date. For this reason, we assume a rather more parsimonious definition of temporal distance which allows for some delay in order for beneficiaries to have the money.

When observing a municipality with more than one pay date, we use the earliest pay date to define the distance between payments and interviews. Though this criterion may introduce measurement bias, we also perform additional regressions using the last pay date within the municipalities to re-define temporal distance between payments and interviews. In Section 5.3, however, we perform an additional sensitivity analysis to check whether results hold when using exact payment dates.

Figure 1 depicts hours worked in the reference week for distinct groups of beneficiaries according to the distance (in weeks) between pay dates and the reference week. The first group is composed of individuals who received the cash transfer two or more weeks before they were interviewed (i.e., received the transfer at least two weeks before the reference week). Similarly, the second, third, and fourth groups are composed of individuals for whom the cash transfer occurred one week before, during, and one week after the reference week, respectively. The decline of hours worked during the reference week is

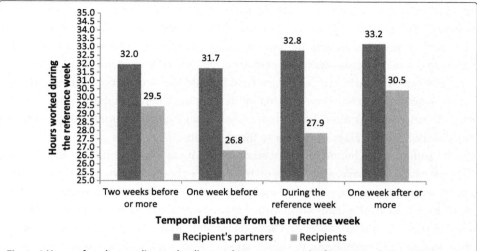

Figure 1 Hours of work according to the distance between pay and reference week. *Notes*: Dark grey bars correspond to hours of work during the reference week of recipient's partners. Light grey bars correspond to hours of work during the reference week of benefit recipients (housewives). Each pair of bars represents weekly hours of work according to the temporal distance (in weeks) between the pay and interview dates. "Two weeks before or more" implies that the payment was observed to occur at least two weeks before the reference week. "One week before" implies that the payment occurred one week before the reference week. "During the reference week" denotes that the payment occurred in some day corresponding to the reference week. "One week after or more" denotes that the payment will occur one week after the individual is surveyed.

linked to the week in which the transfer is received for all individuals included in our sample, and this decline is largest among those who receive the cash transfer one week before the reference week. Furthermore, this decline is larger for cash recipients than for their partners. This greater decline in weekly hours worked can be interpreted as containing effects of (i) time spent in going to withdraw the money, (ii) time taken to spent the money once it is received (i.e., purchasing consumption goods), and (iii) income effects. The first two effects are related to the program's features, and do not represent disincentives to work. Thus, we are particularly interested in isolating the third effect from the overall labor supply response to welfare transfers.

Based on the graphical evidence and exploiting within-municipality differences between pay dates and interview dates (reference week), we estimate the following model:

$$y_{ij} = \alpha + \sum_k \delta_k d_{ij} + X_i'\beta + \lambda_j + \mu_{ij}, \tag{1}$$

where y_{ij} is the outcome variable (labor force participation, hours of work, etc.) of individual i living in municipality j, d_{ij} denotes the distance (in weeks) between the payment and the reference week, X_i is a vector of individual characteristics, λ_j is a vector of municipality fixed effects, and μ_{ij} is an error term capturing all other omitted factors. Our parameters of interest are denoted by δ_k, which measures the effect of the distance between pay dates and interview dates. Therefore, these parameters are recovered using across-municipalities variation in pay dates and within-municipality variation in interview dates. In what follows, the omitted category is that the payment takes place at least two weeks before the reference week (i.e., the first dummy variable).

In this specification, each dummy may capture a specific effect related to the distance between pay dates and the reference week. For instance, the second dummy variable, "payment occurs one week before the reference week", might capture effects related to purchasing consumable goods with the cash received, whereas the third dummy variable, "payment occurs during the reference week", could capture effects related to the time spent in going to the bank and picking up the money. The fourth dummy variable, "payment occurs one week after the reference week", may capture additional changes in working effort of individuals in days prior to the cash transfer.

There are some caveats in our empirical strategy which are worth describing with further detail. First, we only have information on pay dates established by *Juntos* but we fail to observe the actual date the beneficiary went to the bank to withdraw the money. For this reason, we assume that recipients withdraw the money within the week in which the cash transfer was made available[9]. Second, it may be possible that when interviewers arrive to a given municipality, they begin to survey families who work less (i.e., those who are almost always present at home) and then survey families who work harder. If this were the case, our estimates should be seen as a lower bound (in absolute terms), since those who were surveyed earlier are more likely to be captured in the omitted category of distance between pay and interview dates, and by construction, all our parameters of interest are interpreted as a function of the omitted category. Thus, this omitted category captures the average working intensity of individuals who were surveyed earlier, and are presumed to have a lower labor intensity[10]. Finally, our indicators of distance between pay and interview dates may capture other effects not related to the transfer but correlated with other unobservable variables. For instance, it could be the case that pay days are established on days when labor supply is low for a different reason than the transfer (e.g., holidays). To check this is not the case, we perform falsification tests in Section 5.3.

Variation in pay and interview dates is crucial to our strategy. In Table 1, we present the distribution of payment dates associated with the cash transfer from *Juntos*. Regarding the day of the month, we do not find any special pattern. If anything, we could say that there is a slight concentration around the third week of the month, between the 16th and the 20th day. Regarding the day of the week, it seems that Mondays are the most common day of payment while Sundays are the least frequent. The distribution of interview dates is presented in the bottom half of the table. The frequency of dates looks pretty balanced throughout the month. It is also worth noticing that almost all interviews are conducted on Sundays, when most of the family members stay at home. Finally, the survey process within a municipality has an average duration of 30 days.

4.2 Data

Our primary source of information is the ENAHO conducted in 2009 by INEI. The ENAHO collects individual level information and is a nationwide representative survey, both in urban and rural areas. We use information from the employment and income registry, which restricts the sample only for individuals aged 14 or older. The ENAHO has three important features. First, it includes several questions which allow us to accurately identify households receiving monetary transfers from *Juntos*. This is particularly important since the program design refers to women as the benefit recipients. Second, this survey includes questions regarding relationship with the family head, enabling us to distinguish the potential impact for different household members, say male heads and

Table 1 Distribution of payment and interview dates

Panel A: Payment dates	Frequency	Percentage
Day of the month		
1-5	323	8,5
6-10	485	12,8
11-15	726	19,2
16-20	1006	26,6
21-25	712	18,8
26-31	529	14,0
Day of the week		
Sunday	178	4,7
Monday	1,099	29,1
Tuesday	512	13,5
Wednesday	490	13,0
Thursday	648	17,1
Friday	449	11,9
Saturday	405	10,7
Panel B: Interview dates	**Frequency**	**Percentage**
Day of the month		
1-5	664	17,0
6-10	579	14,8
11-15	892	22,9
16-20	556	14,3
21-25	624	16,0
26-31	584	15,0
Day of the week		
Sunday	3,780	99,97
Monday	1	0,03

Sources: Juntos administrative data (payment dates) and ENAHO surveys (interview dates).

female spouses (cash recipients). Finally, this dataset provides a rich set of variables that allows us to construct different labor supply outcomes and include a wide set of controls in our regressions.

To precisely estimate the impact of the proximity to the payment date on labor supply outcomes we need a representative sample of all municipalities which are beneficiaries from *Juntos*. By 2009, 638 municipalities were part of the program. Given that the ENAHO follows a stratified sampling procedure, this survey collected information in 260 municipalities enrolled in *Juntos* in this particular year. This represents roughly 40.8% of the municipalities in which the *Juntos* program was present in 2009. Nevertheless, when expanding the sample using the survey weights from the sampling design, Perova and Vakis (2012) find that the number of households which report receiving cash transfers from *Juntos* surveyed in the ENAHO 2009 is very close to the actual number of beneficiary households listed in the program's official records. We therefore use sample weights in all of our regressions and correct standard errors taking into account ENAHO's sampling design.

As an additional concern we check whether the transfer conditions are consistently reproduced in each of the surveyed households. In other words, we check that (i) the benefit recipient is the mother (female household head or the head's spouse), (ii) women report to receive 100 Peruvian Nuevos Soles (around 37 U.S. current dollars), and (iii) the frequency of transfers is monthly. Around 98% of the cash recipients in our sample are women satisfying the mentioned conditions.

We also check that surveyed households who are receiving monetary transfers from *Juntos* satisfy the eligibility conditions. Despite the fact that eligible households should be below the poverty line in order to receive the transfer, our sample suggests that around 19% of the households are above the poverty line defined by INEI. We exclude non-poor households from our empirical analysis below and discuss in Section 5.3 how including these households can affect our results[11].

Information on pay dates comes from administrative records provided by *Juntos* managers[12]. As mentioned in Section 4.1, payment schedules are reported at the village level. Unique municipality identifiers are used to match the information of payment dates from the administrative dataset, previously collapsed at the municipality level, to the beneficiaries sample built up from the ENAHO 2009. Our final sample contains information of 1,995 individuals living in 1,087 households enrolled in *Juntos*. Of these individuals, 1,615 live in poor conditions, whereas 380 are not poor according to the standard per-capita daily expenditure measure. Variable averages and standard errors (reported in parentheses) are shown in Table 2. Each column reports summary statistics of all individuals included in each of our four dummy variables defining temporal distance between pay and interview dates.

4.3 Outcome variables

We focus on three different measures of labor supply: participation (extensive margin) weekly hours worked (intensive margin) and working for paid activities. As described above, each of the outcome variables are measured for the week before (reference week) the interview (which usually takes place on Sundays).

Labor participation is a dummy variable which is equal to one when the individual reported having worked or searching for a job any time during the reference week. To measure labor intensity, we take the total number of hours worked during the same reference week. Lastly, the indicator for working for paid activities is relevant for evidencing changes in labor supply alternative margins once the payment has already been done or is about to occur (for instance, household members could reallocate time to family or home production related unpaid activities once the cash has been transferred). The last two outcome variables are defined only for those who reported having been employed during the reference week.

Given that we have information of the number of hours worked on each day of the reference week, we are also able to test whether individuals change their labor supply behavior in a given day or whether they balance their labor intensity throughout the whole week. This insight will be helpful when interpreting our main results.

5 Results
5.1 Main results

Table 3 reports the results for the equation of labor force participation. Each row indicates the distance between the cash transfer receipt and the reference week. Columns (3), (6), and (9) are our preferred specifications since they control for municipality fixed effects as well as individual covariates (sex, age, educational level, marital status, indicators for mother tongue, indicators for poverty status, an indicator for rural residence, and

Table 2 Descriptive Statistics (according to temporal distance between pay and reference week)

Variable	Temporal distance between pay and reference week			
	At least two weeks before	One week before	During the reference week	At least one week after
Age	43.53	41.70	42.53	42.27
	(12.16)	(10.60)	(12.29)	(11.68)
Male	0.47	0.48	0.46	0.46
	(0.50)	(0.50)	(0.50)	(0.50)
Education level: No education	0.19	0.18	0.17	0.19
	(0.39)	(0.39)	(0.38)	(0.39)
Education level: Primary	0.60	0.67	0.64	0.63
	(0.49)	(0.47)	(0.48)	(0.48)
Education level: Secondary	0.21	0.14	0.18	0.17
	(0.40)	(0.34)	(0.38)	(0.37)
Education level: Tertiary	0.01	0.01	0.01	0.01
	(0.11)	(0.12)	(0.11)	(0.11)
Mother tongue: Spanish	0.30	0.28	0.33	0.27
	(0.46)	(0.45)	(0.47)	(0.44)
Mother tongue: Quechua	0.61	0.71	0.62	0.68
	(0.49)	(0.46)	(0.49)	(0.46)
Mother tongue: Other	0.09	0.01	0.05	0.05
	(0.28)	(0.09)	(0.22)	(0.22)
Poverty condition: Extremely poor	0.40	0.47	0.43	0.47
	(0.49)	(0.50)	(0.50)	(0.50)
Poverty condition: Poor	0.37	0.39	0.36	0.35
	(0.48)	(0.49)	(0.48)	(0.48)
Poverty condition: Non poor	0.22	0.14	0.21	0.18
	(0.42)	(0.35)	(0.41)	(0.39)
Lives in rural area	0.90	0.77	0.83	0.86
	(0.30)	(0.42)	(0.37)	(0.35)
In labor force	0.95	0.93	0.93	0.95
	(0.21)	(0.25)	(0.26)	(0.22)
Weekly hours worked	30.66	29.25	30.19	31.77
	(15.68)	(15.91)	(17.97)	(16.22)
Worked for paid activities	0.55	0.58	0.53	0.55
	(0.50)	(0.49)	(0.50)	(0.50)
Observations	563	425	442	565

interactions between indicators of distance between the payment date and the reference week and the dummy variable determining whether or not the individual is the household head). Results from these columns suggest that there are no effects of the cash transfer receipt on labor force participation, even when splitting the sample by recipients and recipients' partners.

Table 4 shows results for the equation of hours worked in the reference week. For the sample as a whole, there are no significant effects on the intensive margin. However, we find that having received the cash transfer within the seven days before the reference week reduces about 5.7 hours of work in the reference week for recipients only - see column (6). Recall that the effect of the transfer among recipients may be driven by two possible confounding factors: time spent in transportation from the

Table 3 Effects of temporal distance between pay and reference week on labor force participation

Transfer occurred:	All individuals			Recipients			Recipients' partners		
	(1)	(2)	(3)	(4)	(5)	(6)	(7)	(8)	(9)
One week before the reference week	-0.028*	-0.009	-0.009	-0.072**	-0.044	-0.044	0.015*	0.006	0.148
	(0.016)	(0.030)	(0.030)	(0.029)	(0.060)	(0.060)	(0.009)	(0.007)	(0.203)
During the reference week	-0.027	-0.011	-0.011	-0.054*	-0.046	-0.046	0.002	0.019	0.162
	(0.017)	(0.032)	(0.032)	(0.029)	(0.059)	(0.059)	(0.012)	(0.016)	(0.206)
At least one week after the reference week	-0.011	-0.007	-0.007	-0.029	-0.024	-0.024	0.010	-0.001	-0.319
	(0.014)	(0.024)	(0.024)	(0.024)	(0.047)	(0.047)	(0.010)	(0.009)	(0.336)
Municipality fixed effects	No	Yes	Yes	No	Yes	Yes	No	Yes	Yes
Additional controls	No	No	Yes	No	No	Yes	No	No	Yes
Observations	1,615	1,615	1,615	859	859	859	756	756	756
R-squared	0.003	0.144	0.144	0.008	0.284	0.284	0.005	0.280	0.280

Notes: Robust standard errors in parentheses. Additional controls include: an indicator for sex, an indicator for marital status (married or living together), age, indicators for educational level (primary, secondary, tertiary), an indicator for Spanish mother tongue, an indicator for poverty status, an indicator for living in rural areas, and interactions terms between an indicator for household head and temporal distance between pay and reference week.
***p < 0.01, **p < 0.05, *p < 0.1.

location of residence to the bank and time spent in purchasing the goods or consuming the money once it has been withdrawn from the bank. If those who were paid during the reference week have also anticipated the transfer date (and, therefore, have reduced their working hours) and have spent some time in receiving the transfer, then the resulting point estimate for those who were paid one week before

Table 4 Effects of temporal distance between pay and reference week on weekly hours of work

Transfer occurred:	All individuals			Recipients			Recipients' partners		
	(1)	(2)	(3)	(4)	(5)	(6)	(7)	(8)	(9)
One week before the reference week	-0.558	-1.899	-1.756	-1.640	-4.192*	-5.618**	0.241	-0.425	-0.726
	(1.131)	(1.840)	(1.832)	(1.398)	(2.284)	(2.397)	(1.789)	(2.903)	(2.916)
During the reference week	-0.294	-1.234	-0.972	-0.790	-0.594	-1.836	0.196	-1.537	-1.155
	(1.164)	(1.849)	(1.835)	(1.414)	(2.213)	(2.367)	(1.872)	(3.017)	(3.012)
At least one week after the reference week	1.308	0.678	0.996	0.992	3.802	2.573	1.614	-3.312	-2.332
	(1.073)	(1.825)	(1.806)	(1.300)	(2.206)	(2.295)	(1.729)	(2.918)	(2.919)
Municipality fixed effects	No	Yes	Yes	No	Yes	Yes	No	Yes	Yes
Additional controls	No	NoZ	Yes	No	No	Yes	No	No	Yes
Observations	1,577	1,577	1,577	827	827	827	750	750	750
R-squared	0.002	0.259	0.259	0.005	0.395	0.395	0.001	0.419	0.436

Notes: Robust standard errors in parentheses. See additional notes on Table 3.
***p < 0.01, **p < 0.05, *p < 0.1.

the reference week is not driven by these particular confounding effects. Nonetheless, time spent in purchasing goods with the received money could also be affecting our estimates[13].

Table 5 reports the results for the equation of "working for paid activities". Results do not show a clear pattern regarding the effects of the distance between pay and interview dates on working in a paid-job, even for different household members. Moreover, these effects are statistically insignificant. One possible interpretation for the lack of effects of the cash transfer receipt on the probability of working for paid activities is that there may exist some rigidities in switching from unpaid to paid jobs in the very short run.

Given the results, all the remaining analysis is based on the short run effects of cash transfers on hours of work. In the following lines we try to disentangle the potential *income* effect generated by the welfare transfer from the aforementioned confounding effects. To do so, we begin by exploring whether the reduction in working hours brought up by the welfare transfer is evenly distributed along the whole week or if it is concentrated in a particular day or days of the reference week. Under the hypothesis that the reduction in hours of work is being driven by time spent in purchasing goods (once we control for the potential anticipation and transportation effects), one should expect that the effect of the transfer is grouped in a particular day of the week (say, the day which is closer to the payment date).

In Table 6 we report the resulting coefficients for every day of the reference week. Consistent with the estimates shown in Table 4, we find negative and significant effects for those who are paid within the seven days before the reference week. Specifically, we find that working hours are reduced by roughly 1.3 hours in every day except for Sundays. In addition, we find that hours of work on Thursday are reduced by 1 hour if payment occurs during the reference week.

Overall, results show a decrease in hours worked when payment occurs in the reference week. This reduction is most likely to be driven by time spent on going to the bank.

Table 5 Effects of temporal distance between pay and reference week on working for paid activities

Transfer occurred:	All individuals			Recipients			Recipients' partners		
	(1)	(2)	(3)	(4)	(5)	(6)	(7)	(8)	(9)
One week before the reference week	0.027	0.070	0.070	-0.019	-0.015	-0.015	0.004	0.028	0.027
	(0.035)	(0.065)	(0.065)	(0.037)	(0.062)	(0.062)	(0.016)	(0.024)	(0.024)
During the reference week	-0.020	-0.062	-0.062	-0.030	-0.086	-0.086	-0.026	-0.003	-0.005
	(0.037)	(0.065)	(0.065)	(0.037)	(0.064)	(0.064)	(0.021)	(0.026)	(0.026)
At least one week after the reference week	0.005	-0.029	-0.029	0.001	-0.081	-0.081	-0.003	0.001	0.010
	(0.034)	(0.065)	(0.065)	(0.035)	(0.065)	(0.065)	(0.016)	(0.019)	(0.021)
Municipality fixed effects	No	Yes	Yes	No	Yes	Yes	No	Yes	Yes
Additional controls	No	No	Yes	No	No	Yes	No	No	Yes
Observations	1,577	1,577	1,577	827	827	827	750	750	750
R-squared	0.001	0.047	0.047	0.001	0.358	0.358	0.004	0.402	0.436

Notes: Robust standard errors in parentheses. See additional notes on Table 3.
***p < 0.01, **p < 0.05, *p < 0.1.

Table 6 Effects of temporal distance between pay and reference week on daily hours of work (recipients only)

Transfer occurred:	Sunday	Monday	Tuesday	Wednesday	Thursday	Friday	Saturday
	(1)	(2)	(3)	(4)	(5)	(6)	(7)
One week before the	0.828*	-0.732	-0.810*	-1.269**	-1.319***	-1.334***	-0.982*
reference week	(0.452)	(0.494)	(0.491)	(0.498)	(0.497)	(0.514)	(0.535)
During the reference	1.231**	-0.183	-0.760	-0.783	-0.994*	-0.644	0.297
week	(0.500)	(0.531)	(0.527)	(0.520)	(0.534)	(0.548)	(0.552)
At least one week after	1.341***	0.342	0.225	0.019	-0.084	0.074	0.656
the reference week	(0.487)	(0.453)	(0.458)	(0.470)	(0.493)	(0.459)	(0.533)
Municipality fixed effects	Yes	Yes	Yes	Yes	Yes	Yes	Yes
Additional controls	Yes	Yes	Yes	Yes	Yes	Yes	Yes
Observations	827	827	827	827	827	827	827
R-squared	0.398	0.366	0.395	0.373	0.366	0.379	0.345

Notes: Robust standard errors in parentheses. See additional notes on Table 3.
***p < 0.01, **p < 0.05, *p < 0.1.

However, when payment takes place one week before the reference week, the reduction in labor intensity is evenly distributed along the reference week which is inconsistent with the hypothesis that our results are mainly driven by transportation from the household to the bank. We interpret these results as if the dummy variable representing that the payment was made "one week before the reference week" reflects the immediate disincentives to work generated by the having received the cash transfer.

5.2   Heterogeneous effects

We next explore whether the decline in hours worked during the reference week is homogeneous across all recipients or if they differ according to their observable characteristics. First, in Table 7 we divide the sample of recipients according to their marital status (married and non-married). Interestingly, we find that the reduction in working hours of recipients when the transfer was observed to happen one week before the reference week is driven by the sub-sample of married women. The point estimate for married women is -11.3 and is statistically significant at the 1% level, whereas the coefficient of the sub-sample of non-married women is not statistically significant. One plausible explanation for this difference is that married women also rely on their husbands' income and this allow them to reduce their working intensity more than non-married women.

Second, we analyze if there exists heterogeneity between old and young recipients. In order to keep a balanced sample in both groups, we say that a recipient is young if she is 40 years old or younger and she is old, otherwise. Table 8 presents results from this specification. Results suggest that younger women (i.e., recipients aged 40 or less) reduce more their working hours relative to older women. In fact, working behavior of older women seems to be unaffected by the cash transfer receipt, since all the coefficients are statistically insignificant. On the other hand, younger women reduce working intensity by around 12 hours when the payment occurs one week before the reference week.

Third, we distinguish between recipients who have children aged 5 or less and those who do not. This distinction is important because the presence of young children at home is a major determinant in female labor supply. Results from splitting the sample according to children's age are presented in Table 9. As expected, recipients with children aged 5 or less reduce their labor supply more than recipients with older children. The point estimate

Table 7 Effects of temporal distance between pay and reference week on weekly hours of work by marital status (recipients only)

Transfer occurred:	Married		Non-married	
	(1)	**(2)**	**(3)**	**(4)**
One week before the reference week	-2.318	-11.293***	-2.825	-2.620
	(1.875)	(3.667)	(2.068)	(4.647)
During the reference week	-2.165	-6.788	0.088	3.899
	(2.058)	(4.599)	(2.325)	(4.557)
At least one week after the reference week	-1.310	-1.808	3.246	5.252
	(1.745)	(3.823)	(2.023)	(4.344)
Municipality fixed effects	No	Yes	No	Yes
Additional controls	Yes	Yes	Yes	Yes
Observations	446	446	381	381
R-squared	0.072	0.540	0.063	0.540

Notes: Robust standard errors in parentheses. See additional notes on Table 3.
***p < 0.01, **p < 0.05, *p < 0.1.

of having received the cash transfer one week before the reference week is -9.96 hours for recipients with young children. This could suggest that recipients reduce their hours of work in order to spend this additional time in activities related to child rearing.

5.3 Robustness analysis

5.3.1 Changes in the sample and different specifications

Though distance between program's pay dates and ENAHO's interview dates is presumably exogenous, the estimates in the previous section may be capturing some confounding effects. First, the way we construct the temporal distance when observing more than one pay date in a given municipality could introduce measurement bias, attenuating our estimated effects. Second, there still some additional effects which have not been discarded in previous estimates, downwardly biasing our results. In particular, the way in which time spent in going to withdraw the money can affect the results has not been discussed, and can erroneously be interpreted as a disincentive effect to work. Third, results can be sensitive to the inclusion of non-poor beneficiaries in the sample. Finally, our measures

Table 8 Effects of temporal distance between pay and reference week on weekly hours of work by age group (recipients only)

Transfer occurred:	Young (under 40)		Old	
	(1)	**(2)**	**(3)**	**(4)**
One week before the reference week	-4.224**	-11.985***	-0.502	-2.088
	(2.035)	(4.350)	(1.919)	(4.887)
During the reference week	-3.163	-8.396*	0.841	4.143
	(2.211)	(4.671)	(2.186)	(4.883)
At least one week after the reference week	-0.897	-2.033	1.881	7.796
	(1.845)	(3.750)	(1.893)	(4.814)
Municipality fixed effects	No	Yes	No	Yes
Additional controls	Yes	Yes	Yes	Yes
Observations	411	411	416	416
R-squared	0.061	0.544	0.058	0.553

Notes: Robust standard errors in parentheses. See additional notes on Table 3.
***p < 0.01, **p < 0.05, *p < 0.1.

Table 9 Effects of temporal distance between pay and reference week on weekly hours of work by children's age (recipients only)

Transfer occurred:	With children aged 5 or less		With children aged 6 or more	
	(1)	(2)	(3)	(4)
One week before the reference week	-4.346**	-9.962**	-0.637	-6.152
	(1.822)	(3.878)	(2.209)	(4.867)
During the reference week	-0.336	-3.830	-2.747	-2.149
	(1.903)	(4.900)	(2.664)	(5.689)
At least one week after the reference week	0.686	1.870	-0.624	4.646
	(1.618)	(3.548)	(2.256)	(5.791)
Municipality fixed effects	No	Yes	No	Yes
Additional controls	Yes	Yes	Yes	Yes
Observations	447	447	354	354
R-squared	0.080	0.511	0.042	0.563

Notes: Robust standard errors in parentheses. See additional notes on Table 3.
***p < 0.01, **p < 0.05, *p < 0.1.

of distance between pay and interview dates can be capturing effects other than *income* effects, affecting the interpretation of our results.

We begin our robustness checks by exploring whether the inclusion of non-poor families in our sample could yield different results. To the extent that poor beneficiaries can live in more remote areas and have less access to transportation, results shown in the previous section can represent lower-bound estimates. In Table 10 we report the results for weekly hours of work after including non-poor beneficiaries in our sample. Results correspond to recipients only. All the estimated coefficients are negative and statistically significant at the 1% level. In our most preferred specification (i.e., including municipality fixed effects and controlling for individual characteristics), we find that having been paid one week before the reference week reduces working intensity by around 6 hours.

The estimated effects are also larger than those presented in Table 4, where we exclude non-poor families. This additional evidence suggests that the decline in hours of work is not driven by the time needed to withdraw the money, since non-poor beneficiaries are more likely to spend *less* time going from home to the bank. Moreover, this difference

Table 10 Effects of temporal distance between pay and reference week on weekly hours of work, including non-poor beneficiaries (recipients only)

Transfer occurred:	(1)	(2)	(3)
One week before the reference week	-2.632	-4.881**	-5.998**
	(1.329)	(2.466)	(2.408)
During the reference week	-1.564	-0.685	-1.948
	(1.319)	(2.583)	(2.597)
At least one week after the reference week	1.024	3.071	2.251
	(1.225)	(2.251)	(2.275)
Municipality fixed effects	No	Yes	Yes
Additional controls	No	No	Yes
Observations	1,015	1,015	1,015
R-squared	0.009	0.340	0.354

Notes: Robust standard errors in parentheses. See additional notes on Table 3.
***p < 0.01, **p < 0.05, *p < 0.1.

may suggest that non-poor beneficiaries' labor supply is more elastic (with respect to cash transfers) than that of poor beneficiaries.

As an attempt to dissipate concerns related to measurement errors, we next construct a different measure of distance between pay and interview dates. Recall that our measure of "recentness" of the cash transfer is defined as the distance in weeks between the pay date and households' interview dates within a given municipality. Nevertheless, a municipality could have more than one pay date, since *Juntos* payment schedule is defined at the village level. Up until now, we have used the earliest date to construct our measures of distance between pay dates and the reference week.

In Table 11 we present results when constructing the indicators of distance using the last date of payment within the municipality. We only include recipients in the regressions. In columns (1) to (3) we exclude non-poor recipients while in columns (4) to (6) we include them in the sample. When controlling for recipients characteristics, results suggest that poor beneficiaries reduce their weekly hours of work by 4.85 (statistically significant at the 5% level) when the cash transfer occurred one week before the reference week. This reduction in weekly hours of work is larger (-5.97 hours) when including non-poor households in the sample (column 6) and is statistically significant at the 5% level. Coefficients reported in columns (3) and (6) of Table 11 are similar to those reported in column (6) of Table 4 and column (3) of Table 10, respectively, where we use the same samples and the first date of payment within the municipality to define temporal distance. The evidence presented on this table suggests that the impact of having received the cash transfer one week before the reference week on hours of work does not significantly change when we modify the definition of the municipality-payment date.

A major threat to our identification strategy is that the dummy variables denoting the distance between payment and interview dates may be capturing other factors not related to the cash transfer, but to the specific date of the payment. For instance, it could be the case that payment dates are established on days when the labor supply is low for a different reason than the transfer (e.g., holidays). This potential correlation between dates and unobservable variables that affect hours of work would invalidate our strategy. To check that this is not the case, we perform a falsification test using available data from non-beneficiaries. If the dummy variables representing the distance between payment

Table 11 Effects of temporal distance between pay and reference week on weekly hours of work using the last pay date within municipalities (recipients only)

	Poors			Poors and non-poors		
Transfer occurred:	(1)	(2)	(3)	(4)	(5)	(6)
One week before the reference week	-1.229	-3.781	-4.847**	-2.118	-5.194*	-5.970**
	(1.646)	(3.171)	(2.461)	(1.570)	(2.983)	(2.905)
During the reference week	-1.049	1.595	0.817	-1.503	0.803	-0.094
	(1.612)	(3.344)	(3.437)	(1.506)	(2.957)	(3.016)
At least one week after the reference week	-0.951	2.238	1.550	-0.450	1.538	1.044
	(1.346)	(2.718)	(2.187)	(1.287)	(2.536)	(2.520)
Municipality fixed effects	No	Yes	Yes	No	Yes	Yes
Additional controls	No	No	Yes	No	No	Yes
Observations	827	827	827	1,015	1,015	1,015
R-squared	0.001	0.392	0.432	0.003	0.339	0.384

Notes: Robust standard errors in parentheses. See additional notes on Table 3.
***p < 0.01, **p < 0.05, *p < 0.1.

and interview dates were correlated with other variables that affect labor supply, they should also have an impact on the hours of work of non-beneficiaries.

We perform regressions for weekly hours of work including in the sample spouses of household heads who are not beneficiaries from *Juntos* but who live in treated municipalities. Table 12 presents the results from these regressions. Results show that none of the dummies measuring the distance between pay and interview dates are significant at any conventional level. We interpret these results as if our indicators of distance are not correlated with omitted variables that may affect labor supply by alternative channels.

Finally, we perform an additional specification that allows us to rule out the hypothesis that our results may be driven by the time spent picking up the money. In particular, we perform two separate regressions according to the program's payment method in order to rule out this possibility. Recall that there exist two payment methods: deposits to bank accounts and delivering cash in armored van. The former implies that beneficiaries go to the bank and withdraw the money through ATM, whereas armored vans distribute the money to beneficiaries in the main square of their village. This second payment method was introduced to reach the most remote places of the Peruvian territory and does not require beneficiaries to move long distances in order to pick up the money. Thus, the effect of temporal distance between interview and payment dates on labor supply for beneficiaries who received the cash transfer via armored vans does not contain confounding factors such as time spent in withdrawing the money.

Table 13 reports the results for weekly hours of work divided according to the payment mechanism. Columns (1) and (2) correspond to the bank account mechanism, and columns (3) and (4) correspond to payment through armored vans. All the regressions are performed for recipients only. Coefficients for "bank account" are not statistically significant at any conventional level. In contrast, coefficients for "armored van" are statistically significant at the 1% level when including the full set of controls. In particular, work intensity of individuals for whom the cash transfer was made by armored vans is reduced by 8.8 hours when the transfer occurred 1 week before the reference week. We interpret this result as if the reduction in hours of work is purely due to an income effect and is not related to the time spent going to the bank.

Table 12 Effects of temporal distance between pay and reference week on weekly hours of work (non-beneficiary housewives)

Transfer occurred:	(1)	(2)	(3)
One week before the reference week	-0.054	-0.799	-0.210
	(1.542)	(3.021)	(3.024)
During the reference week	-1.603	-2.155	-1.997
	(1.557)	(2.831)	-(2.793)
At least one week after the reference week	3.352	2.211	2.099
	(1.663)	(2.848)	(2.790)
Municipality fixed effects	No	Yes	Yes
Additional controls	No	No	Yes
Observations	927	927	927
R-squared	0.010	0.333	0.348

Notes: Robust standard errors in parentheses. See additional notes on Table 3.
***p < 0.01, **p < 0.05, *p < 0.1.

Table 13 Effects of temporal distance between pay and reference week on weekly hours of work by payment mechanism (recipients only)

	Bank		Armored van	
Transfer occurred:	(1)	(2)	(3)	(4)
One week before the reference week	-3.195*	-0.913	-2.335	-8.807**
	(1.839)	(4.353)	(2.087)	(3.056)
During the reference week	-0.670	7.421	-2.835	-6.207
	(2.275)	(4.529)	(2.119)	(3.864)
At least one week after the reference week	0.201	11.202*	-0.418	-1.006
	(2.082)	(6.448)	(1.763)	(2.667)
Municipality fixed effects	No	Yes	No	Yes
Additional controls	No	Yes	Yes	Yes
Observations	369	369	458	458
R-squared	0.086	0.478	0.060	0.400

Notes: Robust standard errors in parentheses. See additional notes on Table 3.
***p < 0.01, **p < 0.05, *p < 0.1.

5.3.2   An alternative measure of temporal distance

Additional concerns about the econometric approach can be related to the way temporal distance is defined. In this section, we construct an alternative measure of temporal distance based on the exact date of payment and interview dates. More specifically, since we observe hours of work for every day of the reference week and the municipality payment date, we can calculate the exact number of days between the pay day and each of the days in the reference week. Moreover, since we have exactly 7 different observations for each individual (associated to the seven days of the reference week), we can perform fixed effect regressions at the individual level using temporal distance in days as the independent variable.

Panel A of Table 14 reports the results from the linear specification. Columns with even numbers include only poor recipients, whereas columns with odd numbers allow for the inclusion of non-poor recipients in the sample. The first two columns use the earliest pay date and the last two columns use the last payment date within a given municipality to define the number of days between the cash transfer and the "reference day" (the day for which hours of work are reported). That is, each individual's hours of work are measured in 7 different reference days. The point estimate for poor recipients is 0.127 (statistically significant at the 1% level), suggesting that hours of work go up by 0.127 hours per day when the cash transfer occurs after the reference day. When including non-poor beneficiaries in the sample, the point estimate rises to 0.131, and is also statistically significant at the 1% level. A similar pattern is observed when using the last payment date within the municipality.

In Panel B of Table 14 we present the estimated coefficients associated to dummy variables indicating the number of days between the pay day and the reference day. For the sake of simplicity, we construct 10 such variables, each representing the number of days between the cash transfer and the reference day. In particular, we include in the regressions indicators for cash transfer occurring 1 day, 2 days, 3 or 4 days, 5 or 6 days, and 7 or more days after (or before) the reference day. The omitted category is when the pay day and the day of report are the same (i.e., temporal distance between pay and the reference day is equal to zero). Results show that working hours are reduced when the cash transfer occurs before the day in which individuals report their working behavior. The largest

Table 14 Effect of temporal distance between pay and reference day on daily hours of work (recipients only)

| | Payment date within municipalities | | | |
| | Earliest pay date | | Latest pay date | |
	(1)	(2)	(3)	(4)
Panel A				
Coefficient on linear specification	0.127***	0.131***	0.119***	0.123***
	(0.014)	(0.013)	(0.025)	(0.039)
	[0.523]	[0.546]	[0.489]	[0.557]
Panel B				
Transfer occurred (with respect to the reference day):				
At least 7 days before	0.157***	0.109***	0.123**	0.173***
	(0.044)	(0.034)	(0.041)	(0.053)
5or 6 days before	-0.288**	-0.268*	-0.230*	-0.196*
	(0.116)	(0.156)	(0.101)	(0.091)
3 or 4 days before	-0.434**	-0.489**	-0.339	-0.432**
	(0.228)	(0.204)	(0.243)	(0.213)
2 days before	-0.251	-0.266	-0.252	-0.209
	(0.237)	(0.212)	(0.212)	(0.221)
1 day before	0.053	-0.067	-0.039	0.051
	(0.234)	(0.209)	(0.249)	(0.219)
1 day after	0.180	0.174	0.178	0.263
	(0.244)	(0.219)	(0.256)	(0.227)
2 days after	0.343	0.313	0.442*	0.448**
	(0.247)	(0.223)	(0.257)	(0.230)
3 or 4 days after	0.243	0.203	0.326	0.380*
	(0.231)	(0.209)	(0.242)	(0.217)
5 or 6 days after	0.829***	0.818***	0.962***	1.023***
	(0.263)	(0.241)	(0.278)	(0.252)
At least 7 days after	1.132***	1.203***	1.267***	1.134***
	(0.276)	(0.253)	(0.294)	(0.277)
	[0.520]	[0.610]	[0.519]	[0.537]
Individual fixed effects	Yes	Yes	Yes	Yes
Observations	5,789	7,105	5,789	7,105
Number of individuals	827	1,015	827	1,015

Notes: Robust standard errors in parentheses. R-squared in brackets.
***p < 0.01, **p < 0.05, *p < 0.1.

decline in hours of work occurs when the payment was observed to happen 3 or 4 days before the day of report, and becomes negligible when the pay day gets closer to the day of report of working behavior.

In Figure 2 we plot the estimated coefficients along with their 95% confidence intervals according to the distance (in days) between the pay day and the reference day. We use day 0 (i.e., cash transfer occurred the reference day) as the benchmark dummy variable. The figure clearly describes a U-shaped pattern, implying that working intensity is reduced when the cash transfer was made within 5 days before the reference day and remains at its *normal* level when cash transfers occur after the reference day.

6   Discussion

Along the document, we have argued that, although CCTs may not have long-term or permanent effects on labor supply of adults, it may be the case that individuals reduce

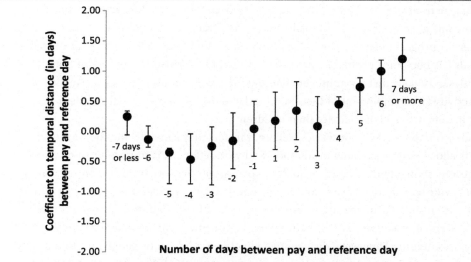

Figure 2 Coefficients on temporal distance (in days) between pay and reference day. *Notes*: Each point in the graph corresponds to a coefficient associated to a dummy variable measuring the temporal distance between pay and reference day (day in which the hours of work are reported). The omitted category is "distance between pay and reference day equals 0", which implies that the pay and the reference day are the same.

their working intensity in the short-term as a response to welfare transfers. Our empirical analysis is based on the plausible assumption that payment schedules of *Juntos* are orthogonal to interview dates of ENAHO survey, and, using this identifying assumption, we are able to construct measures of temporal distance to test whether the recentness of cash transfers affects benefit recipients' labor supply. In particular, we find that working hours of recipients are reduced when the cash transfer was observed to happen within one week before the interview took place. In this section we discuss some possible paths through which it is possible to observe short- but not long-term effects of welfare transfers on labor supply of adults.

Results shown in Section 5.3 suggest that declines in working intensity are mostly driven by married women in their childrearing ages. As discussed by Moffitt (1992), there is a voluminous empirical literature supporting the idea that divorced or separated women have a more inelastic labor supply relative to women living in husband-wife (or maritally stable) families. There exist several explanations for these observed differences. The absence of a male with income to help support the children is the most common explanation. Two-parent families not only have the capability of generating more income since both parents can work for paid activities, but can also allocate more efficiently the time devoted to parenting practices. In contrast, child bearing and work in female-headed houses are both mutually exclusive activities. Therefore, the *income* effect generated by the welfare transfer is more likely to affect women living in husband-wife families.

Time not devoted to work can be re-allocated to parenting activities or, more broadly, home production. However, this implies that activities in which beneficiaries are involved might be such that they can *freely* switch between home production and paid job at any point of time (highly flexible activities). In the specific case of the Peruvian *Juntos* program, del Pozo and Guzmán (2011) find that the welfare transfers increase the likelihood of owning small animals, such as poultry and guinea pigs, as well as the use of land for growing natural grasses (which are used to feed guinea pigs). Moreover, authors find that income generated by selling small animals as a fraction of household total income is greater for program beneficiaries relative to non-treated households. Since raising small animals has become a profitable business that might be carried out as part of household activities, it is likely that program beneficiaries - in particular housewives - have turned to this activity as a compliment of their home-related duties, and which allow them to earn labor income while taking care of their children.

Aside from the working incentives welfare transfers may generate and the way in which time is allocated across home production and work effort, it is important to emphasize that results shown in the empirical analysis correspond to short-term responses of working behavior to welfare transfers and might not be taken as program's average treatment effects. As discussed in the literature review, most of the studies evaluating the effect of CCTs on labor supply (in Latin America) do not find significant changes in working behavior of adults. However, "disincentive effects on adult labor supply are found only for the program that made the most generous transfers, the *RPS* in Nicaragua" (Fiszbein and Schady 2009). This piece of evidence suggests that *income* effects generated by welfare transfers may depend on the amount of the transfer relative to individual's earned income[14].

The observed decrease in working effort of recipients in the short run can be explained from consumption patterns over time. If the welfare transfer allows households to achieve a higher consumption bundle over a certain period of time (say, during periods in which the cash transfer has recently been made) but not permanently, it is likely that the *income* effect would be visible only in the short run. However, when the cash transfer has been totally spent, labor supply must increase in order to afford the initial (i.e., out-of-welfare) consumption bundle. Put it differently, welfare transfers can "buy" leisure as long as a certain level of consumption has been achieved. Below this threshold, labor supply increases and returns to its initial level. Thus, if the cash transfer is sufficiently large to afford higher levels of consumption during a long period of time, then this would generate a permanent decrease of labor supply of individuals. This insight can explain why CCTs giving more generous stipends are observed to have disincentive effects on labor supply of adult beneficiaries.

7 Conclusion

It is well-known that welfare programs in developed countries may have unintended effects on labor supply (Ashenfelter 1983; Moffitt 2002). Conditional Cash Transfer programs are not the exception. However, empirical evidence from Latin American countries does not seem to be consistent with the *income* effect predicted by the standard model of labor supply. Evidence drawn from experimental and quasi-experimental evaluation methods is associated with the long term effects of program participation on adult labor supply. Although these empirical approaches allow researchers to accurately identify average treatment effects of welfare programs on different set of outcomes, it does not come without its drawbacks. In the specific case of adult labor supply, particular concerns should be given to general equilibrium effects potentially introduced by program's benefits, and indirect effects generated by the reduction in child labor.

In this paper we adopt a novel empirical approach which allow us to estimate short term effects of cash transfers on adults' working effort. In particular, we exploit within municipality exogenous variation introduced by the temporal distance between payment schedules of the Peruvian *Juntos* program and interview dates of the Peruvian National Household Survey to explore whether the monthly receipt of cash transfers affect working behavior. Despite the fact that we cannot estimate average treatment effects, this empirical approach is useful for isolating immediate effects on labor supply generated by program stipends from other potentially confounding factors.

We find that women's (but not men's) weekly hours of work are reduced by almost 6 hours in the week following the payment date. This effect is mainly driven by married (maritally stable) women and by mothers with children aged 5 or less. However, no effects are found for labor force participation, nor for working for paid activities. These results are robust to changes in the sample, different specifications, and alternative measures of temporal distance.

Some interesting implications arise from our findings. From an academic perspective, we reconcile empirical evidence with the theoretical predictions of the standard model of labor supply. In this regard, although *income* effects are not observed in previous studies analyzing the impact of CCTs on adult labor supply in the sense of working disincentives, we do find that, in the short run, these effects are likely to appear. The absence of long term effects of cash transfers on working effort can be attributed to transfer's generosity and consumption patterns over time. The latter implies the way households maximize consumption in days near pay dates relative to more distant days.

For evaluation purposes, special attention should be paid to general equilibrium effects and changes in the labor market composition potentially introduced by CCTs. With respect to the former, it is possible that, within targeted communities, reductions in labor force participation generated by the introduction of welfare transfers can increase wages, thereby mitigating the predicted *income* effects. In fact, Alzúa et al. (2013) find that household earned income increase as a result of increases in wages among male beneficiaries when analyzing the Mexican *PROGRESA* program. Regarding labor market composition, there is some evidence on changes in working activities. For instance, del Pozo and Guzmán (2011) find that women are more likely to work closer to home. Likewise, Adato and Roopnaraine (2004) find that adult males work longer in their own parcels relative to their counterparts when assessing the Nicaraguan *RPS*.

From a policy perspective, different issues arise. First, changing the amount and frequency of the payments could, as suggested by Fiszbein and Schady (2009), amplify the immediate labor supply response to cash transfers. Second, as an attempt to minimize the decrease in hours of work, pay dates could be defined on days when labor supply is expected to be low (e.g., weekends). Third, policy makers should take into account the trade-off they face in terms of payment methods: bank deposits can be operationally cheaper but they impose larger transportation costs (not only money but also time) than delivering cash in armored vans.

Finally, we believe that our empirical approach could be useful to answer other related outcomes that might respond to the receipt of the cash transfer. For instance, we could examine if households change their regular consumption pattern during the week after the payment (e.g., going to restaurants instead of eating at home). Also, it would be relevant to check whether cash recipients do not lose control over the money once they arrive home. If potential disputes within the household arise after the payment, we could test whether there is an increase in domestic violence during these days. It would also be relevant to examine whether children's school attendance (or education-related expenses) increase after the pay date. These are promising avenues for future research that may expand the discussion about the benefits and limitations of CCTs.

Endnotes

[1] In general, welfare programs can be divided according to the type of benefits: cash and in-kind transfers. Ashenfelter (1983), Moffitt (1992), and Moffitt (2002) provide outstanding reviews of cash transfer programs. For a review of the relationship between in-kind benefits and labor supply, see Currie (1994), Yelowitz (1995), Blundell and MaCurdy (1999), Moffitt (2002), and Hoynes and Schanzenbach (2009).

[2] Other studies suggest that individuals are likely to invest in agricultural related productive assets. In a recent article, Duflo et al. (2011) document that demand for agricultural tools tend to increase on days close to pay dates

[3] In order to qualify, children must be 18 years old or under (with few exceptions accepting families with children "permanently and totally disabled" aged 19 or above), must be somehow related to the claimant (blood, marriage or law), and must be resident of the United States.

[4] Other See Eissa and Hoynes (2006) and references therein.

[5] This is not the case for the Chilean *Chile Solidario* program, since one of the conditions for eligibility is that unemployed household members should be enrolled in local employment offices.

[6] See Moffitt (2002) for a further examination of this particular scenario.

[7] There does not exist an extensive literature evaluating *Juntos* impacts on program beneficiaries. Most of the studies evaluating *Juntos* are based on qualitative analysis of program's impacts (Escobal and Benites 2012, Alcázar 2010). Until this date, Perova and Vakis (2012), Sánchez and Jaramillo (2012), and del Pozo and Guzmán (2011) constitute the only quantitative studies of this program. The latter two studies evaluate program's impacts on nutritional status of infants and household's productive investments and agricultural production, respectively.

[8] See the Appendix for further detail on variables definition.

[9] It is worth noting, however, that this would be true only in villages where the payment method is through bank deposits, but not in villages where beneficiaries go to the main square on the pay day and wait for the armored van. We use this feature of the program to perform additional sensitivity tests in Section 5.3.

[10] Cash transfers were usually made available during the third week of the month, and interviews in a given district usually began during the first days of the calendar month and lasted almost 30 days. Based on this information, those who were interviewed at the end of the month, are more likely to be captured in the dummy variables encompassing individuals who received the transfer "during the reference week" or "one week after the reference week".

[11] The reason underlying the filters of non poor households as part of the Juntos beneficiaries can be explained based on poverty transitions (households being initially poor and then escaping from poverty once they had already been selected as beneficiaries) and program administrative failures (non poor households selected as beneficiaries even when the program was initially targeted to households below the poverty line).

[12] This information is also available at: http://www.juntos.gob.pe/cronograma_transportadora.php.

[13] It is worth noting, however, that the reduction in working hours occurs in the reference week. This implies that, if there exists an effect encompassing time spent in consumption of goods, then it is likely that this effect should appear just after the transfer has been done, but not in the reference week (seven days after the payment date).

[14]One important consideration regarding the lack of evidence of negative effects of welfare transfers on labor supply is the timing in which program evaluations are made. As discussed by Fiszbein and Schady (2009), most of the existing studies use data collected shortly after the households have become eligibles to participate in the program for the first time. However, it may take some time before households adjust their working behavior to welfare benefits.

Appendix

Program's features

Eligibility Consists of three stages: (i) selection of eligible municipalities (based on poverty level, under age 5 chronic malnutrition, and exposure to violence during 1980s and 1990s); (ii) selection of eligible households (based on Logit model measuring the probability of a household living in poverty); (iii) community validation (community assemblies carried out by local authorities and government representatives)

Cash transfer 100 Nuevos Soles (US$ 37) per month

Conditions (i) children ages 6–14 attend at least 85% of yearly school classes; (ii) children ages 0–59 months old get fully immunized and attend periodically to growth controls; (iii) children ages 3–36 months get nutrition supplements; (iv) pregnant women visit health clinics for prenatal care; (v) nursing women visit health clinics for postnatal care; (vi) parents attend health clinics to receive information about nutrition, health and hygiene; (vii) parents without ID (identification) attend to program Mi nombre (*My name*).

Payment methods (i) bank deposit and (ii) cash delivery with armored van

Variables definition

Reference week Seven days before the interview day

Reference day The day of the reference week for which hours of work is reported

First pay date The first (earliest) pay date within a municipality

Last pay date The last (latest) pay date within a municipality

Outcomes (i) participation: a dummy variable which is equal to one if the individual had a job or looked for one in the reference week, and zero otherwise; (ii) hours of work: hours worked in the reference week (or in the reference day); (iii) working for paid activities: a dummy variable which is equal to one if the individual had a paid-job in the reference week, and zero otherwise

Variables of temporal distance between pay dates and the reference week (i) payment takes place, at least, two weeks before the reference week; (ii) payment occurs one week before the reference week; (iii) payment takes place during the reference week; (iv) payment occurs after the reference week. Omitted category: payment takes place, at least, two weeks before the reference week

Additional samples

Placebo sample Non-treated housewives (female heads who are not enrolled in the program) who live in municipalities covered by *Juntos*

Abbreviations
CCTs: Conditional Cash Transfer programs; Juntos: Conditional Cash Transfer program in Peru; ENAHO: Encuesta Nacional de Hogares (Peruvian National Household Survey); INEI: Instituto Nacional de Estadistica (Peruvian National Institute of Statistics).

Competing interests
The IZA Journal of Labor & Development is committed to the IZA Guiding Principles of Research Integrity. The authors declare that they have observed these principles.

Acknowledgements
This paper updates and supersedes "Conditional Cash Transfers, Payment Dates and Labor Supply: Evidence from Peru" (available as CEDLAS Working Paper N. 140, Jan. 2013). We are indebted to Leonardo Gasparini for his invaluable guidance, comments and support. We also thank David Lam and an anonymous referee for very useful suggestions on previous drafts. We are grateful for comments to César Calvo, Viviana Cruzado, Rosamaria Dasso, Albrecht Glitz, Marc Goñi, Hugo Ñopo, Ingo Outes-Leon, Renato Ravina, Laura Ripani, Alan Sánchez, Leopoldo Tornarolli, José Valderrama and seminar participants at the Central Bank of Peru, the LACEA/IDB/WB Network of Inequality and Poverty 2013 (UNLP-Argentina), the Peruvian Ministry of Economy and Finance, Universidad de Piura, and Universitat Pompeu Fabra. Nicolás Dominguez provided excellent assistance processing the data on the payment schedule from Juntos. We gratefully acknowledge financial support from the II Contest of Essays on Labor and Social Issues in Latin America - 2012, organized by CEDLAS (UNLP-Argentina) and IDRC (Canada). All remaining errors are ours.
Responsible editor: David Lam

Author details
[1]Inter-American Development Bank, 1300 New York Avenue NW, Washington, D.C. 20577 USA. [2]Vancouver School of Economics, Vancouver, Canada.

References
Adato M, Roopnaraine T (2004) Sistema de Evaluación de la Red de Protección Social de Nicaragua: Un Análisis Social de la 'Red de Protección Social' (RPS) en Nicaragua. Washington, DC, International Food Policy Research Institute
Alcázar L (2010) Algunas Reflexiones sobre el Programa JUNTOS. In: Portocarrero F, Vásquez E, Yamada G (eds) Politicas Sociales en el Perú: Nuevos Desafíos. Red para el Desarrollo de las Ciencias Sociales en el Perú
Alzúa ML, Cruces G, Ripani L (2013) Welfare programs and labor supply in developing countries: experimental evidence from Latin America. J Popul Econ 26(4): 1255–1284
Angelucci M, De Giorgi G (2009) Indirect effects of an aid program: how do cash transfers affect ineligibles' consumption? Am Econ Rev 99(1): 486–508
Ardington C, Case A, Hosegood V (2009) Labor supply responses to large social transfers: longitudinal evidence from South Africa. Am Econ J: Appl Econ 1(1): 22–48
Ashenfelter O (1983) Determining participation in income-tested social programs. J Am Stat Assoc 78(383): 517–525
Becker GS (1981) Altruism in the family and selfishness in the market place. Economica 48(189): 1–15
Bertrand M, Mullainathan S, Miller D (2003) Public policy and extended families: evidence from pensions in South Africa. World Bank Econ Rev 17(1): 27–50
Blundell R, MaCurdy T (1999) Labor supply: a review of alternative approaches. Handb Labor Econ 3: 1559–1695
Camerer C, Babcock L, Loewenstein G, Thaler R (1997) Labor supply of New York City Cabdrivers: one day at a time. Q J Econ 112(2): 407–441
Currie J (1994) Welfare and the well-being of children: the relative effectiveness of cash and in-kind transfers. Tax Policy Econ 8(1): 1–43
del Pozo C, Guzmán E (2011) Efectos de las transferencias monetarias condicionadas en la inversión productiva de los hogares rurales en el Perú. Consorcio de Investigación Económica y Social - CIES
Duflo E, Kremer M, Robinson J (2011) Nudging farmers to use fertilizer: theory and experimental evidence from Kenya. Am Econ Rev 101(6): 2350–2390
Eissa N, Hoynes HW (2006) Behavioral responses to taxes: lessons from the EITC and labor supply. Tax Policy Econ 20(1): 73–110
Escobal J, Benites S (2012) Transferencias y condiciones: efectos no previstos del programa JUNTOS. Lima: Niños del Milenio; Young Lives. Boletín de políticas públicas sobre infancia, 7
Fehr E, Goette L (2007) Do workers work more if wages are high? Evidence from a randomized field experiment. Am Econ Rev 97(1): 298–317
Fiszbein A, Schady NR (2009) Conditional cash transfers: reducing present and future poverty. World Bank Publications, Washington DC
Foguel M, Paes de Barros R (2010) The effects of conditional transfer programmes on adult labor supply: an empirical analysis using a time-series-cross-section sample of Brazilian municipalities. Estudios Economicos 40(2): 259–293
Galasso E (2006) With their effort and one opportunity: alleviating extreme poverty in Chile. Dev Research Group, World Bank, Washington DC
Goette L, Huffman D, Fehr E (2004) Loss aversion and labour supply. J Eur Econ Assoc 2(2): 216–228. Papers and Proceedings of the Eighteenth Annual Congress of the European Economic Association
Hoynes HW, Schanzenbach DW (2009) Consumption responses to in-kind transfers: evidence from the introduction of food stamp program. Am Econ J: Appl Econ 1(4): 109–139
Lundberg S, Pollak RA (1993) Separate spheres bargaining and the marriage market. J Pol Econ 101(6): 988–1010
Lundberg, S, Pollak RA (1994) Noncooperative bargaining models of marriage. Am Econ Rev 84(2): 132–137

Lundberg S, Pollak RA, Wales TJ (1997) Do husband and wives pool their resources? Evidence from the United Kingdom child benefit. J Human Resour 32(3): 463–480

Maluccio J (2010) The Impact of Conditional Cash Transfers on Consumption and Investment in Nicaragua. Journal of Development Studies, Taylor & Francis Journals 46(1): 14–38

Maluccio JA, Flores R (2005) Impact evaluation of a conditional cash transfer program: the Nicaraguan Red de Protección Social. Research reports 141, International Food Policy Research Institute (IFPRI). Washington DC

Manser M, Brown M (1980) Marriage and household decision-making: a bargaining analysis. Int Econ Rev 21(1): 31–44

Mastrobuoni G, Weinberg M (2009) Heterogeneity in intra-monthly consumption patterns, self-control, and savings at retirement. Am Econ J: Econ Policy 1(2): 163–189

McElroy M, Horney MJ (1981) Nash-bargained household decisions: toward a generalization of the theory of demand. Int Econ Rev 22(2): 333–349

Moffitt R (1992) Incentive effects of the US welfare system: a review. J Econ Lit 30(1): 1–61

Moffitt, R (2002) Welfare programs and labor supply. Handb Public Econ 4: 2393–2430

Parker S, Skoufias E (2000) The impact of Progresa on work, leisure, and time allocation. International Food Policy and Research Institute, Washington DC

Perova E, Vakis R (2012) 5 years in Juntos: new evidence on the program's short and long-term impacts. Economía 35(69): 53–82

Samuelson PA (1956) Social indifference curves. Q J Econ 70(1): 1–22

Sánchez A, Jaramillo M (2012) Impacto del programa Juntos sobre la nutrición temprana. Revista Estudios Económicos 23(1): 53–66

Segovia G (2001) Efectos del Programa JUNTOS en la Economía Local de las Zonas Rurales a Cinco Años de Intervención en las Regiones de Apurimac, Ayacucho, Huancavelica y Huánuco. Programa Nacional de Apoyo Directo a los Más Pobres - JUNTOS

Shapiro JM (2005) Is there a daily discount rate? Evidence from the food stamp nutrition cycle. J Public Econ 89(1): 303–325

Skoufias E, Di Maro V (2008) Conditional Cash Transfers, Adult Work Incentives, and Poverty. Journal of Development Studies, Taylor & Francis Journals 44(7): 935–960

Yelowitz AS (1995) The medicaid notch, labor supply, and welfare participation: evidence from eligibility expansion. Q J Econ 110(4): 909–939

8

Displacement and education of the next generation: evidence from Bosnia and Herzegovina

Christoph Eder

Correspondence:
christoph.eder@jku.at
Department of Economics,
Johannes Kepler University Linz,
Altenberger Str. 69, 4040 Linz,
Austria

Abstract

In this paper, I study the effect of displacement (in the sense of forced migration) of parents during a violent conflict on investment in their childrens' education years later. Using the ethnic division during the Bosnian War as a natural experiment, I plausibly identify exogenously displaced households and compare them to households who did not have to move because of the war. Displaced parents spend between 20 and 30% less on the education of their children in primary and secondary school. The result also holds for single expenditure positions like textbooks, school materials and annual tuition in secondary school. A number of robustness checks and nearest-neighbor matching is performed to confirm the finding. A decomposition of the causal effect shows that differences in income and the stock of durable goods can at most explain one third of the finding. Potential explanations for the reduced spending of displaced parents on education include altered preferences through the exposure to violence, increased uncertainty about the future, and financial constraints.

JEL Classification: I25; J15; O15
Keywords: Displacement; Conflict; Education

1 Introduction

Violent conflict is a regular phenomenon in the developing world and its long-term consequences can be substantial through the destruction of human and physical capital, damage to infrastructure, and forced population movements. However, research on the economic consequences of wars and other violent events have only recently gained momentum as micro-level data from conflict areas become available. This is an important line of research as it indicates to policy makers the direct consequences of violent conflicts and which issues need to be dealt with once a conflict is over.

The findings in this literature offer interesting insights into peoples' lives in war-torn countries and on the effects of exposure to conflict. However, forced migration has seen relatively little attention, even though the UNHCR counts 10.4 million refugees and 36 million people of concern in 2009 in their Global Report (UNHCR 2009). In this paper I study the effects of displacement of parents on educational expenditure on their children.[1]

I use the ethnic division during the Bosnian War between 1992 and 1995 as a natural experiment for displacement. The war divided the previously ethnically mixed Bosnia and

Herzegovina into two parts and through "ethnic cleansing" resulted in two areas of homogeneous ethnic make-up. The resulting displacement of part of the population enables me to uncover its causal effects. The identification strategy circumvents the problem of endogenously migrated households by using only households who moved across the front line during the war. No significant difference in time invariant household characteristics support the assumption that treatment was exogenous.

The short time span between the end of the war and the collection of the data set does not allow me to evaluate educational outcomes of children of displaced parents. However, the education system of Bosnia and Herzegovina requires parents to provide textbooks, uniforms, school materials etc. to their children, which gives me the chance to look at inputs in educational production. In particular, I am interested in parents' education expenditure on their children.

I find that displaced parents spend significantly less on the education of their children five years after the end of the war than comparable households that were not displaced. The estimates of the reduction in spending on education range from 20 to 30%. Considering that the average household in Bosnia and Herzegovina spends more than half a monthly household income on the education of a child per year, this is quantitatively a large difference. The finding is robust to a number of specifications and nearest-neighbor matching estimates confirm the magnitude. Displaced parents also spend significantly less on single expenditure positions like annual tuition in secondary school, textbooks, and other school materials.

Recent experimental evidence suggests that students' test scores react positively to additional educational inputs within a given institutional setting (Das et al. 2013), confirming an intuition that has been challenged in the past.[2] As small an investment as $3 per student spent mostly on child's stationary, classroom materials, and practice books can increase test scores by 0.1 standard deviations in India (Das et al. 2013). As Hanushek (2003) points out, there is evidence that increased school quality has positive effects on labor market outcomes and productivity.

Exploring the causal channels through which displacement influences education expenditure, I show that at most one third can be explained by differences in income and wealth levels. The employment status of parents also fails to explain a major part of the difference, so there is no evidence that displaced parents substitute school inputs for increased parental effort as found by Houtenville and Smith Conway (2008). Potential explanations for the reduced spending of displaced parents on education include altered preferences through exposure to violence, increased uncertainty about the future, and tighter financial constraints.

The paper is organized as follows: The next section reviews the literature, Section 3 discusses the background of the study in Bosnia and Herzegovina, as well as the data and the identification strategy, while Section 4 presents the main results. Section 5 discusses some channels through which displacement works and Section 6 concludes.

2 Literature review

The availability of micro-data from a large number of developing countries has greatly increased the possibilities of researchers to investigate the effects of violent conflicts at the individual and household level. A large number of papers look at the effects of exposure to violence on school attainment (eg. Akresh and de Walque 2008; Swee 2009; Shemyakina

2011; Chamarbagwala and Morán 2009; Merrouche 2006; Rodriguez and Sanchez 2009). Most of these studies find a negative effect for at least a subgroup of the population even after the end of the violent spell. Justino (2011) surveys this literature. Swee (2009) analyzes the case of Bosnia and Herzegovina and finds lower completion rates in secondary school through exposure to a violent conflict. However, he argues the effect is driven by youth soldiering and should not have long-run consequences. Since displacement is a direct consequence of potential exposure to violence, my findings contribute to the understanding of why educational production is affected even after the end of the violence.

The destruction of schools during periods of violence often fails to explain the reduction in educational attainment as that would affect boys and girls in the same way, which is often not the case (Shemyakina 2011). Swee (2009) argues that youth soldering has prevented older males from attending school, while Shemyakina (2011) explains that girls were kept at home to avoid sexual assaults and harassment on their way to school. León (2012) finds evidence that the death of teachers and the health status of parents could be the causal mechanism.

In a recent addition to the literature Pivovarova and Swee (2012) suggest that all these findings could be driven by "selection into victimization", ie. wartime displacement changes the composition of the population.[3] For the case of Nepal, Pivovarova and Swee (2012) show with panel data that the problem is empirically relevant.

Exposure to violence also has impacts on peoples' preferences. Bellows and Miguel (2009) find that it increases civil participation, while Voors et al. (2012) find that preferences towards risk, the discount rate, and altruistic behavior towards neighbors are affected.

The effects of displacement have also been studied in a number of papers. Fiala (2009) finds that displaced households have in general fewer assets and lower consumption quality. Only the previously poorest are marginally better off after displacement. Lower asset holdings of displaced households are also confirmed by Rahim et al. (2013). Kondylis (2010) shows that displacement makes men more likely to be unemployed and women more likely to be out of the labor force in the case of Bosnia and Herzegovina.

In the long-run Sarvimäki et al. (2009) find positive effects on income for displaced agricultural workers in Finland, which is confirmed by Bauer et al. (2013) for Germany. However, the latter find lower income for the rest of the displaced even for the second generation. The positive long-run effects of displacement found in Sarvimäki et al. (2009) and Bauer et al. (2013) are likely due to increased sector and geographic mobility of the displaced population. With the exception of Bauer et al. (2013), the above mentioned contributions focus on the effect on the generation of the displaced, however the negative consequences of displacement do not need to end there.

3   Context, data, and identification

3.1   The Bosnian war

Bosnia and Herzegovina became independent in the Fall of 1991 after the breakdown of former Yugoslavia. The three major ethnic groups, Bosniaks, Serbs, and Croats, were struggling to gain power and eventually the conflict turned violent in April 1992. Initially all three ethnic groups were fighting each other, with the Serbs in control of the army of the former Yugoslavia (Silber and Little 1996, p.222). In February 1994, Croats and

Bosniaks reached a peace agreement and eventually joined forces against the Serbs. With air support from the NATO, Bosniaks and Croats were able to push the Serbs back and regain control of large areas. The Bosnian War ended in December 1995 with the Dayton Agreement, according to which Bosnia and Herzegovina was divided into two entities along the front line at the end of the war: the *Federation of Bosnia and Herzegovina* and the *Republika Srpska*. During the war about 100,000 - 110,000 people were killed and an estimated 1.3 - 1.8 mio. were displaced (the total population in 1991, the year of the last official census, was 4.38 mio.).

The extensive displacement during the war led to mostly ethnically homogeneous geographic areas. After the war most Bosniaks and Croats lived in the Federation of Bosnia and Herzegovina and most Serbs in the Republika Srpska. Those two entities are like separate states with their own administration and they currently cooperate only in a few areas. As Dahlman and Tuathail (2005) show with two examples, in ethnically mixed municipalities that were split between the two entities, the ethnic groups were almost completely segregated by 1998 along the entity borders, which was not the case before the war. However, the Dayton Agreement declares that all refugees and displaced persons have the right to return to their homes of origin and get their property returned (Tuathail and O'Loughlin 2009, p.1047). The return migration peaked in the years 2002-03, but a large fraction of the displaced population does not plan to return to their pre-war homes. Also the majority of the properties of displaced households in their home municipalities was occupied by others, destroyed, or damaged (Tuathail and O'Loughlin 2009, p.1051).

3.2 The education system in Bosnia and Herzegovina

The education system in Bosnia and Herzegovina faces many challenges and changes these days. As of 2001, primary education lasts for 8 years, where during the first 4 years the entire material is taught by one teacher and in grades 5-8 each subject has its own teacher. Secondary education is divided into vocational training and gymnasium (more academically oriented), where curricula are taught in 3-5 year programs (UNESCO 1996; UNESCO 1997). In general, primary schools have no annual tuition, but textbooks, school materials, etc. still need to be payed for by the parents. Only few municipalities ensure that textbooks for disadvantaged are provided (OECD 2006). Low or non-existent incomes, migration, and difficult post-war conditions are common reasons why parents are unable to be "active parents" and fail to provide school equipment, supplies, and textbooks (UNESCO 1996).

The post-war financial situation for schools in Bosnia and Herzegovina was constrained, to say the least, as this paragraph from a report about the education system in the Republika Srpska illustrates (UNESCO 1997, p.ii.):

"Primary education is, in theory, free, and is financed from the government budget. In practice the government is often unable to pay salaries, and school repairs have often become the responsibility of the municipal authorities. At the secondary level the central government is expected to pay the salaries of personnel, and the municipality all other charges. It was reported that in December 1996 public sector employees, including teachers, had not been paid for 4 to 5 months. The education system today is largely dependent on financial sacrifices made by teachers and families. Textbooks, for example, are extremely expensive: an average primary school text costing DM 1-3.4 [DM = Convertible Mark] and a secondary one as much as DM 7".

Reports show that the curriculum for primary school is designed for a child equipped with 10 textbooks per grade. For most parents that seems hardly affordable, given that a qualified teacher earned in 1996 only 120 Convertible Mark per month (UNESCO 1996) and unemployment is high.[4] In the years following the publication of these reports, some reforms concerning the curriculum took place and in 2004 primary school was extended to 9 years (Swee 2010). International aid has certainly improved some issues, but it is unclear if this reduced the parents' financial burden of having children in school. A project report on the education reform in Bosnia and Herzegovina by the European Union from 2008 observes (EU 2008): "The education reform process evolves at an uneven and slow pace".

3.3 Data

For this study I use household survey data from the "Living Standard Measurement Survey" (henceforth LSMS) (State Agency for Statistics of BiH et al. 2001) of Bosnia and Herzegovina. The data collection started in 2001 in 25 municipalities with about 5,400 households. From 2002-2004 about half of the households were reinterviewed each year to form a 4-year panel data set. The LSMS covers a wide range of topics. The different sections ask questions about housing, education, health, labor, credit, migration, and social assistance. There are also sections on consumption, household businesses, and agricultural activities. For most of this paper, I use the cross-sectional data from 2001. I do this for two reasons: First, the sample size is reduced in the panel data to half the number of households, and second, the 2002-2004 interviews cover a limited number of topics. I will go into more detail about data issues in the respective sections.

3.4 Identification

In order to seriously estimate an effect of displacement on household behavior, the treatment of displacement must be at random, ie. ex ante, households in both, treatment and control group, do not differ in their characteristics, neither observable nor unobservable. Given that displacement is a form of migration, this is a strict requirement to satisfy. In this section I argue that the Bosnian War provides a rare, although sad, opportunity to study this by-product of violent conflict. I think of displacement as a version of migration, where the instinct of self-preservation dominates all economic considerations. The single most important push-factor is survival, while pull-factors of certain destinations do not pose a problem to the estimation of a causal effect, as municipality fixed effects are always included in the regressions.

My identification strategy, in a nutshell, is that in Bosnia and Herzegovina ethnicities were mixed before the war. The Bosnian War introduced a line of division along which two ethnically homogeneous territories emerged. The front line was not drawn by economic motives and people did not sort themselves into displacement but were forced by their instinct of self-preservation. The random course of the line of division and the absence of self-selection allow me to identify the effect of displacement on household behavior by comparing households that crossed the front line to households that did not move during the war.

At the time when Bosnia and Herzegovina was part of former Yugoslavia, the population was a mix of Bosniaks, Serbs, and Croats in most municipalities. The ethnic conflict in Bosnia and Herzegovina between 1992 and 1995 caused many people to leave their home and take refuge on the other side of the front line. Table 1 describes this homogenization of the two entities of Bosnia and Herzegovina. The share of Serbs in the Federation of Bosnia and Herzegovina shrank to 2.3% from 17.6%, while the share of Bosniaks (Croats) went down to 2.2% from 28.1% (1% from 9.2%). Serbs were leaving from the Bosnian/Croatian side of the front line to the Serb side and Bosniaks/Croats the other way round.

During the war, Bosniaks and Croats in the Serb territory were at risk of being killed, what became to be known as "ethnic cleansing". A main goal of Serb forces was to create an ethnically homogeneous territory within Bosnia and Herzegovina. Serbs beyond the front line faced a similar fate and were abandoning whole villages within a few days (Silber and Little 1996, p.358). Even after the Dayton Agreement was signed, displacement did not come to a halt. Several villages in the Federation of Bosnia and Herzegovina and suburbs of Sarajevo are reported to have been abandoned after the local Serbs realized they were trapped in Bosniak territory (Silber and Little 1996, p.30). Thus displacement during and after the war produced for the most part ethnically homogeneous regions.

Of course displacement status is not a question in the LSMS and has to be inferred from the data. The data include the municipality of residence right before the war and the location of residence in 2001. When a person did not move at all, he/she enters the control groups of non-movers. If a person resided on the other side of the front line before the war than he/she does in 2001, the person is considered displaced. People who changed their location of residence but did not cross the front line or people who returned to their pre-war residence are dropped. A household enters either the control or treatment group when both, the household head and his/her spouse, did not move or got displaced.

Note that the identification strategy implies the ethnicity of a person. A person living in the current Republika Srpska before the war and is now living in Federation of Bosnia and Herzegovina, the person is considered to be a displaced Bosniak. Conversely, a person, who has moved from the Federation of Bosnia and Herzegovina before the war to

Table 1 Main ethnic groups in Bosnia and Herzegovina

Bosnia and Herzegovina (Overall)			
	Bosniaks	Serbs	Croats
1991	43.5%	31.2%	17.4%
1996	46.1%	37.9%	14.6%

Federation of Bosnia and Herzegovina			
	Bosniaks	Serbs	Croats
1991	52.3%	17.6%	21.9%
1996	72.5%	2.3%	22.8%

Republika Srpska			
	Bosniaks	Serbs	Croats
1991	28.1%	55.4%	9.2%
1996	2.2%	96.8%	1.0%

Source: Official census in 1991 and unofficial census conducted by the UN in 1996.

the Republika Srpska after the war, is considered to be a displaced Serb. However, information about the ethnicity of a person is not available in the first wave of the data set, but only in the smaller second wave. Hence, I can test this prediction of the ethnicity by the migration pattern only on this smaller sample. Table 2 reports the ethnicities of the groups of non-movers and displaced people. Out of 1,040 displaced individuals, there is one Croat and no Serb in the Federation of Bosnia and Herzegovina and one Bosniak and one Croat in the Republika Srpska. The ethnicity mix in the sample of non-movers is not as clear-cut, which probably originates in the presence of enclaves in both, the Republika Srpska and the Federation of Bosnia and Herzegovina. However, these enclaves do not pose a threat to my identification, because these people did not got "treated" by forced displacement, neither did they endogenously decide to migrate. The evidence in Table 2 is a strong argument in support of my identification strategy.[5]

The first main threat to the identifying assumptions would be a systematic course of the front line so that economically different areas were divided. If economically undeveloped areas were targeted and conquered during the war, the displaced households were poorer than their non-mover counterparts already before the war. Kondylis (2010, p.241f) discusses this possibility and concludes that the war was "determined more by geo-strategic motives rather than economic motives". The Serb invasion followed the goal to connect the Serb stronghold around Banja Luka with the Serb nation. In addition, Kondylis (2010) provides evidence that pre-war educational attainment is uncorrelated with war casualties (and hence developed areas were not more contested) and there is no clear connection between the pre-war ethnic mix and war intensity.

The second key assumption implies that, ex ante, displaced households were not different from non-mover households. One possibility is that households of a certain type could have moved into areas, where they were especially exposed to the risk of displacement. This includes, for instance, a Bosniak family moved to Banja Luka (now the capital of the Republika Srpska) before the war so the household head could take a good position there. The data does not suggest evidence of sorting before the war in Bosnia and Herzegovina, as 70% of the household heads in the data still lived in their municipality of birth just before the war. Considering the small size of the average municipality in Bosnia and Herzegovina of 373 km^2, this suggests that households generally do not exhibit high mobility. Moreover, the results of the paper are not sensitive to restricting the sample to households who still resided in their birth municipality just before the war. If the results

Table 2 Displacement by ethnic groups

		After-war entity of residence	
		Federation of Bosnia and Herzegovina	Republika Srpska
Displaced	Bosniak	285	1
	Serb	0	747
	Croatian	1	1
	Other	5	0
Not moved	Bosniak	2,847	59
	Serb	121	2,306
	Croatian	614	22
	Other	108	39

Ethnicity data are from the second wave of the the LSMS on Bosnia and Herzegovina, which only includes half of the household from the first wave. The number of observations is reported.

are purely driven by pre-war geographic sorting, the findings would vanish in such a selected sample.

Another potential problem is that households with certain characteristics were displaced, while others at the same location and of the same ethnicity did not move, and hence displacement was not a life-saving treatment as suggested earlier. In terms of observable characteristics displaced and non-mover households do not differ as the descriptive statistics in Table 3 show. While Serbs in the sample were more likely to be displaced, there is no significant difference in other household characteristics. There is also no difference in the distributions of the highest level of education achieved and the age of the household head using a Kolmogorov-Smirnov equality of distributions test.[6] The column "Regression" reports the point estimate of a regression of the household characteristic on the displacement indicator and municipality fixed effects. However, regional differences are not a problem as municipality fixed effects are included in all regressions.

Table 4 tests whether the pre-war household characteristics are jointly correlated with displacement. In a regression of the displacement indicator on the characteristics, only the dummy variable for the Serb territory is a good predictor of displacement. The variables of household and child characteristics (the number of children of the family in school, a dummy variable for the oldest child of the family, a dummy for female children, years of education and age of the household head) are unable to significantly explain displacement. A joint test of the five household/child characteristics can not reject the hypothesis that displacement is a non-selective process. The results do not change when municipality fixed effects are included in column 2.

Even if household characteristics of displaced and non-movers are not significantly different from each other, pre-war experience could still affect education decisions. Although, each ethnicity has nominally their own language, there are only minor differences in the spoken word (Mappes-Niediek 2009, p.30). One might argue that the

Table 3 Descriptive statistics and exogeneity of displacement

	All	Not moved	Displaced	Difference	Regression
Displaced Family	0.189	0	1		
Republika Srpska	0.44	0.40	0.61	0.21***	
				(0.037)	
Number of Children	1.81	1.81	1.81	0.00	0.09*
of Family in School				(0.056)	(0.054)
Oldest Child	0.41	0.41	0.40	-0.01	-0.01
of Family				(0.023)	(0.025)
Female Child	0.47	0.47	0.48	0.01	0.02
				(0.028)	(0.030)
Education of	10.30	10.34	10.10	-0.25	-0.22
Household Head				(0.279)	(0.305)
Age of	45.74	45.80	45.47	-0.33	-0.87
Household Head				(0.735)	(0.834)
Municipality FE					Yes
Observations	1,952	1,584	368	1,952	1,952

Significance levels: * :10% ** : 5% *** : 1%.
Standard errors clustered at the household level in parenthesis.
The column "Regression" reports the point estimate of a regression of the household characteristic on the displacement indicator and municipality fixed effects.

Table 4 Regression output: displacement

	Dep. variable: displaced family	
Republika Srpska	0.136***	
	(0.0239)	
Number of Children	-0.000	0.021
of Family in School	(0.0150)	(0.0148)
Oldest Child	-0.011	-0.009
of Family	(0.0154)	(0.0140)
Female Child	0.008	0.011
	(0.0080)	(0.0110)
Education of	-0.004	-0.004
Household Head	(0.0038)	(0.0036)
Age of	-0.002*	-0.002
Household Head	(0.0012)	(0.0012)
Municipality FE		Yes
Observations	1,952	1,952
R-squared	0.031	0.162
F-value	0.70	1.19
(p-value)	(0.622)	(0.310)

Significance levels: * : 10% ** : 5% *** : 1%.
Standard errors clustered at the household level in parenthesis.
The F-value (p-value) corresponds to a test of the joint hypothesis that the effects of the five control variables (not the geographic control for the Republika Srpska) are zero.

group of displaced were ethnic minorities before the war and were ousted by the majority population. This is true at the entity level, but in more narrowly defined regions the displaced were often the ethnic majority but had to flee nevertheless. As Mappes-Niediek (2009, p.44f) describes it is a myth that households were driven out by neighbors of different ethnicity, but mostly by militants form other parts of Yugoslavia or soldiers. Reports describe ethnically different neighbors to have been close friends and attempted to protect each other from attacks. Since the three different ethnic groups have lived together in Bosnia and Herzegovina for a long time (the geographic distribution of ethnic groups in 1910 is very similar to the one in 1991) and the lack of major conflicts between those groups indicates that no group was suppressed by another one. Hence, there is limited reason to suspect a systematic pre-war difference of the later displaced population to the non-movers. Put differently, the pattern of displacement in a certain municipality was arguably driven by the geopolitical situation and not by the characteristics of a certain group in that municipality.

A final concern to identification is international migration/displacement. The Ministry for Human Rights and Refugees (MHHR 2003) reports the number of international refugees as 1.2 million between 1992 and the end of the war, which is more than a quarter of the total population in Bosnia and Herzegovina before the war. About half of this group returned to their home country until 2003. This is potentially a threat to the identification strategy if the families who left Bosnia and Herzegovina during the war have a characteristic that is different to the people who stayed in the country and if the treatment and control groups are unequally affected.

For this purpose I compare the displaced Serbs in Bosnia and Herzegovina to the residents of the Republic of Serbia who lived in Bosnia and Herzegovina in 1991 using the LSMS of Serbia in 2002. Serbs living in the future Federation of Bosnia and Herzegovina (the Bosniak territory) before the war had the choice between internal displacement and displacement/migration to the Republic of Serbia. I find that household heads and their spouses in the Republic of Serbia have on average 1.4 years more of education and are 4 years younger (results not shown).

These numbers suggest that the internally displaced are different from the externally displaced, which confirms the finding of Kondylis (2010) for migration to Western European countries. However, the fact that within Bosnia and Herzegovina the displaced and the non-movers are indistinguishable in terms of education and age (Table 3) indicates that my treatment and control groups were equally affected by internal displacement/migration and international displacement/migration is therefore not a problem for identification. Anyways, the problem of international migration/displacement is common in the literature on conflicts, because micro data set usually restrict the sample to a country.

4 Main results

The treatment effect of displacement on education expenditure is estimated by Ordinary Least Squares (OLS) of the estimating equation

$$y_{i,j} = \delta d_{i,j} + X_{i,j}\beta + \eta_j + \varepsilon_{i,j}, \tag{1}$$

where $y_{i,j}$ is the log. of education expenditure on child i in municipality j, $d_{i,j}$ is the displacement indicator, $X_{i,j}$ are exogenous control variables (ie. exogenous in the sense that they are not influenced by displacement as well as uncorrelated with the error term), η_j is a municipality fixed effect, and $\varepsilon_{i,j}$ is an error term. The standard errors are clustered at the household level to account for intra-household correlation of the error term.

The selection issues discussed in the previous sections would be a problem if $d_{i,j}$ and $\varepsilon_{i,j}$ are correlated. However, the discussion showed that many issues can be ruled out. I also employ nearest neighbor-matching as an alternative estimation method to check the robustness of the OLS findings.

4.1 Preliminary evidence

In a first step, I plot the Kernel density function of education expenditure of displaced and non-mover households against each other. Panel (a) in Figure 1 shows the unconditional densities while Panel (b) depicts deviations from municipality means. It is clearly visible that the whole distribution of the displaced households is shifted to the left of the distribution of the non-mover households, both, unconditionally and in deviations from municipality means.

Table 5 reports descriptive statistics for the various expenditure groups per child in Convertible Mark, the local currency. In a regression of the expenditure category on the displacement indicator and municipality fixed effects, only few categories show a significant difference. A simple difference of means between non-movers and displaced households would not be informative due to regional variation in education expenditure, therefore the regression.

Education expenditure is not a trivial part of total expenditure for households in Bosnia and Herzegovina. The average annual expenditure on education per child is 267.1 Convertible Mark, while the average total household income per month in the data set is 481 Convertible Mark. On average 4.6% of the annual total household income is spent on the

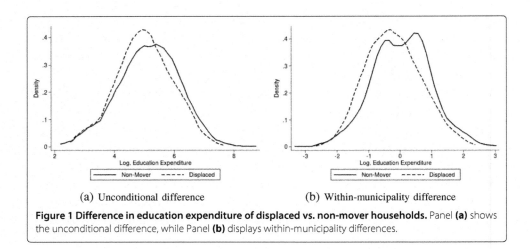

(a) Unconditional difference   (b) Within-municipality difference

Figure 1 Difference in education expenditure of displaced vs. non-mover households. Panel **(a)** shows the unconditional difference, while Panel **(b)** displays within-municipality differences.

education of a child. This a high price to pay for generally "free" education, which causes Mooney and French (2005) to suggest financial support for the education of children of displaced households.

In most specifications I use the sum of all expenditure classes, because of the group called "Total cost (not included in previous classes)". This expenditure class forms a pool for expenses, that parents cannot classify or do not bother to split up into the exact

Table 5 Descriptive statistics: education expenditure by classes

	Mean	Standard deviation	Regression
Annual Tuition	12.1	(58.9)	-3.6
			(2.39)
Special Tuition	2.1	(25.2)	1.6
			(1.99)
Membership Fee for Parent's Association	0.7	(16.5)	-0.1
			(0.22)
School Uniforms and other School Clothing	36.5	(89.4)	-7.7
			(4.98)
Textbooks	35.3	(53.6)	-2.5
			(4.51)
Other School Materials	31.5	(34.5)	-2.4
			(2.55)
Food and Lodging	44.2	(104.0)	-16.3***
			(5.7)
Other Costs	19.9	(71.9)	-13.6***
			(4.27)
Total Costs (not included in previous classes)	84.9	(275.5)	-28.8**
			(14.62)
Expenditure on Education (sum of all groups)	267.1	(316.4)	-73.4***
			(17.18)
Municipality FE			Yes
Observations			1,952

Significance levels: * : 10% ** : 5% *** : 1%.
Standard errors clustered at the household level in parenthesis.
Values are denoted in *Convertible Mark*. The column "Regression" reports the coefficient of a regression of the expenditure category on the displacement indicator and municipality fixed effects. A direct comparison of means between non-movers and displaced households is not informative due to regional variation in education expenditure.

groups. The problem is that the group "Total cost (not included in previous classes)" is negatively correlated with all other groups, which suggests that some households do not take the effort to split up the expenditures into the various classes and put everything into this group. Since dropping such households would reduce the sample size considerably, I use the sum of all groups in the main specifications to avoid the loss of many observations. In additional specifications, I restrict myself to a number of selected groups and drop the households that use the class "Total cost (not included in previous classes)".

4.2 Total causal effect

In this section, I present the estimation results for the total causal effect of displacement on education expenditure. The robustness checks show that the difference in spending on education holds across various specifications. An exact interpretation of dummy variables in semi-logarithmic regressions is provided in the row "Transformation" following van Garderen and Shah (2002). However, the exact interpretation deviates from the regression coefficients only slightly and also statistical significance remains unchanged.

The main results are reported in Table 6: the findings indicate a highly significant and robust drop in education expenditure in all specifications. Quantitatively, the difference in education expenditure between displaced parents and parents that did not move during the war is in the ballpark of 25 to 30% depending on the specification. Column (1) reports the difference controlling only for the entity of residence. Including control variables for child and parent characteristics (column (2)) hardly changes the estimated effect. The inclusion of municipality fixed effects increases the effect to a difference of almost 30%, which is identical between the two entities as column (4) shows.

Column (5) tests whether displaced parents discriminate between boys and girls, but shows that there is no significant difference. In column (6) I interact the displacement variable with the secondary school variable to test whether the difference in education expenditure originates in primary or secondary school. The point estimate of the interaction term is zero and hence displaced parents spend less in both, primary and secondary school.

In column (7), I control for the grade of school the child is in. This variable might be influenced by displacement, as children of displaced parents might only attend lower grades and therefore education might be cheaper. Then the difference in education expenditure would not be a decision of the parents, but imposed by the system. However, when the grade of the school is included in the regression, the point estimate increases to a difference of almost 33%.

In Table 7, I estimate the effect of displacement using a nearest-neighbor matching estimator. This method pairs individuals of ex ante comparable observable characteristics who differ only by treatment status and calculates the difference in the outcome variable (matching by covariates). The matching estimator may improve upon simple regression by comparing only individuals with similar observable characteristics and by doing so hopes to also balance unobservable characteristics. Hence, matching can reduce a potential bias of the estimated treatment effect due to selection issues if the distribution of observable characteristics contains information on the distribution of unobservable characteristics.

The average treatment effect in column (1) is a difference in education expenditure of 33%, while the average treatment effect on the treated in column (2) is 44%. These

Table 6 Regression output: education expenditure I

| | Log. of education expenditure | | | | | | |
	(1)	(2)	(3)	(4)	(5)	(6)	(7)
Displaced Family	-0.250***	-0.240***	-0.294***	-0.299**	-0.346***	-0.299***	-0.329***
	(0.0699)	(0.0697)	(0.0670)	(0.1187)	(0.0763)	(0.0722)	(0.0663)
Displaced Family × Republika Srpska				0.009			
				(0.1434)			
Displaced Family × Female Child					0.111		
					(0.0977)		
Displaced Family × Secondary School						0.000	
						(0.1197)	
Secondary School						0.285***	
						(0.0558)	
Grade of School							0.074***
							(0.0074)
Republika Srpska	0.461***	0.455***					
	(0.0536)	(0.0540)					
Number in Children of Family in School		0.083*	0.030	0.030	0.030	0.021	-0.003
		(0.0430)	(0.0347)	(0.0347)	(0.0346)	(0.0345)	(0.0344)
Oldest Child of Family		0.236***	0.246***	0.245***	0.244***	0.205***	0.153***
		(0.0430)	(0.0394)	(0.0394)	(0.0394)	(0.0402)	(0.0407)
Female Child		0.058	0.064	0.064	0.043	0.069*	0.065
		(0.0444)	(0.0412)	(0.0412)	(0.0470)	(0.0410)	(0.0402)
Education of Household Head		0.014*	0.021***	0.021***	0.021***	0.018**	0.016**
		(0.0084)	(0.0079)	(0.0080)	(0.0079)	(0.0079)	(0.0077)
Age of Household Head		0.008***	0.010***	0.010***	0.010***	0.007***	0.004
		(0.0029)	(0.0027)	(0.0027)	(0.0027)	(0.0027)	(0.0027)
Transformation	-22.29***	-21.56***	-25.64***	-26.39***	-29.47***	-26.03***	-28.21***
	(5.423)	(5.458)	(4.974)	(8.705)	(5.376)	(5.334)	(4.753)
Municipality FE			Yes	Yes	Yes	Yes	Yes
No. Observations	1,952	1,952	1,952	1,952	1,952	1,952	1,952
R-squared	0.054	0.071	0.201	0.201	0.202	0.215	0.244

Significance levels: * : 10% ** : 5% *** : 1%.
Standard errors clustered at the household level in parenthesis.
The line "Transformation" reports approximate unbiased estimator of the percentage change of a dummy variable in a semi-logarithmic regression (Kennedy 1981) and its standard error following van Garderen and Shah (2002).

numbers confirm the OLS results and are actually larger than those. The results are robust to an increase in the number of neighbors the treated observations are matched to. Column (3) includes only an indicator for the Republika Srpska and finds a difference of 22%, which is comparable to the OLS estimate. The inclusion of regional control variables actually pose a violation of the assumptions of matching where the matching variables must be unaffected by the treatment. However, displacement affects the location of residence by definition. Column (4) tests the case without regional control variables and finds a similarly significant result. Hence, if matching is better able to deal with selection into treatment than OLS and it produces similar results, selection does not seem to drive the main findings of Table 6.

A closer look at some education expenditure groups is taken in Table 8. For this table, I restrict the sample to the 1,325 children, whose parents split up all their costs to the detailed expenditure groups and did not use the category "Total Costs (not included in

Table 7 Regression output: nearest-neighbor matching

	Log. of education expenditure			
	(1)	**(2)**	**(3)**	**(4)**
Displaced Family	-0.330***	-0.440***	-0.222***	-0.205***
	(0.0822)	(0.0772)	(0.0701)	(0.0653)
Average Treatment Effect	Yes		Yes	Yes
Average Treatment Effect on the Treated		Yes		
Municipality FE	Yes	Yes		
Control for Republika Srpska			Yes	
No. Observations	1,952	1,952	1,952	1,952

Significance levels: * : 10% * * : 5% * * * : 1%.
Standard errors in parenthesis.
Nearest-Neighbor-Matching is performed on the basis of the usual control variables (number of children in school in the family, indicator for the oldest child, indicator for a female child, the education of the HHH, and the age of the HHH). Every treated observation is matched to a single untreated one.

previous classes)". Including a child with zero reported expenditure on textbooks, for instance, and a single position in the group of unclassified expenditures would lead to unreasonable results in these regressions.

In primary school (grades 1-8) only few parents pay annual tuition and as column (1) shows, there is no significant difference in spending. However, in secondary school, where areas of specialization are offered, there is a large and significant difference between children of displaced and non-mover parents. Regression (2) shows a reduction by about 80%. In terms of other school material, which includes notebooks, pencils, etc., there is a difference of 17.1%. The spending on textbooks in column (4) is conditional on positive spending on textbooks by anyone in the municipality, because in some municipalities textbooks are provided by the municipality or the federal government. The difference is still a significant 21.4%. Adding up these three groups, which seem to be especially important for the quality of education, I estimate a difference of 14.6%.

These results suggest that displaced parents restrict expenditures on the education of their children wherever they can, that is even in matters like the choice of the secondary school and the provision of study materials.

Table 8 Regression output: education expenditure II

	Annual tuition	Annual tuition	Other school materials	Textbooks	Important groups
	(1)	**(2)**	**(3)**	**(4)**	**(5)**
Displaced Family	0.148	-0.805***	-0.171**	-0.214**	-0.146**
	(0.1371)	(0.2937)	(0.0759)	(0.0910)	(0.0617)
Primary School Only	Yes				
Secondary School Only		Yes			
Controls	Yes	Yes	Yes	Yes	Yes
Municipality FE	Yes	Yes	Yes	Yes	Yes
No. Observations	984	341	1,325	1,101	1,325
R-squared	0.078	0.278	0.164	0.724	0.428

Standard errors clustered at the household level in parenthesis.
Significance levels: * : 10% ** : 5% *** : 1%.
Control variables include number of children in HH enrolled in school, education of HHH, age of HHH and dummy variables for being the oldest child and females. Only households with zero expenditure in the residual category "Total Costs (not included in previous columns)" are used in all regressions. In the regression "Textbooks", only municipalities with some positive expenditures were used. "Important Groups" is the sum of the previous three groups. All independent variables are in measured in logs.

The specifications in Table 9 perform some robustness checks. If someone outside the household paid for education expenditures and that is the reason why parents spend less, the difference in education expenditure could be inconsequential for educational output. Das et al. (2013) show that anticipated public supply of additional school inputs in India and Zambia is offset by an expenditure reduction of parents. Fortunately, the LSMS records the expenses paid from someone outside the household, however only as the total amount. Including these expenditures and running the baseline regressions with the new dependent variable in column (1) reduces the difference in education expenditure to 23.8% but remains highly significant. Restricting the sample to the households without any outside funds for education in column (2) shows a slightly increased difference of 30.6%. These findings imply that the reduced education expenditure is not driven by displaced households who are substituting for additional external funds.

In column (3) dummy variables for rural and mixed municipalities are interacted with the displacement dummy, while the base group are urban municipalities. The interaction terms produce positive, but insignificant point estimates, while the difference in the base group is estimated at 37%. When the sample is restricted to households that still lived in their municipality of birth just before the war, one can rule out that some households self-selected to a higher risk of displacement through migration before the war and now drive the main finding. This can be ruled out as the restricted sample, that did not migrate before the war, also spends 29.1% less on the education of their children.

To sum up, I find a strong negative relationship between displacement and the spending on the education of their children. The result is robust to a number of sample restrictions and the inclusion of various control variables.

Table 9 Regression output: education expenditure III

	Log. of education expenditure			
	All funds (1)	Original (2)	Original (3)	Original (4)
Displaced Family	-0.238***	-0.306***	-0.370***	-0.291***
	(0.0723)	(0.0721)	(0.0971)	(0.0830)
Displaced Family × Rural Municipality			0.151	
			(0.1646)	
Displaced Family × Mixed Municipality			0.183	
			(0.1563)	
No Funds from Outside of Household		Yes		
Never Moved before War				Yes
Controls	Yes	Yes	Yes	Yes
Municipality FE	Yes	Yes	Yes	Yes
No. Observations	1,947	1,827	1,952	1,454
R-squared	0.170	0.202	0.202	0.184

Standard errors clustered at the household level in parenthesis.
Significance levels: * : 10% ** : 5% *** : 1%.
Control variables include number of children in HH enrolled in school, education of HHH, age of HHH and dummy variables for being the oldest child and females. "All Funds" includes education expenditures paid by someone from outside the household. Column (2) restricts the sample to households that do not receive funds for education from outside the household. Column (4) restricts the sample to households who still lived in their municipality of birth before the war.

5 Channels

So far the paper focused on estimating the total causal effect of displacement on education expenditure, but has not offered a channel through which this effect might work. However, it is of great interest to researchers and policy makers alike to understand the mechanisms through which displacement operates. I first start with some econometric considerations to guide the analysis.

5.1 Econometric considerations

The estimation of the channel through which displacement works faces two issues: First, including a variable of a channel introduces an endogenous variable and hence OLS produces biased estimates. And second, the proper counterfactual of an evaluation of a channel changes the interpretation of the estimation results.

5.1.1 Evaluating the indirect effect

The following two equations describe the effect of displacement through an intermediary variable m_i (eg. income) on education expenditure. Municipality fixed effects are omitted for simplicity.

$$y_i = \delta_1 d_i + X_i\beta_1 + \rho_1 m_i + \theta_1 m_i d_i + \varepsilon_{1i} \tag{2}$$

$$m_i = \delta_2 d_i + X_i\beta_2 + \varepsilon_{2i} \tag{3}$$

In these equations, displacement has a direct effect δ_1 on education expenditure, changes the intermediary variable through δ_2, and might influence the effect of the intermediary variable on education expenditure through θ_1. Simply including the intermediary variable and its interaction with displacement introduces an endogeneity problem as $Cov(\varepsilon_{1i}, \varepsilon_{2i})$ might be nonzero. In the case of $Cov(\varepsilon_{1i}, \varepsilon_{2i}) \neq 0$, the OLS estimates in equation (2) will be biased (Angrist and Pischke 2009, p.64). However, the bias can be signed: Using income as an example, it is most likely that $Cov(\varepsilon_{1i}, \varepsilon_{2i}) > 0$, as high income households are more likely to value education more. This causes the estimate of ρ_1 to be biased upwards, ie. the indirect channel of displacement-on-income-on-education expenditure captures too much of the total effect and hence results in a downward bias of δ_1.

5.1.2 Counterfactual

The second problem in these regressions concerns the proper counterfactual. The question I want to answer with these regressions is: "Would the household spend less on education even if displacement would not have changed the intermediary variable?" In a usual regression of education expenditure on a displacement indicator, the intermediary variable, and its interaction with displacement, one has to do some calculations to get a precise answer to the question above and hypothesis testing gets more difficult. However, when the intermediary variable is redefined a single parameter delivers a sufficient answer.

The conditional expectation function is (control variables X_i omitted)

$$E\left[y_i | d_i, m_i\right] = \alpha + \delta d_i + \rho m_i + \theta m_i d_i.$$

Redefine the intermediary variable by subtracting the average of the intermediary variable of the non-displaced households:

$$\tilde{m}_i = m_i - E[m_i|d_i = 0]$$

Then the expected difference in education expenditure between displaced and non-movers, given no change of the intermediary variable by displacement is

$$E\left[y_i|d_i = 1, \tilde{m}_i = E\left[\tilde{m}_i|d_i = 0\right]\right] - E\left[y_i|d_i = 0\right] = \delta + (\rho + \theta)\tilde{m}_i - \rho\tilde{m}_i$$
$$= \delta \tag{4}$$

since $E\left[\tilde{m}_i|d_i = 0\right] = 0$.

Therefore the transformation of the intermediary variable allows me to estimate the difference in education expenditure under the assumption of no change of the intermediary variable through displacement with the single parameter δ. All other estimators remain unchanged because variances and covariances do not change by subtracting a constant.

5.2   Income, the stock of durable goods, and the housing situation

One of the most natural explanations for the difference in education expenditure is that displaced families have lower income and wealth. It is not surprising that displaced households have lower labor income and wealth, especially real estate, than households that did not have to move during the war. When households get displaced, they usually do not have time to sell their real estate, which is often the most valuable asset of a family. If displaced families rent a dwelling while the non-mover families have inherited a house to live in, it would not be surprising that displaced households spend less on education of their children.

The descriptive statistics in Table 10 document that displaced households experience a significant reduction in income, the stock of durable goods, and are less likely to own the dwelling they live in. Total income is lower for displaced households, but higher non-labor income (pensions and allowances) partly counterbalance the reduction in labor income. Also the share reporting zero labor income of 36.1% is a lot higher than that of non-movers of 19.1%. A large difference is in the stock of durable goods, which can be considered as a proxy for wealth as data on financial assets is not available.

The last three rows show the limited information on the housing situation available. The share of families that own the dwelling they live in is almost eight times as high for the non-movers than it is for the displaced. Displaced families mostly rent the place they live in, but a share of almost 16% live in a place without paying for it (either on loan from friends or families, as illegal occupants in abandoned houses, or in emergency lodges). These differences are prime candidates to explain the large reduction in education expenditure found earlier.

Income and wealth is controlled for with several different variables. Household labor income measures the sum of labor income reported for the last month by household members. Household non-labor income measures the sum of pensions and allowances per month received by household members, while total household income is composed of the sum of the two aforementioned variables. The variable durables is the sum of the values of reported durable goods in the household, but not financial assets or real estate. Dummy variables for a reported value of zero for any of those variables are included in the regressions to allow for more flexibility. The housing situation is coded in three indicator

Table 10 Descriptive statistics: income, durable goods, and housing

	All	Not moved	Displaced	Difference
Total HH Income	481	492	437	-54**
				(27.3)
Total HH Income	527	539	473	-66**
(conditional on > 0)				(28.2)
Share with Zero Total	0.086	0.088	0.075	-0.013
HH Income				(0.016)
HH Labor Income	404	426	313	-113***
				(27.4)
HH Labor Income	521	527	490	-37
(conditional on > 0)				(33.9)
Share with Zero	0.224	0.191	0.361	0.170***
HH Labor Income				(0.024)
HH Non-Labor Income	77	66	124	58***
				(8.9)
HH Non-Labor Income	188	174	229	55***
(conditional on > 0)				(15.7)
Share with Zero	0.590	0.621	0.458	-0.163***
HH Non-Labor Income				(0.29)
Stock of Durable Goods	2,688	2,884	1,852	-1,032***
				(244.7)
Stock of Durable Goods	2,795	3,002	1,915	-1,087***
(conditional on > 0)				(251.8)
Share with Zero	0.038	0.040	0.033	-0.006
Stock of Durable Goods				(0.011)
Housing Situation:	0.655	0.790	0.108	-0.682***
Own Dwelling				(0.023)
Housing Situation:	0.264	0.148	0.733	0.585***
Rent Dwelling				(0.022)
Housing Situation:	0.081	0.062	0.159	0.097***
Live for Free				(0.016)
Observations	1,901	1,541	360	

Standard errors in parenthesis.
Significance levels: * : 10% ** : 5% *** : 1%.
Income is relates to monthly income. All income and wealth values are in *Convertible Mark*.

variables for ownership of dwelling, renting a dwelling, or living in the dwelling without paying for it.

The results of the regressions are shown in Table 11. Remember that the point estimates of the first row estimate the difference to the counterfactual of no reduction of income and/or durables. Also the unexplained part of the displacement effect is a lower bound as discussed above. However, the difference in education expenditure is surprisingly robust to the inclusion of income and durable goods variables. The difference decreases only slightly and rules out income and wealth differences as the main mechanism. Similarly the indicator variables for the housing situation fail to explain the difference in education expenditure.

The dummy variable for displacement remains significant at the one-percent level in most specifications and at the five-percent level in the regressions with the housing variables. The most flexible specification with income and durable goods variables in column

Table 11 Regression output: income, durable goods, and housing

	Log. of education expenditure						
	(1)	(2)	(3)	(4)	(5)	(6)	(7)
Displaced Family	-0.293***	-0.233***	-0.254***	-0.257***	-0.209***	-0.316**	-0.329**
	(0.0676)	(0.0701)	(0.0683)	(0.0669)	(0.0686)	(0.1407)	(0.1384)
Log. HH Total Income[1]	0.074*			0.051			
	(0.0401)			(0.0422)			
Displaced Family × Log. HH Total Income[1]	0.035			0.029			
	(0.0788)			(0.0799)			
Log. HH Labor Income[1]		0.042			0.009		0.001
		(0.0516)			(0.0555)		(0.0583)
Displaced Family × Log. HH Labor Income[1]		0.076			0.072		0.094
		(0.1062)			(0.1128)		(0.1142)
Log. HH Non-Labor Inc.[1]		0.026			0.023		0.015
		(0.0423)			(0.0422)		(0.0448)
Displaced Family × Log. HH Non-Labor Inc.[1]		0.006			-0.001		0.006
		(0.0800)			(0.0799)		(0.0806)
Log. Durable Goods[1]			0.065**	0.052*	0.060**		0.052*
			(0.0266)	(0.0283)	(0.0289)		(0.0306)
Displaced Family × Log. Durable Goods[1]			0.055	0.046	0.015		0.034
			(0.0559)	(0.0568)	(0.0589)		(0.0604)
Own Dwelling[1]						0.161	0.160
						(0.1453)	(0.1502)
Displaced Family × Own Dwelling[1]						0.096	-0.200
						(0.2789)	(0.2820)
Rent Dwelling[1]						0.207	0.233
						(0.1558)	(0.1607)
Displaced Family × Rent Dwelling[1]						0.093	-0.073
						(0.2361)	(0.2398)
Zero Indicator[1]	Yes	Yes	Yes	Yes	Yes		Yes
Displaced Family × Zero Indicator[1]	Yes	Yes	Yes	Yes	Yes		Yes
F-test	7.51***	4.37***	5.92***	4.18***	2.99***	5.61***	2.12**
Controls	Yes	Yes	Yes	Yes	Yes	Yes	Yes
Municipality FE	Yes	Yes	Yes	Yes	Yes	Yes	Yes
No. Observations	1,901	1,901	1,901	1,901	1,901	1,783	1,783
R-squared	0.250	0.253	0.251	0.255	0.258	0.216	0.231

Standard errors clustered at the household level in parenthesis.
Significance levels: * : 10% ** : 5% *** : 1%.
Control variables include number of children in HH enrolled, education of HHH, age of HHH and dummy variables for being the oldest child and females. "F-test" results from a test of joint significance of displacement and all its interactions.
[1] Measured as the difference to the mean of non-movers.

(5) shows a difference in education expenditure of 20.9% after controlling for labor and non-labor income and the stock of durable goods. This is still two-thirds of the total causal effect. When the housing variables are included, there is actually a slight increase from the total causal effect estimated previously.

To conclude, differences in income, the stock of durable goods, and the housing situation can explain at most one third of the total effect, but do not seem to be the main mechanism. There still seems something else to be going on that was induced by displacement of the parents.

5.3   Employment status of parents

Another mechanism to explore is whether differences in the employment status of the parents cause the education expenditure difference. If both parents are working, parents may not have the time to help their children learn and therefore spend more on books and school materials to make up for less personal support (Houtenville and Smith Conway 2008). The descriptive statistics in Table 12 show that displaced parents are less likely to be employed. This mechanism could therefore explain the difference in education expenditure.

I test this hypothesis by including indicator variables for employment status of both parents (or a single parent), the spouse of the household head, and if no parent is employed in Table 13. Interaction terms of the employment indicators with displacement are included as well. Again the mean of the non-movers of each employment variable is subtracted from the indicator variable to interpret the displacement dummy as the aforementioned counterfactual. In the three following columns I add one dummy variable and the interaction term at a time. None of these coefficients is significant at a traditional level as can be seen in Table 13.

As with income, the coefficients show that only a small portion of the difference in education expenditure can be explained by the employment status of the parents, at most about one tenth in the last regression. The main mechanism through which displacement affects education expenditure is still undetected.

5.4   Preferences, uncertainty, and financial constraints

In summary, neither income, the durable goods level, the housing situation nor the employment status of the parents are able to account for the majority of the difference in education expenditure. The natural question is then: How does the effect come about? Unfortunately, I am not able to fully answer this question. This section discusses additional explanations.

A possible explanation is that displaced households are able to buy cheaper school materials and textbooks or share the supplies with other families. Displaced households in an area may build networks to help each other. However, it is hard to imagine that displaced households find a way to save on education expenditure that households who did not move during the war do not find, especially with their social network in place. The non-movers in Bosnia and Herzegovina are not exactly rich to pass up a possibility to save.

Voors et al. (2012) present evidence from field experiments in Burundi showing that exposure to violence affects preferences. In detail they report more altruistic behavior

Table 12 Descriptive statistics: parent's employment status

	All	Not moved	Displaced	Difference
Both Parents Employed	0.29	0.30	0.23	-0.07***
				(0.026)
Spouse of HHH Employed	0.28	0.29	0.23	-0.06**
				(0.026)
No Parent Employed	0.34	0.30	0.48	0.17***
				(0.027)
Observations	1,901	1,541	360	

Standard errors in parenthesis.
Significance levels: * : 10% ** : 5% *** : 1%.

Table 13 Regression output: parent's employment status

	Log. of education expenditure			
	(1)	(2)	(3)	(4)
Displaced Family	-0.281***	-0.290***	-0.276***	-0.274***
	(0.0687)	(0.0682)	(0.0696)	(0.0689)
Both Parents Employed[1]	0.097			0.056
	(0.0674)			(0.0723)
Displaced Family ×	0.165			0.203
Both Parents Employed[1]	(0.1529)			(0.1689)
Spouse Employed[1]		0.095		
		(0.0676)		
Displaced Family ×		0.062		
Spouse Employed[1]		(0.1476)		
No Parent Employed[1]			-0.147**	-0.129*
			(0.0705)	(0.0756)
Displaced Family ×			0.017	0.099
No Parent Employed[1]			(0.1340)	(0.1470)
F-test	9.74***	9.34***	8.08***	6.14***
Controls	Yes	Yes	Yes	Yes
Municipality FE	Yes	Yes	Yes	Yes
No. Observations	1,901	1,901	1,901	1,901
R-squared	0.202	0.200	0.202	0.204

Standard errors clustered at the household level in parenthesis.
Significance levels: * : 10% ** : 5% *** : 1%.
Control variables include number of children in HH enrolled, education of HHH, age of HHH and dummy variables for being the oldest child and females. "F-test" results from a test of joint significance of displacement and all its interactions.
[1] Measured as the difference to the mean of non-movers.

towards neighbors, more risk taking, and a higher discount rate. For my purpose the higher discount rate is of special interest. If displaced households were more exposed to violence than non-movers, as can be expected, then displaced parents could have a higher discount rate than parents who were not displaced. Individuals with a higher discount rate would invest less in projects that generate a payoff in the future - such as education. Unfortunately, with the crude consumption data available, such a hypothesis can not be tested seriously.

Two other potential explanations come to mind. First, displaced households face a lot of uncertainty about the future and try to prepare themselves by cutting down spending on every non-vital position, which includes education expenditure. In a simple two period model, an agent with convex marginal utility reduces consumption in the first period if the risk of period 2 income increases. Kimball (1990) calls this phenomenon prudence and defines it as "the propensity to prepare and forearm oneself in the face of uncertainty". In 2001 the restitution of property to internally displaced households and the possibility to return to their homes from before the war was still an issue in Bosnia and Herzegovina. Many displaced households probably faced a highly uncertain future. On the other hand one could argue that increased uncertainty through displacement prompts households to invest more in highly mobile assets, such as human capital, which they could take with them if they ever had to change location again.

The second potential explanation are financial constraints. Displaced households could face tighter financial constraints due to the loss of their social network for credit or the lack of property they could use as collateral. Unfortunately, financial assets are not included in the survey to infer about financial constraints. Even if financial constraints are not binding now, the expectation that they will bind in the future would already induce households cut back on expenditures today (Deaton 1991).

However, I am not able to give a full explanation how the difference in education expenditure comes about. A change in the discount rate of displaced households, increased risk, and financial constraints are consistent with the findings of this paper, but other channels through which displacement works can not be ruled out in general.

6 Conclusion

This paper contributes to the literature on the consequences of violent conflicts by looking at the effect of displacement, in the sense of forced migration, on investment in education. I find a robust statistical relationship between the displacement status of parents and the amount spent on the education of their children. The reduction of education expenditure through displacement is in the range of 20 to 30% compared to parents who did not move during the war. The estimated difference in education expenditure is robust to many specifications and a series of tests indicate that selection bias is not the source of the result. Nearest-neighbor matching on covariates finds quantitatively similar effects.

A number of channels of how displacement might affect education expenditure are discussed. Differences in income and durable goods levels can explain at most one third of the baseline result. A lower ownership rate of housing among displaced households also fails to explain the main finding. The employment of parents and support from outside the household can also be ruled out as the main mechanisms.

I further discuss recent experimental findings on the effect of exposure to violence on preferences, the hypothesis that the displaced households face more uncertainty about the future, or more rigid financial constraints than non-movers. That would lead them to cut back spending on every non-vital position, including the education of their children.

More work needs to be done to fully understand how violent conflict influences peoples lives. Research has shown negative consequences of exposure to violence and displacement, but how exactly the changes in economic outcomes come about is not fully understood yet.

Endnotes

[1] The term "displacement" refers to forced migration and is different to job loss, which the labor literature often refers to as displacement.

[2] As Das et al. (2013) show, when parents expect to receive additional resources, they substitute out of their own educational expenditure and therefore the total educational inputs available to students do not increase much. This substitution is likely responsible for the failure to find positive effects in previous experimental studies.

[3] A problem for the estimation of causal effects emerges as the often used difference-in-difference approach between birth cohorts of treatment and control regions does not account for non-random wartime displacement. This generates a sample correlation between outcomes and conflict intensity that is not the causal effect of exposure to conflict.

[4] Detailed reports about conditions at schools during the academic year 2000-01 are, to my knowledge, not available.

[5] Croats are hardly found as displaced people in the data, because households of Croats who found them self in Serb territory likely moved to the - then newly formed - Republic of Croatia (IDMC 2009). I will therefore focus on Bosniaks and Serbs from now on.

[6]This is also true for the larger sample of all household heads and their spouses in the LSMS data set, not just the ones with children in school that is used here.

Competing interests

The IZA Journal of Labor & Development is committed to the IZA Guiding Principles of Research Integrity. The author declares that he has observed these principles.

Acknowledgements

The research presented in this article was conducted as part of my PhD dissertation at Simon Fraser University. My senior supervisor, Anke Kessler, contributed by providing comments on research design and exposition, while the junior supervisors, Simon Woodcock and Chris Muris, help with comments on the exposition of the research. I also thank Gustavo Bobonis, Alex Karaivanov, Krishna Pendakur, and conference participants at the Atlantic Summer Conference on Public Policy Research, the Development Conference of the German Economic Association, the conference of the European Association of Labour Economists, seminar participants at Johannes Kepler University, the editor (Hartmut Lehmann), and four anonymous referees for helpful comments. All remaining errors are mine.

References

Akresh R, de Walque D (2008) Armed Conflict and Schooling: Evidence from the 1994 Rwandan Genocide. HiCN Working Paper 47. http://www.hicn.org/wordpress/wp-content/uploads/2012/06/wp47.pdf. Accessed 23 Jun 2014

Angrist J, Pischke J (2009) Mostly Harmless Econometrics. Princeton University Press, Princeton NJ

Bauer T, Braun S, Kvasnicka M (2013) The Economic Integration of Forced Migrants: Evidence from Post-War Germany. Econ J 123:998–1024

Bellows J, Miguel E (2009) War and Local Collective Action in Sierra Leone. J Public Econ 93:1144–1157

Chamarbagwala R, Morán H (2009) The Human Capital Consequences of Civil War: Evidence from Guatemala. HiCN Working Paper:59. http://www.hicn.org/wordpress/wp-content/uploads/2012/06/wp59.pdf. Accessed 23 Jun 2014

Das J, Dercon S, Habyarimana J, Krishnan P, Muralidharan K, Sundararaman V (2013) School Inputs, Household Substitution, and Test Scores. Am Econ J Appl Econ 5:29–57

Dahlman C, Tuathail G (2005) Broken Bosnia: The localized geopolitics of displacement and return in two Bosnian places. Ann Assoc Am Geograph 95:644–662

Deaton A (1991) Savings and Liquidity Constraints. Econometrica 59:1221–1248

EU (2008) Institutional and Capacity Building of Bosnia and Herzegovina Education System. http://www.cep.edu.rs/sites/default/files/Education_Strategy_2008_-_2015.pdf. Accessed 23 Jun 2014

Fiala N (2009) The Consequences of Forced Displacement in Northern Uganda. HiCN Working Paper:65. http://www.hicn.org/wordpress/wp-content/uploads/2012/06/wp65.pdf. Accessed 23 Jun 2014

Hanushek E (2003) The Failure of Input-Based Schooling Policies. Econ J 113:64–98

Houtenville A, Smith Conway K (2008) Parental Effort, School Resources, and Student Achievement. J Hum Resour 43:437–453

IDMC (2009) A profile of the internal displacement situation: Croatia. http://unpan1.un.org/intradoc/groups/public/documents/untc/unpan016823.pdf. Accessed 23 Jun 2014

Justino P (2011) Violent Conflict and Human Capital Accumulation. HiCN Working Paper:99. http://www.hicn.org/wordpress/wp-content/uploads/2012/06/wp99.pdf. Accessed 23 Jun 2014

Kennedy P (1981) Estimation with correctly interpreted dummy variables in semilogarithmic equations. Am Econ Rev 71:801

Kimball M (1990) Precautionary Savings in the Small and in the Large. Econometrica 58:53–73

Kondylis F (2010) Conflict Displacement and Labour Market Outcomes in Post-War Bosnia and Herzegovina. J Dev Econ 93:235–248

León G (2012) Civil conflict and Human Capital Accumulation: The Long Term Consequences of Political Violence in Perú. J Hum Resour 47:991–1022

Mappes-Niediek N (2009) Die Ethno-Falle. Christoph Links Verlag, Berlin

Merrouche O (2006) The Human Capital Cost of Landmine Contamination in Cambodia. HiCN Working Paper:25. http://www.hicn.org/wordpress/wp-content/uploads/2012/06/wp25.pdf. Accessed 23 Jun 2014

MHHR (Ministry for Human Rights and Refugees) (2003) Comparative Indicators on Refugees, Displaced Persons and Returnees, Property Law Implementation, and Reconstruction in BiH from 1991 to 30 June 2003. http://www.mhrr.gov.ba/PDF/LjudskaPrava/common%20core%20document%20BH-rev-ENGLISH.pdf. Accessed 23 Jun 2014

Mooney E (2005) Access to Education for Internally Displaced Children. The Brookings Institution-University of Bern. http://www.brookings.edu/fp/projects/idp/20050111_mooney.pdf. Accessed 23 Jun 2014

OECD, Mission to Bosnia and Herzegovina (2006) Action Plan on School Enrolment and Completion in Bosnia and Herzegovina. http://www.oscebih.org/documents/osce_bih_doc_2006092510260492eng.pdf. Accessed 23 Jun 2014

Pivovarova M, Swee E (2012) Quantifying The Microeconomic Effects of War: How Much Can Panel Data Help? HiCN Working Paper 116. http://www.hicn.org/wordpress/wp-content/uploads/2012/06/HiCN-WP-116.pdf. Accessed 23 Jun 2014

Rahim A, Jaimovich D, Ylönen A (2013) Forced displacement and behavioral change: An empirical study of returnee households in the Nuba Mountains. HiCNWorking Paper 157. http://www.hicn.org/wordpress/wp-content/uploads/2012/06/HiCN-WP-157_1.pdf. Accessed 23 Jun 2014

Rodriguez C, Sanchez F (2009) Armed Conflict Exposure, Human Capital Investments and Child Labor: Evidence from Colombia. HiCNWorking Paper 68. http://www.hicn.org/wordpress/wp-content/uploads/2012/06/wp68.pdf. Accessed 23 Jun 2014

Sarvimäki M, Uusitalo R, Jäntti M (2009) Long-Term Effects of Forced Migration. IZA Discussion Paper 4003. http://ftp.iza.org/dp4003.pdf. Accessed 23 Jun 2014

Silber L, Little A (1996) The Death of Yugoslavia. Penguin Books, London

State Agency for Statistics of BiH, Statistical Institute of the Federation of BiH, Republika Srpska Statistical Institute and The World Bank (2001) Living Standard Measurement Survey - Bosnia and Herzegovina. http://tinyurl.com/bdetznv. Accessed 23 Jun 2014

Shemyakina O (2011) Education and Armed Conflict in Tajikistan. HiCN Working Paper 106. http://www.hicn.org/wordpress/wp-content/uploads/2012/06/wp1061.pdf. Accessed 23 Jun 2014

Swee E (2009) On War and Schooling Attainment: The Case of Bosnia and Herzegovina. HiCN Working Paper 57. http://www.hicn.org/wordpress/wp-content/uploads/2012/06/wp57.pdf. Accessed 23 Jun 2014

Swee E (2010) Together or Separate? Post-conflict Partition, Ethnic Homogenization, and the Provision of Public Schooling. http://individual.utoronto.ca/swee/ethnic11.pdf. Accessed 23 Jun 2014

Tuathail G, O'Loughlin J (2009) After Ethnic Cleansing: Return Outcomes in Bosnia-Herzegovina a Decade Beyond War. Ann Assoc Am Geograph 99:1045–1053

UNESCO (1996) Review of the education system in the Federation of Bosnia and Herzegovina. http://unesdoc.unesco.org/images/0011/001144/114461eo.pdf. Accessed 23 Jun 2013

UNESCO (1997) Review of the education system in the Republika Srpska - Bosnia and Herzegovina. http://unesdoc.unesco.org/images/0010/001092/109215eo.pdf. Accessed 23 Jun 2014

UNHCR (2009) Global Report 2009. http://www.unhcr.org/gr09. Accessed 23 Jun 2014

van Garderen K, Shah C (2002) Exact interpretation of dummy variables in semilogarithmic equations. Econometrics J 5:149–159

Voors M, Nillesen E, Verwimp P, Bulte E, Lensink R, van Soest D (2012) Violent Conflict and Behavior: A Field Experiment in Burundi. American Economic Review 102:941–964

In search of opportunities? The barriers to more efficient internal labor mobility in Ukraine

Johannes Koettl[1,3*], Olga Kupets[1,2], Anna Olefir[1,3] and Indhira Santos[1]

* Correspondence:
jkoettl@worldbank.org
[1]World Bank, 1818 H Street NW,
Washington, DC 20433, USA
[3]World Bank Country Office in
Moldova, 20/1 Pushkin Street,
MD-2012 Chisinau, Republic of
Moldova
Full list of author information is
available at the end of the article

Abstract

Ukraine's economy lacks dynamism, and this is both the cause and the effect of people not moving across the regions. The rate at which Ukrainians move from one region to another within the country is only half of what would be expected in comparison with other countries. This paper examines the barriers that prevent workers from moving within Ukraine, using information from focus group discussions and expert surveys. It also offers recommendations for creating greater labor mobility in Ukraine through addressing institutional bottlenecks and defines five key areas for improvement, including the population registry system, housing and credit markets, vocational education and training systems, labor market institutions, and the social welfare system.

JEL Classification: J61; J68; P25

Keywords: Internal labor mobility; Housing market; Barriers to migration; Transition economies

1 Introduction

The transition to a market economy in many Eastern European countries has been typically accompanied by a significant shift from widely-dispersed industries to a concentration of capital and production in a few areas. Labor has largely mirrored the movement of capital and production, leading to large economic gains.

In Ukraine, however, labor is not flowing as smoothly to the areas where production and capital are concentrated. Ukrainians do not move often, and when they do move, they don't necessarily go to areas with more jobs and higher wages. Internal mobility is about half of what is expected when comparing Ukraine with other countries, despite large economic differentials. Hence, relatively few people are taking advantage of economic opportunities in other areas, and the challenge is to explain why they fail to seize these opportunities.

A 2004 study of the determinants of inter-regional migration in Ukraine found that that the drivers of internal migration in Ukraine have changed significantly over time, with labor market conditions becoming less and less relevant to people's decision to move (Martynenko 2004). Kupets (2012, 2014a, b) examined why migration flows between some Ukrainian regions were almost non-existent, while between other regions, which are typically very similar in terms of social and economic development, there were substantial flows in both directions, concluding that the geographic distance provides a serious obstacle to residential migration within Ukraine. In particular,

Kupets (2014b) finds that the estimated distance elasticity of migration increased from minus 0.91-0.92 in 2008 to minus 0.96-1 in 2012. Significant effects of the distance between the regions' major cities and of a common land border between regions (used as a proxy for cultural, religious and political proximity in addition to geographic proximity) show that direct and indirect migration costs, including the costs of moving to dissimilar regions in terms of culture, religion, and political attitudes (but not in terms of the language), have deterring effects on residential inter-regional migration in Ukraine. Besides, these empirical studies show that Ukrainians seem to only partially respond to the unemployment and wage differentials, but importantly also to inter-regional differences in local per capita public expenditures on education, health care and social assistance (Kupets 2014a), the number of doctors, crime rate and air pollution (Kupets 2014b). However, the effects of economic, social and environmental variables are not always significant and in the expected direction. Finally, in a study of temporary labor migration and commuting of the employed population, based on labor force survey data, it has been found that although intra-regional flows dominate over inter-regional and international flows in all regions, there were six regions in which workers were more likely to go for temporary employment abroad rather than to some other region within Ukraine (Kupets 2012). This suggests that, in view of more attractive employment opportunities and much higher expected returns, cross-border external migration is often used as a substitute for long-distance migration within Ukraine.

The main objective of this paper is to explore the barriers to internal migration in Ukraine using qualitative information from expert surveys and focus group discussions. To provide insights into the attitudes of migrant workers, the unemployed and employed towards internal migration, as well as their motivations to move and the most salient barriers to internal mobility, nineteen focus group discussions were conducted by the Kiev International Institute of Sociology (KIIS) between March and April 2012. The findings of these focus group discussions were complemented by a survey of nineteen experts, including representatives of trade unions and employers' organizations, and researchers of labor market and migration issues, and by consultations with policymakers, social partners and representatives of the private sector.

The major barriers to internal mobility are found to be mainly institutional. Internal labor mobility is low and inefficient because of weaknesses in five main areas: (i) administrative procedures, reflected in a population registry system that binds people to their place of residence and increases the costs of internal migration; (ii) underdeveloped housing and credit markets that make housing in leading regions unaffordable to potential migrants, particularly the poor; (iii) insufficient human capital, as people in lagging regions often lack the necessary skills to access better economic opportunities in high productivity, modern sectors in the leading regions; (iv) weak formal labor market institutions that sustain labor market and wage rigidities, encourage informality and do not provide workers with enough reliable information about job openings and labor market conditions; and (v) social benefits that are tied to the officially registered place of residence and therefore often discourage relocation to another area. Individual socio-psychological factors such as strong ties to families, friends and local community and overall reluctance of Ukrainians to relocate, even for a better job and living standards, are also important constraints to mobility frequently mentioned by experts and focus group informants.

In the face of weak formal institutions that are supposed to help people connect to economic opportunities, Ukrainians often circumvent these institutions and have to rely on alternative solutions, which are mostly unregulated, do not provide formal protection and entail high levels of uncertainty. Over-reliance on informal social networks, employment, and housing together with corruption are the major examples of these solutions. Although informal networks and practices help many people to solve their social and economic problems, they are suboptimal as they often lead to too costly and risky outcomes.

Hence, the main policy implication is the need to address the existing institutional bottlenecks that affect internal mobility in order to allow people, especially the poor, to move more freely from lagging, job-scarce regions to leading regions with better employment and income opportunities. Given the critical demographic situation in Ukraine, with a population that is rapidly shrinking and aging, the issues of removing existing barriers to internal mobility need to be put high on the present reform agenda because an older population is much less likely to migrate for economic reasons.

Apart from aging, globalization and international competition make more mobility all the more necessary by pressing Ukraine to push ahead with the modernization of its economy. This will require further agglomeration of capital and labor, a process that in Ukraine has so far been slower than in peer countries.

The remainder of the paper is organized as follows. Section 2 offers a brief literature review of how a mobile workforce can benefit the economy and why it is important for Ukraine. Section 3 provides some background information on the magnitude and patterns of internal migration in Ukraine. Section 4 examines the main barriers to migration of Ukrainians within the country. Section 5 offers policy recommendations, and Section 6 concludes.

2 Potential benefits of internal migration: literature review

The concentration of people, capital and production was fundamental in the development of industrialized countries in North America, Western Europe, and Northeast Asia. Because economic prosperity did not happen everywhere at the same time in those countries, people had to relocate to find economic opportunities and productive jobs. This concentration in turn stimulated further growth and rising living standards.

A large volume of theoretical and empirical work from developed and developing countries, summarized in Chapter 5 of the 2009 World Development Report (World Bank 2009a), suggests that voluntary internal migration for economic reasons does not only increase the earnings of migrants but also contributes to aggregate economic growth by improving the distribution of labor, clustering skills and talents, and driving agglomeration spillovers. Studies on migration, development and poverty reduction in Asian countries such as Bangladesh, China, India, Pakistan and Vietnam (International Organization for Migration 2005) also show that, if managed properly, internal migration, particularly from rural to urban areas, plays an important role in poverty reduction in sending areas as the flow of money, goods and services between rural and urban areas increases demand for local agricultural output, stimulates the non-farm economy and absorbs surplus labor. For example, IOM 2005 estimated that labor migration from rural to urban areas in China contributed 16 percent of total GDP growth in the period between 1978 and 1997 (International Organization for Migration 2005, p.70). Similarly, Lall et al. (2006) estimated that 30 percent of India's urban economic growth is accounted for by the movement of more than 20 million Indians from rural to urban areas in the 1990s.

There is also evidence that Canada's economic growth in the 1990s and early 2000s had significantly benefitted from labor migration from the low-productive eastern provinces to highly-productive western provinces (Sharpe et al. 2007). This study asserts that interprovincial migration was responsible for 1.3 percent of real trend GDP growth in Canada over the 1987–2006 period and 2.8 percent of the actual real GDP growth in 2006. At the same time, the authors point out that reallocation of labor between provinces does not produce productivity growth in itself, but it ensures that potential productivity gains resulted from increased human capital, technological advancement, and capital investment are further exploited.

Internal migration also offers societies an opportunity for the convergence in living standards among individuals and regions, while reducing overall macroeconomic volatility and contributing to the absorption of shocks, as suggested by neoclassical economic theory. Proponents of the New Economic Geography, on the other hand, argue that selective migration for economic reasons can lead to a backwash effect and huge divergence rather than convergence between "lucky" and "unlucky" regions (Moretti 2012; Myrdal 1963). The empirical evidence also provides quite mixed results. For example, the 2009 World Development report (World Bank 2009a) argues that recent empirical studies show the positive impact of migration on income convergence in developed and developing economies, often after an initial divergence in low and middle-income countries. At the same time, Vakulenko (2014) concludes that various studies using a similar β–convergence model but different sets of control variables and estimation methods find positive, negative and insignificant relationships between migration and convergence. In the same paper, findings from Russia suggest that there are positive effects of migration on income and wages in sending regions, but the impact is quite small, probably because the regional income convergence in Russia mainly happens through capital mobility and the subsequent development of financial and real estate markets rather than through labor mobility.

It is important to note that there are also potential costs associated with high internal mobility. In fast-growing urban areas in developing countries, traffic congestion and overcrowding, lack of sufficient housing, environmental degradation, increased crime rate, growing inequalities in access to jobs, housing, education, safety, cultural and social amenities are often a problem (International Organization for Migration 2005). At the individual level, both internal and cross-border migration is also associated with many risks and costs that reduce the benefits, especially for poor families. Among the many hardships are: debt bondage as migrants borrow money to migrate; dangerous and difficult working conditions; living in the open or in very poor accommodation with inadequate water and sanitation; crime and personal safety issues; lack of information about rights, entitlements and the applicable law in general; lack of access to health services, education (for migrant's children) and other government services; and discrimination (International Organization for Migration 2008 Chapter 7. Internal migration. In: World migration report 2008). But appropriate urban planning and social policies can help mitigate some of the potential negative effects of internal labor mobility.

To sum up, there are important economic gains that can be realized from intensive and efficient internal migration, both in terms of economic growth but also in terms of living standards of individuals. The potential for mobility of workers to contribute to higher productivity, economic growth and living standards is especially critical for a transition country like Ukraine, whose economy is going through a fundamental process of structural transformation. Yet, so far, the pace of restructuring and modernization has been slow: Among transition economies, Ukraine had one of the least agglomerated economy and population in 1990, but it experienced almost no agglomeration since then. Despite a slight convergence in regional unemployment rates and wages over the last decade, there are substantial regional disparities, particularly in regional output per worker (see Figure 1).

According to the studies on poverty in Ukraine (Brück et al. 2010; United Nations Development Programme 2008; World Bank 2005), the country has not taken full advantage of internal migration of workers and their families for bringing down these regional imbalances. We return to this issue of what keeps Ukrainians from taking advantage of internal migration after a brief discussion on past patterns of migration within the country.

3 Magnitude and patterns of internal migration in Ukraine

The primary source of data on migration flows in Ukraine is administrative data on in-migration (inflows), out-migration (outflows) and net migration (inflows minus outflows) based on population registration of the place of residence (see the details in Section 4.1). This administrative data refers to those changes of residence that are registered with the State Migration Service and published by the State Statistics Service of Ukraine. Therefore, these data refer mainly to residential mobility, but many moves of workers and their families might go unregistered. This means that administrative internal migration data is likely to underestimate actual migration, as corroborated by the survey of labor market experts conducted for this report. However, we complement this source of data with additional microeconomic sources based on household surveys to get a more complete picture of migration patterns.

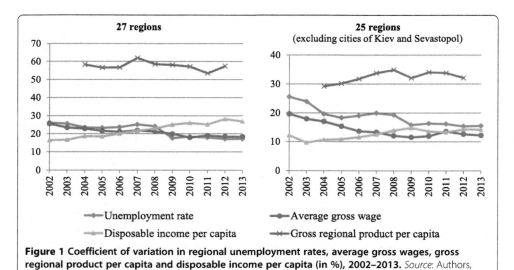

Figure 1 Coefficient of variation in regional unemployment rates, average gross wages, gross regional product per capita and disposable income per capita (in %), 2002–2013. *Source*: Authors, based on the State Statistics Service of Ukraine data.

Official statistics indicate that about 622,000 people changed residency within Ukraine in 2013, which constitutes about 1.37 percent of the total population[1]. Despite some increase in 2010, the gross migration rate is not yet back to its pre-crisis levels (Figure 2). Moves from one region[2] to another (inter-regional migration) represent around 42 percent of total registered internal migration while moves within the same administrative region (intra-regional migration) make up 58 percent.

The highest propensity to migrate is observed among youth aged 15 to 19, followed by the 20 to 24-year-olds, who move from their home places mainly to pursue studies after secondary school. Females and urban young people under 30 years have a higher propensity to migrate than their male and rural counterparts. On the other hand, men and the rural population appear to have a higher propensity of changing their official place of residence in older age when internal migration is more likely to be motivated by labor market reasons rather than by education or marriage. Overall, urban areas gain population through internal migration from both intra- and inter-regional migration. But these net gains have significantly reduced over the last years from about 53,000 people in 2005 to only about 14,000 people in 2013.

An analysis of inter-regional migration flows reveals that in most regions out-migration exceeded in-migration, resulting in negative net migration rates. The regions with the biggest net losses relative to its population were Kirovohrad, Kherson and Luhansk oblasts. There are some regions though that had consistent population gains through internal migration. These are Sevastopol City, Kiev oblast, Kiev City, Odesa, Chernivtsi and Kharkiv oblasts, and the Autonomous Republic of Crimea[3]. These migrant-attracting regions are located in different geographic parts of Ukraine and are not concentrated in certain areas, for example in the industrially developed East.

The rates of internal migration are low in Ukraine when compared to other countries. Using official statistics on internal migration and controlling for the average size of regions, we estimated that actual internal migration rates in Ukraine are about half of what we would expect when compared to other countries[4]. An alternative source of data for international comparison is the joint EBRD/World Bank "Life-in-Transition" survey, a large micro-data set that uses the same questionnaire and methodology across all countries of Eastern Europe and Central Asia and some Western European countries. According to this data, in Ukraine, 0.5 percent of the population moved within

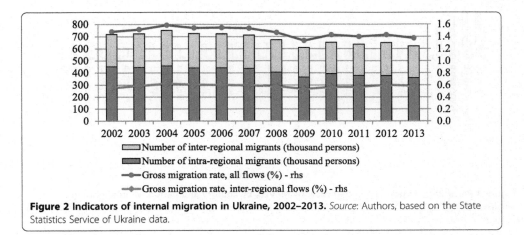

Figure 2 Indicators of internal migration in Ukraine, 2002–2013. *Source*: Authors, based on the State Statistics Service of Ukraine data.

the year preceding the survey in 2010, and 4.5 percent moved within the last five years (Figure 3). Although data in this survey do not distinguish between external and internal migrations, Ukraine's migration rates are clearly at the lower end of the distribution when comparing across countries. Only 11 countries displayed lower migration rates, while 21 countries displayed higher rates than Ukraine.

Not only are Ukrainians not very mobile, it seems that also intentions to migrate are low when compared to other countries. According to Life-in-Transition data, 2 percent of Ukrainians said they planned to move abroad in the near future, and about 0.9 percent said they intended to move to other parts of Ukraine. Only three countries had a workforce that was less inclined to migrate internally, while 29 countries displayed higher rates.

Synovate, a global market research company (integrated into Ipsos in 2012), conducted a survey of labor mobility in Bulgaria, Russia, Serbia and Ukraine (Synovate 2010). The results of the survey confirmed the finding from the Life-in-Transition survey, namely low desire to relocate both in Russia and Ukraine. Specifically, if offered a 50 percent increase in salary, around 80 percent of respondents in Russia and Ukraine would still refuse to relocate. In Bulgaria and Serbia, only 50 percent would refuse.

In an environment of low residential labor mobility, commuting can be a substitute for labor and residential migration in facilitating transitions out of joblessness and smoothing regional disparities. This is precisely the case in Ukraine. According to the labor force survey, the total number of commuters was above 2.6 million employed people in 2010, or 13.2 percent of the employed population in Ukraine (Table 1). But only a small share of workers travel across regions. Inter-regional commuting rate (1.6 percent in 2010) is low in Ukraine when compared to the old EU member states, although it is comparable to those observed in Bulgaria, Poland or Romania (Paci et al. 2007).

Our findings regarding low internal migration in Ukraine, which is based on different data sources, is also consistent with local perceptions. In a survey of labor market experts conducted for this study, 12 out of 19 respondents said that internal mobility rates in Ukraine are low when compared to those of other Eastern European countries.

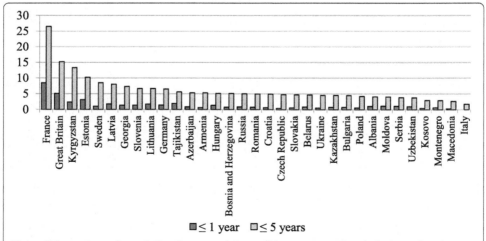

Figure 3 Percentage of population that recently moved, by country and period when migration occurred (in %), 2010. *Note*: Recent moves include both internal and international migrants. *Source*: Authors, based on the European Bank for Reconstruction and Development and World Bank Life-in-Transition Survey.

Table 1 Commuting rate as percent of the employed population (in %), 2005-2010

	2005	2006	2007	2008	2009	2010
Total						
All commuters	10.5	10.8	11.6	13.0	13.2	13.2
Intra-regional	9.2	9.5	10.2	11.1	11.6	11.6
Inter-regional	1.4	1.4	1.4	1.9	1.7	1.6
Urban						
All commuters	6.7	7.0	7.2	7.5	7.0	7.2
Intra-regional	5.2	5.6	5.9	5.9	5.6	5.8
Inter-regional	1.5	1.4	1.3	1.6	1.4	1.4
Rural						
All commuters	18.8	19.2	21.2	25.2	26.3	26.0
Intra-regional	17.7	18.0	19.5	22.6	24.1	24.1
Inter-regional	1.1	1.2	1.7	2.6	2.2	1.9

Notes: Respondents temporarily working abroad are excluded.
Source: Authors, based on labor force survey data.

Only 3 respondents thought internal migration is high, while 4 respondents thought it was at the same level as in peer countries.

Therefore, all surveys confirm that Ukrainians are far less likely to move than workers in other countries. For those Ukrainians who move, one would expect that they move to the most dynamic regions. However, an examination of inter-regional migration data presents a further puzzle: even when Ukrainians do move, they do not always move to the most productive regions with high wages and low unemployment (Figure 4).

Ukrainians changing their place of residence within the country are more likely to move to communities located either within the same region (58 percent of all registered

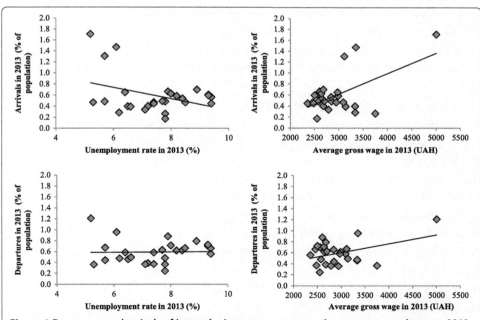

Figure 4 Departures and arrivals of internal migrants versus unemployment rates and wages, 2013.
Source: Authors, based on the State Statistics Service of Ukraine data.

moves within Ukraine in 2012) or to neighboring regions (23.7 percent), which often have similar employment and income opportunities as the place of origin. Those who move to non-neighboring regions choose predominantly the capital city of Kiev, whereas moves between lagging and better-off regions located in different parts of Ukraine are relatively rare (Kupets 2014b). A positive and significant correlation between in-migration and out-migration rates indicates that high in-migration and out-migration rates are usually observed in the same regions, and therefore there is a great deal of churning rather than a genuine reallocation of people between regions.

In summary, Ukrainians do not migrate internally as much when compared to other countries, and those who move are not necessarily going to the regions with better labor market conditions. This begs the questions if there are constraints to internal labor mobility and what they are, which is the subject of the next section.

4 Barriers to relocation of workers within Ukraine

In order to answer these questions, we collected qualitative information using several methods: a Delphi-type survey among Ukrainian experts; focus group discussions; and consultations with Ukrainian policymakers, social partners, and representatives of local and international companies and business associations.

A short questionnaire consisting of 11 closed and open questions on internal mobility was sent to a panel of 46 experts; 19 fully answered questionnaires were returned. The respondents included four trade union representatives, four representatives from employers' organizations and eleven labor market and migration experts from think tanks and universities. The questionnaire focused on two main areas: (i) assessing perceptions in Ukraine on the magnitude and patterns of labor market mobility, and (ii) identifying of the most critical barriers to internal labor mobility in Ukraine.

Focus group discussions were aimed at better understanding the attitudes of migrant workers, the unemployed and employed towards internal migration, motivations to move, and the most salient barriers to internal mobility. They were conducted by the Kiev International Institute of Sociology between March and April 2012 with financial and technical support of the World Bank. There were two different sets of focus group discussions:

Two focus groups among migrant workers in Kiev City, one with highly-skilled employees/self-employed and the other with low-skilled workers. Nineteen participants filled in a prescreening questionnaire; sixteen participated in the focus group discussions. All participants had moved to Kiev for labor reasons from different regions of Ukraine. The two groups were balanced in terms of gender and age.

Seventeen focus groups were carried out among people with different labor market status as background work for the 2013 World Development Report (World Bank 2012b) and the accompanying country study for Ukraine (Kupets et al. 2012). The core questions discussed were about the employment situation in Ukraine, the meaning of a good job, people's appraisal of the availability and access to jobs, the role of jobs in social cohesion, coping strategies used by individuals and households when they are hit by negative shocks, and employment-related social relations between different social groups and generations. Internal and international migration was discussed as one of the possible coping strategies. The fieldwork was carried out in four different regions of

Ukraine. In total, 157 informants participated in these discussions. Table 2 summarizes the key characteristics of these focus groups.

Although not representative and subjective in nature, this exercise provides an insight into the most binding constraints to internal mobility in Ukraine and the people's perceptions on the role of internal labor mobility for Ukraine's economic growth and development.

According to the experts' survey, there are indeed barriers to move. Fifteen out of nineteen experts indicated that given the regional differences in labor market outcomes in Ukraine, more people would like to move than actually did so for labor reasons. In other words, people are constrained in their decisions on internal mobility. The focus group discussions confirm this finding, with most participants indicating that they realized they could improve their job prospects by moving, but they often faced significant obstacles to migration.

In terms of what these barriers are, the experts list the population registry, lack of access to credit and the costs of migration, and the underdeveloped housing and mortgage market as the top three barriers (Figure 5). This finding is again confirmed by the

Table 2 Description of focus groups

Group code	Short group description	Location	Date
I.1	Highly-skilled internal migrants	Kiev	30.04.2012
I.2	Low-skilled internal migrants	Kiev	30.04.2012
II.01	Workers from a mono-industrial town	Ukrainsk, Donetsk oblast	02.04.2012
II.02	Unemployed women aged 45-50	Donetsk	31.03.2012
II.03		Lviv	31.03.2012
II.04	Unemployed men aged 45-50	Donetsk	31.03.2012
II.05		Lviv	30.03.2012
II.06		Simferopol, Crimean AR	07.04.2012
II.07	University graduates entering the labor market (one year after graduation), field of studies: engineering	Donetsk	01.04.2012
II.08	University graduates entering the labor market (one year after graduation), field of studies: information technologies	Lviv	31.03.2012
II.09	University graduates entering the labor market (one year after graduation), field of studies: sociology	Kiev	27.03.2012
II.10	Highly skilled freelancers and self-employed/private entrepreneurs (IT specialists, lawyers, journalists, accountants, consultants, etc.)	Kiev	26.03.2012
II.11	Informally employed women (street market) from the city	Donetsk	01.04.2012
II.12	Informally employed women from the city	Lviv	30.03.2012
II.13	Informally employed men (including casual workers in elementary jobs, e.g. in construction) who are labor migrants from the other parts of Ukraine to Kiev	Kiev	26.03.2012
II.14	Seasonal workers in agriculture	Village Uyutnoe, Saky rayon, Crimean AR	08.04.2012
II.15	Seasonal workers in hotels, restaurants, transport, and other activities related to summer resorts	Evpatoria, Crimean AR	08.04.2012
II.16	Inactive people renting out their apartments during the hot season	Evpatoria, Crimean AR	08.04.2012
II.17	Youth aged 20-24 that are not in employment, education, or training (NEET)	Village Vidnyky, Lviv oblast	31.03.2012

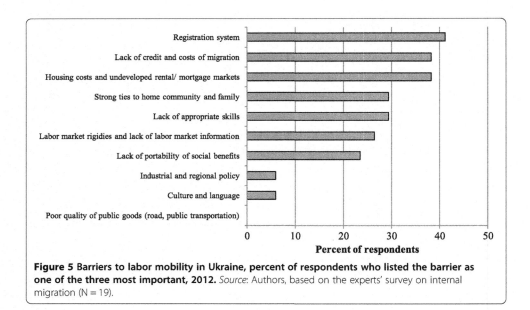

Figure 5 Barriers to labor mobility in Ukraine, percent of respondents who listed the barrier as one of the three most important, 2012. *Source*: Authors, based on the experts' survey on internal migration (N = 19).

focus group discussions. Other potential barriers that featured prominently in both studies are skills, labor market institutions, and the design of social benefits. Interestingly, strong ties to families, friends and home communities, which were not directly mentioned among the suggested alternatives in the survey of experts, are also seen as critical factors hindering internal labor mobility in Ukraine. This is likely to reflect both affective ties to family and communities that bind people to their hometowns, but also the importance of informal social networks to find employment and housing and gather social support. It can be also the case that in view of relatively small differentials of income (adjusted by cost-of-living), workers simply do not have strong economic incentives to move far from their relatives and neighborhoods.

Surprisingly, industrial and regional policies, existing cultural and language differences between regions, poor quality of public goods and infrastructure (including roads and public transportation), ability (or inability) of migrants to integrate at new location, international migration as a substitute to internal migration are considered to be far less important obstacles to migration of workers within Ukraine. We will now discuss the main barriers in turn.

4.1 Population registry

A particular administrative obstacle to workers' mobility – in the form of a requirement that people register their place of residence – was cited most often by labor market experts and workers in our studies as critical in limiting internal mobility in Ukraine. This system of residential registration is an inheritance, albeit reformed, of the Soviet Union's old "*propiska*" system, which regulated the movement of people within the country.

According to the Law on Freedom of Movement and Free Choice of the Place of Residence in Ukraine (effective since January 2004), all residents have to register their place of residence with the State Migration Service within ten days of arrival at the new place of residence. The new place of residence is defined as the administrative-territorial unit where a person lives for at least 6 months during a year. To be registered, a person has to submit a written statement, internal passport, proof of a stamp duty payment, and two copies of the filled deregistration coupon from the previous place of residence. According to this law, it is prohibited to require any other documents for registration.

However, according to the Civil Code of Ukraine, the place of residence is defined as a place where a person permanently or predominantly lives as an owner, under the terms of the rental contract or under other statutory terms. Therefore, to be registered at a particular address (which is recorded then in the registration card and stamped in the internal passport), a person must provide grounds for registration. These grounds for registration are a property certificate, a rental contract, an authorization to occupy a publicly-owned apartment/house ("*order*") or the like. If there are no such documents, the official written consent from the property owner(s), if it is a private property, and from the household head and all the adult members of his/her family registered in this apartment/house, if it is a public or corporate property, is required.

If someone rents an apartment, he/she needs to provide an official rental contract. As became clear in the focus group discussions and in the consultations for this paper, both property owners and renters lack incentives to register rental contracts. For property owners, registering a contract would mean paying additional taxes on rental income and higher utilities costs which are linked to the number of people officially residing at an address. For renters, on the other hand, it would mean paying higher rents because of the aforementioned taxes and utilities. Since tax morale is generally low in Ukraine for a variety of reasons, the vast majority of people prefer informal rental agreements. The consequence is that these agreements protect neither the property owner nor the renter formally. Ultimately, it considerably increases uncertainty on both sides about the true price and the default risks of the rental agreement, and this uncertainty increases the costs of migration, especially to places further away from one's home.

Since the rental market is predominantly informal and the purchase of housing in attractive areas is usually too expensive, migrants most often do not have grounds to officially register at the new location. Individuals actually living at a particular address but who are unable to register may be prevented from access to public services. Although legally, residency is not a requirement for basic public services such as education and health care, many people still think this is the case, maybe due to the discretionary enforcement of the law or simple misinformation. However, this is a serious barrier for private entrepreneurs, voters, applicants to social assistance and housing subsidy, citizens willing to get some official document such as a driver license, tax identification code certificate, and so on because all procedures are tied to the official place of residence according to registration and the respective local office (tax administration, voting district, social assistance department, traffic police etc.).

Results from the focus group discussions echo these concerns regarding the registration system as an obstacle to migration. Difficulties and costs associated with the registration system ranked among the most significant problems encountered by low-skilled migrants. From the focus group discussions, it is also clear that migrants are not completely sure of when residency registration is a requirement:

"Usually, if you have children of pre-school or school age, registration is needed for placing children in a kindergarten or in a school. But in Kiev, this is not a problem. In Kiev, it is better with this issue than in other cities." (FG I.2)

"Nowadays everything should be paid by patients in hospitals, that is why registration is not being asked." (FG I.2)

It should be noted that the registration system per se does not seem to constitute an overwhelming constraint to internal mobility because those who have decided to move have found ways around it. Some of the most popular strategies are: living with relatives or friends and getting their permission for registration; "owning" a miniature share of an apartment, often in non-existent places (with help of intermediaries for additional charge); and not registering at all, with bribing the decision makers if needed. These options, that help mitigate the deterrent effects of the registration system on internal migration, are available to many people. But they are costly and are, therefore, inefficient.

4.2 Access to housing and credit

For internal migrants, two elements are critical: having access to affordable housing and to affordable credit to cover migration costs. Housing-related constraints and limited access to credit are among the most critical barriers to internal mobility in Ukraine according to local experts (Figure 5). Reflecting this fact, focus group participants said that housing was the main obstacle keeping them from moving to places with better opportunities, especially to Kiev:

"For example, when I was working in my hometown, it meant that I lived at home, worked quietly, went to work, and had a small salary. When I arrived to Kiev, I needed to rent an apartment. This rent was very high...Almost all of my first salary went to rent." (FG I.1).

The Synovate survey (Synovate 2010), already mentioned in Section 3, underlines the problem. It found that while Ukrainians were less willing than Serbs or Bulgarians to relocate for a better job, this would change if they were provided with housing. In that case, more than half of the surveyed Ukrainians said they would change their mind and agree to move. In fact, Ukrainians explicitly cited imperfections in the housing market as the key constraint on their mobility. This is a powerful illustration of the housing market's importance in determining labor mobility in Ukraine.

There are several reasons why the housing market significantly affects Ukrainians' decisions to move (Komarov 2012). First, there is a very high home ownership rate. According to the Household Budget Survey in 2010, 95 percent of households owned the home they lived in, and only 2.4 percent of households reported that they rented their dwellings. This partly reflects a legacy from the first decade of transition when publicly owned houses and apartments were transferred to their occupants at little or no cost through privatization. Home ownership can discourage mobility because the perceived cost of staying in one's home, weighted against the anticipated transaction costs of relocating, is low. As income-migration elasticity is likely to be lower for homeowners than for renters, the former are less responsive to a higher salary of a new job. Personal attachments may also make it more difficult to give up an old house or apartment.

Second, there are significant housing price differentials across regions in Ukraine, with housing in leading regions being significantly more expensive than in lagging regions. These differentials make it difficult for people to sell their houses/apartments in lagging regions to finance the acquisition of similar ones at destination. Furthermore, wage or income differentials are not as large to compensate for significant differences in housing prices. To compare these regional differences, Komarov (2012) calculated the housing affordability index in all major cities as a ratio of the average price of an apartment of 54.8 square meters (which is an average usable area per dwelling in Ukraine) to the average annual disposable income per household and the average annual salary. He found that the most unaffordable housing both in terms of the disposable income and salary was in Lviv (11 and 22.5, respectively), Kiev (8.8 and 21.2) and Odesa (11.1 and 19.7) (Figure 6).

There are also significant regional differences in rental costs. Renting an apartment remains hardly affordable for households with a median level of income in most large cities of Ukraine. According to Komarov (2012), the most expensive rent of a benchmark one-bedroom apartment relative to an average household income in the end of 2010 was in Odesa (50.2 percent), Sevastopol (44.1 percent), Simferopol (43.4 percent), Donetsk (42.9 percent) and Dnipropetrovsk (37.4 percent). The relatively more affordable apartments to rent were in Zaporizhia (20.1 percent), Uzhhorod (22.5 percent) and Luhansk (22.8 percent). Due to liquidity constraints, many people cannot leave the poorest regions simply because they are unable to finance the cost of new housing in attractive destinations.

Third, housing in Ukraine is very expensive overall, representing on average more than 15 times annual income (Figure 7). This is the highest ratio in the ECA region after Lithuania and Belarus and seven times higher than in the United States.

Housing-related issues have been found to increase the cost of internal mobility and reduce the incentive to move in other countries as well. Home ownership has often been associated with decreased labor mobility (Bloze 2009; Fidrmuc and Huber 2003; Green and Hendershott 2001). In addition, the availability and cost of housing in other regions helps determine internal mobility (Fidrmuc and Huber 2003; Ghatak et al. 2007).

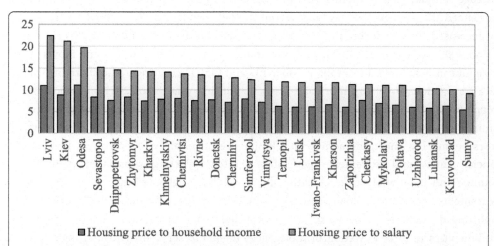

Figure 6 Affordability of housing across Ukrainian major cities, end of 2010. *Note*: Housing cost is calculated as the average housing cost per square meter multiplied by 54.8 square meters, which is an estimated average usable area per dwelling in Ukraine. *Source*: Authors, based on Komarov (2012, Table 4.1). Original data are from the State Statistics Service of Ukraine (on disposable income and salaries) and the joint database of the Association of Realtors of Ukraine (on housing costs).

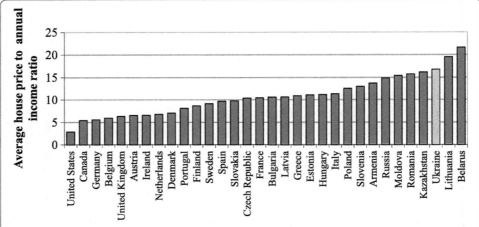

Figure 7 House price to annual income ratio in Ukraine and selected countries, 2010. *Note*: House price to income ratio is the ratio of median house prices to median annual disposable net wage, expressed as years of income. Median house price and median wages are taken on the basis of a sample of cities inside the country. For example, Ukraine is assessed on the basis of 16 cities, including all major oblast centers. For Russia, Poland and the USA, the number of surveyed cities is 24, 22, and around 240 cities, respectively. *Source*: Komarov (2012, Figure 3.1).

A fundamental constraint for affordable housing in leading regions is the lack of access to credit and underdeveloped mortgage markets. Financial markets, together with the services they provide, such as mortgages and other loans, are crucial for labor mobility (Hoj 2011; Coulson and Fisher 2009; Haurin and Gill 2002; van Leuvensteijn and Koning 2004). Well-functioning credit markets can help both in financing the move itself and also in financing housing arrangements at destination. They can be particularly useful in countries like Ukraine, where there are significant price differentials in housing across regions. Improvements in the credit and mortgage markets that result in lower interest rates are likely to have a feedback effect on housing prices.

Yet, Ukraine has a small mortgage market, with basic legislation passed only in 2003. Mortgage lending gained momentum in Ukraine in 2005 while most CEE countries experienced the start of the mortgage boom in the early 2000s. Residential mortgage debt increased sharply during the pre-crisis years and reached its peak of 11 percent of GDP in 2009 (Komarov 2012). This is comparable to the rates in Bulgaria and Slovenia but significantly below those in many other EU and OECD countries. The share of real estate transactions involving mortgage loans in the first quarter of 2011 was about 7 percent of the total number of transactions. This is about 3 percentage points more than in 2010 but over 10 times less than that of the "pre-crisis" year of 2007. The main factors behind low mortgage activity in Ukraine are uncertainty of borrowers in their financial stance and extremely high interest rates reflecting substantial political, economic and inflationary risks. Additionally, banks have tightened up their mortgage requirements regarding the loan value and debt servicing payment-to-income ratio and supporting documents, in response to the weak legislation protecting creditors' rights and difficulties in forced eviction of mortgagees unable to serve their loans if kids (up to 18 years old) or other vulnerable groups of people are registered there, particularly after the anti-crisis measures taken by the Ukrainian authorities in 2008–2009.

It is also important to note that before the economic and financial crisis that hit Ukraine in the end of 2008, most households preferred USD-denominated mortgage loans (less often in Euro or Swiss franc) due to much lower interest rates compared to UAH-denominated loans, even though they received their income in UAH[5]. After almost 40 percent devaluation of the UAH in the second half of 2008, these households faced serious problems with loan payments, and they continue facing similar problems thereafter[6]. As a result, the quality of a mortgage portfolio has deteriorated substantially, with non-preforming loans of over 20 percent in total mortgage lending (Komarov 2012).

Further development of mortgage lending in Ukraine is suppressed by the poorly functioning financial market, which suffers from the lack of long-term funding due to the shallow domestic capital market, absence of institutional investors (e.g. pension funds), and high macroeconomic volatility. Before the global financial crisis, main sources of mortgage funding were short-term deposits and external borrowing (either in the form of Eurobonds or credit lines provided by parent banks to their subsidiaries in Ukraine). But reliance on such sources made the Ukrainian banking system heavily exposed to interest and foreign exchange risks.

Underdeveloped mortgage and credit market leads to high out-of-pocket payments from households' savings or borrowings from relatives, friends or informal intermediaries to cover reallocation costs from one place to another. This is likely to be a tall order for internal migrants, especially youth and the poor.

4.3 Lack of skills

Ukraine has a considerable skills mismatch, with an oversupply in certain occupations (laborers, sales and services, skilled agriculture) and concurrent undersupply in others (certain groups of professionals, particularly health workers; craftsmen and machine operators). Skilled labor shortages have become the second most commonly reported constraint to growth in the enterprise surveys across all countries in the Eastern Europe and Central Asia region (World Bank 2011a). On average, 30 percent of firms considered education and skills to be a major or severe constraint in 2008. Also, it takes firms considerably longer in Ukraine to hire workers with the required skills than in other countries in the region. This is especially true for skilled and non-production workers (World Bank 2009b).

Increasing internal labor mobility can help improve the matching process in the labor markets, but the lack of appropriate and easily transferable skills seems to be a serious obstacle to moving, as suggested by experts' survey (Figure 5). This concern was also echoed in the focus group discussions. As one participant puts it:

> "At home I do get a low salary. But, it is impossible to find a job elsewhere in line with my field of expertise." (FG I.2).

These findings are supported by results from the labor force survey: the composition of jobs even by 1-digit occupation group in the regions with higher wages is significantly different from those in lagging regions (Figure 8). For example, in Ternopil oblast – the region with the lowest average wage in Ukraine – the share of unskilled jobs (elementary occupations) is over 45 percent, whereas the share of the first two groups (Legislators, senior officials and managers and Professionals) is 18.5 percent. In Kiev City, which is the leading region in many respects and the main destination for migrants, the similar shares are 4.7 and 50.6 percent, respectively. Therefore, workers from the lagging regions willing

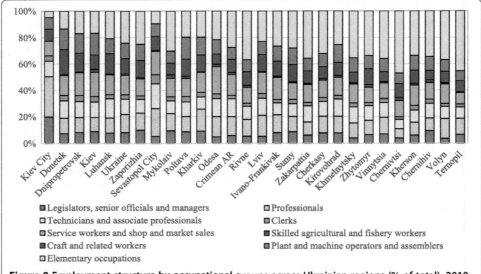

Figure 8 Employment structure by occupational groups across Ukrainian regions (% of total), 2010.
Note: Regions are shown in descending order according to the average monthly wage in 2010.

to get the most productive jobs in leading regions are very likely to lack the skills demanded at these jobs that certainly discourage them from reallocation.

Inadequate basic computer and search skills of workers also deter labor mobility as they limit access of job seekers to information about vacancies in other settlements/ regions available on the Internet (e.g. all-Ukrainian job portal maintained by the Public Employment Service of Ukraine) and contribute to informational asymmetries. The information barrier is particularly important in Ukraine due to the weakness of formal channels for the exchange of labor market information and abundance of informal jobs, information about which is not easily available.

The issues of demand and supply of skills (technical, cognitive and non-cognitive), skills mismatch and overeducation, and their role in employability, earnings and labor mobility have been understudied in Ukraine for data reasons. Hopefully, the ongoing studies based on the recent STEP survey conducted by the World Bank, the latest wave of the Ukrainian Longitudinal Monitoring Survey and the labor force survey will help fill this gap in the literature.

4.4 Labor market institutions

The importance of strong labor market institutions for internal labor mobility is motivated by two facts: first, the lack of dynamism in the Ukrainian labor market, as documented by much lower job creation and reallocation rates than in peer countries (World Bank 2009b); and second, the evidence that informal practices act as a partial, but at times, inefficient substitute for formal institutions in the labor market.

For workers to move, a fluid labor market is essential. High job turnover rates, in terms of recreation of existing jobs and the creation of new ones, increase the chances of employment and the quality of matching between employers and workers. If labor markets are static, people have fewer opportunities to change jobs and, therefore, fewer incentives to look for and move to better jobs, especially when far from home.

Labor market regulations, such as employment protection legislation (EPL), that regulate the hiring and firing process of workers, are a critical determinant of the dynamism of labor markets. Overall, the available evidence in the literature on the impact of labor market institutions and policies on labor market outcomes remains inconclusive and often contradictory. In a comprehensive study of this impact in the transition economies of Eastern Europe and Central Asia, Lehmann and Muravyev (2012) found a robust negative effect of stricter EPL on the employment-to-population ratio and a significant positive impact on youth unemployment. The tax wedge is also found to have a strong depressing impact on the employment-to-population ratio, but not on any of the unemployment types, a result that was interpreted by the authors as "a scenario where high labor costs push workers into informal employment". In Ukraine, where the overall EPL, and protection of regular workers in particular, is very stringent compared to the other successor states of the Soviet Union (Muravyev, 2014), it is an important force deterring dynamism in the labor market and therefore labor mobility.

Ideally, EPL should provide a balance between the much needed flexibility to increase the dynamism of the labor market while offering sufficient protection to workers to have a proper safety net that facilitates labor market transitions. In Ukraine, this balance is not provided, enforcement of the old Labor Code adopted in 1971 is very weak, and employers tend to abuse their power, as confirmed by focus groups discussions for the Ukraine case study on jobs (Kupets et al. 2012). If provisions of EPL that regulate the terms of labor contracts, including the length of contract, payment of wages, working conditions, notice periods for layoffs, and severance pay, are enforced, they ensure a necessary level of security and certainty that increases the expected payoff from labor market decisions, including labor migration[7]. If workers do not have this security because of informal employment or abuse of power by their employers, they are deterred from moving to take up such insecure jobs. The uncertainty of payment of wages and fake probation periods are the most widespread problems mentioned during focus group discussions that adversely affect migration decisions:

"Basically, 90 percent of the construction sector here is in the shadow. And those 10 percent, which are not... Everyone here knows how many guys they employ, these people work 2–3 months and quit, new guys work 2–3 months and quit, and so on. Just because they are not getting paid for their work" (FG II.6)

"Many friends who got a job, mainly found through the Internet, say that they have a probation period. A month, two, three months... After all, employers do not pay because they tell them that they are not satisfied with people's work and say to them "good-bye". Next people come for 2–3 months, next, and so on." (FG II.10)

Besides, strict EPL and inefficient labor market institutions support the existing nationwide wage and labor market rigidities, which limit cost-of-living adjustments in regional wages and, therefore, decrease the net benefits of migration to the leading regions where, as has been shown above, housing and also living costs are much higher. Finally, other by-products of inefficient formal labor market institutions, namely gender, age and ethnic discrimination, work-related violence and exploitation of migrant workers, particularly widespread among the low-skilled, also hamper the ability of people to find decent employment in the other regions and therefore trap them in their low-productive jobs or unemployment in lagging regions.

4.5 Social benefits

Just as with labor regulations, social benefits can either discourage or encourage the open movement of labor. Well-designed unemployment insurance and social assistance benefits can help people overcome financial constraints and secure work in leading regions. On the other hand, poorly designed social benefits may prevent people from entering the labor market and may drive them to remain in lagging areas.

Overall, the social assistance sector has substantial coverage in Ukraine – with over 42 percent of the population receiving directly or indirectly at least one type of social assistance – and has poor targeting performance. Although the overall spending on social assistance went up before the crisis in 2008, there was a contraction of the income-tested program for low-income families in favor of categorically targeted programs such as child-related allowances, privileges to different categories of population, and allowances for people with disabilities. As a result, the overall targeting accuracy of the social assistance sector in Ukraine had deteriorated by 2008, and Ukraine became one of the poorest performers in the Eastern European and Former Soviet Union countries in terms of overall targeting accuracy and cost-effectiveness in alleviating poverty (World Bank 2010).

The receipt of social transfers may alter the labor and migration behavior of household members in two ways. On the one hand, they may reduce their work efforts and stop searching for (better) economic opportunities in other regions because transfers reduce the pressure to work and the rewards from working, particularly if benefits are reduced when household income increases (Grosh et al. 2008). On the other hand, beneficiaries may use the transfer to finance reallocation, cover job search costs, invest in training or small business, etc. But the empirical evidence suggests that participation in social assistance programs has only small or moderate effects on employment in developed countries, and even smaller effects in developing countries, where due to low generosity, most social assistance programs complement rather than substitute for the earnings of able-bodied beneficiaries (Grosh et al. 2008).

This is especially true for the programs with moderate generosity when the benefits represent less than a quarter of household income, as in Ukraine (World Bank 2010). The childbirth grant is probably the only prominent exception in terms of generosity, which seems remarkably high when compared to spending on other beneficiaries. In rare cases, it might indeed prevent people from moving, especially when taking into account the higher purchasing power in lagging and rural areas, but it is not likely to be the main reason against migration.

Another important barrier to internal labor mobility could arise from eligibility criteria for social benefits. If the eligibility is tied to the place of residence, and the benefit is not portable across regions, it could prevent people from moving. Technically, this is not always the case in Ukraine. For example, people can apply for and receive unemployment insurance regardless of where they live; the same is true for access to education and health care services. However, the application to social assistance and various benefits requires personal office visits at the place of official residence. To the extent that people are often not officially registered at the place where they actually live, this might require more or less frequent trips to the place of origin and could act as a – albeit probably small – disincentive to move. These concerns were confirmed by informants of focus groups discussions and our survey of experts (Figure 5).

4.6 Social networks and informal arrangements

As discussion has shown above, people in Ukraine face significant barriers when deciding to move. The institutions that are supposed to help people connect to economic opportunities in other regions – housing markets, government institutions like the population registry, labor market institutions, education and social welfare systems – are underperforming. As a result, Ukrainians often have to rely on alternative solutions, which are mostly unregulated and do not provide formal protection, entail high levels of uncertainty, and use social networks in lieu of formal institutions.

Social networks can be an efficient way of overcoming some of the barriers to internal mobility, but not always. The housing market is a good example. When searching for housing, using social networks can be a very efficient means. But social networks are typically tighter in the close proximity of one's home and therefore an important complement to other channels. But further away, they will be less tight and hence less efficient, and relying only on social networks alone can limit one's options. A fluid and transparent formal housing market is also needed.

The labor market is another, even more telling example. As with housing, social networks can be an efficient complement to formal search channels for jobs. But relying on social networks alone as a substitute for formal search channels limits people's options with regard to job search and could prevent them from connecting to better economic opportunities. The large extent of informal employment in Ukraine further limits people's horizons. Individuals circumvent the formal institutions of the labor market and either work informally or underreport their wages. As a consequence, the payment of wages is associated with high levels of uncertainty, as the focus group discussions show. When looking for a (new) job, Ukrainians use their social networks to get reassurance about the reliability of their prospective employer with regard to promised wage payments and working conditions. If there is no such reassurance, the risks and hence the costs of migration are higher.

Social protection and access to credit are the last examples. In the absence of effective formal social protection mechanisms that support risk management, people will have to rely on informal social risk management mechanisms. Or, in the absence to formal access to credit, they will have to rely on families and friends for loans, including for financing migration. Strong ties to local communities are essential to have access to these informal risk management mechanisms and access to credit. Again, these can be valuable complements to formal institutions, but if they act as a substitute to formal institutions, they can either hold people back, or, maybe even more importantly, influence migrants' destination decisions since people will prefer to go where they can build on an existing network. This might not necessarily be where the economic opportunities are.

5 Policy implications: removing the barriers to internal mobility

Increasing internal mobility in Ukraine is crucial given the challenges it faces in the future: a rapidly declining and aging population. Ukraine's population is declining faster than in in almost any other country in the world, due to high mortality, low birth rates and outmigration. Ukraine's population is projected to fall below 35 million by 2060 (from current 45 million), and over a quarter of the population are expected to be aged 65 years and older by then. If gender-age-specific labor force participation rates remain constant at 2010 levels, Ukraine is expected to lose over 8 million economically active people aged 15 to 64 years between 2010 and 2060, or over 39 percent of its 2010 level (Kupets 2014c). Hence, demographic shifts will have a strong impact on Ukraine's labor market and medium- and long-term economic growth prospects. Greater workforce mobility and better utilization of available human resources across the country are likely to help mitigate their impact.

In order to make Ukrainians more mobile and create the conditions necessary to complete the transition to a market economy, it is important for the government to make lasting changes in policy and create effective institutions that support labor mobility rather than standing in the way. Each change will have a ripple effect on the others, and together they will simplify the current system, reduce uncertainty, and provide protection for workers.

5.1 Reform the registry system

In the previous section, we listed the population registry as one of the major barriers to moving in Ukraine. Although many people have found ways around the inefficiencies created by the registration system, reforming it could change people's perceptions about the barriers to moving and reduce inefficiencies in other markets, such as housing/ rental, which may also limit internal mobility.

Organization for Security and Co-operation in Europe (2009) provides useful guidelines on population registration, setting out the main principles for the establishment and maintenance of functional models of population registration in democratic societies, describing criteria for developing efficient population-registration systems that correspond to the actual needs of the member states and their citizens, and highlighting good practices in the region. Ukrainian authorities and practitioners should follow these guidelines in reforming the national system of population registration. It is important to ensure that after reforming the system, citizens can actually exercise the fundamental human rights guaranteed by the Constitution of Ukraine and international legal instruments, such as those regarding the freedom of movement and free choice of the place of residence; access to social public services like education, health care, and social assistance; the right to vote; privacy and property rights, etc.

But reforming the registration system is not only about changing the legal framework or computerization of the system, it is also about strict implementation of the rules and procedures by all the relevant institutions and removing the incentives for individuals to provide false information about the place of residence or circumvent the system at all. On top of this, there should be public trust and confidence in government and political institutions, which has been very low in Ukraine (Kupets et al. 2012) and which triggered the civil unrest and political turmoil in 2013 – 2014 (Besedina 2014). Building trust of Ukrainians in their government and political institutions by improving governance, fighting corruption, reducing income inequality and strengthening the civil society is, therefore, the first step to increase the willingness of citizens to register their actual place of residence and declare their economic activities/income to the state.

True reform of the registration system also requires coordinated actions from the tax system and the housing/rental markets. Improving the incentives for registering rental contracts would create the necessary institutional backdrop for making renting more transparent and more attractive.

5.2 Ensure a better functioning housing market

Ensuring a better functioning housing market – including its complementary markets such as real estate, rental and credit markets – is fundamental in addressing existing barriers to internal labor mobility in Ukraine. Komarov (2012) suggests a detailed list of policy options directed at improving the overall functioning of these markets in Ukraine. The key area is the development of the rental market, with the necessary re-orientation of the state housing policy goals from promising free homeownership to everyone to providing households with more and better opportunities of rented housing. Komarov (2012) offers the following two supplementary alternatives for developing the public rental sector in Ukraine:

(i) social housing, to be rented out by local authorities to low-income households, disabled, homeless people and other socially vulnerable citizens, at fairly low rates that are largely subsidized by local authorities, and

(ii) affordable housing, i.e. housing offered for rent to the households which are not poor enough to claim social housing but which are not rich enough to buy an apartment/house or get a mortgage loan. Dwellings for affordable housing can be provided from a municipal stock but mainly at the expense of private resources mobilized in the framework of a public-private partnership, funds provided by non-profit organizations and private investors. Amann (2005) suggests to follow good practices of Scandinavian countries, the Netherlands and Austria by establishing an intermediary organization between the market and the state like Housing Finance Agency (so-called Third Sector in housing), which acts in accordance with the market economy principles but helps fulfill policy targets of the state.

The Austrian model of social housing and its financing, with the Limited Profit Housing Associations acting as the Third Sector in housing, has proved to be one of the best models to follow by Central and South Eastern European countries (Amann and Mundt 2005; Amann 2010). A definite advantage of the Austrian social housing model is that it does not restrict policy measures to low-income households, and, as a result, there is a high level of equality in housing cost, quality of settlements and available space and almost no segregation (Amann and Mundt 2005). In addition, competition between the large social housing sector and the private segment of the rental market influences the general price level and fosters overall efficiency in the housing market.

Imposing a real estate tax in Ukraine as a stimulus for housing supply in the higher-demand areas is another promising reform. Without a real estate tax, housing is historically treated as a relatively inexpensive consumption commodity by many insiders (e.g. poor elderly citizens). The imposition of a real estate tax would change the perception of housing from a consumption good to a capital good and expand the rental market for rooms, apartments and houses. This could be particularly beneficial as a source of affordable housing for potential migrants. The real estate tax is also worth considering because in addition to being a source of revenue, it is beneficial for decentralization of public finances – a policy goal that is being pursued by the Ukrainian government with the donor community, and is on the top of the current reform agenda.

The imposition of the real estate tax on 1 January 2013 was envisaged by Article 265 of the New Tax Code of Ukraine, but in mid-2013 it was postponed until 1 January 2014. According to the recent amendments to the Tax Code effective since 1 April 2014, the tax base is the total area of a residential real estate property. For individuals, the tax base may be reduced by 120 square meters for apartments and by 250 square meters for a house. The tax is heavily criticized by experts because of low tax rates[8] and because its base is linked to an apartment size (in square meters) rather than to a market value of the property, which is at odds with standard practice in the world. Furthermore, as usual in Ukrainian legislation, there are many tax exemptions[9]. Hence, it is not a full-fledged property tax that would deliver substantial revenues to local governments and contribute to the efficient reallocation of people between dwellings, municipalities and regions, as in developed countries. This calls for further improvement of the real estate tax in Ukraine, following good practices in the world.

Finally, concerted actions are also needed in the land and financial markets. Currently, distorted land markets (with land and urban zoning restrictions as a speculative asset for shadow economy receipts) and shallow financial markets (with lacking or unaffordable credit for developers and private investors) limit the construction of new and affordable housing. Development of a sustainable mortgage and credit market requires reduction of macroeconomic risks and inflation; creating more options for long-term funding, for example through increased participation of institutional investors in the framework of pension and stock market reforms; improving the legislation regarding the problems of non-performing loans and protection of creditors' rights; etc. The state could also give an impetus to mortgage market development through a restoration of mortgage bonds issued for refinancing of commercial banks through the State Mortgage Institution or a mortgage broker company based on state-owned or commercial banks (Komarov 2012). Overall, policies should support deeper mortgage lending while managing risks better.

5.3 Invest in skills development and education

In order to facilitate labor mobility, people need to be equipped with skills that are transferable across sectors and occupations. For this, people need to have the ability to acquire new knowledge, and for that they need a good foundation of cognitive and non-cognitive skills. For the younger generation, this base of strong cognitive skills can be provided by the education and training system. For the stock of current workers who are already out of the formal education system, the policy challenge is to find effective ways to provide these foundations and encourage re-training in new, modern occupations.

Many of the challenges inherent in improving skills in the workforce and reducing the skills mismatch can be addressed through effective policy interventions in post-secondary education. As discussed extensively in a World Bank report on skills in Eastern European and Central Asian countries (World Bank 2011a), such interventions should focus on overcoming failures in information that lead many people to make sub-optimal skills investments (for example, when few people acquire the skills needed to become engineers, physicists, family therapists, skilled craftsmen that are in high demand and prefer instead "fashionable" fields such as finance, economic sciences, law, political science, etc.) and on quality assurance.

Ukraine also needs to improve the efficiency of its elementary and secondary education systems. It has struggled to reorganize its school networks in the face of shrinking student cohorts, resulting in a misallocation of scarce resources, for example, in maintenance of nearly empty schools rather than in restoring the attractiveness of the teaching profession (Coupe et al. 2011). Reallocating resources would enable the system to provide a good grounding in the skills most needed in a knowledge-based economy. It is also necessary to ensure that pre-school and basic education curricula and pedagogic practice pay adequate attention to the critical development of cognitive and non-cognitive skills. This is important when it comes to setting learning standards and targets, training teachers, and when assessing learning in both cognitive and behavioral dimensions. The experience with related reforms and interventions in Europe and the rest of the world can offer useful lessons.

To meet the challenge of retraining workers, the education and training system needs to become more responsive to labor market needs. This will require more direct involvement of the private sector in the design and provision of education and training and a more active role in providing young workers and older trainees with on-the-job learning and training opportunities. At the same time, workers need to have better access to appropriate labor market data, like prevailing wages, career advancement opportunities, and vacancy rates in order to make informed decisions about their educational investment. Labor market observatories and public and private labor market intermediaries should play an important role in providing this information, especially for potential internal migrants. Life-long learning also becomes increasingly important, given the demographic trends.

In short, it is the formation of the right skills rather than diplomas, efficiency rather than the amount of spending on education, quality rather than quantitative education indicators that should be the focus of reforms of the education and training systems in Ukraine. To that end, though, more evidence is needed on the learning and employment outcomes of students, graduates and adult workers in order to inform policy design and monitoring.

5.4 Rebalance labor market and social welfare institutions

As follows from discussion in Section 4.5, institutional reforms of the labor regulations are extremely important for creating a dynamic labor market in Ukraine. The current labor code that dates from before the transition needs to be replaced by the new one – an issue that has been on the top of the legislative agenda since 2001 but without positive outcome so far. In addition, there are many reforms in the field of labor inspection services, labor taxation, and governance that are also needed in order to reduce informality and improve the overall labor market functioning (World Bank 2011b). The challenge is to rebalance labor regulations to provide the much needed flexibility to increase the dynamism of the labor market while offering sufficient protection to workers to have a proper safety net that facilitates labor market transitions.

As with labor laws, the key for social benefits is to balance the amount of the benefit aimed at support of low-income households with the disincentives it might create to participate in the labor force and seek economic opportunities in leading regions. It is also important to ensure that the eligibility criteria for social benefits and services do not bind people to their current place of residence, and the benefits are easily portable across the country. In other words, existing social benefits and services should be spatially blind in their design and universal in their coverage – i.e. made available to every eligible person or household regardless of its location (World Bank 2009a). In Ukraine, there is also room to reconsider the design of some not well targeted social assistance programs to improve the equity of the social welfare system and save costs that can be channeled into other important programs or areas (World Bank 2010).

6 Conclusion

Ukraine's economy lacks dynamism, with job creation and reallocation rates significantly below those of its peers. This is both the cause and the effect of people not moving. The rate at which Ukrainians move from one region to another within the country is only half of what we would expect it to be when comparing to other countries. Yet even this small stream of mobile workers in Ukraine does not flow to leading regions. Migrants are not leaving lagging areas with poor labor market outcomes, and they are not necessarily going to regions with better job conditions. This suggests that certain barriers prevent people from seeking economic opportunity but also that significant gains could be realized from greater internal labor mobility.

The main barriers to internal mobility in Ukraine are institutional: (i) administrative procedures that require people to be officially registered at their place of residence, although many people prefer not to register a new residence for various reasons; (ii) underdeveloped housing and credit markets, which make it difficult for people to rent or buy housing in leading regions; (iii) inadequate human capital, as people in lagging regions often lack the necessary skills to access better economic opportunities in high-productivity, modern sectors in the leading regions; (iv) weak formal labor market institutions that reduce dynamism in the labor market, stimulate informal work arrangements and do not provide workers with enough reliable information about job openings and labor market conditions; and (v) social benefits and services that are often tied to the place of residence and that could, in some cases, discourage labor force participation and work efforts in the first place.

Addressing these institutional bottlenecks that affect internal mobility will allow people, especially the poor, to access more and better jobs in leading regions. We suggest five key areas for improvement aimed at helping workers to freely pursue job opportunities throughout Ukraine. First, the population registry system needs to be streamlined and modernized. Second, reforms are necessary to improve the functioning of housing and credit markets. Third, reforms in the education and training system aimed at equipping people with relevant and easily transferable skills are needed. Fourth, labor market institutions need to be improved in a way that will spur dynamism in the labor market while still protecting workers and will also provide reliable information about job openings and labor market conditions. Fifth, there is a need for modernization of the social welfare system to make social benefits easily portable across the country and more targeted at the most needy people.

7 Endnotes

[1]Although population registers count migrations (events) rather than migrants (transitions), we use these terms interchangeably assuming that the share of multiple and return migration within a given year is negligible.

[2]Region here refers to the first-level administrative unit which is one of 24 oblasts, Autonomous Republic of Crimea or one of two cities with a special status (Kiev and Sevastopol). Taking into account the average size of Ukrainian regions (about 1,675,000 people in 2013), the administrative division of Ukraine into 27 units is consistent with the NUTS system and corresponds to its second level (NUTS-2). This allows us to compare migration indicators in Ukraine to those in the EU member states.

[3]Regions are shown in descending order in terms of the net internal migrate rate in 2013.

[4]We compared internal migration rates in Ukraine (measured by administrative data at oblast and rayon level) with internal migration rates from other countries. For other countries, the internal migration rates are mainly measured through population registries or, at times, through surveys or the census. The comparison is done controlling for the average size and number of geographical units used to calculate internal migration rates. This is important because the number of migrants recorded fundamentally depends on the number and size of the units into which the territory is divided, and the differences in statistical geography can bias cross-country comparisons. Applying a log-linear trend line across the whole sample yields the expected internal migration rate for a given size of the unit of measurement.

[5]According to the National Bank of Ukraine, mortgage loans denominated in foreign currency made up 88 percent of total mortgage loans in 2010 (Komarov 2012).

[6]For example, from January 2005 to October 2008 the official UAH/USD exchange rate was between 4.84 – 5.3 UAH per 1 USD. In the aftermath of the economic crisis at the end of 2008, the local currency depreciated to about 8 UAH per 1 USD and remained pegged to this rate until the end of 2013. Political and economic turmoil in Ukraine in 2014, together with transition of the National Bank of Ukraine to a floating exchange rate regime in order to meet the IMF requests, turned the Ukrainian hryvnia into one of the worst performers versus the US dollar in the world, with depreciation over 13 UAH per 1 USD in October 2014.

[7]Interestingly, perceived job security in both temporary and permanent private jobs is found to be lower in countries with stricter employment protection legislation. This is probably because strict EPL seems to increase the associated cost of job loss by reducing the re-employment probability and extending duration of unemployment (Clark and Postel-Vinay 2009). At the same time, perceived job security in public jobs, which are usually "insulated from labor market shocks", is uncorrelated with the stringency of EPL.

[8]The fixed rate per square meter is set as a percentage of the minimum salary established by the law as of 1 January of the respective tax year. For residential apartments, the total area of which does not exceed 240 square meters, and residential houses, the total area of which does not exceed 500 square meters, the real estate tax rate for the property not being a land plot must not exceed 1 percent of the minimum wage. In case of an excess of the size of the above area, the tax rate shall be 2.7 percent. The first version of this regulation, effective before April 1, 2014, used only residential (living) area of the residential real estate object instead of its total area.

[9]For example, pursuant to Article 265.2.2 of the Tax Code, the tax is not paid for: residential properties owned by state or territorial communities (their joint ownership); residential properties located in exclusion areas and unconditional (mandatory) resettlement as set forth by law; structures of a family-type orphanage; garden or dacha buildings (but their number should not exceed one such property per taxpayer); residential properties owned by families having many children and foster families having three or more children (but their number should not exceed one such property per family); and dormitories.

Abbreviations
AR: Autonomous Republic; EPL: Employment protection legislation; EU: European Union; GDP: Gross Domestic Product; IOM: International Organization for Migration; NUTS: Nomenclature of Territorial Units for Statistics; OECD: Organization for Economic Cooperation and Development; OSCE: Organization for Security and Co-operation in Europe; UAH: Ukrainian hryvnia (local currency); USA: United States of America; USD: US dollar; UNDP: United Nations Development Programme.

Competing interests
The IZA Journal of Labor and Development is committed to the IZA Guiding Principles of Research Integrity. The authors declare that they have observed these principles.

Acknowledgements
This paper is based on a report conducted as part of the World Bank's analytical and advisory services to Ukraine (World Bank 2012a). The findings, interpretations, and conclusions expressed herein are those of the authors and do not necessarily reflect the views of the Board of Executive Directors of the World Bank or the governments they represent. The authors are grateful to the Bank staff for valuable comments on the earlier drafts of the report, peer reviewers of the final draft, and administrative and logistical support. Vladislav Komarov contributed greatly through his background paper on the key features and weaknesses of the housing market in Ukraine.
The authors are also grateful to the anonymous referee for constructive feedback and suggestions to improve the paper. The authors also thank the participants of a World Bank dissemination workshop in Kiev in December 2012 and the KNOMAD Conference on Internal Migration and Urbanization in Dhaka in April-May 2014 for useful comments and suggestions.
Responsible editor: Hartmut Lehmann

Author details
[1]World Bank, 1818 H Street NW, Washington, DC 20433, USA. [2]Department of Economics, National University of Kyiv-Mohyla Academy, 10 Voloska Street, 04070 Kyiv, Ukraine. [3]World Bank Country Office in Moldova, 20/1 Pushkin Street, MD-2012 Chisinau, Republic of Moldova.

References
Amann W (2005) How to boost rental housing construction in CEE/SEE countries. Hous Finance Int J 12:24–31
Amann W (2010) New policies to facilitate affordable housing in Central and Eastern Europe. Acta Polytechnica 50(1):53–56
Amann W, Mundt A (2005) The Austrian System of Social Housing Finance. Available via IUT. http://www.iut.nu/FindOutMore/Europe/Austria/Socialhousing_finance_Amman_Mundt.pdf. Accessed 17 September 2014
Besedina E Trust and economic reforms. Forum for Research on Eastern Europe and Emerging Economies (FREE) Policy Brief Series. Available via FREE. http://freepolicybriefs.org/2014/05/19/trust-and-economic-reforms. Accessed 17 September 2014
Bloze G (2009) Interregional migration and housing structure in an East European transition country: A view of Lithuania 2001–2008. Baltic J Econ 9(2):47–66
Brück T, Danzer A, Muravyev A, Weißhaar N (2010) Determinants of poverty during transition: household survey evidence from Ukraine. J Comp Econ 38(2):123–145
Clark A, Postel-Vinay F (2009) Job security and job protection. Oxford Econ Papers-New Series 61(2):207–239
Coulson N, Fisher L (2009) Housing tenure and labor market impacts: The search goes on. J Urban Econ 65(3):252–264
Coupe T, Olefir A, Alonso J (2011) Is Optimization an Opportunity? An Assessment of the Impact of Class Size and School Size on the Performance of Ukrainian Secondary Schools. World Bank Policy Research Working Paper No. 5879, World Bank, Washington, DC
Fidrmuc J, Huber P (2003) The Puzzle of Rising Regional Disparities and Falling Migration Rates During Transition. Paper Presented at the 18th Annual European Economic Association Congress and the 58th European Econometric Society, Stockholm. 20–24 August 2003. http://www.eea-esem.com/papers/eea-esem/2003/2010/FidrmucHuberESEM2003.pdf
Ghatak S, Mulhern A, Watson J (2007) Interregional Migration in Transition Countries: The Case of Poland. Economics Discussion Paper 2007/7, School of Economics, University of Kingston, London
Green R, Hendershott PH (2001) Home Ownership and the Duration of Unemployment: A Test of the Oswald Hypothesis. NBER Working Paper 2001/8/2, Cambridge, MA
Grosh M, del Ninno C, Tesliuo E, Ouerghi A (2008) For Protection and Promotion: The Design and Implementation of Safety Nets. World Bank, Washington, DC

Haurin D, Gill L (2002) The impact of transaction costs and the expected length of stay on homeownership. J Urban Econ 51:563–584

Hoj J (2011) Improving the Flexibility of the Dutch Housing Market to Enhance Labour Mobility. OECD Working Paper No. 833, OECD, Paris

International Organization for Migration (2005) Migration, Development and Poverty Reduction in Asia. IOM, Geneva

International Organization for Migration (2008) Chapter 7. Internal migration. In: World migration report (2008) Managing Labour Mobility in the Evolving Global Economy. IOM, Geneva, pp 173–199

Komarov V (2012) Housing Market and Labor Mobility. Available via World Bank. http://documents.worldbank.org/curated/en/2011/09/17013326/housing-market-labor-mobility. Accessed 1 September 2012

Kupets O (2012) Statystychnyj analiz maiatnykovoi trudovoi mihratsii v Ukraini [Statistical analysis of commuting in Ukraine]. In: Formation of the Market Economy, Special Edition "Labour in the 21st Century: New Trends, Social Dimension and Innovative Development", vol 1. Kyiv National Economic University, Kyiv, pp 649–660. in Ukrainian

Kupets O (2014a) Do Ukrainians vote with their feet: Local public expenditures and inter-regional migration. Naukovi zapysky NaUKMA, Ekonomichni nauky [NaUKMA. Sci Proc Econ Sci 159:35–41

Kupets O (2014b) Interregional migration in Ukraine: Spatial, economic and social factors. Demography Soc Econ 2:22. in press

Kupets O (2014c) Labor market challenges of an aging and shrinking population in Ukraine. J Comp Econ Stud 9:99–134

Kupets O, Vakhitov V, Babenko S (2012) Demographic Change. Jobs case study, Ukraine. Available via World Bank. http://siteresources.worldbank.org/EXTNWDR2013/Resources/8258024-1320950747192/8260293-1320956712276/8261091-1348683883703/WDR2013_bp_Jobs_And_Demographic_Change.pdf. Accessed 1 December 2012

Lall SV, Selod H, Shalizi Z (2006) Rural–Urban Migration in Developing Countries: A Survey of Theoretical Predictions and Empirical Findings. World Bank Policy Research Working Paper No. 3915, World Bank, Washington, DC

Lehmann H, Muravyev A (2012) Labor markets institutions and labor market performance: What can we learn from transition countries? Econ Transit 20(2):235–269

Martynenko T (2004) Regional Migration and the Evolution of Regional Unemployment Patterns in Ukraine. EERC (KSE), Kiev, Ukraine

Moretti E (2012) The new Geography of Jobs. Houghton Mifflin Harcourt, New York

Muravyev A (2014) The evolution of the regulation of labour in the USSR, the CIS and the Baltic states, 1985–2009. Eur Asia Stud 66(8):1270–1294

Myrdal G (1963) Economic Theory and Underdeveloped Regions. Methuen & Co, Ltd, London

Organization for Security and Co-operation in Europe (2009) Guidelines on Population Registration. OSCE Office for Democratic Institutions and Human Rights, Warsaw

Paci P, Tiongson E, Walewski M, Liwirnski J, Stoilkova M (2007) Internal Labor Mobility in Central Europe and the Baltic Region. World Bank Working Paper No. 105, World Bank, Washington, DC

Sharpe A, Arsenault A, Ershov D (2007) The Impact of Interprovincial Migration on Aggregate Output and Labour Productivity in Canada, 1987–2006. Research Report 2007–02, Centre for the Study of Living Standards, Ottawa

Synovate (2010) Survey of Labour Mobility in Russia, Ukraine, Bulgaria and Serbia. Synovate, London

Vakulenko E (2014) Does migration lead to regional convergence on Russia? Working paper 53/EC/2014. Basic Research Program, National Research University Higher School of Economics (HSE), Moscow

van Leuvensteijn M, Koning P (2004) The effect of home ownership on labor mobility in the Netherlands. J Urban Econ 55(3):580–596

United Nations Development Programme (2008) Human Development Report. Human Development and Ukraine's European Choice. UNDP Ukraine, Kiev, Ukraine

World Bank (2005) Ukraine Poverty Assessment: Poverty and Inequality in a Growing Economy. Report no. 34631-UA. World Bank, Washington, DC

World Bank (2009a) World Development Report 2009: Reshaping Economic Geography. World Bank, Washington, DC

World Bank (2009b) Ukraine Labor Demand Study. World Bank, Washington, DC

World Bank (2010) Improving Targeting Accuracy of Social Assistance Programs in Ukraine. Technical Note for the Government of Ukraine. World Bank, Washington, DC. Available via World Bank. http://siteresources.worldbank.org/UKRAINEINUKRAINIANEXTN/Resources/UkraineHMTNote.pdf. Accessed on September 17, 2014

World Bank (2011a) Skills, not Just Diplomas. Managing Education for Results in Eastern Europe and Central Asia. World Bank, Washington, DC

World Bank (2011b) Policies to Reduce Informal Employment: An International Survey. Technical Note for the Government of Ukraine. World Bank, Washington, DC. Available via World Bank. http://siteresources.worldbank.org/UKRAINEINUKRAINIANEXTN/Resources/455680-1310372404373/PoliciestoReduceInformalEmploymentEng.pdf. Accessed on September 17, 2014

World Bank (2012a) In Search of Opportunities: How a More Mobile Workforce Can Propel Ukraine's Prosperity (Vol. 1 and 2). World Bank, Washington, DC

World Bank (2012b) World Development Report 2013: Jobs. World Bank, Washington, DC

10

The effects of migration on poverty and inequality in rural Kosovo

Judith Möllers[*] and Wiebke Meyer

* Correspondence: moellers@iamo.de
Leibniz Institute for Agricultural
Development in Transition
Economies (IAMO),
Theodor-Lieser-Str. 2, 06120 Halle,
Saale, Germany

Abstract

The economic wellbeing of a large number of rural Kosovar families depends heavily on migrants' remittances. This paper aims at analysing the impact of migration on rural poverty and inequality in Kosovo. It draws on the 2009 nationally representative Kosovo Remittance Study. Analyses are based on a comparison with counterfactual migrant household incomes derived from Propensity Score Matching. We find that remittances have no impact on the extremely poor, but lift around 40% of migrant households above the vulnerability threshold. Gini coefficients show a tendency to increase due to migration. Determinants of different outcomes of migration are explored in a logit regression on migration success. Household and income structure as well as education play a role in how migrant households climb up the income ladder.
JEL: F22, F24, O15, P36

Keywords: Migration; Remittances; Poverty; Inequality; Kosovo; Propensity score matching

1 Introduction

Migrant remittances are known to be an important and stable source of income, not only in the developing world, but also in many transition economies. Indeed, European transition countries such as Albania, Moldova, and Bosnia and Herzegovina are among the top recipients of remittances as a portion of gross domestic product (GDP) (Mansoor and Quillin 2006).

In Kosovo, around one fifth of households are involved in labour migration, with this proportion slightly higher in rural areas (United Nations Development Programme 2010). Migration is well-known to be a coping strategy and a source of income that compensates for the low employment rates in the country (Corbanese and Rosas 2007). The very high unemployment rate of around 40%, plus the estimated number of 200,000 young people who will enter the labour market within the coming five years, increases the pressure to migrate. Indeed, 50% of the younger generation say they would emigrate if they could (Haxhikadrija 2009). Currently, between 315,000 and 500,000 Kosovars live abroad, of whom about 50% reside in Germany. It is estimated that every third household in Kosovo has family members living abroad (Mustafa et al. 2007; European Stability Initiative 2006).

There is hardly any official and reliable data available on the remitted sums resulting from this migration, because considerable amounts of the money are transferred informally (World Bank 2010). The United Nations Development Programme (2010) estimates the absolute amount of remittances in 2009 as € 443 million. The share of remittances is estimated to represent around 13% of GDP.

Despite its economic importance for the country, relatively little is known about migration and remittances in Kosovo, which have been widely underrepresented in the migration and development literature (Vathi and Black 2007). Although a number of studies have been published recently, most of the analyses are descriptive. The recent report of Gashi and Haxhikadrija (2012) nicely summarises results of available data and migration literature on Kosovo. Havolli (2011) and Meyer et al. (2012) provide more detailed analyses of the drivers of remitting. When the impact of remittances on households in Kosovo is analysed, this is done based on a simple comparison of recipients and non-recipients: for instance, in Haxhikadrija (2009); Möllers et al. (2013); and Elezaj et al. (2012).

In this contribution we highlight the impact of remittances on the welfare and income distribution of the rural population[1]. The paper adds to the debate on the linkages between remittances and poverty and inequality (see, for instance, Taylor 1992; Adams 2011; Lokshin et al. 2010). Unlike earlier studies on Kosovo, we base our analysis on counterfactual incomes derived from Propensity Score Matching (PSM). Our main aim is to quantify the income-related outcomes of migration on (migrant sending) rural households. In addition to changes in poverty and inequality indicators, we also explore factors that determine household based success of migration (measured as an upward shift in income quintiles among migrant households).

The paper is structured as follows: after a brief survey of the literature in Section 2, we introduce our methodology and data in Section 3. Section 4 provides a descriptive comparison of migrant and non-migrant households. The main analytical results are presented in Section 5. We start from a comparison of income groups. Based on headcount indices and using counterfactual incomes, we then determine the share of migrant households that would fall into poverty without remittances. We show if and how the rural income distribution is affected by mixed income structures – and especially by remittances. To analyse the marginal effect of remittances on inter-household income distribution we calculate decomposed Gini coefficients and Gini elasticities. Finally, an econometric analysis of the success factors linked to whether a rural migrant household will climb up the income ladder is presented. The procedure applied for this is a logit regression. Section 6 concludes.

2 A brief survey of the literature

This section briefly introduces migration and poverty related facts about Kosovo and presents some key results and arguments of the discussion on the effect of migration on poverty and inequality.

Kosovo's economic situation is, and for a long time has been, challenging. The country was historically one of the poorest in the region, and it is still struggling with high levels of poverty and low growth rates which, despite progress in recent years, are still too low to significantly affect poverty reduction and extreme unemployment (United States Agency for International Development 2008). The per capita income was estimated at only € 1,760 in in 2009 (Gashi and Haxhikadrija 2012). This is also reflected in the high shares of 34% and 12% of the population falling below the absolute and extreme poverty lines respectively in 2009 (World Bank and SOK 2011); the Gini index is, however, relatively modest at 0.30 (World Bank 2007a). The role that migration and remittances might play in Kosovar households is reflected in the fact that nearly one in ten households in Kosovo indicate that remittances are their main income source

(Statistical Office of Kosovo 2010). The share of the population which receives remittances (around 20%) is substantially higher than the fraction receiving social assistance (about 13%); the average amount of remittances is three times higher than the average values from social protection programmes in recipient households. There is also evidence that rural areas in particular, where poverty is usually more pressing than in urban areas, enjoy higher average amounts of remittances (United Nations Development Programme 2010; World Bank 2007a).

The World Bank (2007b) highlights migration as one of three (complementary) pathways out of rural poverty (the other two being farm intensification and specialisation, and entering local non-farm labour). Indeed, the potential of migration and remittances to significantly reduce acute poverty is widely discussed in the literature (Adams and Page 2005; Lokshin et al. 2010). A large, and growing, number of multidisciplinary micro-studies show that (temporary) migration helps to smooth seasonal income fluctuations, to provide extra cash to meet contingencies, or to increase disposable income (e.g. Mosse et al. 2002; Adams et al. 2008; Lokshin et al. 2010; Verme 2011; for an overview of empirical studies in developing countries see Adams 2011).

While there is not much doubt that remittances increase the incomes of recipient households, their use is also important when discussing impacts on development. There is much evidence that remittances are used primarily to increase consumption, in particular of food and clothing, and less frequently for investment purposes (Davis et al. 2010; Mansoor and Quillin 2006)[2]. Haxhikadrija (2009) reports that in Kosovo the receipt of remittances is often followed by the purchase of leisure goods such as satellite dishes, mobile phones or cameras. Next to daily expenses, rural households primarily use remittances to improve their basic equipment, whereas investment in education seems rather rare; in rural areas the differences in the possession of goods, such as televisions, refrigerators, washing machines and cars, between migrant and non-migrant households are clearly visible. As such expenses frequently flow into imported goods, trickle down effects and thus longer term impacts on development and poverty reduction may be hampered. For farm households in neighbouring Albania, Miluka et al. (2010) suggest that migration is used by rural households as a way out of agriculture. For Kosovo there are, however, no indications that significant amounts of remittances are used for this purpose, yet, those few households that do report business investments often make use of remittances (Möllers et al. 2013; Gashi and Haxhikadrija 2012).

Another much debated issue is about who actually migrates and who receives remittances. The causal link between migration and the wealth status of the labour-sending household has direct implications for poverty and inequality effects. If people are in a position to migrate (and increase their income) because they are better off in the first place, then poverty effects will be lower. Most studies find that richer households receive more remittances (Mansoor and Quillin 2006). However, a clear causal link cannot be made, because the drivers and impacts of migration are complex. Remittance flows depend on different underlying motives for getting involved in migration and for remitting. In the home country household not only the financial flows but also the decision to send migrants induces adjustments in the labour endowment and thus in income (and probably also consumption) strategies (e.g. Meyer et al. 2012; Davis et al. 2010).

Similarly, inequality effects depend on the share of households receiving transfers, the average amounts received (or how much migrants remit), and the distribution of remittances among the population (which households are sending migrants and receiving remittances) (Giannetti et al. 2009). If the economic position of the remittee household is improved through remittances then overall inequality in the communities might rise as a consequence (de Haan and Rogaly 2002). Whether or not migration increases income inequality of the sending households due to the receipt of remittances has not yet been fully clarified. Some researchers expect an increased inequality, for instance if information and education are decisive for the (self-)selection of migrants (Milanovic 1987). Indeed, Adams (2011), who reviews a large number of empirical studies, finds that at the country level international remittances tend to increase income inequality. Others argue that remittances contribute to a more equal income distribution, especially if trickle down effects are at work. Taylor and Wyatt (1996), for instance, find that the indirect effects of remittances affect the household farm income distribution positively. Giannetti et al. (2009) present small but equalising distributional effects for a number of Eastern European countries. Barham and Boucher (1998) argue that inequality outcomes are sensitive to the choice of method. Differences can, for example, be attributed to value judgements regarding the weight attached to certain income groups when constructing inequality measures (Stark et al. 1988).

In summary, the literature does not provide clear directions for the effects of migration on home country households. We base our analysis of Kosovo on the widely accepted hypothesis that migration has positive direct effects on both migrants' rural incomes and rural incomes in general. Thus, we expect remittances to reduce poverty, even if a counterfactual income is used for comparison. We further expect remittances to increase inequality, as migrants tend to be concentrated in better educated and wealthier households.

3 Methodology and data

This paper draws on the recent and representative dataset of the Kosovo Remittance Study (KRS) (United Nations Development Programme 2010). The KRS acknowledges the major importance that remittances play in the economy of Kosovo. Its particular strength is its large sample of 4,000 households which allows for a truly quantitative view on the issue. Our study looks at a subsample of 1,727 rural households from this database[3]. The sample size is reduced due to missing data after casewise deletion for some variables in the econometric analyses.

The analysis focuses on the effect of remittances on poverty and inter-household income inequality. According to Adams (2011), there are at least four methodological problems that confront any economic work on international migration: simultaneity, reverse causality, selection bias and omitted variable bias. Yet, appropriate solutions, although available in theory, are difficult to implement in practice. For instance, experimental designs are almost impossible to obtain, and panel data are rarely available. Sample selection procedures and the use of instrumental variables are the most commonly used solutions. Instrumental variables may, in theory, remove many of the biases that arise from endogeneity, selection bias and omitted variables, but the difficulty comes in specifying good instruments. A fully convincing set of suitable instruments in a migration regime is not available yet; there are many different arguments put forward to support the choice of particular instruments but better conceived instruments are generally lacking (Miluka et al. 2010; Davis et al. 2010).

Furthermore, analytical results on remittances and income depend on whether remittances are treated as a substitute for local earnings or as an exogenous transfer. Thus, this touches on the question of whether or not the opportunity costs of migration are taken into account. This issue can be addressed by constructing a counterfactual situation reflecting what the status of a migrant household would have been had that household not involved itself in migration (McKenzie and Sasin 2007). In our analysis, we apply the method of PSM to estimate counterfactual incomes from which the poverty and inequality effects are assessed. PSM estimators have been developed to correct for non-random (self-)selection and to pair treated observations (with migrants) with similar controls (without migrants). The outcome of the control observation can be interpreted as the counterfactual income of the treated observations (in the absence of treatment) (Jimenez-Soto and Brown 2012).

The applied PSM methodology consists of the following steps. First, a logit or probit model of migrant and non-migrant households is estimated. The parameters of this model, that should be unaffected by treatment and fulfil the unconfoundedness condition, are used in the second step to predict the propensity score, which expresses the predicted probability of a household engaging in migration[4]. Third, migrant and non-migrant households are matched; the observed income of the matched non-migrant household is imputed as the counterfactual income of the migrant household.

In our analysis, we use a set of socio-economic variables to estimate a logit model on the treatment variable (migrant households) (Additional file 1: Tables S1 and S2). For the PSM procedure we use the psmatch2 and teffects psmatch Stata modules; for the choice of variables we relied on recommendations given by Caliendo and Kopeinig 2008). The method by which the matched pairs were formed was the three nearest neighbour procedure allowing replacement. The robustness of the results was tested along different specifications including caliper, radius and kernel matching. Tests for balance and common support were undertaken. Successful matching was checked along the bias reduction and t-test (Additional file 1: Table S3), and Pseudo R2 (Additional file 1: Table S4) (Caliendo and Kopeinig 2008). Furthermore, overlap must be given to ensure the common support assumption. Additional file 1: Figure S1 presents visual analysis results of propensity score distributions. Since the bootstrap standard errors for PSM estimators are not in general found to be valid, we rely on standard errors obtained from Stata teffects psmatch for the calculation of treatment effects; the underlying methodology is based on the work of Abadie and Imbens (2012). Rosenbaum bounds are calculated to test the sensitivity of estimated treatment effects with respect to unobservables (Additional file 1: Table S5).

The derived counterfactual incomes are used in the analysis of poverty and inequality effects as well as in a logit model in which we aim to explore further the success factors of migration.

Poverty is measured not only along income groups (tertiles and quintiles), but also by three standard poverty measures: (1) the *headcount index*; (2) the *poverty deficit index*; and (3) the *poverty severity index* (Foster et al. 1984). The three poverty measures by Foster et al. (1984) are described by

$$P(\alpha) = \frac{1}{n} \sum_{i=1}^{m} \left[\max\left(\frac{z-c_i}{z}, 0\right) \right]^{\alpha},$$ (1)

where z is the poverty line, c_i is the income of the individual i, n is the total number of individuals and m is the number of poor individuals. The parameter α changes depending on the poverty measure. If α is set equal to 0, we obtain P(0), that is, the *headcount index* indicating the proportion of the poor below the poverty line. P(1) displays the *poverty deficit*, a measure that takes into account how far the poor, on average, fall below the poverty line. Finally, if α is set equal to 2, we obtain P(2), called the *poverty severity* measure, which captures the difference in the severity of poverty by giving more weight to the poorest. Thus, *poverty severity* accounts for income differences (World Bank 2000; Coudouel et al. 2000).

The choice of poverty lines is a critical issue, especially if policy conclusions are drawn. Ravallion (1998) discusses alternative approaches to setting and implementing poverty lines. In general, absolute poverty lines, which have a fixed real value over time and space, are preferable to relative poverty lines that rise with the average income and expenditure levels. Poverty lines may be set according to food intake or cost-of-basic-needs. In addition, subjective perceptions are sometimes used to set poverty lines. In our approach we show results for several poverty lines. As a measure of absolute and extreme poverty we use a line that was suggested by the World Bank and SOK (2011) for Kosovo. It is calculated based on a cost-of-basic-needs approach. This poverty line lies somewhat below the commonly used 2-$ per day- line suggested for Eastern European countries (Alam et al. 2005). Another absolute poverty line that has been used for this region is set at US$4.30 per day. This is supposed to reflect a vulnerability threshold in order to identify households which are not suffering absolute material deprivation, but are vulnerable to poverty. Although it seems somewhat arbitrary, it does bear some relationship to empirically observed vulnerability to poverty (Alam et al. 2005). Finally we also present a relative poverty line which is used in, for example, Eurostat statistics. However, we stress that absolute poverty lines are certainly more relevant in the context of our study.

Poverty analyses often refer to adjusted household sizes which are used to calculate per capita incomes that consider economies of scale. Economies of scale arise in many ways in a family, for example by sharing certain expenditures such as housing or a car. There are different methods for estimating equivalence scales. Here we use figures that reflect the so-called modified OECD equivalence scale which is also used by Eurostat. It assigns the coefficient 1 to the household head, 0.5 to other adults in the household, and 0.3 to children under the age of 16.

The effect of certain income sources on income distribution can be determined by Gini coefficients[5] in two ways (Reardon et al. 2000). The most common method is the comparison of a Gini coefficient for all incomes with another Gini coefficient that is calculated excluding the income source of interest (in our case, remittance income). If the latter is smaller than the Gini based on total income, this income source has a negative effect on the income distribution, and vice versa. In addition, decomposition according to different income sources allows conclusions to be drawn regarding the relative distribution effect of certain sources. The contribution of each income source is the product of a concentration coefficient for that income source and the fraction of that income source in total income (Shorrocks 1982; World Bank 2000). Formally G_k^*, the concentration coefficient for income component k, is given by

$$G_k^* = \frac{2}{\mu n^2} \sum_{i=1}^{n} \left(r_i - \frac{n+1}{2} \right) y_{k,i},$$ (2)

where $y_{k,i}$ is the component k of the income of household i. The mean total income is denoted by μ, and r_i is the household's i rank in the ranking of all incomes. The Gini coefficient is a weighted sum of the concentration coefficients G^*

$$G = \sum_{k=1}^{K} \frac{\mu_k}{\mu} G_k^* = \sum_{k=1}^{K} S_k G_k^*, \tag{3}$$

where $S_k = \mu_k/\mu$ is the share of component k in total income. The percentage contribution of income source k to total income equality is found to be

$$P_K = S_k \frac{G_k^*}{G} \times 100\%. \tag{4}$$

The marginal contribution of each income source k to inequality can be described by an elasticity of the Gini coefficient, which is given by Lerman and Yitzhaki (1994) as

$$\in_{G,S_k} = \frac{S_k \left(G_k^* - G \right)}{G}. \tag{5}$$

4 Descriptive statistics: a comparison of migrant and non-migrant households

The objective of this section is to briefly introduce the rural Kosovar household to the reader. Bearing in mind our research question, we present important differences in the demographic- and income-related variables of migrant and non-migrant households in the sample that also inform the main results in Section 5.

Rural households in Kosovo are typically big. The 1,727 rural households of the KRS have, on average, five family members (with considerable variation in the household size)[6]. The average age of the household head is 50 years. Around 28% of the households are categorised as migrant households, meaning that they have at least one family member living abroad; on average the number of migrants is 2.5. About 60% of these migrant households receive remittances. In the overall sample around 17% receive remittances. Table 1 presents socio-economic variables of migrant and non-migrant rural households; the non-parametric Kruskal-Wallis test, indicating whether the mean, frequency or median are equally based on calculated ranks, is used to test for significant differences.

Migration depends on the availability of work force in a household. Therefore it is no surprise that migrant households tend to be bigger, however their dependency ratio is also slightly higher than non-migrant households (0.60 versus 0.49)[7]. Education is sometimes mentioned as a key door opener for migration activities. But although the educational attainment of the rural household heads is generally high (almost eleven years of schooling), it does not differ significantly between migrant and non-migrant households. The same is true for the highest level of education within the household[8].

The average annual household income (excluding remittances) lies at around € 4,800 per annum (Table 1). When remittances are not considered in the household income, differences between migrant and non-migrant households are not significant; if remittances are included, migrant households have significantly higher household and per capita incomes. Per capita incomes that include remittances, calculated based on equivalised household sizes (see Section 3), are 70% higher for migrant households than for non-migrant households (€ 2,633 versus € 1,840).

Table 1 Socio-economic characteristics of rural households with and without migrants

| | All households | Migrant household=1 | | Test statistics |
		1	0	χ^2 / p
Number of rural HH	1727.00	479.00	1248.00	–
HH size	4.97	5.03	4.95	0.677 / 0.411
Dependency ratio	0.52	0.60	0.49	10.067 / 0.002
Age of HH head	49.85	52.47	48.85	23.354 / 0.000
Years of education of HH head	10.95	10.68	11.06	2.132 / 0.144
Number of migrants	0.71	2.54	0.00	1673.087 / 0.000
Highest level of education in HH				
- Primary School (up to 4 years) or lower	2.21	2.30	2.17	0.025 / 0.875
- Secondary General School (~8 years)	8.25	9.81	7.64	2.149 / 0.143
- Vocational or Grammar School (~12 years)	50.35	47.60	51.41	2.005 / 0.157
- University degree	39.20	40.29	38.78	0.333 / 0.564
Household income (€)	4,819	5,177	4,682	0.420 / 0.517
Household income incl. remittances (€)	5,249	6,728	4,682	65.323 / 0.000
PC income, equivalised (€)	1,889	2,017	1,840	2.265 / 0.133
PC income incl. remittances, equivalised (€)	2,060	2,633	1,840	82.672 / 0.000
Income shares (%)				
- Waged employment	66.62	58.83	74.52	106.554 / 0.000
- Self-employment	10.66	6.47	11.22	4.440 / 0.035
- Remittances	5.14	13.15	0.00	811.168 / 0.000
- Other income	17.58	18.16	12.50	15.536 / 0.000

Source: Own calculation based on KRS 2010 data.
Note: N=1,727 rural households; HH=household, PC = per capita.
Test statistics refer to a Kruskal-Wallis-Test.

The major share of rural incomes, around two thirds, stems from waged employment. Indeed, 70% of all rural households have waged employment as their primary income source. The income share is lower for migrant households (59%). Remittances make up on average 13% of their income. Overall, the share of remittances in all households lies at around 5%;[9] remittances make up the largest income share in less than 4% of the rural households[10]. Self-employment is the primary income source of around 11% of all rural households. It plays a slightly bigger role in the income portfolio of non-migrant households (11% income share versus 6% in migrant households). Thus, it does not seem that remittances are a key to open up business opportunities (see also Section 2). Despite the extraordinary agro-ecological potential for agricultural activities, rural households rely to a relatively low degree on farm incomes (unfortunately not included in the KRS database). National statistics show that only around 6% of Kosovar households indicate that farm incomes are their major income source, and the contribution to overall individual incomes is only 1% (Statistical Office of Kosovo 2010). Even for farm households this share at 13% is surprisingly low, most likely due to the small average farm size of less than three hectares and low levels of market orientation (Möllers et al. 2013).

The category 'other income' in Table 1 is mainly derived from pensions or social payments. At the national level, social welfare benefits account for 2% of individual incomes, pensions from Kosovo for 6% and pensions from abroad for 4% of the incomes (Statistical Office of Kosovo 2010). In our KRS data these contribute a surprisingly large share (18%) to total rural household incomes (Table 1); around 14% indicate that 'other income' is their main source of income. The significant difference between migrant and non-migrant households is probably due to former or current migrants having access to pensions from abroad.

In a nutshell, although migrant households do not seem to be better educated, they enjoy higher incomes. The absolute income difference is significant when remittances are considered. For both migrant and non-migrant households waged employment is the most important income source. Migrant households rely less on self-employment, but more on transfers such as from remittances, pensions or social assistance.

5 Main findings: effects of remittances on poverty and inequality in Rural Kosovo

In this section we provide evidence about the welfare effects of remittances on rural households. In the previous section we showed that remittances contribute significantly to absolute incomes of migrant households. Now we look at the overall poverty situation by presenting results on income groups and poverty indices. This is followed by an inequality analysis. Finally, with the aim of understanding how poverty reduction could be addressed more effectively through migration, we explore factors that determine migration success.

Effects on poverty and inequality depend on the number of recipients, absolute remittances amounts, and on who sends migrants and receives remittances. This last aspect, addressing the question of whether proportionally more migrants come from lower or higher income groups (Milanovic 1987) and how these income groups are characterised, is presented in Table 2; we distinguish three income classes (tertiles), where the first tertile is the income class with the lowest per capita income and the third tertile is the richest group.

Indeed, poorer households have significantly fewer migrants, and less than 10% receive remittances at all (Table 2). In particular, the number of migrant households (with at least one migrant) is significantly higher in wealthier households[11]. Accordingly, the percentage contribution of remittances to the income portfolios rises from the poor to the wealthy tertile. In the wealthiest income class more than one quarter of households receive remittances; for 7% of households in the third tertile remittances are their main income source. The absolute value that remittances add to per capita incomes leads to an income rise of 13% compared to 3–4% in the other tertiles. Whether these households have climbed the ladder towards this tertile or were better off in the first place is an important question. One indication for the amount of upward shifting is shown in a comparison for tertile membership in a counterfactual situation (where the observed income of the matched non-migrant household is imputed as counterfactual income of the migrant household) and the actual situation: 6% moved from tertile 1 in the counterfactual scenario towards tertile 2 in the actual scenario. Almost 20% of wealthy households in tertile 3 come from the counterfactual tertiles 1 and 2.

An indicator for the existence of income inequality within rural Kosovar households is shown in Table 2 in the fact that the richest income group earns more than half of all incomes, while the share of the poorest tertile in all household incomes is only 16%.

Table 2 Socio-economic characteristics according to income classes

	All households	Income class (tertile)			Test statistics
		1	2	3	χ^2 / p
Number of rural HH	1727.00	576.00	575.00	576.00	—
Share of remittances receiving HH in %	16.79	9.38	14.43	26.56	72.427 / 0.000
HH size	4.97	5.60	4.90	4.43	0.049 / 0.976
Dependency ratio	0.52	0.65	0.47	0.43	3.078 / 0.215
Age of HH head	49.85	50.10	50.13	49.32	1.766 / 0.414
Number of migrants	0.71	0.42	0.64	1.06	3.998 / 0.135
Share of HH with at least one migrant	27.74	17.19	25.39	40.63	81.249 / 0.000
Years of education of HH head	10.95	10.15	11.18	11.52	4.574 / 0.102
Highest level of education in HH in %					
- Primary School (up to 4 years) or lower	2.21	4.20	1.39	1.04	6.171 / 0.046
- Secondary General School (~8 years)	8.25	13.46	5.39	5.91	49.644 / 0.000
- Vocational or Grammar School (~12 years)	50.35	51.75	52.87	46.43	4.087 / 0.130
- University degree	39.20	30.59	40.35	46.61	28.244 / 0.000
Household income (€)	4,819	2,506	4,255	7,695	8.427 / 0.015
Household income incl. remittances (€)	5,249	2,577	4,469	8,700	8.570 / 0.014
PC income, equivalised (€)	1,889	852	1,599	3,216	9.020 / 0.011
PC income incl. remittances, equivalised (€)	2,060	877	1,667	3,637	9.449 / 0.009
Income shares (%)					
- Waged employment	66.62	54.07	73.28	72.50	2.038 / 0.361
- Self-employment	10.66	14.44	9.96	7.59	3.667 / 0.160
- Remittances	5.14	2.59	4.05	8.77	6.000 / 0.050
- Other income	17.58	28.89	12.72	11.14	2.352 / 0.308
HH with remittances as main income source (%)	3.65	2.08	1.74	7.12	29.688 / 0.000
Household spending (€ per month)	130.80	83.28	130.10	179.66	
Household food expenditures (%)	40.63	44.56	40.70	38.28	
Share in all household incomes (%)	100.00	16.37	28.35	55.28	
Upward shift compared to tertile based on counterfactual migrant incomes	8.51	–	6.09	19.44	

Source: Own calculation based on KRS 2010 data.
Note: N=1,727 rural households; Tertile 1 = Income class with the lowest per capita income (incl. remittances) etc. HH=household, PC = per capita.
The test statistics refer to a Kruskal-Wallis-Test.

Furthermore, the household income (including remittances) of the middle tertile is around 70% higher than that of the first, while the richest group has more than three times as much as the first, and almost double the income compared to the middle tertile. Differences in per capita incomes are even higher. One reason for the income differences may be seen in the better educational attainment in the higher tertiles: the number of years in education of the household head increases from the poor to the better-off. The wealthiest income class has a particularly high share of university education (this indicator looks at the highest level of education in the household). Poor households are represented with a significantly higher share in primary and secondary education and a lower share in university degrees.

Table 3 presents three common income based poverty measures calculated on the basis of three different poverty lines[12]. We have chosen two absolute poverty lines, and one relative poverty line (see Section 3).

The consumption based poverty line of € 1.55 per day in 2009 prices that is used by the World Bank and SOK (2011) seems, from our point of view, very low. This poverty line reflects the social assistance level that a person gets in Kosovo, € 40 per month (Statistical Office of Kosovo 2010), an amount which is, according to what we saw during our survey work, hard to live off in the country. It is also far below the average expenditure of the poorest tertile of the KRS rural households of around € 83 per person per month (Table 2). Thus it clearly reflects extreme poverty. According to this poverty line, 7% of the rural sample are considered extremely poor. The poverty deficit, defined as the average distance of the poor to the poverty line, is 2%. The measure of poverty severity considers income differences by giving more weight to the poorest. In other words, greater weight is given to households that are further away from the poverty line. It lies at 1% for this extreme poverty line.

Vulnerability to poverty is reflected in the PPP-US$ 4.30 line. Here, the vulnerability incidence lies at 45%. For the PPP-US$ 4.30 line the poverty deficit (16%) and poverty severity (8%) are slightly higher than for the measure of extreme poverty. The chosen relative poverty line of 60% of the median[13] of the equivalised per capita income is below the PPP-US$ 4.30 line. It results in a poverty incidence of 20%; poverty deficit is at 6% and poverty severity at 3%.

The impact of migration and remittances on poverty is depicted in the last two columns of Table 3. Obviously, results depend on the poverty line. Differences between a 'naïve' comparison of a headcount index calculated based on incomes without considering remittances and the counterfactual income approach are relatively small. Still, the expected overestimation of the positive impact of remittances on poverty reduction is visible[14]. Overall, poverty levels would rise between 0% and 3% if households were not supported by their family members living abroad (based on counterfactual incomes). Extreme poverty seems to be unaffected by remittances. This may be explained by the self-selection of migrants from the middle and higher income groups. Poverty reduction based on the PPP-US$ 4.30 line from 0.48 and 0.45 reflects an absolute number of 200 rural migrant households (41% of all migrant households) which are lifted out of poverty due to

Table 3 Poverty in rural Kosovo

	Yearly income (€)	Headcount-index	Poverty deficit	Poverty severity	Headcount index	
					Without remittances	Counterfactual incomes
Absolute poverty line						
€ 1.55 line, 2009 prices*	566	0.07	0.02	0.01	0.09	0.07
PPP-US$ 4.30 line	1,453	0.45	0.16	0.08	0.51	0.48
Relative poverty line						
60% of sample median**	930	0.20	0.06	0.03	0.22	0.21

Source: Own calculation based on KRS 2010 data.
N=8,591 rural household members from both subgroups with and without migrants
*Absolute poverty line used by the World Bank (2011) for Kosovo on the basis of a cost-of-basic needs approach for 2009.
**This poverty line corresponds to 60% of the median equivalised per capita income within the sample.

Table 4 Average treatment effect on migrant households

Variable	Sample	Treated	Controls	Difference	Std. Err.	T-stat
Per capita income (pcincequrem)	Unmatched	2578.85378	1834.50793	744.345851	113.049411	6.58
	ATT	1834.50793	1893.62923	685.224549	160.721832	4.26
Test for significance based on AI robust Std. Err. *** according to Abadie and Imbens (2012)				687.5878	157.1407	4.38

Source: Own calculation based on KRS 2010 data.

remittances. For the relative poverty line we find that 85 (18%) of the migrant households are raised above the threshold due to remittances.

The effect of migration on migrant households is also shown in the average treatment effect on the treated that results from PSM analysis. Migration leads to an average income increase of around € 690 per year in migrant households (Table 4).

Table 5 depicts rural Gini coefficients and addresses the question of whether remittances play a role with regards to income inequality. The income distribution was calculated for total equivalised per capita incomes, for per capita incomes excluding remittances, and for the counterfactual scenario. The national Gini coefficient for the year 2005 was about 0.30 (World Bank 2007a). The Gini coefficient of 0.37 for the sample indicates a slightly higher inequality for our rural population. If remittances are not considered ('naïve' approach), the Gini coefficient goes down slightly to 0.36. Using counterfactual incomes, the Gini is 0.35. The examination of partial coefficients calculated on the basis of decomposed Gini coefficients confirms this tendency towards an un-equalising effect of remittances (positive elasticity in brackets in the lower part of Table 5). This is in line with the fact that remittances are the most unevenly distributed income source and, as we have seen, tend to be concentrated in richer income groups. The elasticity figure indicates that a 1% increase in remittances would lead to a 6.9% increase in the Gini coefficient. Yet, if we assume that migrants tend to be concentrated in the upper segments of the income distribution, the effect is most likely overestimated (see Acosta et al. 2008). Similarly to remittances, waged employment increases income inequality. Incomes from self-employment and 'other income' decrease inequality: their elasticities are negative.

We have seen that migration lifts a large proportion of migrant households out of poverty, but not all migrant households are able to achieve a significant upward shift in

Table 5 Income distribution and remittances

Gini coefficient	
• on the basis of equivalised per capita incomes	0.37
• remittances excluded	0.36
• using counterfactual incomes	0.35
Decomposed Gini coefficients (elasticity in brackets)	
• on the basis of waged incomes	0.38 (0.029)
• on the basis of self-employment	0.19 (−0.044)
• on the basis of remittances	0.67 (0.069)
• on the basis of other incomes	0.22 (−0.054)

Source: Own calculation based on KRS 2010 data.
Note: N=1,727 rural households from both subgroups with and without migrants.

incomes. Based on a logit regression we aim to show how a set of variables is related to the success of rural households' migration activities in Kosovo. An underlying hypothesis is that households which can increase their income enough to move at least one quintile upwards differ significantly in their socioeconomic variables. We measure this upward movement as a positive change between the quintile based on counterfactual migrant household income compared to the actual income quintile. The dummy turns one for this positive quintile shift. For households that start from the highest quintile the dummy turns one if they reach a 20% increase in incomes compared to the counterfactual situation. We use a set of classical socio-economic independent variables as typically used in poverty analyses and regress them on our sample of 479 migrant households (389 after casewise deletion). The model presented in Table 6 has an overall good fit. Descriptive statistics can be found in the Additional file 1: Table S6.

A positive shift in quintiles is reached by 185 successful migrant households (48%). These households are characterised by a higher educational level, i.e. a university

Table 6 Logit regression on successful migration (quintile upward move)

Independent variables	Coefficient	Std. Err.	Sig.	Exp(B)	95% Conf. Interval	
agehhh	0.171	0.067	0.011	1.186	1.039	1.353
agehhh2	−0.002	0.001	0.006	0.998	0.997	0.999
genderhhh	0.607	0.419	0.148	1.834	0.807	4.170
eduyhhh	−0.052	0.053	0.328	0.949	0.856	1.053
unemployed	−0.720	0.329	0.028	0.487	0.255	0.927
Albanian	0.702	0.387	0.069	2.018	0.946	4.308
maxeduhigh	0.796	0.326	0.015	2.216	1.170	4.198
depratio	−0.725	0.257	0.005	0.484	0.293	0.801
sumofactive	−0.437	0.112	0.000	0.646	0.519	0.804
nomigr	−0.020	0.068	0.765	0.980	0.857	1.120
munrem2009_2	0.000	0.000	0.000	1.000	1.000	1.000
rem	0.016	0.006	0.010	1.017	1.004	1.029
cfpcinc	−0.002	0.000	0.000	0.998	0.998	0.999
Prishtina	−0.021	0.712	0.976	0.979	0.243	3.949
Mitrovica	−0.763	0.758	0.314	0.466	0.105	2.062
Peje	−0.763	0.768	0.320	0.466	0.104	2.098
Gjilan	−0.612	0.768	0.426	0.542	0.120	2.443
Prizren	−0.056	0.762	0.942	0.946	0.212	4.209
Ferizaj	−0.067	0.748	0.928	0.935	0.216	4.049
constant	−0.037	1.909	0.985	0.964		

Number of observations = 389 migrant households.

chi2(19) = 175.063.

Prob > chi2 = 0.000.

Nagelkerke R2 = 0.484.

Hosmer Lemeshow chi2 (8) = 4.324.

Prob > chi2 = 0.827.

Source: Own calculation based on KRS 2010 data.
Note: Dependent variable: successful migration (dummy that turns 1 if household moves upwards to a higher quintile compared to the counterfactual situation; for migrant household starting from the highest quintile a 20% increase in incomes turns the dummy to 1).

degree of some kind within the household. Interestingly, the variable depicting years of education of the household head is not significant. An upward movement in quintiles is further related to the age of the household head. The probability for the move increases with age, but decreases again from some point on. It is higher for ethnic Albanian households. A dummy variable indicating whether a household head is unemployed or not is significant too: unsurprisingly, unemployment has a negative influence on migration success. With regard to the household composition we find that an increasing number of dependents lowers the probability for a positive shift. However, the same is true for an increasing number of household members of working age. Thus it seems that smaller households with a small share of dependents are best off in terms of achieving the move to a higher quintile. While the regional dummies give no significant results, a variable that displays the squared average absolute remittances received in a municipality is significant. Thus, very high municipality averages are linked to the successful migration of individual migrant households as well. The share of remittances in the current household income increases the probability of moving up the quintiles. Interestingly, the counterfactual income is significant with a negative impact on migration success. We interpret this as follows: our success indicator, an upward shift between quintiles, is comparatively easier to reach for poorer household. This is due to the lower absolute income rise that is needed for the move between lower quintiles compared to the move between the fourth and fifth quintile in particular.

Summing up our main findings, we show that migration has the expected positive effect on rural incomes. However, the poorest tend to benefit less. For the extremely poor, we find no impact on poverty reduction at all. This is explained by the fact that migrants and remittances are more often found in wealthier and better educated households. According to our counterfactual scenario, migrant households increase their income significantly by almost € 700 per year. However, not all migrant households are labelled successful. Those who are able to climb the income ladder often come from small households with not many dependent members in the lower income groups. They are characterised by higher education. The share of remittances in their household income is high, and a location in a municipality with high remittances increases the probability for success. Effects on income distribution point towards an increase in inequality through remittances, which again might be attributed to the fact that remittances tend to flow towards wealthier households and do not reach the poorest.

6 Conclusion

In Kosovo a saying goes, a family needs 'one son for the family, who stays at home, one for migration, who works abroad, and one for the mother country'. Indeed, many rural Kosovar households are involved in migration and they benefit from remittances. But is 'one son for migration' really needed in rural Kosovo to be able to make ends meet? Are remittances helping to find a pathway out of poverty? We cannot give a definite answer to these questions, because this would need longitudinal data, but our counterfactual scenarios strongly indicate that remittances are indeed important in the fight against poverty in rural Kosovar households.

First, we show that migrant households have higher absolute incomes, and the share of remittances in the income of migrant households is significant (13%). Second, poverty indicators calculated based on counterfactual incomes show that, depending on the poverty line chosen, a considerable share of 18% or 41% respectively of migrant families are no longer poor due to their access to remittances. However, the effect is not seen to apply to the extremely poor who generally have less access to remittances. Third, with regard to distributional effects, we find (based on decomposition and a comparison with counterfactual incomes) that migration makes the income distribution more unequal. This can be taken as a hint that those who do not take part in migration activities and do not benefit from remittances fall behind.

According to our counterfactual scenario, migrant households increase their income significantly by almost € 700 per year. However, not all migrant households are able to climb the income ladder. Successful migration certainly depends on various factors, some of them complex or even unobservable. Starting from a set of classical socio-economic factors, we show that the household structure and the wealth status are decisive for the migration outcome. Migrant households which are successful are further characterised by significantly higher education levels than migrant households with lower educational levels. This is not the case for migrant households as a whole where, compared with non-migrant households, differences in education are not significant. This results from the fact that better education is typically found in the upper income tertile, where successful migrant households rather do not come from. We therefore conclude that education is one key for making migration a pathway out of poverty: it allows families to climb the income ladder through migration. Certainly other factors might have an important influence on migration outcomes and thus on poverty too. Our analysis is limited at this stage as we would have liked to include additional relevant variables such as risk behaviour or attitudes of the migrant.

With regard to policy conclusions, first, we stress that the poorest seem to benefit least from migration. Therefore it is necessary to monitor the income distribution. Only if trickle down effects materialise may a drop in income equality be avoided in the longer term. Social security policies are important in supporting those who are most vulnerable and excluded from migration benefits. Second, our analysis shows that migration is not solely beneficial for better off households: in fact within the group of migrant households, poorer households in particular are able to turn migration into success. Making migration a success story is key to poverty reduction based on remittances. Education seems to be among the most important factors to achieve this.

Endnotes

[1] The focus on rural households is justified because it is known that they tend to benefit more from remittances than urban households, and are also more affected by poverty (Haxhikadrija 2009).

[2] However, Göbel (2013) finds for Ecuador that remittance inflows increase expenditures on education, health, and housing.

[3] The subsample refers to the subset of rural households with complete income data. Households with more than ten household members are not included due to missing data in the KRS database (for these households it is not possible to calculate the correct per capita incomes that are needed for the analyses).

[4] PSM assumes that the treatment satisfies some form of exogeneity, meaning that the selection is on observables. The assumption of unconfoundedness implies that systematic differences in outcomes between treated and untreated units with the same value for covariates are attributable to treatment. Thus, it relies on a set of observable variables that

captures all relevant differences between the treated and control group so that the non-treatment outcome is independent of the treatment status, conditional on those characteristics; the possible existence of unobservables correlated with the migration decision is a limitation to the application of the method (Caliendo and Kopeinig 2008, Jimenez-Soto and Brown 2012, Imbens and Rubin 2014).

[5] The Gini coefficient is the most widely used measure of income distribution. Its value varies between zero and one, with zero indicating a perfectly equal income distribution. The higher a Gini coefficient is, the more unequally incomes are distributed. Gini coefficients between 0.25 and 0.35 are considered 'reasonable', while coefficients higher than 0.5 indicate that income distribution is seriously unbalanced (Ellis 2000).

[6] The average household size of five household members is underestimated: it does not include households with more than ten household members because they are excluded from the sample due to missing data in the KRS 2010 database (see above).

[7] Pure pensioner households are excluded because dependency ratios cannot be calculated.

[8] Pastore et al. (2013) point at significant gender differences: young women tend to have a lower level of education and are less likely to be employed.

[9] Milanovic (1987) in his study of Yugoslav households provides remittances income shares for the 1973, 1978 and 1983 in which the percentages for Yugoslavia were given as between 3% and 5%. He stresses that remittances are consistently higher among farm households (10%-15%).

[10] The Statistical Office of Kosovo (2010) estimates this share to be around 10% in Kosovo.

[11] This is also the case if tertiles are calculated based on counterfactual incomes derived from PSM.

[12] Although it is often argued that consumption-based poverty indicators are preferable, we concentrate in our analysis on income-based indicators. While consumption and income differ only moderately for the first two tertiles, the consumption data and income data are strikingly different for the third tertile – probably due to higher investment and saving activities that are not depicted in the KRS database.

[13] We use the sample median income, a number that is expected to be somewhat below the national median because we look at rural households only.

[14] Acosta et al. (2008) confirm this on an empirical basis for a number of Latin American countries. They point out that when no imputations are made for the income of remittance senders, countries where recipients are concentrated at the bottom of the distribution of non-remittance income exhibit much higher reductions in poverty headcounts attributable to remittances. Nonetheless, they stress that the effects of remittances are in either case far from negligible.

Additional file

Additional file 1: Table S1. Descriptive statistics of variables in the PSM logit model. Table S2: PSM logit results - psmatch2: NN (3). Table S3: Testing the balance of covariates and absolute bias reduction. Table S4: R2 of raw and matched model. Table S5: Rosenbaum bounds test for sensitivity. Table S6: Descriptive statistics of variables in the logit model on successful migration. Figure S1: Overlap graph.

Abbreviations

ATT: Average treatment effect on the treated; GDP: Gross Domestic Product; HH: Household; €: Euro; ESI: European Stability Initiative; KRS: Kosovo Remittance Study; PC: Per capita; PSM: Propensity Score Matching; Std. Dev.: Standard deviation; Std. Err.: Standard error; OECD: Organisation for economic co-operation and development; UNDP: United

Nations Development Programme; USAID: United States Agency for International Development; US$: US dollar; SOK: Statistical Office of Kosovo.

Competing interests
The IZA Journal of Labour and Development is committed to the IZA Guiding Principles of Research Integrity. The authors declare that they observed these principles.

Acknowledgements
The authors wish to acknowledge very useful comments from the anonymous referee. We are also thankful to the UNDP for the provision of the data of the Kosovo Remittance Study 2010.
Responsible editor: Hartmut Lehmann

References
Abadie A, Imbens GW (2012) Matching on the estimated propensity score. Harvard University and National Bureau of Economic Research. http://www.hks.harvard.edu/fs/aabadie/pscore.pdf, 18.6.2014
Acosta P, Calderón C, Fajnzylber P, Lopez H (2008) What is the impact of international remittances on poverty and inequality in Latin America? World Dev 36:89–114
Adams RH (2011) Evaluating the economic impact of international remittances on developing countries using household surveys: a literature review. J Dev Stud 47(6):809–828
Adams RH, Page J (2005) International Migration, Remittances and Poverty in Developing Countries. In: MAIMBO SM, RATHA D (eds) Remittances – Development Impact and Future Prospects. The World Bank, Washington DC, USA
Adams RH, Cuecuecha A, Page J (2008) The Impact of Remittances on Poverty and Inequality in Ghana, Policy Research Working Paper No. 4732. The World Bank, Washington D.C.
Alam A, Murthi M, Yemtsov R, Murrugarra E, Dudwick N, Hamilton E, Tiongson E (2005) Growth Poverty and Inequality. Eastern Europe and the Former Soviet Union. The World Bank, Washington DC
Barham B, Boucher S (1998) Migration remittances and inequality: estimating the net effect of migration on income distribution. J Dev Econ 55(2):307–331
Caliendo M, Kopeinig S (2008) Some practical guidance for the implementation of propensity score matching. J Econ Surv 22(1):31–72
Corbanese V, Rosas G (2007) Young People's Transition to Decent Work: Evidence from Kosovo. Employment Policy Papers 2007 (4). International Labour Office, Geneva
Coudouel A, Hentschel JS, Wodon QT (2000) Poverty measurement and analysis. In: Poverty Reduction Strategy Sourcebook. World Bank, Washington, DC
Davis B, Carletto G, Winters P (2010) Migration, transfers and economic decision making among agricultural households: an introduction. J Dev Stud 46(1):1–13
De Haan A, Rogaly B (2002) Introduction: migrant workers and their role in rural change. J Dev Stud 38(5):1–14
Elezaj E, Bislimi F, Duri I (2012) Kosovo Remittance Study 2012. United Nations Development Program (UNDP) – Kosovo, Prishtina, KS
Ellis F (2000) Rural Livelihoods and Diversity in Developing Countries. Oxford University Press, Oxford
European Stability Initiative [ESI] (2006) Cutting the lifeline: Migration, families and the future of Kosovo. European Stability Initiative (ESI), Berlin, D, and Istanbul, TR
Foster J, Greer J, Thorbecke E (1984) A class of decomposable poverty measures. Econometrica 52(3):761–765
Gashi A, Haxhikadrija A (2012) Social impact of Emigration and Rural–urban Migration in Central and Eastern Europe. Final Country Report Kosovo. European Commission, ec.europa.eu/social/BlobServlet?docId=8861&langId=en, accessed May 2014
Giannetti M, Federici D, Raitano M (2009) Migrant remittances and inequality in Central-Eastern Europe. Int Rev Appl Econ 23(3):289–307
Göbel K (2013) Remittances, expenditure patterns, and gender: parametric and semiparametric evidence from Ecuador. IZA J Migr 2(1):1–19
Havolli S (2011) Determinants of migrants' earnings and remittances: evidence from Kosovo. Focus on European Economic Integration Q1(11):90–99
Haxhikadrija A (2009) Diaspora as a driving force in the development of Kosovo: myth or reality? http://www.swiss-cooperation.admin.ch/kosovo/en/Home/Publications, 18.06.2014
Imbens G, Rubin DB (2014) An Introduction to Causal Inference in Statistics, Biomedical and Social Science. Cambridge University press, New York
Jimenez-Soto E, Brown R (2012) Assessing the poverty impacts of migrants' remittances using propensity score matching: the case of Tonga. Econ Rec 88(282):425–439
Lerman RI, Yitzhaki S (1994) Effect of marginal changes in income sources on US income inequality. Public Finan Q 22(4):403–417
Lokshin M, Bontch-Osmolovski M, Glinskaya E (2010) Work-related migration and poverty reduction in Nepal. Rev Dev Econ 14(2):323–332
Mansoor A, Quillin B (2006) Migration and Remittances. Eastern Europe and the Former Soviet Union. The World Bank, Washington DC
McKenzie D, Sasin MJ (2007) Migration, Remittances, Poverty, and Human Capital: Conceptual and Empirical Challenges, World Bank Policy Research Working Paper No. 4272. The World Bank, Washington D.C
Meyer W, Möllers J, Buchenrieder G (2012) Who remits more and who remits less? Evidence from Kosovar migrants living in Germany and the corresponding origin households. Oxf Dev Stud 40(4):443–466
Milanovic B (1987) Remittances and income distribution. J Econ Stud 14(5):24–37

Miluka J, Carletto G, Davis B, Zezza A (2010) The vanishing farms? The impact of international migration on Albanian family farming. J Dev Stud 46(1):140–161

Möllers J, Meyer W, Xhema S, Buchenrieder G (2013) A socio-economic picture of Kosovar migrants and their origin farm households, IAMO Discussion Paper No. 140. Leibniz Institute of Agricultural Development in Transition Economies (IAMO), Halle (Saale), D

Mosse D, Gupta S, Mehta M, Shah V, Rees J (2002) Brokered livelihoods: debt, labour migration and development in tribal Western India. J Dev Stud 38(5):59–88

Mustafa M, Kotorri M, Gashi P, Gashi A, Demukaj V (2007) Diaspora and Migration Policies. Riinvest, Prishtina

Pastore F, Sattar S, Tiongson E (2013) Gender differences in earnings and labour supply in early career. Evidence from Kosovo's school-to-work transition survey. IZA J Labor Dev 2(5):1–34

Ravallion M (1998) Poverty Lines in Theory and Practice, Living Standards Measurement Study Working Paper No. 133. World Bank, Washington, DC

Reardon T, Taylor JE, Stamoulis K, Lanjouw P, Balisacan A (2000) Effects of nonfarm employment on rural income inequality in developing countries: an investment perspective. J Agric Econ 51(2):266–288

Shorrocks AF (1982) Inequality decomposition by factor components. Econometrica 50(1):193–212

Stark O, Taylor JE, Yitzhaki S (1988) Migration, remittances, and inequality: a sensitivity analysis using the extended Gini index. J Dev Econ 28(3):309–322

Statistical Office of Kosovo [SOK] (2010) Household Budget Survey 2009. Series 5: Social Statistics. http://ask.rks-gov.net/ENG/hbs/tables, 18.06.2014

Taylor JE (1992) Remittances and inequality reconsidered: direct, indirect and intertemporal effects. J Policy Model 14 (2):187–208

Taylor JE, Wyatt TJ (1996) The shadow value of migrant remittances, income and inequality in a household-farm economy. J Dev Stud 32(6):899–912

United Nations Development Programme (2010) Kosovo Remittance Study 2010. UNDP, Prishtina

United Nations Development Programme (2011) Kosovo Remittance Survey 2011, Fast Facts. UNDP, Prishtina

United States Agency for International Development [USAID] (2008) Kosovo Economic Performance Assessment. http://pdf.usaid.gov/pdf_docs/PNADL767.pdf, 2.5.2014

Vathi Z, Black R (2007) Migration and poverty reduction in Kosovo, Development Research Centre (DRC) of Migration, Globalisation and Poverty DRC on Migration, Globalisation and Poverty Working Paper No. C 12. Development Research Centre on Migration, Globalisation and Poverty, Brighton

Verme P (2011) The poverty reduction capacity of public and private transfers in transition. J Dev Stud 47(6):870–893

World Bank (2000) Making Transition Work for Everyone: Poverty and Inequality in Europe and Central Asia. The World Bank, Washington, D.C.

World Bank (2007a) Kosovo poverty assessment. Report No. 39737-XK. The World Bank, Washington D.C.

World Bank (2007b) World Development Report 2008: Agriculture for Development. The World Bank, Washington D.C.

World Bank (2010) World Bank indicators: workers' remittances and compensation of employees, received (current US$), retrieved November 4, 2010. http://data.worldbank.org/indicator/BX.TRF.PWKR.CD.DT

World Bank and SOK (2011) Consumption Poverty in the Republic of Kosovo in 2009. The World Bank, Washington D.C.

11

Do parents drink their children's welfare? Intra-household allocation of time between market labour, domestic work and child care in Russia

Gianna Claudia Giannelli[1], Lucia Mangiavacchi[2] and Luca Piccoli[2*]

*Correspondence:
luca.piccoli@uib.es
[2] Department of Applied
Economics, University of the
Balearic Islands, Ctra de Valldemossa
km 7.5, Palma de Mallorca, Spain
Full list of author information is
available at the end of the article

Abstract

The aim of this paper is to investigate whether parental alcohol consumption leads to a reduction of child welfare. To this end, we analyse whether alcohol consumption decreases parents' time spent looking after children and working. Using the Russia Longitudinal Monitoring Survey, we estimate a model of intra-household allocation of time for mono-nuclear families with children under fifteen years of age. We find that fathers' alcohol consumption has a negative impact on their weekly hours spent doing child care, while no significant effect is observed for mothers' alcohol consumption.

JEL codes: D1; I1; J13; J22

Keywords: Child care; Time allocation; Alcohol consumption; Labour supply; Russia

Introduction

It is a widely recognized fact that alcohol consumption is a major risk factor for morbidity and mortality. Higher morbidity and mortality rates, however, are not the only negative consequences of alcohol addiction. Alcoholism is also known as a family disease, since it may lead to serious health and socio-economic problems, not only in the short-run, but also in the long-run, through the transmission of its harmful effects to offspring. Parental alcoholism may negatively affect children in several ways. Many children of alcoholics have common symptoms such as low self-esteem, loneliness, guilt, feelings of helplessness, fears of abandonment, and chronic depression (Berger 1993; Chatterji and Markowitz, 2001). Unfortunately, these and other more dramatic consequences, such as domestic violence, psychological alienation, and deprivation of affection, are difficult to be measured through general purpose socio-economic surveys.

When parents regularly consume alcohol, they may reduce time spent in child care. Furthermore, children may also be affected through the negative effects of one parent's alcohol consumption on the other spouse. Family responsibilities may shift from two parents to one parent and, as a result, the non-alcoholic parent may also reduce time spent in looking after children. In all such cases, a negative impact of alcohol consumption on child care time would imply a welfare loss for the child.

Information on parents' time devoted to child care and on individual alcohol consumption can be fruitfully exploited to infer about the influence of alcohol consumption on parents' effort towards their children. Therefore, one viable way of studying the effects of parents' alcohol consumption on children is through parents' time-use. This is possible thanks to the increasing availability of more detailed data on the use of time within the household. Using time use data, in this paper we propose a model to test the effects of parental alcohol consumption on child care time.

To our knowledge, this is the first study to address the problem of the effects of alcohol consumption on the allocation of time within the household. So far, the economic literature has focused on the effects of alcoholism on individual labour market outcomes, based mainly on U.S. data, finding an unclear effect of alcohol abuse on labour supply. For instance, Mullahy and Sindelar (1991) and French et al (1998) explore respectively gender differences in labour force participation in response to alcoholism and alcohol abuse on the labour supply of young men. Interestingly, Hamilton and Hamilton (1997) find that moderate alcohol consumption leads to higher earnings relative to abstinence, while heavy drinking leads to reduced wages relative to moderate drinking. More recently, and again based on U.S. data, Feng et al (2001) finds that problem drinking has a negative but non-significant impact on employment for women, and a positive and significant impact for men, suggesting the importance of modelling the impact of alcohol consumption on labour supply decisions separately for males and females. French et al (2011) find that alcohol misuse is significantly related to employment problems, suggesting that the transmission mechanism that links alcohol consumption and labour supply works through a conflictive behaviour between supervisor and colleagues.

Russia is a particularly interesting setting in which to study the socio-economic consequences of drinking. Alcohol consumption was the third leading cause of death during the Soviet regime (Baltagi and Geishecker, 2006), and was one of the main causes of increased mortality during the transition decades (Brainerd and Cutler, 2005). Tekin (2004) has exploited the Russia Longitudinal Monitoring Survey (RLMS-HSE) to estimate the effects of alcohol consumption on employment and wages for males and females during transition. His estimates reject the hypothesis of an inverse U-shaped relationship between alcohol consumption and employment outcomes found in Hamilton and Hamilton (1997). Instead, the impact of alcohol consumption turns out to be non-significant as far as labour supply is concerned, yet positive and linear for both male and female wages levels.

Moreover, during the 90s, child care services in Russia declined as a result of economic transition to a market economy, and their cost increased substantially, so that low income families could not afford them anymore. As a result, after transition, Russian couples have to rely massively on child care provided by household members (Lokshin, 2004), and, since child care is so crucial for children's welfare, the question as to whether child care time provided by parents could be affected by alcohol consumption appears particularly relevant.

Our paper uses a sample of households drawn from the RLMS-HSE to investigate whether alcohol consumption reduces the time that parents spend with their children, thus changing the intra-household allocation of time in an unfavourable way for children. In line with recent advances in household economics, we analyse the time allocation decisions of partners under the assumption that this is jointly determined by members of the household across various activities. We estimate an SUR Tobit system using Full Information Maximum Likelihood, accounting for a possible correlation of the errors among time-use equations, simultaneously for the husband and the wife. Our model presents some similarities and some differences with respect to Bloemen et al (2010). It is similar in that it treats the time use choices of both spouses jointly and analyses the same time use categories. It is different in that it allows us to explicitly deal with the problem of sample selection bias in labour supply and to endogenise wages in the decision process.

Our results suggest that a father's alcohol consumption significantly reduces the time he devotes to child care, while no effects are observed for mothers' alcohol consumption. Moreover, we do not find any effect of one spouse's alcohol consumption on the other spouse. We interpret these findings as evidence of a negative impact of fathers' alcohol consumption on child welfare.

The paper is structured as follows: a section on Background literature reviews the relevant economic literature on allocation of time within the household and on the effects of alcohol consumption; a section on Theoretical foundations outlines the theoretical framework; a section on the Empirical strategy describes the empirical specification, while data and variables used are presented in the section on Data. Section Results discusses the findings of the empirical analysis, and the last section concludes.

Background literature

Spouses' allocation of time has been treated jointly since Chiappori (1988, 1992) while time dedicated to domestic tasks has been endogenised since Gronau (1977), Grossbard-Shechtman (1984), Kooreman and Kapteyn (1987) and Apps and Rees (1996), that extended the original time use model proposed by Becker (1965). In the recent empirical literature, it is a common practice to separate child care time from domestic tasks[1].

Studies on the determinants of parental child care have been based mostly on systems of simultaneous equations for paid work and child care time of individuals, as in Kalenkoski et al (2005, 2007, 2009), mainly using the American Time Use Survey and the U.K. Time Use Study. Kimmel and Connelly (2007) include both domestic tasks and child care. They use data for the U.S. to estimate a four-equation system in which the dependent variables are the minutes used in household production, leisure activities, paid work, and child care by mothers. Their main finding is a substantial, positive wage elasticity for care time, while both leisure and household production time decline with increased wages.

One strand of literature studies one partner's choices conditioning on spouse's decisions, distinguishing between different activities and modelling them jointly. Powell (2002), for example, examines the impact of child care prices and wage rates on the joint employment and child care decisions of married mothers in Canada. She finds that wages have a positive impact on the probability of choosing any of the working states and that child care prices for centre, sitter, and relative care reduce the probability of working and using each respective mode of care. Connelly and Kimmel (2009) extend the model proposed by Kimmel and Connelly (2007) considering the effect of spouse's characteristics on time devoted to leisure, child care, and home production of married mothers and fathers. Their results show little effect of one spouse on the unpaid time use of the partner, while the relative wage does not affect time use choices. In Russia, Lokshin et al (2000) and Lokshin (2004) focus again on mothers, modelling simultaneously household demand for child care, mothers' labour force participation and mothers' working hours. Both studies do not restrict the sample to single unit households, so the inclusion of multi-nuclear families implies the need to control for not only the wage of the husband, but also the average wage of all other family members. Their results show that mothers' labour force participation and working hours are responsive to changes in the price of child care and hourly wages. Additionally, (Lokshin 2004) evidences the ineffectiveness of family allowances transfers on a household's choice of child care arrangements.

In a growing number of studies both female and male partners' choices regarding the different types of activities are modelled jointly. Child care time allocation is substantially different between spouses[2], and, since female and male child care times are not orthogonal, they should be modelled jointly. Hallberg and Klevmarken (2003), for example, develop a simultaneous equation framework for child care and paid work. Using panel data for Sweden, they find that a change in the mother's working hours has less influence on the parents' time with their children than a change in the father's working hours. Using a similar methodology, Garcia-Mainar et al (2011) estimate a joint model of parental child care time for five European countries. Bloemen et al (2010) analyse simultaneously the time allocated by husband and wife to paid work, child care and housework in Italy. They find that spouses time allocation is sensitive to personal and household characteristics, such as education and children's age. Men married to more highly educated women spend more time with their children and the husband's own characteristics have little effect on wives' time allocation.

As far as the case of Russia is concerned, during the 90s, child care institutions in Russia, as well as female labour force participation, declined as a result of the economic transition from a socialist to a market economy. At the same time, the cost of child care supplied by the government increased, making daycare services unaffordable for low income families with young children. Lokshin et al (2000) and (Lokshin 2004) use the 1994 - 1996 rounds of RLMS to estimate a model of consumer demand for state provided child care and find that mothers' decisions to send children to formal child care and to participate in the labour market are taken jointly. They find that the cost of private child care is a disincentive to participation, while public transfers in the form of family allowances are ineffective. Similarly, Grogan and Koka (2010) estimate a discrete choice model of mothers' labour force participation for a longer panel and find an even stronger negative effect for having children under 3 in the 2000s. As a result, during the 90s, in-home care increased to levels ranging from 69.4% to 99.9% of total child care time, depending on child age. These findings suggest that Russian couples, after the economic transition, have to rely almost completely on informal child care provided within the household.

As for alcohol consumption, it is well known that in Russia alcohol consumption is high, with effects on health that increase morbidity and mortality. Brainerd and Cutler (2005) suggest that the increase in alcohol consumption is one of the leading causes of the dramatic positive trend in mortality rates during transitional years, accounting for about 25% of the increased mortality[3]. Moreover, consumption of vodka is more likely to be binge rather than moderate drinking (Brainerd and Cutler, 2005; Baltagi and Geishecker, 2006). During the transition to a market economy, positive trends in alcohol consumption patterns were observed by several studies, all of them using RLMS data. Zohoori et al (1998) and Brainerd and Cutler (2005) found that in the early 1990s, per-capita consumption of alcohol doubled in particular among middle-aged men. In the following years, this upward trend was interrupted by an increase in the price of alcohol, until 1998 when it started to rise again (RLMS data suggest an increase of 27% in alcohol consumption in the whole period 1992-2000). The last five waves of RLMS (2006-2010) partially confirm the previous trends, with total daily alcohol intake for drinkers showing a slight increase for males and an essentially stable path for females.

Theoretical foundations

A bulk of literature, starting with Grossbard-Shechtman (1984) for marriage market models and Apps and Rees (1996) within the collective framework, have formulated utility models that account for both the multi-person nature of many households and the inclusion of household production. In these models, time allocation decisions of male and female partners are jointly determined, as well as the allocation of time among the different types of activities.

The model proposed here is grounded in this stream of literature and presents three main features: i) child care time is included as a separate time use category as in Kimmel and Connelly (2007) and Connelly and Kimmel (2009), ii) husbands' and wives' time use are jointly determined as in Bloemen et al (2010), and iii) information on individual alcohol consumption is exploited to test its impact on individual allocation of time and on intra-household distribution of domestic tasks and paid work.

In theory, as was postulated by Becker (1981), parents are assumed to have altruistic preferences towards the other family members. This assumption implies the inclusion of partner's and child's welfare among the arguments of each parent's utility function. In particular, parents have the following altruistic utility functions:

$$U_m = U_m(t_m^l, z_m^a, U_f, U_c)$$
$$U_f = U_f(t_f^l, z_f^a, U_m, U_c)$$
$$U_c = U_c(z^c) \tag{1}$$

where m and f represent male and female partners, t^l is leisure time, z^a is a composite consumption good consumed by each adult (such that $z_m^a + z_f^a = z^a$), produced as a combination of household production time of the two partners and of intermediate goods and services purchased in the market $z^a = g(t_m^d, t_f^d, \mathbf{x})$. z^c is a composite good consumed by the children and produced as a combination of child care time of the two partners and goods and services purchased in the market $z^c = g(t_m^c, t_f^c, \mathbf{x})$. It follows that each parent's utility can, without loss of generality, be rewritten as:

$$U_i = U_i(t_m^l, t_f^l, z_m^a, z_f^a, z^c). \tag{2}$$

Assuming that the adults take responsibility for maximizing family welfare, they maximize household utility subject to the constraints of both their own time as well as that of the household budget:

$$T_m = t_m^w + t_m^d + t_m^c + t_m^l$$
$$T_f = t_f^w + t_f^d + t_f^c + t_f^l$$
$$\mathbf{p}'\mathbf{x} = w_f t_f^w + w_m t_m^w + v \tag{3}$$

where w, d, c and l are time use categories (paid work, domestic tasks, child care and leisure time respectively), v is household non-labour income, and $\mathbf{p}'\mathbf{x}$ is household expenditure on market goods. It is worth noting that such a specification is general and embraces both unitary and collective decision models depending on how household utility is specified. The solution of the model yields the supply functions of the uses of time for both partners:

$$t_i^k = t_i^k(w_i, w_j, v) \tag{4}$$

where, for each individual ($i = m, f$) each time use category ($k = c, d, w, l$) depends on wages (w_i and w_j), household non-labour income (v) and the structure of preferences[4]. Family and personal characteristics, indeed, can be included in the time use functions as preference factors.

The system defined by the paid work, domestic tasks and child care equations for each partner (leisure equations are excluded to avoid collinearity), as previously stated, is potentially compatible with a collective specification (see, for example, Bourguignon, 1999; Mangiavacchi et al, 2010; Dunbar et al, 2013). However, as the data includes no child exclusive goods (for parents we could use the respective leisure times), it would be impossible to identify the child sharing rule. Thus, the use of a collective model would imply an unnecessary burden, at least for the aims of this paper.

As detailed in the next section, our empirical strategy is to estimate the reduced form equation system (4). Even though this strategy does not allow us to fully recover the structural parameters of preferences, it still allows us to determine the impact of an exogenous variable on the time use equations. In our context, child care time directly affects child consumption, and, by consequence, what affects child care time, also affects child welfare. The child's utility depends on the amount of good z^c that the child consumes, which, in turn, have child care time among its production input factors. By assumption, in fact, the time devoted to child care has a strictly positive productivity: a larger amount of time input increases z^c. In turn, z^c has a strictly positive marginal utility for the child. This implies that an exogenous variable that significantly reduces child care time, also significantly reduces z^c. However, since z^c also depends on purchased goods **x**, a parent might renounce to some child care time in favour of paid work time, thus increasing child utility by increasing expenditure on **x**. However, if an exogenous variable negatively affects child care time and has no positive impacts on market labour time of both partner, then there would be an unquestionable negative impact on child welfare. We apply this line of reasoning to understand the transmission mechanism of the effects of alcohol consumption on child welfare.

Empirical strategy

The empirical specification of the system of equations (4) involves considering several factors to avoid biased estimates. Each time use equation is left censored, since, for some individuals, the minimum amount of child care, domestic tasks or paid work is zero. A suitable econometric model in this case would be a type-1 Tobit (Amemiya, 1985). This specification, however, may be problematic. In fact, non-workers' potential wages must be estimated, and the empirical literature widely recognizes the possibility of a sample selection bias. One solution is to estimate wages independently for men and women in a first stage using a Heckman selection model (Heckman, 1979). Moreover, estimating the wage equations using a Heckman selection model implies estimating a labour participation equation. So, labour supply equations in (4) could also be estimated more precisely if estimated jointly with this labour participation equation. This is possible using a system in which one participation equation is used by two different equations, namely the wage and labour supply equations. Finally, our theoretical model requires the reduced form equations to be estimated jointly, allowing for possible correlation among the error terms. In fact, since our unit of observation is the family, we have to take into account that the amount of time devoted to one activity by one individual not only depends on time spent in other activities, but also on time spent in this and other activities by his/her partner. For example, the mother's child care time will depend on her paid work status (being on leave, working part time or full time, and so on), but also on her husband's paid work: if he works more hours, she might carry out more child care, and vice-versa.

In sum, our empirical specification is a SUR consisting of four equations for the partners' child care and domestic tasks (specified as type-1 Tobit, since almost all individuals participate in these activities, so that the number of censored observations is reasonably small), and six equations for the partners' labour participation, labour supply and wages (specified as a type-5 Tobit). Each partner has five equations two of which are for child care and for domestic tasks and are specified as:

$$t_i^{k*} = \beta_0 + \beta_{a_i}a_i + \beta_{a_j}a_j + \beta_{w_i}w_i + \beta_{w_j}w_j + \beta_v v + \beta_{P_i}'\mathbf{P_i} + \beta_{F_i}'\mathbf{F} + u_{i,k}$$
$$t_i^k = t_i^{k*} \text{ if } t_i^{k*} > 0$$
$$t_i^k = 0, \text{ otherwise,} \tag{5}$$

with $i, j = f, m$ indicating the partner, either female (f) or male (m), $k = d, c$ representing domestic tasks (d) or child care (c), $a_{i,j}$ being individual alcohol consumption, and $\mathbf{P_i}$ and $\mathbf{F}$ personal and family characteristics[5]. The other three equations are for labour market participation, labour supply and wage, and are specified as:

$$d_i^* = \beta_{X_i}'\mathbf{X_i} + e_i$$
$$w_i^* = \beta_{Z_i}'\mathbf{Z_i} + v_i$$
$$t_i^{w*} = \beta_0 + \beta_{a_i}a_i + \beta_{a_j}a_j + \beta_{w_i}w_i + \beta_{w_j}w_j + \beta_v v + \beta_{P_i}'\mathbf{P_i} + \beta_{F_i}'\mathbf{F} + u_{i,w}$$
$$d_i = 1 \text{ if } d_i^* > 0$$
$$d_i = 0 \text{ otherwise}$$
$$t_i^w = t_i^{w*} \text{ if } d_i^* > 0$$
$$t_i^w = 0, \text{ otherwise}$$
$$w_i = w_i^* \text{ if } d_i^* > 0$$
$$w_i = 0, \text{ otherwise,} \tag{6}$$

with the dummy d_i^* indicating the participation equation, w_i^* the wage equation and t_i^{w*} the labour supply equation for member i.

The exogenous variables, presented in the next section, include economic variables, such as partners' potential wages and non-labour income, and other individual and household characteristics, including our relevant variable of interest, namely, alcohol consumption by each partner.

It is worth stressing that, in our model, parents' attitude towards alcohol might be endogenous. One weakness of our analysis is that we were not able to find a suitable instrument to apply an instrumental variable estimation technique[6].

The whole system is composed by 10 equations: 6 for the use of time (paid work, t_i^w, domestic tasks, t_i^d and child care, t_i^c, for $i = m, f$), 2 labour market participation equations

Do parents drink their children's welfare? Intra-household allocation...

245

and 2 wage equations. The resulting error structure is slightly more complex than a standard SUR. The error terms are drawn from a multivariate normal distribution with zero mean and a 10×10 covariance matrix, correlation between the error terms is allowed between time-use equations and own-wage equations, but participation equations are allowed to be correlated only with their own labour supply and wage equation. So, for the avoidance of doubt, correlation is not allowed between female labour market participation and male wage, or between male labour market participation and male child care time. Correlation is allowed for all other equations, so, for instance, the error term in the female wage equation may be correlated with the error term in the female domestic tasks equation.

The covariance matrix, thus, takes the following form

$$
\begin{array}{c}
\begin{array}{cccccccccc}
t_m^c & t_f^c & t_m^d & t_f^d & t_m^w & t_f^w & d_m & d_f & w_m & w_f
\end{array} \\
\begin{array}{c}
t_m^c \\ t_f^c \\ t_m^d \\ t_f^d \\ t_m^w \\ t_f^w \\ d_m \\ d_f \\ w_m \\ w_f
\end{array}
\left[
\begin{array}{cccccccccc}
\sigma_1^2 & \sigma_1\sigma_2\rho_{1,2} & \sigma_1\sigma_3\rho_{1,3} & \sigma_1\sigma_4\rho_{1,4} & \sigma_1\sigma_5\rho_{1,5} & \sigma_1\sigma_6\rho_{1,6} & 0 & 0 & \sigma_1\sigma_9\rho_{1,9} & 0 \\
 & \sigma_2^2 & \sigma_2\sigma_3\rho_{2,3} & \sigma_2\sigma_4\rho_{2,4} & \sigma_2\sigma_5\rho_{2,5} & \sigma_2\sigma_6\rho_{2,6} & 0 & 0 & 0 & \sigma_2\sigma_{10}\rho_{2,10} \\
 & & \sigma_3^2 & \sigma_3\sigma_4\rho_{3,4} & \sigma_3\sigma_5\rho_{3,5} & \sigma_3\sigma_6\rho_{3,6} & 0 & 0 & \sigma_3\sigma_9\rho_{3,9} & 0 \\
 & & & \sigma_4^2 & \sigma_4\sigma_5\rho_{4,5} & \sigma_4\sigma_6\rho_{4,6} & 0 & 0 & 0 & \sigma_4\sigma_{10}\rho_{4,10} \\
 & & & & \sigma_5^2 & \sigma_5\sigma_6\rho_{5,6} & \sigma_5\sigma_7\rho_{5,7} & 0 & \sigma_5\sigma_9\rho_{5,9} & 0 \\
 & & & & & \sigma_6^2 & 0 & \sigma_6\sigma_8\rho_{6,8} & 0 & \sigma_6\sigma_{10}\rho_{6,10} \\
 & & & & & & \sigma_7^2 & 0 & \sigma_7\sigma_9\rho_{7,9} & 0 \\
 & & & & & & & \sigma_8^2 & 0 & \sigma_8\sigma_{10}\rho_{8,10} \\
 & & & & & & & & \sigma_9^2 & \sigma_9\sigma_{10}\rho_{9,10} \\
 & & & & & & & & & \sigma_{10}^2
\end{array}
\right]
\end{array}
$$

where σ_i^2 indicates the variance of error term i, $\sigma_i\sigma_i\rho_{i,j}$ indicates the covariance between two error terms i and j, and $\rho_{i,j}$ indicates the correlation coefficients, with $i,j = 1,\ldots,10 \equiv u_{m,c}, u_{f,c}, u_{m,d}, u_{f,d}, u_{m,w}, u_{f,w}, e_m, e_f, v_m, v_f$.

The system is estimated by Full Information Maximum Likelihood using the aML statistical software[7].

Data

The empirical analysis is based on four rounds (XV to XVIII, spanning from 2006 to 2009) of the Russia Longitudinal Monitoring Survey (RLMS-HSE), conducted by the Higher School of Economics and ZAO Demoscop together with the Carolina Population Center, University of North Carolina at Chapel Hill and the Institute of Sociology RAS[8]. The survey has two phases: during the first phase of the project (1992 -1994), the RLMS collected four rounds of data; in the second phase, until 2011, the RLMS collected sixteen further rounds of data. Households participating in the survey were selected trough a multi-stage probability sampling procedure in order to guarantee national representativeness. Within each selected primary sample unit, the population was stratified into urban and rural substrata in order to guarantee representativeness of the sample in both areas. Between rounds XV and XVIII, the data covers approximately 5,000 households, 12,000 adults and 2,000 children per wave.

Since the RLMS was originally designed to monitor the health impact of economic transition in Russia, it contains detailed information on alcohol consumption of the respondents, use of time and labour supply. The RLMS permits the identification of the relationship between each member in the household, not only with respect to the head of the household. This allows us to select only households with no more than one nuclear family, avoiding problems due to the presence of more than one family with children in the same household[9]. This could amount to a serious issue, since, as was found by Lokshin et al (2000) and Lokshin (2004), the share of extended families in Russia increased substantially during the transition period, and more than half of Russian children live in extended families. The availability of the relationship between all household members also permits the identification of the number of potential suppliers of non-parental informal child care in the family, such as grandparents. Therefore, even if multifamily households are excluded from the analysis, we have kept in the sample households with co-resident grandparents.

Individual alcohol consumption is recorded by the RLMS for all rounds of Phase II. However, only from round XV it is possible to identify the actual monthly consumption. The dataset is also rich in time-use information, even if time spent in domestic activities and informal care is recorded only from rounds XV to XVIII[10]. In these four rounds, time use is recorded within the labour module of the survey, where people declared minutes spent per day in different activities in the last 30 days both during working days and weekends.

It is worth noting that, due to the sampling design, it was not possible to construct a household panel data-set, because families are not uniquely identified over time. While it is rather easy to track individuals, a unique family identifier cannot be constructed. For example, consider two subsequent waves in which a household splits because a son gets married. It is not possible to follow this family over time because: i) the two new families maintain the old household identification number that refers to the previous wave, but for the current wave one keeps the same identification number and the other gets a new one, ii) cross sectional identification numbers may be different in the way they are constructed (in round XV the family identifier received one more digit, and a change in the sample design in round XVIII implied that identification numbers are constructed using different stratification variables). The combination of these two conditions together with the explicit recommendation of HSE to not reconstruct a certain wave identification number using a different wave stratification data, prevented us from building a household panel data-set[11].

So, despite the advantages of a panel data-set, we were forced to pool the four waves into a cross section. In particular, we took all families present in round XVIII and added families from the previous waves that were not present in that round[12].

The dependent variables included in the system of equations are the logarithms of weekly hours spent respectively in child care[13], domestic tasks[14] and paid work. Even though time-use patterns may differ between weekdays and weekends, weekly amounts are used since alcohol consumption is not recorded separately for weekends and weekdays. Regarding time-use categories, as previously mentioned, to identify the effect of parental alcohol consumption on child welfare we separate child care from domestic tasks, as in Kimmel and Connelly (2007), Connelly and Kimmel (2009) and Bloemen et al (2010). Average weekly child care hours are 9.7 hours for men and 15.3 hours for women. Domestic tasks time is 12.9 hours for men and 22.8 hours for women, and paid work time on average is 42.1 hours for men and 31.4 hours for women (see Table 1).

Table 2 shows the joint distribution of time use categories and alcohol consumption for the sample under analysis[15]. It can be seen that fathers rarely carry out more child

Table 1 Overall scores across all the thirty-nine participants under each condition

Individual variables	Husband		Wife	
	Mean	SD	Mean	SD
Weekly childcare hours	9.6805	10.6318	15.3346	13.1642
Weekly domestic work hours	12.9085	12.4256	22.8007	12.8250
Weekly market work hours	42.0895	20.3362	31.3644	20.1227
Grams of alcohol per day / BMI	0.5379	0.9884	0.1314	0.4132
Ln of wage rate	4.2715	0.7401	3.9438	0.6884
Age	35.3745	7.4685	32.8741	7.1889
Non-Russian	0.2727	-	0.2448	-
Pension (not retired)	0.0505	-	0.0249	-
Primary education	0.2821	-	0.4367	-
Tertiary education	0.3963	-	0.2580	-
Occasional drinker	0.7172	-	0.5975	-
Frequent drinker	0.0583	-	0.0054	-
Pregnant	-	-	0.0163	-
Self-reported health status (cat.)	2.5144	0.5964	2.6169	0.5995
Disability + Chronic illness	0.3326	0.5063	0.3691	0.5063
Number of cigarettes	11.3108	10.2433	2.2688	5.0365

Household variables	Mean	SD
Number of children [0–1]	0.0785	0.2719
Number of children [4–6]	0.6263	0.6206
Number of children [0–3]	0.3737	0.5329
Presence of a nursery in the community	0.5975	0.4906
Community males/females ratio	0.9987	0.0572
Community male/female wage ratio	1.2138	0.1224
Community average wage	50.0878	13.3053
Receive help with childcare (cat.)	0.4476	0.5904
Ln of non labour income	6.0025	3.5253
Dwelling dimension (cat.)	1.9751	0.7072
Number of grandparents	0.0505	0.2426
Number of uncles	0.0186	0.1709
Dwelling dimension (cat.)	1.9829	0.7096
Owner of dwelling	0.6807	-
Female headed household	0.0016	-
Region 1 - Metropolitan area	0.0948	-
Region 2 - Northern area	0.0824	-
Region 3 - Central area	0.1748	-
Region 4 - Volga	0.1810	-
Region 5 - Caucas	0.1298	-
Region 6 - Ural	0.1399	-
Region 7 - West Siberia	0.0925	-
Region 8 - East Siberia	0.1049	-
Round XV	0.0824	-
Round XVI	0.1033	-
Round XVII	0.0948	-
Round XVIII	0.7195	-

1287 observations.

care than mothers, but still almost 60% of them dedicate at least 5 hours weekly to child care. This figure rises to 75.4% for mothers. The domestic tasks rely even more heavily on women. Almost 42% of husbands do less than 10 weekly hours of domestic tasks,

Table 2 Joint distribution of child care, domestic tasks, paid work and alcohol consumption

Childcare		Wives				
		0	(0–5]	(5–20]	>20	Total
Husbands	0	10.3	2.6	6.1	2.4	21.4
	(0–5]	1.0	4.4	11.7	2.6	19.7
	(5–20]	2.3	3.0	24.9	15.3	45.5
	>20	0.5	0.5	4.7	7.5	13.4
	Total	14.1	10.5	47.5	27.9	100

Domestic tasks		Wives				
		0	(0–10]	(10–30]	>30	Total
Husbands	0	0.5	1.6	5.8	2.3	10.3
	(0–10]	0.0	7.4	25.6	8.3	41.3
	(10–30]	0.2	5.3	22.6	11.7	39.7
	>30	0.0	0.5	4.7	3.5	8.8
	Total	0.6	14.8	58.7	25.8	100

Paid work		Wives				
		0	(0–32]	(32–45]	>45	Total
Husbands	0	4.4	1.5	4.2	2.4	12.5
	(0–32]	0.3	0.5	1.6	0.2	2.6
	(32–45]	8.3	4.6	26.4	7.6	46.9
	>45	10.6	3.7	15.9	7.9	38.0
	Total	23.6	10.2	48.2	18.0	100

Alcohol consumption		Wives				
		0	(0–2]	(2–10]	>10	Total
Husbands	0	14.8	4.0	3.3	0.6	22.7
	(0–2]	3.3	2.6	0.8	0.1	6.8
	(2–10]	12.6	10.8	9.2	0.9	33.5
	>10	8.9	8.0	14.8	5.3	37.0
	Total	39.7	25.4	28.0	6.9	100

1287 observations. In hours per week (childcare, domestic tasks and paid work) and grams of pure alcohol per day.

while almost 85% of wives do more than 10 hours. The situation changes respect to paid work, where only 15% of fathers are unemployed or part-time workers, with an impressive 38% of overtime workers. Women, however, do show large percentages of full-time and overtime work: 48% and 18% respectively.

As to the drinker's profile, drinking is mostly a male phenomenon (see Baltagi and Geishecker, 2006). Table 1 shows that in our sample more than 77% of men reported drinking, either occasionally (71.7%) or frequently - drinking every day or almost every day - (5.8%). For women, these figures are 59.8% and 0.5%, respectively. A substantial difference is also present in the level of consumption. As shown by Figure 1, male drinkers drink at least twice as much as women. Baltagi and Geishecker (2006) also show that male drinkers are likely to be married, to have children, to be well educated and to have a higher household income than non-drinkers.

In the RLMS, individual alcohol consumption is self-reported by the respondent in the health module. In Russia, alcohol consumption is measured in grams instead of litres, so each respondent is asked to declare how many grams of beer, wine, fortified wine, home-made liquor, vodka, and other alcoholic beverages they usually drink per day during the last 30 days. However, only from round XV it is possible to identify the actual monthly consumption, since respondents have also to declare the days per month they have been drinking. Following Baltagi and Geishecker (2006), these amounts are adjusted for pure alcohol content in order to make the various types of alcoholic beverages comparable and then summed up to compute total individual alcohol consumption. The weights used are 5% for the alcohol content of beer, 10% for wine, 19% for fortified wine, 45% for home made liquor, 40% for vodka, and 20% for other alcohol. Finally, the alcohol variables included in the equations are computed as the logarithm of grams of total alcohol intake per week, and divided by the body mass index of the person, in order to control for the possibly different impact of similar amounts of alcohol on different sized individuals. As to the possible doubts on the validity of self-reported measures of alcohol consumption, we follow the idea, again found in Baltagi and Geishecker (2006), that self-declared alcohol consumption in Russia should not be under-reported, since there is no social stigma

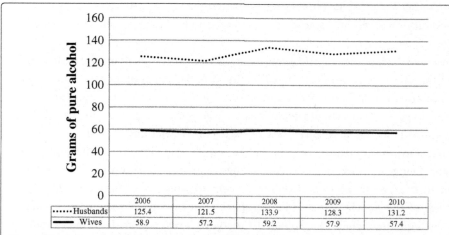

Figure 1 Evolution of alcohol consumption, 2006-2010. Note: Average daily grams of pure alcohol consumed by drinkers.

attached to alcohol consumption within the country. Recall errors are still possible, but at least there should not be a clear negative bias in the declared quantities.

The figures presented in Table 2 confirm that alcohol in Russia is mainly a male phenomenon. More than 70% of fathers drink more than 2 grams of pure alcohol per day (on average) and 37% more than 10 grams (that corresponds to 25 grams - a small glass - of vodka). 10% of males drink more than 30 grams of alcohol per day (not shown in the table). Women drink much less, most of them (65%) consuming less than 2 grams of alcohol per day, which amounts approximately to one glass of vodka per week. Only a few consume more than one glass of vodka per day (less than 7%) and almost 40% are abstemious (compared with 23% of males).

Although the focus of this paper is on the effects of alcohol on child welfare, wages are a critical variable that needs special attention in the analysis. As already discussed, previous analyses on the relation between alcohol and wages suggest a positive correlation (see Tekin, 2004). Thus a wage equation for each of the spouses is included in the system, and to correct possible self-selection bias, correlation between the error terms of the wage equation and the equation for labour participation is allowed.

Other explanatory variables included in the model (see Table 1) are the number of children in the age ranges of 0–1, 0–3 and 4–6, the number of grandparents and uncles living in the household, a dummy for being an entrepreneur, the health status (a categorical indicator equal to one in presence of chronic illness or disability and 2 if both of them are present, and a dummy indicating if receiving some pension, excluding retirement pension), whether the household receives help with child care by relatives not living in the household, the number of cigarettes per day and a standard list of individual demographic controls (age, education, nationality). We also control for the economic condition of the household, using non-labour income, dwelling ownership, and dwelling size. Finally, some regional variables are included, namely, average males/females ratio, male/female wage ratio, average wage, regional dummies and a dummy indicating the presence of a nursery in the community.

The sample selection starts by keeping mothers and fathers in the age 17–65 with children younger than 15 for the four waves and excluding multi-nuclear families (approximately 4400 households). Repeated households are then dropped by the sample (about 3100). Eliminating inconsistent observations, for example those with zero salary and a positive amount of worked hours, leads to the final sample, which is composed of 1287 households.

Given the complexity of the empirical specification, it is worth specifying the exclusions restrictions that help identifying the model[16]. First, the participation equation includes variables that are excluded both from the labour supply and the wage equations. In addition, the wage equation should include some variables not present in the labour supply equation. Thus, we have three sets of exclusion restrictions. The first set concerns the participation equation with the labour supply equation where the excluded variables are: being an occasional drinker, being pregnant (wives only), the number of children in the age range 0–1, dwelling ownership, and three dummies identifying the waves of the panel. The second set of restrictions concerns the participation with the wage equation, where the excluded variables are: average males/females ratio, receive help with child care, number of grandparents, being pregnant, number of children aged 0–3, being non-Russian and being in bad health conditions. Finally, the third set of restrictions concerns the wage equation with the labour supply equation, and the excluded variables are: being an occasional drinker, having only primary education, number of children aged 0–1, dwelling ownership, and the three waves dummies.

Results

Tables 3 and 4 present the estimated parameters of the empirical model introduced in Section "Theoretical foundations". As to the joint nature of the decision processes, the significance of cross equation correlations and of most of the reciprocal variables suggest that the choice of the joint estimation approach is appropriate.

As to the main focus of this paper, our results suggest that the amount of consumed alcohol is a relevant factor in determining fathers' child care time, influencing negatively and significantly (at 5%) their weekly hours spent in this activity. Manually computing the average partial effect[17] of one additional gram of pure alcohol per day for the average male drinker -who drinks 9.7 grams of pure alcohol per day and has a BMI of 25.9- implies a reduction of 2.5 minutes of child care time per week. In our opinion this is a rather large effect. Indeed, drinking one more grass of vodka per day, which contains about 10 grams of pure alcohol, reduces fathers' child care time by almost half an hour. Along this line, drinking 5 glasses more would imply a reduction of more than two hours with respect to an average of 9.7 hours.

According to our theoretical specification, this effect can be interpreted as a negative effect of the father's alcohol consumption on child welfare. Alcohol reduces the time fathers devote to children, thus reducing the amount of child composite good z^c produced and, therefore, children's utility. Mothers' alcohol consumption, instead, has no significant effect on child care. Also, for both parents, it has no significant effect on household income, either through hours of work or in regards to wages, so that we do not observe a compensation for the welfare loss through an increase in market goods expenditure, **x**. This result is in line with Tekin (2004), who finds that alcohol consumption has no significant effect on employment and wages for either males or females.

We find, however, a positive effect of moderate drinking on paid work that is probably linked to the social aggregation value that occasional drinking may generate, especially in a country like Russia, where drinking is not associated with social stigma. This is observed through a positive and significant effect of being an occasional drinker on labour participation for husbands and wives. Moreover, being an occasional drinker has a positive effect on wives' wages. Again, this is in line with previous findings of a positive association between moderate drinking and earnings (Berger and Leigh,1988; Zarkin et al, 1998; MacDonald and Shields, 2001).

In the absence of other studies on the effects of alcohol consumption on the couples' use of time, a comparison can be done with a recent study on the effects of alcohol consumption on the intra-household distribution of resources in Italy (Menon et al, 2012). The authors find that husbands' alcohol consumption significantly reduces wives' shares of economic resources (while the reverse is not true), thus significantly affecting wives' well-being.

The presence of a nursery in the community positively influences participation to the labour market for both parents, and significantly increases the hours of paid work by the wife. This is expected, but it produces a further positive result that at first might seem

Table 3 SUR Tobit estimation

	Childcare		Domestic tasks		Paid work		Labour participation		Wage	
	Husband	Wife	Husband	Wife	Husband	Wife	Husband	Wife	Husband	Wife
Constant	-2.4704	-1.3490	2.6235	0.8920	3.3917***	4.1657***	0.4759	-4.8002***	3.0383***	1.8864
	(2.2833)	(2.1725)	(1.9897)	(1.0965)	(.63356)	(.83443)	(1.9652)	(1.6746)	(.74643)	(1.2547)
Alcohol	-0.0973**	-0.0079	0.0011	0.0717	0.0168	0.0005			0.0378	0.0315
	(.04751)	(.15193)	(.04072)	(.08889)	(.01363)	(.03917)			(.03354)	(.25665)
Alcohol-partner	-0.0612	-0.0649	0.1009	-0.0182	-0.0102	0.0055				
	(.17791)	(.04909)	(.16485)	(.02012)	(.02972)	(.01292)				
Occasional drinker					0.0059	0.0530*	0.2875***	0.2602***	0.0213	0.2328***
					(.02411)	(.03018)	(.10298)	(.09161)	(.05861)	(.08779)
Presence of nursery	0.2220**	0.1101	0.1015	-0.0060			0.2354**	0.3068***	0.2318***	0.1172
	(.09292)	(.09385)	(.08241)	(.04067)			(.1067)	(.09302)	(.05938)	(.10549)
Males/female ratio	-0.5220	0.1580	-1.8410	-0.2930	1.2559**	0.0845	0.6353	0.4532		
	(1.7697)	(1.6817)	(1.6965)	(.71607)	(.54703)	(.59898)	(1.4627)	(1.487)		
Male/female wage ratio	2.5636***	1.6303*	-0.0695	0.6723	0.0417	-0.1316				
	(.85723)	(.84098)	(.7761)	(.4211)	(.19615)	(.26162)				
Average wage	0.0226	0.0104	0.0061	0.0154*	-0.0139**	-0.0056			-0.0025	-0.0145
	(.02217)	(.02155)	(.02025)	(.00848)	(.00606)	(.00652)			(.01056)	(.01715)
Help with childcare	0.1065	0.1359*	-0.0176	-0.0340	-0.0045	0.0138	0.1179	0.0996		
	(.08128)	(.08081)	(.06574)	(.0267)	(.01713)	(.02067)	(.08511)	(.08261)		
Number of grandparents	0.3474*	0.1051	-0.2256*	-0.2156***	-0.0689	0.0387	-0.2152	-0.1534		
	(.20054)	(.21086)	(.12052)	(.06058)	(.05016)	(.05845)	(.19973)	(.19119)		
Age	-0.2966	0.0860	0.0073	0.0908	0.0090	-0.1501	0.2021	2.6074***	0.4643	1.2394**
	(.45831)	(.3836)	(.40631)	(.19774)	(.10083)	(.18565)	(.5941)	(.46815)	(.31869)	(.61251)
Age squared	0.0200	-0.0399	0.0106	-0.0118	-0.0001	0.0167	-0.0424	-0.3543***	-0.0636	-0.1529
	(.05946)	(.0524)	(.05426)	(.02855)	(.01351)	(.02597)	(.07642)	(.06497)	(.04227)	(.09475)
Age ratio	0.1530	0.0601	0.0248	0.2205*	-0.0054	0.1011				
	(.28802)	(.2829)	(.24641)	(.11664)	(.07074)	(.08344)				
Wage rate	0.1653***	0.0629**	0.0820***	-0.0077	-0.0401	-0.0021				
	(.02927)	(.02763)	(.02797)	(.01196)	(.05082)	(.00839)				
Wage rate - partner	0.0531**	0.1408***	0.1277***	0.1560***	-0.0164***	0.0274				
	(.02521)	(.02792)	(.02029)	(.01198)	(.00615)	(.05179)				

Table 3 SUR Tobit estimation (Continued)

	(1)	(2)	(3)	(4)	(5)	(6)	(7)	(8)	(9)	(10)
Non-labour income	-0.0091 (.01243)	0.0072 (.01183)	0.0186* (.01071)	0.0027 (.00528)	-0.0046 (.00285)	-0.0043 (.00359)				-0.1645 (.11351)
Primary education	0.0777 (.10471)								-0.1410** (.06987)	
Tertiary education	0.1695* (.0935)	0.1546* (.09346)	0.0124 (.04059)	-0.0114 (.02297)	-0.0319 (.02807)				0.0078 (.08135)	0.0104 (.10996)
Tertiary education - partner	-0.0371 (.09415)	-0.0512 (.07986)	0.0469 (.04188)	0.0202 (.02077)	0.0350 (.02915)					
Pregnant								0.9923** (.43138)		
Number of children [0–1]							0.1190 (.23312)	0.3339* (.17092)	-0.1292 (.09264)	-0.3364** (.13405)
Number of children [0–3]	0.7903*** (.11242)	0.4580*** (.08873)	0.2182** (.09068)	-0.1899*** (.0412)	-0.0048 (.02293)	-0.0241 (.03386)	-0.1412 (.14257)	-0.5732*** (.12271)		
Number of children [4–6]	0.5140*** (.10317)	0.0611 (.08489)	0.0754* (.04281)	0.0191 (.02234)	0.0266 (.03155)	0.1072 (.11866)		0.1366 (.09601)	0.0053 (.05592)	-0.2427*** (.08659)
Non-Russian	-0.1540* (.09169)	-0.3392*** (.08075)	-0.0776 (.08378)	0.0309 (.03984)	0.0184 (.02526)	0.0167 (.0299)	-0.1382 (.15053)	-0.3769*** (.12322)		
Bad health	0.1299 (.35899)	-0.1640 (.29125)	-0.0622 (.26532)	-0.0561 (.13324)	-0.1589 (.39767)	-0.1622** (.07518)		0.1131 (.07532)		
N. of cigarettes	0.0004 (.00367)	-0.0067* (.00348)	0.0010 (.00362)	0.0020* (.00104)	0.0028 (.00244)	0.0017 (.00517)		-0.0277*** (.00823)	-0.0097*** (.00254)	0.0148 (.0104)
Pension (not retired)	0.2441 (.23874)	0.4322 (.33354)	-0.2520 (.18329)	0.1800 (.24143)	-0.0473 (.17239)	-0.0108 (.06597)				
Dimension of dwelling	-0.2221*** (.05602)	0.0528 (.05795)	0.0022 (.02301)	-0.0037 (.0143)	-0.0118 (.01867)					
Owner of dwelling							-0.1531 (.11509)	0.0549 (.09406)	0.0408 (.05923)	-0.0004 (.08528)
Region 1 (Metropolitan area)	-0.2783 (.79398)	0.0206 (.77319)	-0.1243 (.72494)	-0.4387 (.30198)	0.5077** (.22991)	0.0761 (.24192)	0.7092*** (.24644)	-0.0894 (.14753)	0.7735** (.35939)	0.7359 (.59509)
Region 2 (Northern area)	-0.7659 (.67548)	-0.0966 (.66009)	-0.0949 (.61927)	-0.3970 (.26159)	0.4676** (.1886)	0.1597 (.20537)	0.2667 (.19294)	0.4829** (.19836)	0.5052* (.30064)	0.6558 (.48866)

Table 3 SUR Tobit estimation (Continued)

Region 3 (Central area)	0.8178***	0.3788	0.1882	0.2344**	-0.0859	0.1561	0.0710	0.0470	-0.0664
	(.25745)	(.24344)	(.24919)	(.10998)	(0.0602)	(0.2337)	(.22816)	(.08147)	(.11721)
Region 4 (Volga)	0.5802*	0.4764	0.0215	0.3732***	-0.1434*	0.2689*	0.1229	-0.1828	-0.2506
	(.30451)	(0.2932)	(.27678)	(.12313)	(.07561)	(.14719)	(.12529)	(.12893)	(0.1958)
Round 2						0.1999	0.2315	0.1192	0.0312
						(.24159)	(.20336)	(.12315)	(.25126)
Round 3						-0.0783	0.1053	0.5002***	0.2038
						(.26127)	(.20395)	(0.1282)	(.24058)
Round 4						-0.1593	0.0481	0.4897***	0.1240
						(.21641)	(.16216)	(.10348)	(.20468)

1287 observations. *Significance at the 10% significance level; ** Significance at 5%; *** Significance at 1 Standard error in parenthesis.

Table 4 Errors variance/covariance matrix for the SUR Tobit estimation

Variance/covariance matrix	Childcare		Domestic tasks		Paid work		Labour participation		Wage	
	Husband	Wife	Husband	Wife	Husband	Wife	Husband	Wife	Husband	Wife
Child care - husband	1.2624***	0.4741***	0.2334***	0.1192***	-0.0389	-0.0277	0.0000	0.0000	0.0727**	0.0000
	(.04129)	(.02274)	(.02865)	(0.0294)	(0.0416)	(0.0359)	(-)	(-)	(.03403)	(-)
Child care - wife		1.1733***	0.1038***	0.2084***	0.0416	-0.0895**	0.0000	0.0000	0.0000	-0.0280
		(.03532)	(.03131)	(.03001)	(.04315)	(.04442)	(-)	(-)	(-)	(.04654)
Domestic tasks - husband			1.0834***	0.1307***	-0.0202	0.0623	0.0000	0.0000	0.1533***	0.0000
			(.02657)	(.03288)	(.04223)	(.04157)	(-)	(-)	(.03572)	(-)
Domestic tasks - wife				0.4984***	0.0544	-0.1085*	0.0000	0.0000	0.0000	-0.1771***
				(.00902)	(.04014)	(.05668)	(-)	(-)	(-)	(.04442)
Paid work - husband					0.2524***	0.0264	-0.3262***	0.0000	-0.1210	0.0000
					(.00585)	(.04478)	(0.1031)	(-)	(0.1468)	(-)
Paid work - wife						0.2939***	0.0000	0.8627***	0.0000	-0.2366
						(0.0132)	(-)	(0.2845)	(-)	(.17484)
Labour participation - husband							1.0000	0.0000	0.0921	0.0000
							(-)	(-)	(.08512)	(-)
Labour participation - wife								1.0000	0.0000	-0.8781***
								(-)	(-)	(.08751)
Wage - husband									0.7466***	0.1819***
									(.01251)	(.03883)
Wage - wife										1.0645***
										(.02265)

1287 observations; *Significance at the 10% significance level; **Significance at 5%; ***Significance at 1% Standard error in parenthesis.

counter-intuitive: an increase in husbands' hours of child care. The most likely mechanism that explains this result is that indeed the nursery offers a useful service that allows mothers to work more, but given the rigidities in the labour market contracts - such as the scarce implementation of flexible time contracts - and the inability of nurseries to fully cover the weekly hours of work, husbands may need to compensate with more hours of child care.

As to the other individual variables included in the model, at variance with Kimmel and Connelly (2007), age has no effect on child care and domestic tasks, while it has a positive (quadratic) impact on wives' labour participation (the greatest impact is at around 35 years). The husband/wife age ratio is significant and positive in determining wives' domestic tasks, meaning that wives with a much older husband tend to do more domestic tasks. This is to be expected, since this situation may be a proxy of a very traditional household type.

The individual's and partner's wage rate is positively and significantly associated with more child care for both spouses. This seems to suggest that child care has a positive value *per-se* and the time spent with children increases with the family's social position (in terms of paid work status). Wages also significantly affect domestic tasks, and in particular the partner's wage rate increases the hours of domestic tasks - a result similar to Bloemen et al (2010). If the estimated model was a collective specification this would have been a sign of the increased bargaining power of the partner when he/she has a larger wage rate. Finally, the wage rate of the wife reduces husband's hours of paid work, while the opposite effect is not observed.

Women with higher education carry out more child care: they may be more conscious that the time parents spend with their children is a strong contribution to a child's development. Husbands' education level, on the other hand, is positively related to time spent in domestic tasks. This may be sign of more modern, non-patriarchal households types. Having no more than a primary education tends to reduce husbands' wage rate. For Italian couples, Bloemen et al (2010) find negative signs for the coefficients of primary school education, both in the husband's and wife's child care equations. On the other hand, for American mothers Kimmel and Connelly (2007) and Connelly and Kimmel (2009) find a negative impact of education on child care time. This discrepancy may be due to the differences in the level of efficiency of the three labour markets. The American labour market is efficient and education allows workers to achieve higher wage rates, while in the Russian and Italian labour markets return on education is low and the opportunity cost of work is small even for educated workers. Moreover, in Russia people with only primary education are still a significant part of the population, as shown in Table 1.

Among household characteristics, household composition is, as expected, one of the main determinants of both child care and domestic tasks. The number of young children, aged 0–3 and 4–6, have a positive impact on fathers' and mothers' hours of child care, with a larger impact for younger children. The number of children aged 0–3 has an impact on domestic tasks, increasing husbands' and reducing wives' hours of domestic tasks. This is a plausible results: when children are small, husbands may substitute for their wives in doing more domestic tasks. Grandparents in the household clearly help with household production, reducing hours of domestic tasks for both males and females, not reducing, however, parents' child care. Finally, non-Russian parents dedicate less time to their children and non-Russian wives participate less to the labour market.

The correlation coefficients of the error terms capture the correlation between unobservable factors - both unobserved individual preferences and omitted variables - that influence the equations in the system (5 and 6).

In line with Bloemen et al (2010), Table 4 shows that almost all the estimated correlation coefficients are statistically significant. This means that unobserved preferences of husband and wife can be correlated, which is also a feature of the underlying theoretical model presented in Section "Theoretical foundations". Focusing on child care equations, unobservables of the equation for father's child care are positively correlated with mother's child care, suggesting similar tastes, rather than complementarity, with respect to child care. Positive correlation for child care and domestic tasks between spouses seems to indicate a positive assortative mating, namely, individuals marry each other if they have similar (unobserved) preferences. The same is not true for paid work, since we observe no significant correlations, except for a negative correlation between female child care and paid work, and female domestic tasks and paid work. This is a sign that the explanatory variables were unable to capture all the existing trade-offs between domestic activities and paid work for women. Finally, labour participation is significantly correlated with hours of work for both partners and with the wage equation for wives, confirming the presence of self-selection in the sample.

Conclusions

The main contribution of this article consists of assessing the influence of alcohol consumption on parental child care. To our knowledge, this is the first study to address the problem of the effects of alcohol consumption on the allocation of time within the household. Building on Becker's hypothesis of altruistic preferences, we assume that parents' utility functions depend on their children's welfare. In turn, the latter is determined by a composite child good that is produced in the household through market goods and child care time. This way, studying the determinants of time spent doing child care, domestic tasks and paid work, permits one to deduce parental preferences towards child welfare.

Empirically, we estimate a system of time supply equations (hours of child care, of domestic tasks and of paid work) integrated with labour market participation and wage equations. Our results show that alcohol consumption of the husband negatively affects his time spent doing child care, but has no effects on his or his spouse's labour supply or wage. In our model, child welfare is determined by child's consumption of a composite good produced by the parents using child care time and market goods. We find that fathers' alcohol consumption significantly reduces child care time without affecting family income, thus reducing child welfare through a reduction of the composite good consumed by his children. We find no effects of mother's alcohol consumption on any time use category, labour participation or wages.

Overall, our findings confirm that alcohol consumption is mainly a male phenomenon, and that it negatively affects other family members. In particular, it seems that fathers' preferences for their children's welfare are reduced by alcohol intake, with a welfare loss for the more vulnerable components of the household. This, jointly with the increasing medical and psychological evidence on the damages of alcohol consumption, should be a matter of thorough discussion at the institutional level.

Endnotes

[1] For a conceptual definition of child care in time use surveys, see Folbre and Yoon (2007).

[2] See Garcia-Mainar et al (2011), and Giannelli et al (2012) for a recent cross-country comparison of intra-household allocation of child care and domestic tasks time.

[3] The authors have explored all the possible causes of the dramatic swings in mortality in the country and found that one of the most important factor is alcohol consumption, especially as it relates to external causes of death such as homicide, suicide and accidents.

[4] Note that the solution of the maximization problem would also provide Marshallian demand functions for market goods, provided that goods expenditure and prices are observed and that a household production technology is assumed. In that case, time use function should also depend on market price of goods. In our empirical setting, however, market good expenditures and prices are not available and $\mathbf{p'x}$ is treated as an endogenously determined total household expenditure and prices are not included in the time use equations.

[5] To avoid notation abuse we do not index observations.

[6] Among the inspected variables, as suggested by previous literature, we tested: average regional alcohol price (in several specifications), average regional alcohol consumption, percentage of alcoholics in the region, past disruptive events (job loss and year of loss), suffering chronic illness (diabetes), and so on. None of these variables were significant in determining alcohol consumption.

[7] Lillard, Lee A. and Constantijn W.A. Panis. 2003. aML Multilevel Multiprocess Statistical Software, Version 2.0. EconWare, Los Angeles, California.

[8] RLMS-HSE site: http://www.cpc.unc.edu/projects/rlms-hse.

[9] For instance, there may be reciprocity of child care between families. Furthermore, it would not be possible to identify whether child care is provided to a subject's own children, or to those of other families within the household.

[10] The first four rounds of Phase II also record time use information, but the measures are not directly comparable and a separate analysis of those years should be carried out, which could be the subject of a future study.

[11] To our knowledge, at the time of writing the only panel study at the household level using RMLS is Lacroix and Radtchenko (2011). Indeed, constructing the household panel is possible only at the cost of dropping conflicting households and the households appearing only once in the sample. Some exploratory investigations led to a drastic reduction of the sample size. This implies that obtaining any meaningful result would have been barely possible.

[12] To clarify, we keep all families in the last round (XVIII). If one of these families is present in other waves we keep only the observation that corresponds to the last wave. Then we add families of round XVII that are not present in XVIII and so on. This way, in the pooled data-set each family appears just once, avoiding over-weighting repeated families. This reduces by a substantial amount the sample size because the majority of the households are present in more than one wave.

[13] Child care time is computed as the sum of two time use questions: 1) Played, occupied, spent your leisure time with children or grandchildren who live with you, and 2) Looked after children or grandchildren who live with you- bathed them, fed them, led them to lessons.

[14] Time devoted to domestic tasks is computed as the sum of 8 time use questions: 1) Purchased food goods, 2) Prepared food, 3) Washed dishes, 4) Did laundry, 5) Cleaned rooms 6) Did a small repair of house or dacha, or repaired a car, 7) Did repair work of

house, dacha and 8) Drove a car with "family" purposes Ű for trips to a store, to the dacha.

[15] Clearly, these figures should not be generalized for the entire Russian population, as they were computed on a restricted sub-sample.

[16] It is well known that identification based uniquely on non-linearity is possible but likely to be problematic.

[17] The aML statistical software does not include facilities for computing marginal/partial effects so we proceeded manually. In doing so we accounted for the censored nature of both child care time and alcohol consumption, and for the logarithmic specification of child care time.

Competing interests
The IZA Journal of Labor & Development is committed to the IZA Guiding Principles of Research Integrity. The authors declare that they have observed these principles.

Acknowledgments
The authors thank Tindara Addabbo, Olga Lazareva, the participants to the XXVII National Conference of Labor Economics (AIEL), the participants to the 26th Annual Conference of the European Society for Population Economics, and an anonymous referee for their useful comments and suggestions. Lucia Mangiavacchi and Luca Piccoli acknowledge financial support from the Spanish Government (Grant ECO2011-28999).
Responsible editor: Hartmut Lehmann

Author details
[1] Department of Economics, University of Florence and IZA, Via delle Pandette 9, Firenze, Italy. [2] Department of Applied Economics, University of the Balearic Islands, Ctra de Valldemossa km 7.5, Palma de Mallorca, Spain.

References
Amemiya T (1985) Advanced econometrics. Harvard university press

Apps P, Rees R (1996) Labour supply, household production and intra-family welfare distribution. J Pub Econ 60(2): 199–219

Baltagi BH, Geishecker I (2006) Rational alcohol addiction: evidence from the Russian longitudinal monitoring survey. Health Econ 15(9): 893–914

Becker GS (1965) A theory of the allocation of time. Econ J 75(299): 493–517

Becker GS (1981) A Treatise on the Family, enlarged edn. Harvard University Press, Cambridge

Berger G (1993) Alcoholism and the family, franklin watts edn. Franklin Watts, New York

Berger M, Leigh J (1988) The effect of alcohol use on wages. Appl Econ 20(10): 1343–1351

Bloemen H, Pasqua S, Stancanelli E (2010) An empirical analysis of the time allocation of Italian couples: are they responsive? Rev Econ Household 8(3): 345–369

Bourguignon F (1999) The cost of children: may the collective approach to household behavior help? J Popul Econ 12: 503–21

Brainerd E, Cutler D (2005) Autopsy on an empire: Understanding mortality in Russia and the former Soviet Union. J Econ Perspect 19(1): 107–130

Chatterji P, Markowitz S (2001) The impact of maternal alcohol and illicit drug use on children's behavior problems: evidence from the children of the national longitudinal survey of youth. J Health Econ 20(5): 703–731

Chiappori PA (1988) Rational household labor supply. Econometrica 56(1): 63–90

Chiappori PA (1992) Collective labor supply and welfare. J Pol Econ 100(3): 437–67

Connelly R, Kimmel J (2009) Spousal influences on parents' non-market time choices. Rev Econ Household 7(4): 361–394

Dunbar G, Lewbel A, Pendakur K (2013) Children's resources in collective households: identification, estimation, and an application to child poverty in Malawi. Am Econ Rev 103(1): 438–71

Feng W, Zhou W, Butler J, Booth B, French M (2001) The impact of problem drinking on employment. Health Econ 10(6): 509–521

Folbre N, Yoon J (2007) What is child care? Lessons from time-use surveys of major English-speaking countries. Rev Econ Household 5(223–248)

French M, Zarkin G, Mroz T, Bray J (1998) The relationship between drug use and labor supply for young men. Labour Econ 5(4): 385–409

French M, Maclean J, Sindelar J, Fang H (2011) The morning after: alcohol misuse and employment problems. Appl Econ 43(21): 2705–2720

Garcia-Mainar I, Molina J, Montuenga V (2011) Gender differences in childcare: time allocation in five European countries. Feminist Econ 17(1): 119–150

Giannelli G, Mangiavacchi L, Piccoli L (2012) GDP and the value of family caretaking: how much does Europe care? Appl Econ 44(16)(16): 2111–2131

Grogan L, Koka K (2010) Young children and women's labour force participation in Russia, 1992-2004. Econ Trans 18(4): 715–739

Gronau R (1977) Leisure, Home Production, and Work-the Theory of the Allocation of Time Revisited. J Pol Econ 85(6): 1099–1124

Grossbard-Shechtman A (1984) A theory of allocation of time in markets for labour and marriage. Econ J 94(376): 863–882

Hallberg D, Klevmarken A (2003) Time for children: A study of parent's time allocation. J Pop Econ 16(2): 205–226

Hamilton V, Hamilton B (1997) Alcohol and earnings: does drinking yield a wage premium? Can J Econ: 135–151

Heckman J (1979) Sample selection bias as a specification error. Econometrica 47(1): 153–162

Kalenkoski C, Ribar D, Stratton L (2007) The effect of family structure on parents' child care time in the United States and the United Kingdom. Rev Econ Household 5(4): 353–384

Kalenkoski C, Ribar D, Stratton L (2009) The influence of wages on parents' allocations of time to child care and market work in the United Kingdom. J Popul Econ 22(2): 399–419

Kalenkoski CM, Ribar DC, Stratton LS (2005) Parental child care in single-parent, cohabiting, and married-couple families: time-diary evidence from the United Kingdom. Am Econ Rev 95(2): 194–198

Kimmel J, Connelly R (2007) Mothers' time choices. J Hum Resour 42(3): 643–681

Kooreman P, Kapteyn A (1987) A disaggregrated analysis of the allocation of time within the household. J Pol Econ 95: 223–249

Lacroix G, Radtchenko N (2011) The changing intra-household resource allocation in Russia. J Popul Econ 24(1): 85–106

Lokshin M (2004) Household childcare choices and women's work behavior in Russia. J Hum Resour 39(4): 1094–1115

Lokshin M, Harris K, Popkin B (2000) Single mothers in Russia: Household strategies for coping with poverty. World Dev 28(12): 2183–2198

MacDonald Z, Shields M (2001) The impact of alcohol consumption on occupational attainment in England. Economica 68(271): 427–453

Mangiavacchi L, Perali F, Piccoli L (2010) Child Welfare in Albania Using a Collective Approach. Tech. rep., Universitat de les Illes Balears, Departament d'Economía Aplicada, WP no 41

Menon M, Perali F, Piccoli L (2012) The Passive Drinking Effect: A Collective Demand Application. University of Verona, Department of Economics, Working Paper no. 05/2012

Mullahy J, Sindelar J (1991) Gender differences in labor market effects of alcoholism. Am Econ Rev 81(2): 161–65

Powell L (2002) Joint labor supply and childcare choice decisions of married mothers. J Hum Resour 37(1): 106–128

Tekin E (2004) Employment, wages, and alcohol consumption in Russia. South Econ J: 397–417

Zarkin G, French M, Mroz T, Bray J (1998) Alcohol use and wages: new results from the national household survey on drug abuse. J Health Econ 17(1): 53–68

Zohoori N, Mroz T, Popkin B, Glinskaya E, Lokshin M, Mancini D, Kozyreva P, Kosolapov M, Swafford M (1998) Monitoring the economic transition in the Russian Federation and its implications for the demographic crisis–the Russian Longitudinal Monitoring Survey. World Dev 26(11): 1977–1993

Permissions

The contributors of this book come from diverse backgrounds, making this book a truly international effort. This book will bring forth new frontiers with its revolutionizing research information and detailed analysis of the nascent developments around the world.

We would like to thank all the contributing authors for lending their expertise to make the book truly unique. They have played a crucial role in the development of this book. Without their invaluable contributions this book wouldn't have been possible. They have made vital efforts to compile up to date information on the varied aspects of this subject to make this book a valuable addition to the collection of many professionals and students.

This book was conceptualized with the vision of imparting up-to-date information and advanced data in this field. To ensure the same, a matchless editorial board was set up. Every individual on the board went through rigorous rounds of assessment to prove their worth. After which they invested a large part of their time researching and compiling the most relevant data for our readers.

The editorial board has been involved in producing this book since its inception. They have spent rigorous hours researching and exploring the diverse topics which have resulted in the successful publishing of this book. They have passed on their knowledge of decades through this book. To expedite this challenging task, the publisher supported the team at every step. A small team of assistant editors was also appointed to further simplify the editing procedure and attain best results for the readers.

Apart from the editorial board, the designing team has also invested a significant amount of their time in understanding the subject and creating the most relevant covers. They scrutinized every image to scout for the most suitable representation of the subject and create an appropriate cover for the book.

The publishing team has been an ardent support to the editorial, designing and production team. Their endless efforts to recruit the best for this project, has resulted in the accomplishment of this book. They are a veteran in the field of academics and their pool of knowledge is as vast as their experience in printing. Their expertise and guidance has proved useful at every step. Their uncompromising quality standards have made this book an exceptional effort. Their encouragement from time to time has been an inspiration for everyone.

The publisher and the editorial board hope that this book will prove to be a valuable piece of knowledge for researchers, students, practitioners and scholars across the globe.

List of Contributors

Paul Cichello
Economics Department, Boston College, 140 Commonwealth Ave, Chestnut Hill, MA 02467, USA

Hala Abou-Ali
Faculty of Economics and Political Science, Cairo University, Cairo, Egypt

Daniela Marotta
World Bank, 1818 H Street NW, Washington, D.C 20433, USA

Pablo Ibarraran
Inter-American Development Bank (IDB), Washington, DC and IZA, Bonn, Germany

Laura Ripani
Inter-American Development Bank (IDB), Washington, DC, USA

Bibiana Taboada
Inter-American Development Bank (IDB), Washington, DC, USA

Juan Miguel Villa
University of Manchester, Manchester, England

Brigida Garcia
Professor at the Universidad Autónoma de Santo Domingo, Santo Domingo, Dominican Republic

Jason Gagnon
OECD Development Centre, Paris Cedex 16, France

Theodora Xenogiani
OECD Directorate for Employment, Labour and Social Affairs, Paris Cedex 16, France

Chunbing Xing
Beijing Normal University, Beijing, China

Babatunde O Abidoye
Department of Agricultural Economics, Extension and Rural Development, University of Pretoria, Pretoria 0002, South Africa

Peter F Orazem
IZA and Department of Economics, Iowa State University, Ames, IA 50010, USA

Milan Vodopivec
IZA, International School for Social and Business Studies, Celje, Slovenia and University of Primorska, Faculty of Management, Koper, Slovenia

Tanika Chakraborty
Indian Institute of Technology, Kanpur, India

Anirban Mukherjee
University of Calcutta, Calcutta, India

Sarani Saha
Indian Institute of Technology, Kanpur, India

Ebrahim Azimi
Department of Economics, Simon Fraser University, 8888 University Drive, Burnaby, British Columbia, Canada

Fernando Fernandez
Inter-American Development Bank, 1300 New York Avenue NW, Washington, D.C. 20577 USA

Victor Saldarriaga
Vancouver School ofEconomics, Vancouver, Canada

Christoph Eder
Department of Economics, Johannes Kepler University Linz, Altenberger Str. 69, 4040 Linz, Austria

Johannes Koettl
World Bank, 1818 H Street NW, Washington, DC 20433, USA
World Bank Country Office in Moldova, 20/1 Pushkin Street, MD-2012 Chisinau, Republic of Moldova

Olga Kupets
World Bank, 1818 H Street NW, Washington, DC 20433, USA
Department of Economics, National University of Kyiv-Mohyla Academy, 10 Voloska Street, 04070 Kyiv, Ukraine

Anna Olefir
World Bank, 1818 H Street NW, Washington, DC 20433, USA
World Bank Country Office in Moldova, 20/1 Pushkin Street, MD-2012 Chisinau, Republic of Moldova

Indhira Santos
World Bank, 1818 H Street NW, Washington, DC 20433, USA

Judith Möllers
Leibniz Institute for Agricultural Development in Transition Economies (IAMO), Theodor-Lieser-Str. 2, 06120 Halle, Saale, Germany

Wiebke Meyer
Leibniz Institute for Agricultural Development in Transition Economies (IAMO), Theodor-Lieser-Str. 2, 06120 Halle, Saale, Germany

Gianna Claudia Giannelli
Department of Economics, University of Florence and IZA, Via delle Pandette 9, Firenze, Italy

Lucia Mangiavacchi
Department of Applied Economics, University of the Balearic Islands, Ctra de Valldemossa km 7.5, Palma de Mallorca, Spain

Luca Piccoli
Department of Applied Economics, University of the Balearic Islands, Ctra de Valldemossa km 7.5, Palma de Mallorca, Spain

CPSIA information can be obtained
at www.ICGtesting.com
Printed in the USA
BVOW10*1103040716

454361BV00002B/210/P

9 781682 852484